MĀYĀ IN PHYSICS

Māyā in Physics

N.C. Panda

MOTILAL BANARSIDASS PUBLISHERS
PRIVATE LIMITED • DELHI

Reprint : Delhi, 1996, 1999, ***2008***
Corrected Edition : 2005
First Indian Edition : Delhi, 1991

ISBN : 978-81-208-0698-6

MOTILAL BANARSIDASS
41 U.A. Bungalow Road, Jawahar Nagar, Delhi 110 007
8 Mahalaxmi Chamber, 22 Bhulabhai Desai Road, Mumbai 400 026
203 Royapettah High Road, Mylapore, Chennai 600 004
236, 9th Main III Block, Jayanagar, Bangalore 560 011
Sanas Plaza, 1302 Baji Rao Road, Pune 411 002
8 Camac Street, Kolkata 700 017
Ashok Rajpath, Patna 800 004
Chowk, Varanasi 221 001

PRINTED IN INDIA
By Jainendra Prakash Jain at Shri Jainendra Press,
A-45, Naraina, Phase-I, New Delhi 110 028
and Published by Narendra Prakash Jain for
Motilal Banarsidass Publishers Private Limited,
Bungalow Road, Delhi 110 007

For my youngest son,

BIBHAS

CONTENTS

Part II: ADVAITA VEDĀNTA

Part III: CONFLUENCE

PROLOGUE

IT IS VERY OFTEN felt that religious culture is at variance with scientific culture and both are incompatible. Such a notion is not totally baseless, although many things in religions do not support or contradict science at all. A few religious things that do contradict science are too serious to be ignored. It is not possible on the part of science to compromise with religions on those few things. Hence synthesis of religions and science does not seem to be a practical proposition.

It is further felt that humanistic culture and scientific culture are to be fused in order that science may be beneficial to mankind without any malignant side-effect. If science is compared with a race-horse, humanities may be compared with the reins. Science and technology are to be restrained with humanities for the balanced progress of mankind. Both are to be parallel in movement for the furtherance of the culture and civilization of man and for peace and happiness. But, unfortunately, humanities have developed a tendency to toe the line of science and technology. There does not seem to be any humanizing influence of humanities on man. As a result of the failure of humanities and the one-sided pull of science and technology, the march of mankind has been staggering. It seems man has been dehumanized.

The intellectuals of the world have already realized that mankind may commit suicide at any moment. This would-be disaster is of course avoidable. Science and spirituality are to be fused. An integral philosophy is to be developed. This philosophy is to be one for living, not for theorizing only.

Advaita Vedānta is found to be the only philosophy that has the capacity to be scientific. It can absorb all the modern concepts of science without any contradiction. It can also go beyond science and can fill up the gaps which science cannot. Advaita Vedānta and modern science can be fused to give rise to a synthetic, integral philosophy, which, when translated to action of living, becomes cosmic religion.

In the 1970s and '80s, a few books have been written on Eastern mysticism and science. Books such as *The Tao of Physics* of

Fritjof Capra (1975), *The Dancing Wu Li Masters* of Gary Zukav (1979), *The Eye of Shiva* of Amaury de Reincourt (1980) and 'Brahman→E=MC²' of James Wallace (1985) are worth mentioning here. Capra, being himself a physicist, has successfully stimulated the intellectuals of the world to rethink in terms of spiritualizing science. *The Turning Point*, the second book of Capra, is also thought-provoking and is likely to rationalize human thought.

This book *Māyā in Physics* is not an additional one to repeat what has been written earlier. Although there are many common elements in this book and the books mentioned here, the purpose of writing this book is totally different. It is not the main objective of this book to focus on the Eastern mysticism and the similarities encountered in modern science. The whole of Advatia Vedānta has been re-interpreted here in the light of modern science. Attempt has been made to bring about a fusion of Advaita Vedānta and modern science. The deficiencies of modern science have been made up by the supplementation of Advaita Vedānta. In this integral approach, a total vision has been presented with analysis of concepts and phenomena. The cosmic phenomena have been explained. The recognition of the noumena at the bottom of the phenomena has been justified. The concepts of God and Māyā have also been coherently presented. The problems of cosmology and cosmogony have been hopefully solved. All these things have been fitted in one integral philosophy that does not contradict modern science and rather supports and supplements it. This book is an elaboration of Advaita Vedānta in the framework of modern science. It brings about a synthesis of science and spirituality.

There are many common currents in quantum physics and Vedānta. But the fundamentality of Vedānta is at variance with quantum physics. The concept of Brahman is fundamental in Vedānta. The phenomenal universe of names and forms is illusory. Its substratum is Brahman which is the nondual Reality, Being without becoming. This Reality is formless, actionless, attributeless, changeless, beginningless and endless. The Reality is ungraspable to the senses. It is unknowable, but realizable directly, without any mediation. In contrast to this philosophy of Advaita Vedānta, Buddhism or Taoism has a philosophy that puts emphasis on void (*Śūnya*) or nothingness. The phenomenal universe, in the latter philosophy, is a stream of momentary events. This philosophy does not accept a single timeless entity as reality. Its reality consists of multiple entities that exist and occur for a moment and change to others in the next moment. In this concept of dynamic state of flux, the cosmic stream of events is eternal without the eternality of any individual entity or event. In general, in the philosophy of Buddhism, there is no reality other than the constantly changing and everflowing cosmic stream of events. This concept has similarity with that of quantum physics, but differs from that of Advaita Vedānta that recognizes an unchangeable entity as Reality. The present book has tried to establish an integral philosophy with the fusion of the fundamental concepts of Advaita Vedānta and modern science. Attempt has been made to demystify philosophy and religion and dematerialize science.

There is a second interpretation of the concept of *śūnyatā* (void) or *Nirvāṇa* of Buddhism. According to this, the void is the full and *the* Reality. This concept conforms to the concept of Reality in Advaita Vedānta. Those quantum physicists who recognize nothing as real, for whom things appear from nowhere and disappear into nowheıe, and who are subjectivists, solipsists or nihilists do not serve any meaningful purpose by attempting to demonstrate parallelism among some concepts of quantum physics and Advaita Vedānta.

This is not a book on physics although it incorporates concepts of physics. Any technical physicist, interested in physics only, without any faith in spirituality, may not justifiably condemn it since a book, synthesizing spiritual thoughts and scientific thoughts, can be written. This is not a book on technical philosophy either. If any materialistic philosopher, with empirical attitude and antispiritual faith, does not find *his* philosophy in this book, he may not resent.

An old school of philosophy, viz., Advaita Vedānta, has been re-interpreted in the format of modern science and, in such an endeavour, a new philosophy of science has been presented. This philosophy, if adopted, would avoid the probable disaster of the suicidal extinction of mankind and improve the quality of man.

ACKNOWLEDGEMENTS

I AM INDEBTED to Dr. Pramod Chandra Samal, Dr. Bijoy Kumar Sahu, Dr. Hemant Chandra Mohapatra, Dr. Prabin Kumar Dehury, Dr. Antaryami Mohanty and Dr. Sarat Chandra Mishra, who have helped me in many ways in the process of the preparation of the manuscript. My thanks are due to Mr. Hrudananda Behera and Mr. Bishnu Charan Swain for their secretarial assistance.

The expenditure for the production of the manuscript and part of the cost of the publication of the original edition (1991) of the book were met with the generous donations of a number of benevolent persons. They are: Dr. D.V.R. Prakasha Rao (Madras), Dr. Bishnu Charan Joshi (U.S.A.), Dr. Sitakantha Dash (U.S.A.), Mr. Sibendu Shekhar Mishra (Cuttack), Mr. Rahas Bihari Mohanty (Cuttack), Dr. Radhakanta Mishra (U.S.A.), Dr. V.G. Dev (U.S.A.), Dr. Haralal Choudhuri (U.S.A.), Mr. Biranchi Narayan Chau Pattanaik (Cuttack), Mr. Sudhanshu Mohan Das (Bhubaneswar), Mr. Ranjit Kumar Ray (Bhubaneswar), Dr. Udayanath Sahu (Bhubaneswar), Dr. Brundaban Panigrahi (U.S.A.) and Dr. Rasikananda Tripathy (U.S.A.). I ever owe to them.

I gratefully acknowledge the permissions of the following authors and publishers for quoting materials from their works:

Academic Press, Orlando, Florida

DeWitt, B.S. in "*Foundations of Quantum Mechanics*", ed., B. d'Espagnat, 1971.

Addison-Wesley Publishing Co., Mass.

Wheeler, J., *Some Strangeness in the Proportion*, ed., Harry Woolf, 1980.

Alfred A. Knopf, New York

1. Einstein, A., quoted by Frank, P. in "*Einstein: His Life and Times*", 1947.

2. Monod, J., *Chance and Necessity*, 1971.

American Elsevier Publishing Co., Inc., New York

Walker, E.H., "*The Nature of Consciousness*", Mathematical Biosciences, Vol. 7, 1970.

American Institute of Physics, New York

Einstein, A., *The Physical Review*, Vol. 47, 1935.

Arnold Heinemann Publishers, Delhi
Metha, D.D., *Positive Sciences in the Vedas*, 1974 (Prof. McDonell's rendering).
Blackie & Son Ltd., Glasgow
Born, M., *Atomic Physics*, 1969.
Cambridge University Press, Cambridge
1. Bhor, N., *Atomic Theory and Description of Nature*, 1934.
2. Eddington, S.A., *The Nature of the Physical World*, 1928.
3. Einstein, A. in "*The Evolution of Physics*" by Einstein, A. and Infeld, L., 1971.
4. Jeans, J., *Physics and Philosophy*, 1948.
5. Schrödinger, E., *What is Life & Mind and Matter*, 1980.
6. Schrödinger, E. in "Proceedings of the Cambridge Philosophical Society", Vol. 31, 1935.

Chatto & Windus Ltd., London
Eddington, S.A., quoted by Sullivan, J.W.N. in "*The Limitations of Science*", 1938.
Clarkson Potter (now Crown Publishing Inc.), New York
Heisenberg, W., *On Modern Physics*, 1961.
Collins, London
1. Capra, F., *The Tao of Physics*, 1976.
2. Zukav, G., *The Dancing Wu Li Masters*, 1980.

Cosmo Publications, New Delhi
Banerji, P., *Natarāja, the Dancing God*, 1985.
Crown Publishers, New York
Einstein, A., *Ideas and Opinions* (Translated by Sonja Bargmann), 1954.
J.M. Dent & Sons, London
1. Bohr, N., quoted by Davies, P. in "*God and the New Physics*", 1983.
2. Wheeler, J., quoted by Davies, P. in "*God and the New Physics*", 1983.

W.H. Freeman & Co., Salt Lake City, Utah
Wheeler, J.A. in "*Gravitation*" by Wheeler, J.A., Throne, K.S. and Misner, C., 1973.
Harper & Row, New York
1. Heisenberg, W., *Physics and Philosophy*, 1958.
2. Russell, B., quoted by Heisenberg, W. in "Across the Frontiers", 1974.

Holt, Rinehart & Winston, Inc., New York
Bentham, J., *Great Political Thinkers*, 1969.
Indiana University Press, U.S.A.
1. Jennings, H.S., *Behaviour of the Lower Organisms*, 1965.
2. Wigner, E.P., ed., *Symmetries and Reflections*, 1967.
John Wiley, New York
1. Bohr, N., *Atomic Theory and Human Knowledge*, 1958.
2. Jammer, M., *The Philosophy of Quantum Mechanics*, 1974.
Kluwer Academic Publishers, Dordrecht, Holland
D. E'spagnat, B., *The Physicist's Conception of Nature*, ed., J. Mehra, 1973.
The Library of Living Philosophers, Inc., Evanston, Illinois
Albert Einstein. Autobiographical Notes. In: P.A. Schilp (ed.) *Albert Einstein: Philosopher-Scientist*, 1949.
Macdonald, London
Sagan, C., *Cosmos*, 1981.
Macmillan, New York
1. Crease, R.P. and Mann, C.C., *The Second Creation*, 1986 (Also permitted by the Balkin Agency, New York).
2. Einstein, A., quoted by Born, M. in "*The Born-Einstein Letters*", 1971.
Michael Joseph Ltd., London
Weinberg, S., quoted by Pagels, H.R. in "*The Cosmic Code*", 1983.
Mir Publishers, Moscow
Alekseev, G.N., *Energy and Entropy*, 1986.
M.I.T. Press, Cambridge, Mass.
Wigner, E.P., ed., *Symmetries and Reflections*, 1970.
Oxford University Press, London
1. Freud, S., quoted by Coulson, C.A. in "*Science and Christian Belief*", 1964.
2. Oppenheimer, J.R., *Science and the Common Understanding*, 1954.
3. Radhakrishnan, S., *Dhammapada*, 1950.
Pan Books, London
Huxley, S.J., quoted by Hitchings, F. in "*The Neck of the Giraffe*", 1982.
Penguin Books, Harmondsworth
Russell, B., *Has Man a Future*? © 1961 by permission of the Estate of Bertrand Russell.

Philosophical Library, New York
Einstein, A., *Out of My Later Years*, 1950.
Progress Publishers, Moscow
1. *ABC of Dialectical and Historical Materialism*, 1978.
2. Afanasyev, V.G., *Marxist Philosophy*, 1980.
3. *The Fundamentals of Marxist-Leninist Philosophy*, 1974.
Rhineholt, Div. of International Thompson Publishing Corp., New York
Capek, M., *The Philosophical Impact of Contemporary Physics*, 1961; and Einstein, A., quoted by Capek, M. in the same book.
Routledge & Kegan Paul, London
Wittgenstein, L., *Tractatus Logico-philosophicus*, 1961.
Simon & Schuster, New York
1. Einstein, A., quoted in "*The Evolution of Physics*", 1938, by Einstein, A. and Infeld, L.
2. Russell, B., *Human Knowledge, Its Scope and Limits*, 1962.
Souvenir Press, London
Riencourt, A.D., *The Eye of Shiva*, 1980.
Sterling Publishers, New Delhi
Bahadur, K.P., *The Wisdom of Mīmāṁsā*, 1983.
Talreja Publication, Bombay
Talreja, K.M., *Philosophy of Vedas*, 1982.
Transworld Corgi and Wildwood House, London
Gribbin, J., *In Search of Schrödinger's Cat*, 1984; and Einstein, A., quoted by Gribbin, J. in the same book.
Unwin Hyman, London
1. & 2. Heisenberg, W., *Physics and Philosophy*, 1959; and *Physics and Beyond*, 1971.
3. & 4. Russell, B., *Mysticism and Logic*, 1963; and *The Autobiography of Bertrand Russell*, 1975.

My sincere thanks are due to Mr. K. Ramamurthy, I.A.S. (Retd.) and Ex-Vice-Chancellor of Orissa University of Agriculture and Technology, for his constant encouragement. Mr. Om Prakash of Modern Book Depot, Bhubaneswar, has made reference books available in a dedicative spirit. I am thankful to him. I shall fail in my duty if I do not record my gratitude to M/s. Motilal Banarsidass Publishers Pvt. Ltd., Delhi, who have been glad to publish this book. Mr. N.P. Jain of this famous Publishing House deserves special thanks.

I wrote this book while I was living with my wife, children and grand-children (Manorama, Shephali, Smita, Snigdha, Sudhir, Prakash, Bikash, Bibhas, Nivedita, Madhusmita, Lopamudra) and still I had experiences of my self-afflicted mental isolation. They were glad to bear with me. Their loving support transformed my agonizing labour into creative ecstasy. My hearty thanks to them.

Bhubaneswar
October, 1989

NRUSINGH CHARAN PANDA

LIST OF ABBREVIATIONS

AĀ	Aitareya Āraṇyaka
ABrā	Aitareya Brāhmaṇa
ABS	Advaita-Brahma-Siddhi
Ait	Aitareya Upaniṣad
APR	Aparokṣānubhūti
AV	Atharva Veda
BDP	Brahmāṇḍa Purāṇa
BG	Bhagavadgītā
BGŚB	Bhagavadgītā Śāṅkarabhāṣyam
Bhā	Bhāgavatam
BP	Brahma Purāṇa
Bṛ	Bṛhadāraṇyaka Upaniṣad
BS	Brahmasūtra
BSŚB	Brahmasūtra Śāṅkarabhāṣyam
Chā	Chāndogya Upaniṣad
DBhā	Devī Bhāgavata
DDV	Dṛg-Dṛśya-Viveka
GBrā	Gopatha Brāhmaṇa
GP	Garuḍa Purāṇa
HV	Harivaṁśa
JBrā	Jaiminī Brāhmaṇa
JS	Jaiminī Saṁhitā
Kaṭ	Kaṭhopaniṣad
Ken	Kenopaniṣad
KKU	Kauśitakī Upaniṣad
KLU	Kaivalya Upaniṣad
KP	Kūrma Purāṇa
KS	Kaṭhaka Saṁhitā
Mā	Māṇḍukya Upaniṣad
MĀ	Maitrāyaṇī Āraṇyakam
Mai	Maitrī Upaniṣad
MaiU	Maitreyī Upaniṣad
MāKā	Māṇḍukya Kārikā of Gauḍapāda
MBh	Mahābhārata
MkP	Mārkaṇḍeya Purāṇa

MnU	Maitrāyaṇa Upaniṣad
MP	Matsya Purāṇa
MS	Manusmṛti
Mu	Muṇḍaka Upaniṣad
NB	Nyāya Bhāṣya
NP	Nārada Purāṇa
NS	Nyāya-Sūtra
PD	Pañcadaśī
PP	Padma Purāṇa
Pr	Praśnopaniṣad
PYD	Pātañjala Yoga Darśana
ṚV	Ṛgveda
ŚB	Śāṅkara Bhāṣyam
ŚBrā	Śatapatha Brāhmaṇa
ŚP	Śiva Purāṇa
SPS	Sāṅkhya-Pravacana-Sūtra
SrP	Saura Purāṇa
TĀ	Taittirīya Āraṇyaka
Tai	Taittirīya Upaniṣad
TBrā	Taittirīya Brāhmaṇa
TdBrā	Taṇḍya Brāhmaṇa
TS	Taittirīya Saṁhitā
VāP	Vāyu Purāṇa
VaS	Vaiśeṣika Sūtra
VB	Vyāsa-Bhāṣya
VC	Vivekacūḍāmaṇi
VjS	Vājasaneya Saṁhitā
VP	Viṣṇu Purāṇa
VPDA	Vedānta Paribhāṣā of Dharmarāja Adhvarīndra
VS	Vedānta-Sāra of Sadānanda
YV	Yajurveda
YVā	Yogavāsiṣṭha

PART I

PHYSICS

(Classical and Modern)

CHAPTER I

CLASSICAL PHYSICS

Whence arises all the order and beauty we see in the World?

Isaac Newton

I want to know how God created this world.

Albert Einstein

I had no need of this hypothesis.

Pierre Laplace to Napoleon Bonaparte

THE CURRENT OF THOUGHT about the physical nature of the universe has one single course for a long period of about three thousand years. It had its origin in the prehistoric era around 1000 B.C. Strictly speaking, the ideas developed about the composition of the universe from 1000 to 500 B.C. were speculative rather than experimental. But speculations during this early period continued to influence thought all over the world for the next two thousand and four hundred years. Only in the early part of the nineteenth century did Dalton re-open the chapter of the microconstituents of matter, when he developed his atomic concepts in connection with chemistry. Thus classical physics with its two branches, (a) the Democritean microphysics and (b) the Newtonian macrophysics, has a long span of history until the beginning of the twentieth century when modern physics was born. But in a short span of its life, modern physics has revolutionized the concepts of man about the universe and his own place in it.

Quest for the Building Blocks

From days of yore to the modern time, whenever man sees an object, he is tempted to know about the materials of which the object is made. Whether it is a garment, furniture, building or equipment, air or water, the component parts of which the material is made are inquired into.

We take a piece of rock and break it into smaller pieces. We take a smaller fragment of the rock and break it into still smaller fragments. We continue with the process and get smaller and smaller particles. Even though the fragmented particles are very small, each one has its own dimensions. Each particle has length, breadth and height or thickness. Each particle has mass. Where will our dividing and re-dividing activity stop, then? Can we continue *ad infinitum*? Is the process never-ending? Is there no final stage beyond which further sub-division is impossible? The early philosophers posed this problem before themselves. In their mind they could visualize the smallest particulate stage where their analysis would stop—had to stop. Whatever name they gave to this smallest particle, that was the basic, the fundamental and the primary constituent of matter. That was the primary building block of the universe.

Opinion differed about the kind of building block. Some persons said that there was only one kind of primary building block. Others said that the primary building blocks were more than one or numerous in kind. However, irrespective of the monistic or the pluralistic views on the microstructure of the universe, the fundamentality of the ultimate microconstituent(s) of the universe was not questioned.

Atomic Concept of Ancient India

Kaṇāda of India wrote the *Vaiśeṣika Sūtra* in the fifth or fourth century B.C., but it is quite possible that he wrote it between the sixth and the tenth century before Christ. He gave and elaborated the atomic concept. It seems he had some other proper name. The literal meaning of 'Kaṇāda' is 'giver or expounder of particle concept'. It cannot be a coincidence that the parents of Kaṇāda gave such a name to their baby who, in his adult life, propounded the atomic theory. The philosopher might have been known by this name after he earned fame for his philosophy of atomic pluralism.

According to the Vaiśeṣika view, there are nine substances, viz., earth, water, light, air, *ākāśa,* time, space, soul and *manas* (mind). Distinction is maintained, in this philosophy, between space and *ākāśa*. Although *ākāśa* fills all space, it is not space itself. *Ākāśa* is a simple, continuous and infinite substance. It is not made of discrete, particulate components. It is eternal and omnipresent. It is inactive. It is the substratum of sound.[1] All corporeal bodies are conjoined with *ākāśa*.[2] Out of these nine substances, only four, viz., earth, water, light and air are composed of atoms.

The Vaiśeṣikas recognize five types of *bhūtas* (phenomenal products). These *bhūtas* are: earth, water, light, air and *ākāśa*. Matter is a mixture of these five *bhūtas*, containing one or the other in a predominant degree. Some modern interpreters translate '*bhūta*' as 'element' of chemistry. This is, however, not correct. Etymologically, '*bhūta*' (*bhū+kta*) means "that which has become". The five *bhūtas* are the five states of matter. Earth, water, air, light and *ākāśa* symbolically represent the solid, liquid, gaseous, luminous or thermal and etheric states of matter, respectively.

One notable difference between the Indian and the Greek concepts is worth mentioning here. The early Greeks did not think of *ākāśa* as one of the constituents of the world. Rather they thought it to be void or not-being. In contrast, the Indians considered *ākāśa* as one of the states of matter.

Some uncritical writers blame the Vaiśeṣikas on two grounds. *Tejas* which literally stands for light or heat is a form of energy. It is alleged that the Vaiśeṣikas erroneously considered energy as a form of matter. These writers also criticise the Vaiśeṣikas for taking *ākāśa* as a form of matter; for *ākāśa*, in their view, is nothing else than void. The sharp distinction between matter and energy was maintained in the scientific world until 1905, when Einstein announced his equation ($E=mc^2$) for the interconversion of matter and energy. Now matter is considered as packet of energy and difference between matter and energy has vanished. Again, Einstein was the scientist who declared that space is not void. With the 'field' concept in modern physics, *ākāśa* is being considered as field. The so-called void of *ākāśa* is really full; from it micro-particles jump out to appear and they dip into it to disappear. Thus *ākāśa* is a non-perceptible form of subtle matter.

Even today in books of modern physics, the existence of three states of matter is recognized. These states are: solid, liquid and gaseous. The Vaiśeṣika philosophers could talk about five states of the phenomenal world. They did not talk separately about matter or energy. In their opinion, the five states of the world-stuff are solid, liquid, gaseous, energetic and ethereal or *ākāśic*.

The five *bhūtas* are the five states of the world-stuff, but the Vaiśeṣikas do not recognize them as the ultimate constituents of the universe. The four *bhūtas*, viz., earth, water, light or heat and air, are made of *paramāṇus* or atoms. Only *ākāśa*, being simple and continuous, is not composed of atoms. The atoms are imperceptible, indestructible and eternal.[3] They are globular (*parimāṇ-*

ḍalya) in shape. There are four types of atoms. With reference to earth, water, light and air, the respective sense-perceptions of touch, taste, sight and smell are generated by the atoms. Each type of sense-perception is generated by one class of atoms.

The Democritean World

Many Greek philosophers, before Democritus, could reflect on the primordial substance of which the world is made. This substance was water for Thales (625-546 B.C.), air for Anaximenes (before 494 B.C.) and fire for Heraclitus (535-475 B.C.). Instead of a single subtance, Xenophanes thought of two substances, viz., earth and water as the material cause of the world. Empedocles (495-435 B.C.) declared that earth, water, fire and air are the four primordial substances out of which all things have arisen.

These early Greek thinkers never used the word 'element' for the so-called primordial substances. Modern writers term these substances as elements. But this concept of element should not be confused with the modern concept of element in chemistry or physics.

That the primary building blocks of the world are atoms was declared in the Greek world by Leucippus and his pupil Democritus[4] (460-370 B.C.). The Democritean concepts prevailed in Greece during the last half of the fifth century B.C. Democritus declared that the basic constituents of all things are Being and Not-Being, the full and the empty. The full is divided into innumerable particles. These particles are too small to be perceptible. They are called atoms. Atoms are indivisible. Etymologically the word 'atom' means "that which cannot be divided" (a = not, temnein or temes = cut). The atom was thought to be an absolutely solid unit without any space inside. Although the impenetrable atom was visualized not to have any space inside, the atoms were separated from one another by space which was considered empty, void or Not-Being. Democritus did not believe in the existence of a Creator. His atoms neither came into being nor will they cease to be. They are indestructible and eternal. They are infinite in number and kind. They vary in shape and size. They are eternally in motion in the void which the Greeks considered as of the nature of *Not-Being*. What the Greek atomists called the void was later termed as absolute space by Newton.

The Greek concept of the atom differs from the Indian concept on every point except one. Both the Greeks and the Indians declare that atoms are imperceptible. This is the only point which is common. In the Vaiśeṣika system, each kind of atom has got distinct individuality. The atoms of Kaṇāda are primarily at rest. They are distinguished from souls. Both atoms and souls are co-eternal. The early Vaiśeṣikas did not openly declare the existence of God. However, they accepted *dharma* or *adṛṣṭa* (moral law) as the central principle of their system. They did not consider *ākāśa* as void or not-being. It was a reality for them. On the contrary, the Democritean concepts of atom are different from those of the Vaiśeṣikas. The atoms of Democritus are not qualitatively different. They differ in figure, size, weight, position and arrangement. These differences are quantitative only. The Greeks believed that atoms by nature are in motion. The space is a void or not-being for them. It is a receptacle for the atoms in motion. The Greek atomists were atheists. They did recognize souls, but, in their belief, the atoms constitute souls. They did not accept any moral law that could regulate the atomic activities. They had a mechanistic view of the world. According to Democritus, events that take place in Nature are caused mechanistically.

Both the Indian and Greek schools of atomic pluralism declare that all substances in the world are made of atoms that are too small to be perceptible. Deeper analysis of the two systems, however, reveals that they have more dissimilarity than similarity.

No Birth and Death of the World-Stuff

The early Indian atomists did not mention anything about God. The Greek atomists refuted the existence of God. The idea of uncreatability and indestructibility of the atoms was prevalent in both the systems.

According to Judaism and Christianity, God creates the world out of nothing (*creatio ex nihilo*). From the empirical point of view such an idea seems untenable. From the logical point of view creation *ex nihilo* is impossible. Hence it is safe to deduce that to create something out of nothing is impossible even on the part of the Almighty God.

There are others who believe that both the Creator and the primary material for creation are co-eternal. Some others believe that the Creator, the primary material for creation and souls are co-eternal. Both these groups of believers emphasize on the unavoidability of an agent. In their opinion, whatever is made has got a maker. If there is an object, there must be a subject. The world we see, the world we live in is an object. We human beings are also objects. We must have got a maker. That maker is God.

Atheists question the validity of this argument of God-believers. They use the argument of the theists against the latter. If everything that exists must have got a maker, who is the maker of God? And who is the maker of the maker of God? We go on asking such questions. We can never reach a final stage. Such questions will lead to a logical fallacy, *regressus ad infinitum* (*anavasthā doṣa*). The theist asserts that we have to stop at the level of God. The atheist says: "If we are to stop at some level, why not stop at the level of the world itself?" The atheist believes that the world-stuff was never created and that it will never be destroyed. It is unborn and eternal.

Kapila, the founder of Sāṅkhya philosophy, expounded the doctrine of the uncreatability and indestructibility of the world-stuff in clear, unambiguous terms. "Nothing is eternal. Yet no thing can spring out of nothing nor can it be reduced to nothing, for when things are destroyed they do not disappear altogether but turn into stuff from which other things are made."[5] Thus Kapila arrives at the conclusion that there exists some material which can neither be created nor destroyed, and of which all things are formed, namely matter.

Lenin, while agreeing with Kapila, gives deep atheistic meaning to the concept of matter. He says: "If matter is primary and eternal it is uncreatable and indestructible, it is the inner final cause of everything existing. In a world where matter is the primary cause, the primary foundation of everything, there is room neither for God nor any other super-natural forces......... In the material world there is not a single thing, however minute, which can arise out of nothing or disappear without trace. The destruction of one thing gives rise to another and this to a third, and so on *ad infinitum*. Concrete things change, they are transformed one into another, but matter neither disappears nor is it created anew in the process."[6]

In science two separate laws were considered fundamental and inviolate. They were: (1) Law of Conservation of Matter; (2) Law of Conservation of Energy. The first law says: "Matter is neither created nor destroyed. The sum-total of matter in the universe is constant. There may be transformation of matter from one form to another." The second law says: "Energy is neither created nor destroyed. The sum-total of energy in the universe is constant. There may be transformation of energy from one form to another."

These two conservation laws were sacred till the year 1905. In that year, Einstein announced his mass-energy equation. This equation is symbolically expressed as $E = mc^2$, where E is energy in ergs, m is mass in grams and c is velocity of light, i.e., 10^{10} cm per second. According to this equation mass can be converted to energy and *vice versa*. Thus the distinction between matter and energy was discarded for ever. The contemporary idea is that matter is a packet of energy.

After 1905, the two conservation laws mentioned above were fused together to make it a single law, viz., Law of Conservation of Mass and Energy. This modified law says: "Matter including energy is neither created nor destroyed. There may be only transformation among the different forms of matter and energy."

The conservation laws of matter and energy were revised in 1905. But today in the same century some persons cast doubt into the revised law. When scientists observe the dancing of the micro-particles, their appearance from 'nowhere' and disappearance into 'nowhere', they become reluctant to accept the conservation law. This difficulty has arisen due to our objectified concept of matter and energy. When something becomes something else which is neither matter nor energy, we call it void which is our 'nowhere' here. Whatever we perceive by our senses or, in other words, whatever is manifested to us is our objectified something. Whatever becomes imperceptible to our senses or, in other words, whatever is unmanifested to us is our nothing or void. But the so-called void may be full. Hence scientists who don't rely on the conservation laws have no reason to say that something becomes nothing or nothing becomes something. The Bhagavadgītā propounds one conservation law which cannot be refuted on empirical grounds. This law says: "That which exists does not originate from what does not exist; what exists is not converted to nothing."[7] This is a formal law. It can never be invalidated. Violation of this law implies logical contradiction. This law does not say anything about what exists in the universe and does not specify matter, energy or micro-particles to be conserved. It says this much that whatever exists exists (in any form or no form) and that whatever does not exist does not exist.

Dalton's Atomic Concept

The Indian and the Greek concepts of atom remained confined to the domain of philosophy for not less than 2,000 years. It became a topic of science in the early part of the nineteenth century, about 1803, when John Dalton, an English chemist, stated his famous atomic theory of matter. Dalton was a school teacher. He developed the first modern theory of atoms. He declared that atoms are the smallest particles of elements and molecules are the smallest particles of compounds. An element contains only one kind of atom. An element cannot be changed to simpler substances since its atoms, being the simplest and indivisible, cannot be broken down. The theories of Dalton may be summarized in the following way: (1) All matter is made of tiny unit particles called atoms that are indivisible and indestructible. (2) The atoms of any given element are all alike. (3) A chemical reaction involves either combination of atoms or separation of already combined atoms, without any change in the atoms themselves. (4) Atoms unite in small whole-numbered ratios to form molecules. These concepts of Dalton were considered to be correct in entirety for about one hundred years. Although some of his concepts have not yet been discarded, it was felt necessary towards the last part of the nineteenth century to revise his atomic theory. Especially the concept of the indivisibility and indestructibility of atom was discarded due to emergence of contrary experimental findings.

The Newtonian World

Isaac Newton (1642-1727) is the father of classical physics. He did not start from nowhere. The Greek atomists had already laid the foundation of this physics. But the Democritean concepts could remain in a quiescent stage for many centuries due to the great influence of Aristotle (384-322 B.C.) who could be accepted by the Christian Church. Scientists began to free themselves from this influence during the period of Renaissance. Classical mechanics began with Newton. It is, however, not entirely correct to attribute classical mechanics to Newton alone. Many great thinkers during the Renaissance dedicated themselves to enquiries that later formed the basis of classical mechanics. Leonardo da Vinci, Galileo Galilei, Simon Stevin and Blaise Pascal were the intellectuals who contributed significantly to classical mechanics. But Newton did deserve special credit. In addition to his own original studies, he made a synthesis of all the scattered studies of other workers and constructed a single unified and harmonious theory.

Classical mechanics was born in the year 1687, when Newton published his book "Philosophiae Naturalis Principia Mathematica." For the first time he formulated the three basic principles of classical mechanics. These three principles were later called Newton's laws. These laws may be just mentioned here:

> A body remains at rest or, if already in motion, remains in uniform motion with constant speed in a straight line, unless it is acted on by an unbalanced external force. This is Newton's first law of motion.
>
> The acceleration produced by a particular force acting on a body is directly proportional to the magnitude of the force and inversely proportional to the mass of the body. This is Newton's second law of motion.
>
> Whenever one body exerts a force on a second body, the second body exerts a force on the first body. These forces are equal in magnitude and opposite in direction. This is Newton's third law of motion.

Before discussing the central idea of Newtonian physics, it is worth mentioning the influence of three intellectuals on the work of Newton. They are Nicolas Copernicus (1473–1543), Galileo Galilei (1564–1642) and René Descartes (1596–1650).

The Christian Church has been preaching geocentric and anthropocentric ideas. Copernicus wrote a book that was published in 1543 on the very day of his death. He suggested in that book that it was the Sun and not the Earth that was the centre of the universe. Thus our planetary system is the solar system ('Sol' means 'the Sun' in Latin) or the heliocentric system ('Helios' means 'the Sun' in Greek). Copernicus imagined the planetary orbits to be perfect circles. In 1609, Johannes Kepler (1571–1630) declared that the planetary orbits are ellipses instead of circles. In 1608, Galileo invented the telescope. He observed the motions of the planets and declared that the Earth revolves round the Sun. For this declaration, which was considered 'impious' by the Christian Church, he was seized by the Inquisition shortly before the birth of Newton.

The philosophy (science) of Kaṇāda and Democritus was speculative. The speculative method continued up to the end of the fifteenth century. Galileo resorted to experimentation for the discovery of the laws of Nature. He laid emphasis on quantification in experimental observation. He was a mathematician, a genius, the father of differential calculus. He was the first to express empirical findings in mathematical terms and, for this reason, he is recognized as the father of modern science. His mathematical approach to science is well reflected in his own words: "Philosophy (he meant science) is written in the great book which ever lies before your eyes; but we cannot understand it if we do not first learn the language and characters in which it is written. This language is mathematics, and the characters are triangles, circles, and other geometrical figures."[8]

The world owes a great deal to Galileo who discovered the first law of motion, though, to some extent, he was anticipated by Leonardo da Vinci. This law says: "A moving body will continue to move in the same direction with the same velocity until it is stopped by something." Before Galileo, an altogether different view prevailed regarding motion of a lifeless body. It was thought that any lifeless body would not move on its own and had to be set in motion by a living agency but would gradually come to rest on its own. Life was associated with the movement of the body without the help of any external agency. Aristotle thought that the heavenly bodies were set in motion by God. He also explained the downward movement of earth and water and the upward movement of air and fire as 'natural' to dead matter.

Francis Bacon (1561-1626) was a contemporary of Galileo. While Galileo was doing his experiments in Italy, Bacon was devising his scientific methods in England. Bacon was an empiricist. He was the first to formulate the inductive methods. The methodology of experimentation, the process of drawing general conclusions from experimental observations and the testing of conclusions by further experimentation were laid down in detail by Bacon. He advocated the inductive method of reasoning as opposed to the deductive.

René Descartes, the seventeenth century French philosopher,

is usually regarded as the founder of modern philosophy. He was a brilliant mathematician. He invented analytic geometry and applied his geometrical methods to philosophy. Physics and astronomy profoundly influenced his philosophy. In turn, his ideas influenced science in the centuries to come until quantum physics was developed in the twentieth century.

Descartes was a rationalist. He believed in innate ideas, i.e., ideas that are not derived from experience, but inhere in man and are known intuitively. His methods were deductive as opposed to the inductive ones of Bacon. Descartes started his philosophical meditation in order to arrive at absolutely certain truth. He could doubt the reality of the world, of God, even of his own body. But even when he had bracketed out every phenomenon, he could not bracket out his own 'I'. He could not doubt his 'I'. And so he said: "Cogito, ergo sum" (I think, therefore, I am). He could be certain about the existence of the 'I' that thinks. Descartes' *cogito* made mind more certain for him than matter. Mind and matter were two separate and fundamentally different entities for him. This was the dualism of Descartes. This Cartesian division between mind (*res cogitans*—thinking thing) and matter (*res extensa*—extended thing) has had a profound effect on Western thought. Descartes was a believer of God. The existence of God was a necessity in his scientific philosophy. He conceived of mind and matter as creations of God. But he gave a higher ontological status to mind than to matter. He asserts that the essence of human nature lies in thought and that whatever we conceive clearly and distinctly is true. Only that knowledge which is derived from evident intuition and necessary deduction is true and certain for Descartes, as he says: "The conception of the pure and attentive mind is intuition. There are no paths to the certain knowledge of truth open to man except evident intuition and necessary deduction."

Descartes looked at the material universe as a great machine. He did not see any purpose, life and spirituality in matter. The great machine of Nature, he says, consists of smaller component parts and works according to mechanical laws. The working of the world-machine can be explained in terms of the arrangement and movement of its parts. This Cartesian idea that Nature is a perfect machine which is governed by exact mathematical laws guided all scientific thoughts in the seventeenth, eighteenth and nineteenth centuries until twentieth century physics brought about a radical change.

Descartes' method is analytic. He broke up thoughts and problems into pieces and arranged those in their logical order. This analytic method of reasoning, as advocated by Descartes, was a contribution to science. Of course, when extended to the extreme, this method distorts our vision and conceals the integral and holistic picture. This was exactly what happened in natural and social sciences and also in humanities. This has led to the widespread attitude of reductionism—the notion that every complex phenomenon can be reduced to its constituent parts in order that its true nature be made transparent. Such a notion is erroneous. The knowledge that water is made of hydrogen and oxygen is useful to us; but neither hydrogen nor oxygen can quench our thirst, and also the physical and chemical properties of water are totally different from those of hydrogen and oxygen. The descriptions of the elephant by the six blind men were correct according to the theory of reductionism, but not a single blind man could get the holistic picture of the elephant. Analysis is an important tool in the hands of an investigator in science or humanities, but when it is done at the cost of synthesis, we end in wrong vision.

Like Galileo, Descartes believed that the language of Nature is mathematics. In the realm of mathematics, analytic geometry was his celebrated discovery. He said with great pride: "My entire physics is nothing other than geometry." For him, knowledge of science was certain. He has written: "All science is certain, evident knowledge. We reject all knowledge which is merely probable and judge that only those things should be believed which are perfectly known and about which there can be no doubts."[9]

In the notion of scientism, there is a belief that science can do anything and everything, that there is nothing impossible in science and that all science is certain. Cartesian philosophy is the basis of this scientism. In this regard, the words of Descartes may be quoted here: "I admit nothing as true of them that is not deduced, with the clarity of a mathematical demonstration, from common notions whose truth we cannot doubt. Because all the phenomena of nature can be explained in this way. I think that no other principles of physics need be admitted, nor are to be desired."[10]

Descartes split the person into physique and psyche or body

and mind. The former is the container and the latter is the content. Both the container and the content, according to him, exist independently. This 'Cartesian' division of the world into mind and matter modulated the thinking of Western scientists who visualized all the objects of the world as dead parts assembled into a huge machine. Descartes thought that the universe and every thing in it are automata. He supported this philosophy by his mathematics. He extended his mechanistic view of matter even to living organisms. In his view, plants, animals and human beings are simply machines. He visualized a separate rational soul, sitting in each human being in the pineal gland in the brain. He tried to show that all living organisms were nothing but automata. He said: "We see clocks, artificial fountains, mills and other similar machines which, though merely man-made, have nonetheless the power to move themselves in several different ways... I do not recognize any difference between the machines made by craftsmen and the various bodies that nature alone composes."[11] This Cartesian division has led to endless confusion in the life sciences especially with regard to the relation between mind and brain. This has not spared even the physicist. The founders of quantum physics experienced extreme difficulty in the interpretations of their observations of atomic phenomena so long as they did not discard Cartesian dualism. In this connection Werner Heisenberg has said: "This partition has penetrated deeply into the human mind during the three centuries following Descartes and it will take a long time for it to be replaced by a really different attitude toward the problem of reality."[12] The certainty of scientific knowledge and the rejection of probable knowledge, as founded by Descartes, influenced the world of science for three centuries (17th, 18th and 19th) until the evolution of quantum physics in the twentieth century. Quantum physics recognized the principle of indeterminacy and probability instead of certainty of the occurrence of events.

The mechanistic world view of Descartes exerted profound influence on Isaac Newton and his classical physics. The mechanistic Newtonian model of the universe dominated the scientific thinking of the world from the second half of the seventeenth to the end of the nineteenth century.

Two opposing trends were prevalent before Newton in the scientific thinking of the seventeenth century. Bacon's method was empirical and inductive. On the other hand, Descartes' method was rational and deductive. Newton could bring about a synthesis of these opposing trends in his *Principia*. In his opinion, neither experiments without systematic interpretation nor deduction from first principles without experimental evidence will lead one to reliable conclusion. He unified the two trends by synthesis of systematic experimentation and mathematical analysis and developed a methodology of science that is still operative.

Newton was a believer in Christianity. He believed that the world was created by God Who created and assembled all the different objects into a huge machine. In devising the world-machine, God created the material particles, the forces between them and the fundamental laws of motion. In the beginning, he breathed into this machine the first impulse so that the machine would run, and since that time the world-machine ever runs by God's immutable laws. The natural laws that are discovered by the scientists are, according to Newton, divine laws that are invariable and eternal. The laws of Nature are manifestations of God's perfection. God rules the world from above. He transcends the world, his creation.

Of course, Newton did not feel the constant necessity of God to rule the cosmic machine which is automatic. In the beginning, the world machine was set into motion by God and after that everything is determined. According to this mechanistic determinism of Newtonian physics, from the moment the universe was created and set into motion, everything that has happened, is happening and will happen in it, is already determined. Newton, being a true Christian, was very much worried about the fact that the cosmic machine is no longer in need of the God Almighty after He created the world and applied the first impulsive force to it. When he came to realize that it does not make any difference for the cosmic automata whether God exists or not, it made him sick. He managed to cling to the idea that the Almighty does exercise power to interfere with the working of the world machine when something goes wrong. Occasionally, He corrects the irregularities of misbehaving planets and stars. Newton wrote: "...the diurnal rotations of the planets could not be derived from gravity, but required a divine arm to impress it on them."[13] It was Laplace who could strike a blow on religion in discarding the slightest supernatural cause in the working of the physical universe. He proved conclusively that the cosmic machine is self-correcting. When he presented his monumental work on celestial mechanics to Napoleon, he was reproached for failing to mention God. Laplace replied, "Sire, I have no need for that hypothesis."[14]

Newton postulated absolute space and absolute time. He conceived of space as void that served as a receptacle for the objects of the world. His space was always at rest, infinite, indefinite, extending infinitely to all directions, invariable, unchangeable and eternal. This was the three-dimensional space of Euclidean geometry. In Newton's own words, "Absolute space, in its own nature, without regard to anything external, remains always similar and immovable."[15] His time was eternal, without beginning and end. Newtonian time flows uniformly and smoothly from the past through the present to the future. All changes in the physical world take place in time which, according to Newton, is absolute, having no connection with the material world. "Absolute, true and mathematical time", said Newton, "of itself and by its own nature, flows uniformly without regard to anything external".[16] This flow of time, in the Newtonian concept, does not depend upon events that are external to it and does not vary for various observers. "Absolute time", wrote Newton, "flows equably".[17] His absolute space and absolute time were separate, without having any connections at all.

Both Democritus and Newton believed in the full and the void. The atoms of which matter is made were considered as the full. Space was thought to be completely empty. In both Democritean and the Newtonian models the particles always maintained their identity in mass and shape. Matter was considered to be passive and conserved in both the models. Newton has written in his 'Optiks' about the atoms in the following words: "It seems probable to me that God in the beginning formed matter in solid, massy, hard, impenetrable, movable particles, of such sizes and figures, and with such other properties, and in such proportion to space, as most conduced to the end for which He formed them; and that these primitive particles, being solids, are incomparably harder than any porous bodies compounded of them; even so very hard, as never to wear or break in pieces; no ordinary power being able to divide what God Himself made one in the first creation".[18]

Newton's concept of atom differed from that of modern physics.

Newtonian atoms were made of the same material substance. Newton's matter was homogeneous. In order to explain the difference between one type of matter and another type, he did not conceive of difference in atoms due to difference in weights or densities, but he ascribed the difference to variation in packing of atoms. He assumed the basic building blocks of matter to be one 'stuff' only, varying in sizes.

The Newtonian atomism differed from the Democritean one in description of the gravitational force. This is an attractive force acting among the material particles. In the quantification of this force, Newton, in 1684, worked out a mathematical expression which is known as Newton's law of gravitation. This is stated algebraically as follows:

$$F = G\frac{m_1 m_2}{d^2}$$

Here m_1 and m_2 are the masses of two bodies, d is the distance between them and G is the gravitational constant. This law says: "Every particle in the universe attracts every other particle with a force directly proportional to the product of the two masses and inversely proportional to the square of the distance between them." According to Newton, this gravitational force was created by God and this acts instantaneously over a distance.

In Newton's view, the motion of particles is caused by the force of gravity, which acts instantaneously over a distance. The material particles and the forces acting between them could be thought of as fundamentally different in nature. In Newtonian mechanics, all physical phenomena are reduced to the motion of material bodies, and this motion is caused by their mutual attraction, i.e., by the force of gravity. The effect of this force on particles or material bodies can be mathematically described as the laws of motion, which form the basis of classical mechanics. Thus, according to Newton, the universe is a giant cosmic machine which is completely causal and determinate. Whatever happens in this machine has a definite cause and every cause has a definite effect. With full knowledge of the system, the future of the world machine can be predicted with absolute certainty. This is the rigorous determinism of Newtonian mechanics.

This action-at-a-distance was a big puzzle for Newton. He

could realize that this could be described, but could not be explained. He wrote in *Philosophiae Naturalis Principia Mathematica*: "I have not been able to discover the cause of those properties of gravity from phenomena, and I frame no hypotheses...it is enough that gravity does really exist, and act according to the laws which we have explained, and abundantly serves to account for all the motions of the celestial bodies."[19] In a letter to Richard Bently, Newton wrote: "...that one body may act upon another at a distance through a vacuum without the mediation of anything else, by and through which their action and force may be conveyed from one to another, is to me so great an absurdity that, I believe, no man who has in philosophic matters a competent faculty of thinking could ever fall into it."[20]

What has been described in the foregoing paragraphs is Newtonian absolutism in a nutshell. In this mechanistic model, space and time that are separate and absolute are pre-existent to matter. All the separate objects in the universe are separate parts of the cosmic machine. But the separate parts of the single machine do not have any single substratum. Newtonian science makes effort, not to establish identity of the separate parts, but to find the relationships among the separate parts. These relationships are expressed through the laws of Nature. On the surface, Nature seems to be chaotic, as if there is no order in the universe. But, according to Newton, God Who created matter in the world also created laws of Nature to regulate Nature. Thus Newton's world view was a picture of order beneath chaos. His matter was transformable, but not destructible. He thought that the mass of a body remains constant irrespective of the condition whether it is at rest or in motion. The Newtonian physics assumes that there is an external world which exists apart from us. It further assumes that we can observe, measure and speculate about the external world without in any way changing or influencing it. According to this view, the external world is indifferent from us and our needs. The concept of absolute objectivity that prevailed in science for about three centuries rested upon this assumption of the bifurcation of the phenomenal world into the subjective 'I' and the external world.

A significant contribution to the philosophy of science was made by Newton through his experimental approach. He said: "I make no hypotheses (*Hypothesae non fingo*)." He laid stress on observations and reproducibility of experimental results. The Christian Church expressed unhappiness over this position of Newton. The Church had preached the revealed truth for one and a half millennia and resisted all attempts to correct that 'truth' through experimental results. According to the Church, no method can challenge the truth revealed by God Himself. Newton's method of experimental verification, in effect, was a direct challenge to the power of the Church, although he never intended to antagonize the religious scripture.

In the following three chapters, viz., particle physics, relativity and quantum physics, it will be seen that many concepts of Newton are wrong. However, it is not correct to say that Newtonian mechanics is to be discarded altogether. Newtonian model is still valid and will remain valid in the macro-world. For objects consisting of a large number of atoms and for velocities which are small in comparison to the speed of light, Newtonian model is operative. Relativity and quantum mechanics are operative in the micro-world. Quantum theory is applicable to the sub-atomic particles. Relativity theory is applicable when high velocities comparable to the speed of light are concerned. Neither of these two models is absolutely accurate for all ranges of cosmic phenomena. Each one of these models works for a certain range of phenomena and hence is both valid and not valid if the totality of the cosmic phenomena is considered. Hence, without reference to the macro-world or the micro-world, it would not be correct to say whether one model is 'right' and the other is 'wrong'. Werner Heisenberg has rightly said: "Every word or concept, clear as it may seem to be, has only a limited range of applicability."[21] The correct understanding and humble opinion of great thinker like Einstein are truly reflected in the following sentences: "...creating a new theory is not like destroying an old barn and erecting skyscraper in its place. It is rather like climbing a mountain, gaining new and wider views, discovering unexpected connections between our starting point and its rich environment."[22]

Historians of science have called the sixteenth and seventeenth centuries the Age of the Scientific Revolution. This revolution began with Nicolas Copernicus who overthrew the geocentric view of Ptolemy and the Bible. The man who completed this revolution was Isaac Newton. He developed a complete mathematical formulation of the mechanistic view of Nature. He made a synthesis of the works of Copernicus, Kepler, Galileo, Bacon and Descartes. Physics, as worked out by Newton in the seventeenth century, remained as the solid foundation of the grand edifice of science well into the twentieth century. The achievement of this great genius has been aptly praised by Einstein as "perhaps the greatest advance in thought that a single individual was ever privileged to make."[23]

NOTES

1. VaS, II.1.27, 29-31.
2. NS, IV.2.21-22.
3. NB, IV.2.16.
4. Russell, B., *History of Western Philosophy*, George Allen & Unwin, London, 1975.
5. *ABC of Dialectical and Historical Materialism*, Progress Publishers, Moscow, 1978, p. 79.
6. Afanasyev, V.G., *Marxist Philosophy*, Progress Publishers, Moscow, 1980, pp. 40-41.
7. BG, II.16.
8. Galileo, G., Quoted by Capra, F. in "*The Turning Point*", Fontana/Collins, London, 1983, p. 39.
9. Descartes, R., Quoted by Capra, F., as in [8], p. 42.
10. Descartes, R., Quoted by Capra, F., as in [8], p. 43.
11. Descartes, R., Quoted by Capra, F., as in [8], p. 47.
12. Heisenberg, W., *Physics and Philosophy*, Harper & Row, New York, 1962, p. 81.
13. Newton, I., Quoted by Capra, F., as in [8].
14. Laplace, Quoted by Capra, F. in "*The Tao of Physics*", Fontana/Collins, London, 1981, p. 59.
15. Newton, I., Quoted by Capra, F., as in [14], p. 56.
16. *Ibid.*
17. Newton, I., Quoted by Zukav, G. in "*The Dancing Wu Li Masters*", Fontana/Collins, London, 1980, p. 170.
18. Newton, I., Quoted by Capra, F., as in [8], p. 52.
19. Newton, I., Quoted by Zukav, G., as in [17], p. 49.
20. *Ibid.*
21. Heisenberg, W., *Physics and Philosophy*, Allen & Unwin, London, 1963, p. 125.
22. Einstein, A. and Infeld, L., *The Evolution of Physics*, Cambridge University Press, Cambridge, 1971, p. 152.
23. Einstein, A., Quoted by Capra, F., as in [8], p. 49.

CHAPTER II

PARTICLE PHYSICS

By getting to smaller and smaller units, we do not come to fundamental units, or indivisible units, but we do come to a point where division has no meaning.

Werner Heisenberg

The Lord is subtle, but he is not malicious.

Albert Einstein

God used beautiful mathematics in creating the world.

Paul Dirac

THE INDIVISIBLE AND indestructible atom of Kaṇāda and Democritus was a philosophical conjecture. This speculative concept was accepted as fact in science by Newton and Dalton. For almost a century, Dalton's atomic theory was accepted by the scientific world in its totality. In the last decade of the nineteenth century, cracks appeared in the so-called indivisible atom. A series of discoveries within a short span of time shattered the idea of the indivisibility and indestructibility of atom. These discoveries were X-ray in 1895, radioactivity in 1896, electron in 1897 and radium in 1898.

Discovery of Electron, Proton and Neutron

In 1891, Stoney proposed the name electron for the elementary unit of electric charge. In those years, J.J. Thomson was conducting experiments on cathode rays. In 1897, he declared that the cathode rays are actually a stream of particles carrying negative electrical charges. It was later confirmed that each of such units carrying a negative charge was a minute particle. This particle was named electron.

Scientists could visualize a positively charged particle corresponding to the negatively charged one. After the discovery of the electron, intensive search was made to detect the positively charged particle. A number of workers were independently investigating on the deflection behaviour of positive charged particles in electric and magnetic fields. E. Goldstein in 1886, J. Perrin in 1895 and W. Wein in 1898 reported their observations on the deflection behaviour of something which was positively charged. In 1907, J. J. Thomson proposed the name 'positive rays'. Rutherford, in 1914, suggested that this something that was positively charged or the positive ray of Thomson was a particle. He gave the name 'positive electron' to it. The word 'proton' was assigned to this particle by 1920. A proton carries a unit positive charge whereas an electron carries a unit negative charge. But a proton is much heavier than an electron. The weight of a proton is 1836 times that of an electron.

In the year 1920, suggestion came from three widely separated sources about the existence of an entirely new particle that plays important role in the structure of atoms. W.D. Harkins of U.S.A., Orme Masson of Australia and E. Rutherford of England got evidences for the existence of an uncharged particle. This hypothetical particle was called neutron by Harkins in 1921. The actual discovery of neutron had, however, to wait till 1932 when James Chadwik, an associate of Rutherford, could identify this particle conclusively. The neutron does not carry any electric charge.

With the discovery of these three subatomic particles, the Democritean and the Newtonian atom was no longer considered as indivisible and indestructible. It was realized that atom was not the primary building block of the universe. Atom is made of still smaller particles. These micro-particles are the electron, the proton and the neutron. The neutron is slightly heavier than the proton. For all practical purposes, the neutron and the proton may be considered to have equal weights. But the electron is much lighter, 1836 times lighter than the proton. In the 1930s electron was considered as the smallest particle in the world.

Considering both the natural and the artificial elements in the world, the total number of elements on the Earth is one hundred and odd. It is not safe to specify the exact number since newer and newer man-made elements are occasionally added to the list. Nevertheless, this is not a large number when we realize that all objects, living or non-living, in the universe are made of these few elements only. Again, it is surprising to know that all these elements are made of three micro-particles only, viz., proton, electron and neutron. The diverse elements that have got widely different appearances and properties are made of these three micro-particles only. Whether the element is oxygen or nitrogen, zinc, iron, copper, silver or gold, sulphur, phosphorus, sodium, potassium or calcium, or, radium, plutonium, thorium or uranium, only proton, neutron and electron are the bricks of which the buildings of the atoms of all the elements are made.

Keeping the atomic constituents in view, we may like to know what an element is. An element is a substance all of whose atoms have the same atomic number. The number of positive charges or protons in the atom is its atomic number. Thus each element has its specific atomic number. Like the roll numbers or registration numbers of students in a class, elements have got their respective atomic numbers. The element hydrogen has got only one proton and hence its atomic number is one. The element carbon has got six protons; its atomic number is six. The atomic weight of the same element may vary due to varying number of neutrons. As for example, there are three types of hydrogen atoms, viz., usual hydrogen with one proton and one electron, deuterium with one proton, one neutron and one electron, and tritium with one proton, two neutrons and one electron. When the atomic number changes, in other words, when the number of protons in the atom changes, the element becomes something different. When the atom contains two protons instead of one, it no longer remains a hydrogen atom, but becomes a helium atom. The atomic number is different from the mass number of the atom. The number of protons plus neutrons, or, in other words, the number of nucleons in the nucleus of the atom is the mass number of the atom. The atomic number of carbon is six by virtue of its having six protons, but its mass number is twelve since it contains six protons and six neutrons.

How the different elements that seem to have very little in common are really not compositionally alien to one another may be realized by perusal of Table 2.1.

Atoms are too small. The subatomic particles are still smaller. Their dimensions cannot be measured by inch, centimetre or millimetre. The usual weights of grams or milligrams are too large to express the mass of the micro-particles. Hence special devices have been made to express both these parameters.

The smallest atom in Nature, viz., hydrogen atom, has a diameter of 1×10^{-8} cm. Uranium atom, which is relatively large, has a diameter of 2.5×10^{-8} cm. The radii of most atoms are in the vicinity of 2×10^{-8} cm. The radius of the electron is 2.8×10^{-13} cm. These smaller dimensions are expressed in Angstrom (Å) units.

Table 2.1 : Proton and Neutron Contents in the Atoms of Some Common Elements

Element (most abundant isotope)	*Atomic number*	*Mass number*	*No. of protons*	*No. of neutrons*	*Average atomic weight (awu)*
Hydrogen	1	1	1	—	1.00797
Helium	2	4	2	2	4.0026
Lithium	3	7	3	4	6.939
Beryllium	4	9	4	5	9.0122
Boron	5	11	5	6	10.811
Carbon	6	12	6	6	12.01115
Nitrogen	7	14	7	7	14.0067
Oxygen	8	16	8	8	15.9994
Phosphorus	15	31	15	16	30.9738
Sulphur	16	32	16	16	32.064
Iron	26	56	26	30	55.847
Copper	29	63	29	34	63.54
Silver	47	107	47	60	107.870
Gold	79	197	79	118	196.967
Uranium	92	238	92	146	238.03

One Angstrom unit is 1×10^{-8} cm. The diameter of hydrogen atom is one Angstrom (1A).

The weights of atoms and subatomic particles are expressed in atomic weight units (awu). In this connection, carbon-12 has been accepted as standard and has been assigned twelve atomic weight units. Thus one atomic weight unit is defined as one-twelfth the weight of one carbon-12 atom. The weight of hydrogen atom (with one proton and one electron) is 1.673×10^{-24} g in conventional units and 1.0078 awu in the carbon-12 standard. The masses and the charges, along with some other characteristics, of the subatomic particles are given in Table 2.2.

Table 2.2 : Some Characteristics of the Elementary Particles within an Atom

Particle	*Symbol*	*Relative mass*	*Rest Mass in conventional units g*	*Rest Mass in atomic weight units awu*	*Electric charge*	*Spin relative to photons*	*Life*
Electron	e^-	1	9.1083×10^{-28}	0.000549	—	$\frac{1}{2}$	Infinite
Proton	p	1836	1.67239×10^{-24}	1.007593	+	$\frac{1}{2}$	Infinite*
Neutron	n	1839	1.67470×10^{-24}	1.008982	0	$\frac{1}{2}$	12 to 15 minutes approx.

*Proton decays. Its half-life is 10^{32} years.

Thus the electron was considered to possess the lowest weight among the micro-particles during the 1930s. It will be discussed later that the electron is not the smallest particle and that there are massless particles too.

Discovery of Anti-Particles

In 1928, P.A.M. Dirac, an English mathematical physicist, presented some theoretical arguments in favour of the existence of a particle which is the opposite of an electron. This theoretical anti-electron was supposed to have a mass similar to that of the electron, but to carry a charge opposite to that of the electron. This theoretical prediction of Dirac was soon proved true experimentally by C.D. Anderson who was studying cosmic rays in cloud chamber at the California Institute of Technology. He detected positive electron in cosmic ray in 1932. The positive electron or anti-electron carries a positive charge. It was later known as positron.

When an electron and a positron unite, the two opposite charges neutralize each other and the particles are annihilated, leaving only energy in the form of radiation, similar to gamma rays. The life of a positron is transient. Its average life is in the order of a billionth part (10^{-9}) of a second.

Dirac's theory was extended to other micro-particles. It was thought that existence of particle-pairs might be a universal phenomenon. And hence intensive search was made for the discovery of opposite particles of proton and neutron.

The antiproton was discovered in 1955. At the Lawrence Radiation Laboratory in Berkeley, California, O. Chamberlain, E. Segre, C.E. Weigand and T. Ypsilantis detected this antiparticle whiie working with Bevatron. Antiproton has a mass similar to that of proton, but a charge opposite to that of proton. When the proton and the antiproton unite, the positive and the negative charges neutralize each other and the two particles are annihilated with liberation of energy similar to gamma ray.

The time gap between the discovery of antiproton and that of antineutron was one year only. In 1956, the discovery of antineutron was announced by B. Cork, G.R. Lambertson, O. Piccioni and W. Wenzel. This finding was confirmed by E. Segre and W.M. Powell at Berkeley in 1958. Both neutron and antineutron have similar mass and both are electrically neutral. Still they form a pair of anti-particles that mutually annihilate, with liberation of energy, when they unite. When the neutron and the antineutron spin in the same direction, they produce oppositely directed magnetic fields.

Anti-Matter and Anti-Universe

The existence of antimatter was postulated after the discovery of anti-particles. Matter or 'normal' matter is made of three particles, viz., negatively charged electron, positively charged proton and electrically neutral neutron. In the same analogy, antimatter made of positively charged electron or positron, negatively charged antiproton and electrically neutral antineutron could be conceived of. The normal particles are abundantly present in the world in which we live and hence is the ubiquity of the ordinary matter. The rarity of antimatter in our world is well anticipated since the rare emergence of antimatter is bound to be short-lived in the midst of ubiquitous ordinary matter. Co-existence of matter and antimatter in spatial approximation for appreciable length of time is not possible due to the mutual annihilation with subsequent liberation of energy. But the capability of the existence of antimatter in this world of ours cannot be logically ruled out. Around 1928, Dirac proposed the concept of negative energy states. According to his theory, for every particle there exists an anti-particle. As particle and anti-particle unite to liberate energy, so also, if enough energy is available, particles and antiparticles can be created out of pure energy in the reverse process of annihilation. The acceptance of this theory implies that creation of antiparticles in the world we live in is not rare, although their presence is not abundant. A number of physicists became active to detect the presence of antimatter in our world. In 1965, an international group of physicists, under the direction of L.M. Lederman of Columbia University, confirmed the possibility of antimatter.

Antideuteron, which is an antimatter, was artificially created in the laboratory. An ordinary proton and a neutron form a deuteron which is an isotope of hydrogen. It was experimentally established that an antiproton and an antineutron can form antideuteron. In the nucleus of normal atom, attractive strong forces exist among the nucleons (protons and neutrons), i.e., between protons and protons, neutrons and neutrons and protons and neutrons. With the experimental formation of antideuteron, it was established that equivalent attractive strong force between antiproton and antineutron inside the nucleus of antideuteron does exist. It is natural to expect analogous attractive forces between antiproton and antiproton, antineutron and antineutron, and antiproton and antineutron.

It seems highly probable that all objects within our galaxy, the Milky Way, are entirely made of ordinary matter. This probability is due to the fact that matter and antimatter cannot co-exist because their co-existence means their mutual annihilation and liberation of energy. But the probability of all the objects consisting exclusively of antimatter in some other galaxy is not inconceivable. Everything in that antigalaxy might be made of antimatter consisting of anti-elements composed of anti-atoms into whose constitution might have entered antiprotons, antineutrons and positrons.

But, how come, the galaxy and the antigalaxy do not get mutually annihilated? The great distance intervening between two galaxies probably prevents the collision of matter and antimatter. In a galaxy there is gravitational attraction among bodies of normal matter. It is expected that there is gravitational attraction among bodies made of antimatter in an antigalaxy. But gravitational repulsion instead of attraction is likely to exist between matter of our galaxy and antimatter of some other antigalaxy. Maybe, there is an insulation layer of gamma rays between a galaxy and an antigalaxy. Matter of our galaxy and antimatter of an antigalaxy, in the contiguous boundary region, might have united to be mutually annihilated to release the insulating layer of gamma rays. This may explain the co-existence of our galaxy and a neighbouring antigalaxy without mutual annihilation. In our galaxy matter is stable and antimatter is unstable. In an antigalaxy antimatter may be equally stable whereas matter may be quite unstable there. It may also be assumed that symmetry exists in the formation of matter and antimatter. In that case, formation of matter in one location may be simultaneous with that of antimatter elsewhere. As a consequence, there may exist an anti-universe as a counterpart of our normal universe instead of the existence of galaxies and antigalaxies in the universe in which our galaxy is located.

Thomson's Model of Atomic Structure

In 1898, J.J. Thomson created the first model of the atom. In this model, atoms were clouds of positive charge within which floated negative electrons equal in number to the positive charges so that the total atom was balanced to be charge-neutral. The atom was supposed to be a sphere uniformly charged with positive electricity, in which electrons were embedded. In Thomson's own words, it was something like plum pudding. The structure of the atom that Thomson envisaged is diagrammatically represented in Figure 2.1.

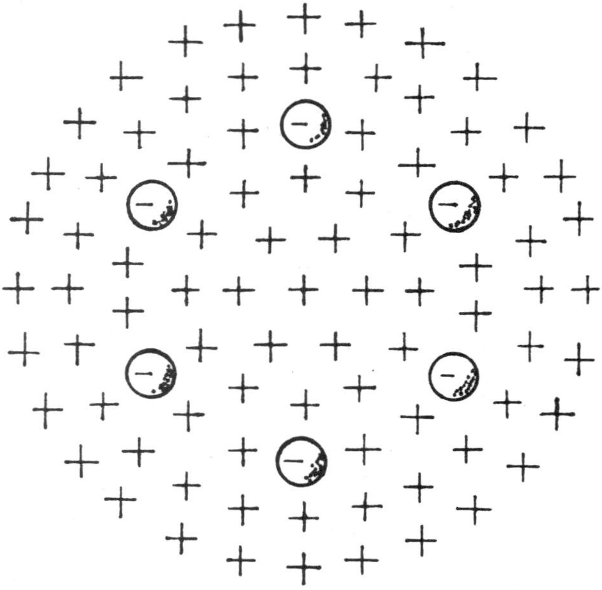

Fig. 2.1: Thomson's model of atomic structure.

Rutherford's Model of Atomic Structure

Alpha rays that were newly discovered were known to consist of positively charged particles. Ernest Rutherford used the alpha rays of radioactive materials to bombard atoms of various substances. He wanted to observe scattering of alpha particles by the bombarded atoms. Had the atoms been solid spheres, the alpha particles would push them aside while forcing their way through them. They would naturally collide with a host of the atoms and, in doing so, would change their direction hundreds and thousands of times. This, however, did not happen in the experiment of Rutherford. He was surprised to see that most of the alpha particles passed with almost no deviation from the straight path. A few alpha particles were deflected at large angles or occasionally repelled backwards. The scattering of the alpha particles by the atoms has been illustrated in Figure 2.2. Deflection of alpha particles occurred as a result of repulsion of the positively charged alpha particles and the positively charged nucleons (protons) inside the nucleus of the bombarded atom.

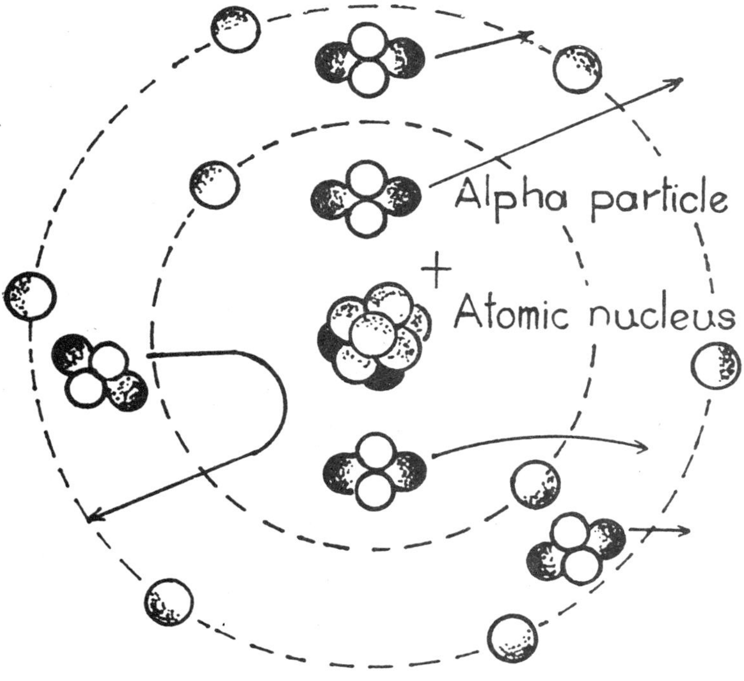

Fig. 2.2: Scattering of alpha-particles by an atom.

Rutherford studied this phenomenon in detail and concluded finally that the atoms were practically empty. He suggested his planetary model of the atom in 1911. According to this model, which is diagrammatically presented in Figure 2.3, the whole positive charge and practically all the mass of the atom are concentrated in the centre of the atom in a small volume. This is the core or the nucleus of the atom. The diameter of an atom is about one hundred millionth of a centimetre. The nucleus occupies about one hundred thousandth of the cross-section of the atom. Thus major portion of the volume of the atom is empty. This concept was contrary to that of the old Democritean and Newtonian solid atoms moving in empty space. With Rutherford's discovery, atom was no longer considered to be impenetrably solid.

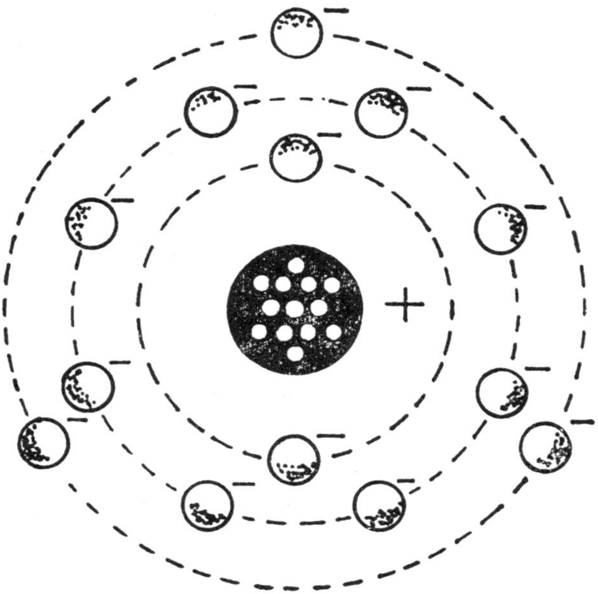

Fig. 2.3: Rutherford's planetary model of the atom.

The total atom is neutral in charge. The number of positive charges in the atomic nucleus equals the number of negatively charged electrons that are extranuclear. Rutherford visualized the atom similar to our solar system. The electrons revolve around the nucleus like the planets around the Sun. The electrons are bound to the nucleus by electric forces. Relatively speaking with respect to masses, the distances of the electrons from the nucleus are enormously greater than those of our planets from our Sun.

Bohr's Model of Electronic Arrangement

The atomic nucleus, although massive, is still tiny. On the other hand, the electrons which contribute hardly any mass to the atom occupy practically all the space of the atomic volume. This situation is quite anomalous. Physicists were very much perplexed in the elucidation of the electronic arrangement. There must be something special in the arrangement of the electrons around the atomic nucleus. In solving this puzzle, studies of atomic spectra by Niels Bohr, measurement of ionization energies of atoms by James Frank and Gustav Hertz and discovery of the periodic table helped the physicists immensely. Finally Niels Bohr unlocked the mystery of electronic structure in 1913. For this marvellous piece of work, he was awarded the Nobel Prize in 1922.

The Bohr atom is described as a tiny solar system, with the nucleus as the Sun in the centre surrounded by the planetary electrons in various orbits. The electrons in unexcited atoms are arranged in one to seven major energy levels, depending on the complexity of the atom. The energy levels or shells are designated by numbers as 1, 2, 3, 4, 5, 6 and 7 or by letters as K, L, M, N, O, P and Q. The first energy level, K, is closest to the nucleus. The electrons on this energy level are held very strongly. With the progressive increase in the distances of the energy levels from the atomic nucleus, the attractive forces of the nucleus on the electrons correspondingly decrease.

There are also energy sublevels in the main energy level. The number of sublevels in a main energy level is equal to the number of that level. Thus, there is only one energy level in the first main level; in the second main level there are two energy sublevels, in the third main level there are three energy sublevels, and so on. The sublevels are named as sharp (s), principal (p), diffuse (d) and fundamental (f). Table 2.3 presents the energy levels with sublevels and the number of electrons therein for a sample of thirty elements.

The electrons in a sublevel are in constant motion. They move in definite regions of space called orbitals. The square of the number of designation of a main energy level gives the number of orbitals in that level. Thus in the second main energy level there are four (2^2) orbitals and in the third main energy level there are nine (3^2) orbitals. More than two electrons cannot occupy a single orbital. Thus the number of orbitals multiplied by two gives the maximum number of electrons in a main energy level. The maxi-

Table 2.3: Electronic Configuration of Some Elements

Atomic No.	*Element*	*K*	*L*		*M*			*N*				*O*				*P*				*Q*			
		1	2		3			4				5				6				7			
		s	*s*	*p*	*s*	*p*	*d*	*s*	*p*	*d*	*f*	*s*	*p*	*d*	*f*	*s*	*p*	*d*	*f*	*s*	*p*	*d*	*f*
1	Hydrogen	1																					
2	Helium	2																					
3	Lithium	2	1																				
4	Beryllium	2	2																				
5	Boron	2	2	1																			
6	Carbon	2	2	2																			
7	Nitrogen	2	2	3																			
8	Oxygen	2	2	4																			
9	Fluorine	2	2	5																			
10	Neon	2	2	6																			
11	Sodium	2	2	6	1																		
12	Magnesium	2	2	6	2																		
17	Chlorine	2	2	6	2	5																	
18	Argon	2	2	6	2	6																	
19	Potassium	2	2	6	2	6	—	1															
20	Calcium	2	2	6	2	6	—	2															
29	Copper	2	2	6	2	6	10	1															
35	Bromine	2	2	6	2	6	10	2	5														
36	Krypton	2	2	6	2	6	10	2	6														
47	**Silver**	**2**	**2**	**6**	**2**	**6**	**10**	**2**	**6**	**10**	**—**	**1**											

		K	L		M			N				O				P				Q
48	Cadmium	2	2	6	2	6	10	2	6	10	—	2								
56	Barium	2	2	6	2	6	10	2	6	10	—	2	6	—	—	2				
70	Ytterbium	2	2	6	2	6	10	2	6	10	14	2	6	—	—	2				
71	Lutetium	2	2	6	2	6	10	2	6	10	14	2	6	1	—	2				
79	Gold	2	2	6	2	6	10	2	6	10	14	2	6	10	—	1				
80	Mercury	2	2	6	2	6	10	2	6	10	14	2	6	10	—	2				
86	Radon	2	2	6	2	6	10	2	6	10	14	2	6	10	—	2	6			
88	Radium	2	2	6	2	6	10	2	6	10	14	2	6	10	—	2	6	—	—	2
90	Thorium	2	2	6	2	6	10	2	6	10	14	2	6	10	—	2	6	2	—	2
101	Mendelevium	2	2	6	2	6	10	2	6	10	14	2	6	10	13	2	6	—	—	2

mum number of electrons in the s, p, d and f sublevels are 2, 6, 10 and 14 respectively.

The maximum number of electrons each shell can accommodate is fixed and is given in Table 2.4. If the atom has more electrons than the first shell can accommodate, the excess electrons start filling up the second shell. If the atom has more electrons than the first and the second shells can accommodate, the excess ones go to the third shell, and so on.

Table 2.4 : Maximum Number of Electrons in the Different Shells

Shell No.	*Number of orbitals*	*Maximum number of electrons*
1	$1^2=1$	$1\times2=2$
2	$2^2=4$	$4\times2=8$
3	$3^2=9$	$9\times2=18$
4	$4^2=16$	$16\times2=32$
5	$5^2=25$	$25\times2=50$
6	$6^2=36$	$36\times2=72$
7	$7^2=49$	$49\times2=98$

Not only the electrons revolve around the nucleus in definite orbitals, but they also spin in the process. The spinning of the electrons is inferred from the results of magnetic studies. Any single orbital has a maximum number of two electrons that spin in opposite directions.

Atomic Spectra

Each atom has got its characteristic spectrum. When the atoms of an element are heated, say with white light, and the emerging beam of light is passed through a prism, a spectrum is observed. In the spectrum a number of black lines are noticed.

Niels Bohr was working on the spectrum of hydrogen. When he made the light shine from excited hydrogen gas through a spectroscope, he got over one hundred lines of colour in a distinct pattern. He was very much perplexed to see so many lines. His problem was: Hydrogen is the simplest element with one proton and one electron in its atom. How can it account for such a complex spectrum?

Bohr could visualize the sudden jump of an electron from inner to outer shell and vice versa. As long as an electron remains in a given orbit, it neither gains nor loses energy. Normally electrons are in places of relatively low energy, called ground states. The electron of hydrogen atom usually stays in the first shell closest to the nucleus. This is the lowest energy state or ground state of a hydrogen atom. The electron of an atom can be excited by subjecting it to high temperature or to bombardment by other electrons. The excited electron jumps to outer orbital of higher energy state. For this jumping it absorbs energy. Depending upon the quantity of energy absorbed, the electron's new position in the outer shell is decided. It may jump from shell 1 to shell 2; it may jump directly from shell 1 to shell 3, 4, 5, 6 or 7.

The excited electron does not continue to remain in that excited state. It loses energy and falls back to any of the inner orbitals of lower energy level. In the unexcited state finally the electron returns to the ground state. While returning to the inner shells the electron emits energy in the form of light that is observed as white line in the spectrum. The inward jump of the electron may be from an outer shell to the next inner shell, or it may be a multi-shell jump at one stretch, depending upon the quantity of emitted energy. In between two definite shells, the quantity of energy absorbed for outward jump is exactly the same as that emitted for inward jump.

Bohr published his theory of atomic spectra in 1913. He worked with hydrogen only. Soon after this, other physicists worked on the atomic spectra of other elements. Although the spectral pictures were much more complicated in the case of other elements, the principle of atomic spectra worked out by Bohr was found to be the same.

In 1900 Max Planck described radiant energy in terms of quanta. These quanta or packets of energy are not emitted or absorbed in continuous series, but are done in discrete series. This concept of energy absorption or emission in definite packets helped Niels Bohr immensely in the solution of the energy requirement for electron jump from one shell to another.

Figure 2.4 is a diagrammatic representation of the atomic shells around the nucleus. Let us suppose that an electron from shell 6 with energy level E_L will jump to shell 7 with energy level E_H. The electron will absorb a quantity of energy equivalent to the difference of E_H and E_L, i.e., $E_H - E_L = \triangle E$. When the electron returns to shell 6 from shell 7, it emits energy quantitatively equivalent to $\triangle E$. This $\triangle E$ is constant for all atoms of a particular element. For the same element, $\triangle E$'s between different pairs of shells are different, although each particular $\triangle E$ is constant. This provides explanation for the radiant energies emitted by a given element to have always the same frequencies or the same wavelengths.

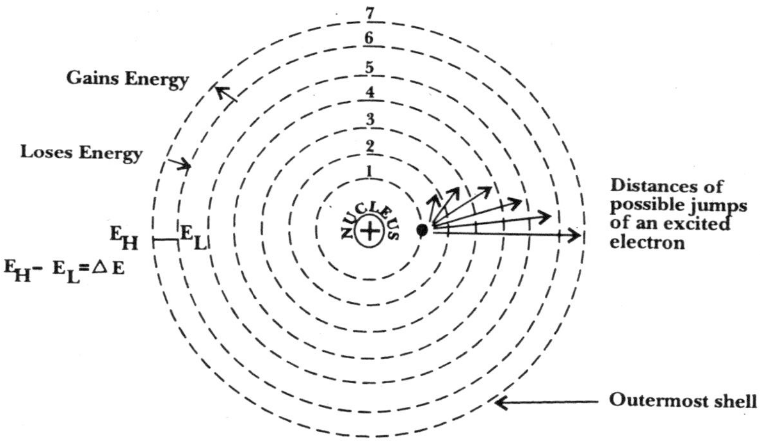

Fig. 2.4 : Electronic shells around the atomic nucleus.

Radioactivity

In 1896, Becquerel showed that uranium salt emitted rays even when it was not exposed to sunlight. This was the discovery of radioactivity, although no such term was coined at that time. Marie Curie coined the term 'radioactivity' in 1898. Following Becquerel's discovery, other radioactive elements such as thorium, polonium, radium, actinium, etc., were soon identified.

Negatively charged particles in radiation were discovered in 1899 simultaneously by Becquerel, by S. Meyer and E. von Schweidler and by F. Giesel. At about the same time Ernest Rutherford declared the existence of alpha and beta rays in radiation from uranium compound. In 1900, Becquerel could identify the beta rays as negatively charged electrons.

That the alpha rays consist of positively charged particles was announced by E. Rutherford in 1903. He could guess in 1906 that the alpha particles might be helium ions carrying two units of positive charges. In 1909, E. Rutherford and T. Royds confirmed that the alpha rays consist of helium ions with two protons and two neutrons.

The so-called alpha rays and beta rays are not really rays, but are particles. The alpha particles are positively charged. The beta particles are negatively charged. There is a third type of radiation that has no charge. This is the gamma radiation. In 1900, P. Villard discovered the gamma rays. The gamma radiation consists of gamma rays that are similar to the X-rays.

All the three types of radiation, viz., the alpha particles, the beta particles and the gamma rays, originate in the respective atomic nuclei and are called nuclear radiations. The origin of these three types of radiations may briefly be discussed here.

The alpha particle is ejected from the atomic nucleus. Since the alpha particle is helium ion with two protons and two neutrons, after each emission the atomic number is reduced by two and the atomic mass is reduced by four. Thus each emission brings about the formation of an atom of a different element.

Naturally occurring radioactive elements emit radiations spontaneously. A natural radioactive series is a collection of elements that are formed from a single radioactive element by successive emissions of alpha or beta particles. The parent element begins its radioactive decay that continues from atom to atom till some non-radioactive atom is formed. Uranium-238 $\left({}^{238}_{92}\mathrm{U}\right)$ may be taken as an example. It emits radioactivity in fourteen stages successively. After each emission it changes to atom of a different element. Finally it becomes lead-206 $\left({}^{206}_{82}\mathrm{Pb}\right)$ which is non-radioactive. This is the stable end-product in the series of transformations. It may be noted here that certain members may decay by the emission of either an alpha or beta particle.

In beta radiation the electron is ejected from the neutron situated in the nucleus of the atom. In this process the neutron, by losing a negatively charged electron, transforms into a proton. Along with an electron, a massless(?) particle called neutrino is created and ejected in beta decay. As a matter of fact, the massless particle created in beta decay is not the neutrino, but its antiparticle, the antineutrino.

Gamma rays are emitted from the excited daughter nucleus which remains after the parent has ejected either an alpha or a beta particle. Thus gamma radiation accompanying alpha or beta decay is due to transitions between energy levels in the daughter nucleus, rather than in that of the parent. This phenomenon is diagrammatically represented in Figure 2.5.

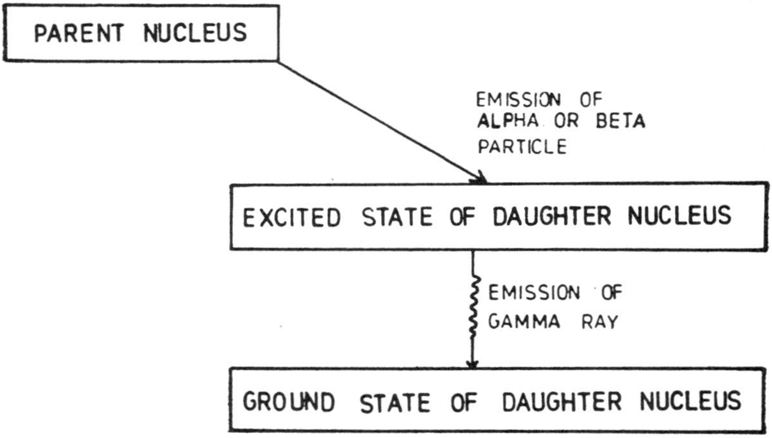

Fig. 2.5 : Emission of gamma radiation in radioactive decay.

The velocity of each type of radiation may be expressed as percentage of the velocity of light. For this purpose, the velocities of the alpha particle, the beta particle and the gamma ray may be designated numbers of 5, 95 and 100, respectively. The approximate relative penetrating powers of alpha, beta and gamma radiations are in the proportion of 1 : 100 : 10,000. Thus gamma ray has the highest penetrating power.

The discovery of radioactivity discarded the older concept of the eternality and indestructibility of the atom. The atom could be broken by extraneous forces such as alpha radiation and neutron bombardment. Even without any extraneous force, the radioactive elements spontaneously break and transform into atoms of newer elements.

Study of Micro-particles

Matter consists of atoms, which in turn, are composed of only three particles, viz., the proton, the neutron and the electron. In the early 1930s, the physicists accepted these three particles as the final list of the elementary particles of all matter. But newer discoveries increased the number of particles from three to six by 1935, and then to eighteen by 1955. Today no physicist of the world would venture to give any definite number of micro-particles. There does not seem to be any definite number.

It has been accepted that particles are created in pairs—particle and its corresponding anti-particle. Accordingly, every particle has got an anti-particle. When particles are created out of pure energy, they always appear in pairs of particle and corresponding anti-particle. Hence when we talk about proton, neutron, electron and other particles, it is understood that we do recognize the existence of the corresponding anti-particles. Of course, a few particles like the photon act as their anti-particles.

All the particles other than the stable ones have transient existence. They decay after a very short time into other particles, some of which may further decay until a combination of stable particles remains. Most of these unstable particles live less than a millionth of a second. It becomes cumbersome to use human second for the particles and hence physicists use the term "particle second" which is equivalent to 10^{-23} seconds.

In spite of the creation and annihilation of multitude of particles, subatomic particles of the same type are absolutely indistinguishable. Thus it is impossible to distinguish one proton from another proton and one electron from another electron. However, there are some distinguishing characteristics to recognize the subatomic particles of different types. Mass, charge and spin are important criteria to distinguish one type of subatomic particle from another.

When we express mass of a subatomic particle without any qualifying term, we mean thereby its rest mass. Any mass other than the rest mass is the relativistic mass. The mass of a particle increases with its velocity and hence it is possible for a particle to acquire any number of relativistic masses.

The masses of particles, whether at rest or in motion, are measured in electron volts. An electron volt is a unit of energy. It is defined as the amount of energy acquired by any particle, with one unit of charge, falling through a potential difference of one volt. When expressed in this unit, the rest mass of an electron is 0.51 million electron volts (Mev) and that of a proton is 938.2 million electron volts.

For the purpose of easy comparison, the mass of an electron is taken as one and the masses of other particles are expressed by numbers which are multiples of the mass of an electron.

Particles like photon and graviton are massless. It means that they have zero rest mass. All of the energy of a massless particle is the energy of its motion. Whenever a photon is created, it instantly travels at the speed of light. It cannot be slowed down since it has no mass to slow. It cannot be speeded up since nothing can travel faster than the speed of light. (Tachyon that is supposed to travel faster than light has not so far been experimentally detected.)

The second characteristic by which one type of subatomic particle is distinguished from another type is its charge. Every subatomic particle has charge—positive, negative or neutral. When neutral, the particle has no electrical charge at all. When positive or negative, the particle has either one whole unit or two whole units of electrical charge.

The third characteristic of a subatomic particle is its spin. Like a spinning top, a subatomic particle spins about an axis. But whereas a spinning top can spin either faster or slower, a subatomic particle spins at exactly a definite rate. The rate of spin is a fundamental characteristic of a subatomic particle. If the spin rate is altered, the particle itself is destroyed.

The spin of subatomic particles is calculated in terms of angular momentum which depends upon the mass, size and rate of rotation of the spinning object.

The actual angular momentum of a subatomic particle is not actually used for describing its spin. The spin of photon is taken as one. The spins of other subatomic particles are indicated by comparison with the spin of photon. The entire family of leptons has a spin of $\frac{1}{2}$, which means that their angular momentum is half of that of a photon. The same is true for the entire family of baryons. The spins of the members of meson family are, however, diverse. Their spins may be 0, 1, 2, 3, etc. in relation to the spin of photon. But they don't have spin values in between two whole numbers.

The existence of some particles has been detected directly,

whereas that of some others has been inferred indirectly. Those particles whose tracks can be seen in bubble chamber pictures belong to the former class. There are other particles that live for considerably shorter duration and decay in a few particle-seconds. During their transient existence they cannot travel farther than a few times their size. As a result, they cannot be seen in the bubble chamber. Although the existence of these resonance particles has not yet been detected directly, it has been inferred indirectly.

One may be interested to know the device(s) by which the properties of the micro-particles are studied. This is done by two ways, viz., by study of cosmic radiation and by artificial collision of particles accelerated to the required energies by particle accelerator in the laboratory. In most natural phenomena on Earth, the energies are not high enough to create massive particles. Hence is the need for an artificial device in which the particles are accelerated to very high energies. Before the invention of particle accelerators, study of the cosmic radiation was the only source of detection of new particles.

Everything about cosmic ray such as its source and its detailed contents has not been definitely known. Subatomic particles occur in large numbers in the stellar centres. It is a natural phenomenon in the centres of the stars for the micro-particles to collide with others with high velocities like the collision in the particle accelerators. As a result of this collision process, extremely strong electromagnetic radiation is produced in some stars. This radiation includes radio waves, light waves or X-rays. Interstellar space and intergalactic space are filled with electromagnetic radiation of various frequencies. In addition to protons of various energies, cosmic radiation contains various kinds of massive particles. The origin of these particles is still a mystery. Protons constitute majority of the massive particles in cosmic rays. Some of these protons have energies much higher than those achieved in the most powerful particle accelerators. When the highly energetic cosmic rays hit the Earth's atmosphere, they collide with the nuclei of air molecules. This produces a great variety of secondary particles which either decay or collide further. This process may go on until the last particle(s) reaches the surface of the Earth. The particles reaching the Earth may find their way into the bubble chamber by accident. And so we are able to detect the particles which originate through cosmic radiation.

Creation, annihilation and dancing of particles are now being studied by computerized particle accelerator and bubble chamber. It is necessary to bring about high-energy collisions of micro-particles for this purpose. The particle that smashes is called the projectile. The particle that is smashed is called the target. The projectile particle travels with high velocity in the accelerator to acquire enormous kinetic energy. The accelerator is a huge circular machine with circumference of many kilometres. In this machine protons are accelerated to velocities near the speed of light. These accelerated protons are made to collide with other protons or neutrons. As a result of the collision, many types of micro-particles are created. Most of them live for an extremely short time—much less than a millionth of a second. For their detection a device called a bubble chamber is necessary. The particle accelerator sends both the projectile and the target particles towards a common collision point which is located inside a bubble chamber. As a jet plane makes a vapour trail in the sky, so also particles leave tracks in the bubble chamber. The particle tracks can be photographed. The bubble chamber is located inside a magnetic field. Particles with positive charge, due to the magnetic field, curve in one direction, and particles with negative charge curve in the opposite direction. The points from which several tracks emanate are points of particle collisions. The tracks appear as beautiful lines, spirals and curves. A computer-triggered camera makes photographs of all the tracks of the micro-particles in the bubble chamber. This is how the micro-particles are detected and their properties are studied. Without this expensive and elaborate arrangement, it is not possible to detect the subatomic particles.

Search for the Ultimate Particle

In the history of science, man's search for the building stone(s) of the universe has taken a prominent place. Man wanted to know and is still trying to know the *fundamental* constituent of the universe, the *primary* building unit, the *ultimate* constituent of the universe. The atoms were discovered. They were considered to be the primary building blocks. Later on the subatomic particles, viz., the proton, neutron and electron, were discovered. As a result, atom was no longer considered as the primary building block. Another question was puzzling the scientist all along. He was interested to know the smallest particle in the world. Of the three important atomic constituents, viz., proton, electron and neutron, electron was found out to be the smallest particle. But particles smaller than the electron were discovered. Again, the existence of massless particles could be known. Hence the idea of the smallest particle remained a myth. Another question which has been baffling the scientist is: How many types of particles are there in the universe? This last question may be discussed first.

Particles may be subdivided into two classes, viz., hadrons and leptons. The former are relatively heavier; the latter are lighter.

'Hadron' is a Greek word. Etymologically it means 'strong'. Hadrons are particles with strong nuclear interactions. There are an infinite number of hadrons. Most of them are highly unstable. They disintegrate in less than a billion-billionth of a second into more stable hadrons.

There are two types of hadrons, viz., baryons and mesons. Baryons are relatively heavier than mesons. Baryons have half-integer spin ($\frac{1}{2}$, $\frac{3}{2}$,...) whereas mesons have integer spins (0, 1, 2,...). Both proton and neutron have got spin $\frac{1}{2}$; they are examples of baryons. Pion and kaon with spin 0 are examples of mesons.

In the atomic structure of elements, electrons are external to the nucleus whose components are protons and neutrons. Thus atom is a composite structure. It has been accepted that the electron is a fundamental particle without internal structure. Does it also hold good with the proton and the neutron? Are these baryons non-composite, primary particles? Or, are they also made of further smaller units? If there are still smaller units, are they also primary and non-composite? How far do we go in searching for the constituent units of particles? In principle, we can go on *ad infinitum*. Some physicists, in the 1960s, did not like this idea of never-ending search for the rock-bottom to the level of matter and held the view that hadrons do not have any definite structure. This gave birth to the 'bootstrap hypothesis'. According to this hypothesis, a level of matter, being both elementary and composite, may 'lift itself up into existence by pulling on its bootstraps'. The hadrons are indeed composite. But their constituent units are particles of the same kind. We may illustrate this by an example. There are three hadrons called A, B and C. All of them are composite. A is made of B and C; B is made of A and C, and C is made of A and B. The three particles are all mutually composite. This notion was extended to an infinite set of hadrons. In this process, no new fundamental particles were thought of. The same old hadrons could be constituents of one another and no hadron was more fundamental than any other. Thus a full-stop was put to the 'endless' regress.

The bootstrap hypothesis was given up in the same 1960s. It was realized that the hadrons are not the final particles. A final particle may be defined here as one which is not made out of still smaller particles. It was discovered that hadrons had component parts. In 1961, Murray Gell-Mann and Yuval Neeman independently noticed a pattern—the eightfold way. By the mid-1960s, this eightfold way and the mathematical symmetry which it implied answered to the riddle of the hadrons. Murray Gell-Mann, and independently George Zweig, could show that hadrons were made out of more fundamental particles. Gell-Mann gave the name 'quark' to these particles. This discovery could point out that hadrons are quark molecules. In 1969, Murray Gell-Mann won a Nobel Prize for his work.

Quarks are point quantum particles similar to the electron. They have the same spin of $\frac{1}{2}$ like the electron. But, whereas an electron has got one unit of electric charge, a quark has a fractional electric charge.

All the hadrons can be built out of three quarks and their antiquarks. These quarks are up (u), down (d) and strange (s) and their antiparticles—antiup ($\bar{u}$), antidown ($\bar{d}$) and antistrange ($\bar{s}$).

Three quarks combine together to make a baryon. The baryon structure may be given as qqq, where q stands for either u, d or s. In the same analogy, antibaryons are made of three antiquarks ($\bar{q}$ $\bar{q}$ $\bar{q}$). Any meson is a combination of a quark and an antiquark ($\bar{q}$ q).

Although hadrons are combinations of quarks and a quark has got fractional electric charge, all hadrons have got integer electric charge (0, ± 1, ± 2). Quarks are combined together in such a way that the total electric charge is an integer.

Three quarks, viz., u, d and s, were enough for the physicist to explain the internal structure of the hadrons. They were satisfied with this fact. However, their search for more quarks was unabated. Around 1973, the existence of a fourth quark was predicted by Sheldon Glashow and his collaborators at Harvard University. Glashow dubbed it as 'charmed'. This charmed quark was experimentally detected in 1974 independently by Sam Ting and collaborators at Brookhaven National Laboratory, and Burton Richter and co-workers at Stanford University. Both the teams independently discovered a new meson made of a charmed quark and its antiquark ($\bar{c}c$). Charmed quark can also combine with u, d or s quark to form new meson (uc, $\bar{d}c$, $\bar{s}c$).

In 1978, a fifth quark was discovered. It was named as 'bottom' or 'beauty'. A group led by Leon Lederman, at the Fermi National Laboratory near Chicago, found a meson made by the combination of bottom quark and its antiquark ($\bar{b}$ b). This bottom quark can combine with any of the other four quarks.

Theoretical physicists are still predicting a sixth quark which has been named as 'top' ('truth'). It is believed that it is more massive than the heaviest bottom quark. It has been searched for, but not yet found. Perhaps it exists at energies higher than we can currently achieve.

Six quarks have been described here. They are the building blocks of hadrons. Atoms are made of subatomic particles, viz., protons, neutrons and electrons. The atomic nucleus is made of nucleons, viz., protons and neutrons. The nucleons that are baryons are made of quarks. What are the quarks made of? Are they primary units without composite parts? Only future can answer this question. Are there only six flavours of quarks and not more than six? No one knows for sure.

Although five quarks have been detected so far, no quark has been observed in a free state. They are always bound up inside the hadrons. In spite of this fact, the real existence of quarks has ceased to be debatable since 1968. Shortly before 1968, a new instrument—linear electron accelerator—was built in the hills behind Stanford University. By conducting a series of experiments with the help of this instrument, physicists proved that hadrons are made of quarks.

Some characteristics of the quarks have been given in Table 2.5. The u and d quarks are very light. The strange quark is about fifty times more massive.

The total number of hadrons (baryons and mesons) cannot be given. There is no such thing as total number of hadrons. Their number is infinite. In contrast to the hadrons, the number of leptons seems to be finite. There are only four leptons. They are: electron, neutrino, muon and tauon. Lepton is a Greek word, which means 'light'.

Table 2.5: Mass and Charge of Quarks

Name	Symbol	Mass in units of electron's mass	Electric charge in units of proton charge
Up	u	2	2/3
Down	d	6	−1/3
Strange	s	200	−1/3
Charm	c	3,000	2/3
Bottom	b	9,000	−1/3
Top	t	?	2/3

Hadrons interact with each other very strongly. By contrast, leptons have weak interactions. Quarks do not exist in a free state; they are always bound together inside the hadrons. Leptons can exist in the free state. Unlike the hadrons, leptons have never revealed any internal structures. They are non-composite. Even at the highest energies, they behave as pure point particles. Physicists so far believe that leptons are truly elementary. Each lepton has a spin of $\frac{1}{2}$.

Electron was discovered as a particle way back in 1897. It has the lightest mass among the electrically charged quanta. It seems to be absolutely stable. Its electric charge is absolutely conserved. The electron is negatively charged whereas its anti-particle (anti-electron or positron) is positively charged.

The muon was discovered in 1937. It is the major component of cosmic radiation at the surface of the Earth. It is negatively charged whereas the anti-muon is positively charged.

Neutrino is the lightest of all leptons. It is almost massless. It is without electric charge. Like all other leptons, it has a spin of $\frac{1}{2}$. The existence of neutrino was predicted by the theoretical physicist, Wolfgang Pauli back in the 1930s. During the time, physicists who were studying the radioactive decays of nuclei were distressed to note that the law of conservation of mass-energy was violated. The energy after the disintegration of the nucleus was less than what was before. Pauli suggested that a new elusive particle was carrying off the undetected energy. Pauli's suggestion was not accepted by many physicists at that time. Eventually experimental evidence for the existence of neutrino was obtained. Fermi named it 'little neutral one' (neutrino). The interaction of neutrino with the rest of matter is extremely weak. Electron neutrino is associated with electron. Muon neutrino is associated with muon. Like photons, neutrinos move at the speed of light.

Most fundamental quanta are mixtures of half left-handed and half right-handed versions. But all neutrinos are left-handed. Right-handed neutrinos do not exist. This violates the conservation of parity. According to it, if a particle exists, its mirror image must also exist. The violation of parity conservation in the case of neutrino was accepted as fact by Chen Ning Yang and Tsung Dao Lee, two Chinese-American physicists. They proposed an experiment to test their hypothesis. On hearing about this experiment, Pauli remarked, "I do not believe that God is a weak left-hander". An experiment was actually conducted by Chien Shiung Wu and her collaborators at Columbia University. The results showed that Pauli was wrong in this case. Yang and Lee received Nobel Prize.

Neutrinos are not really massless; they have got a tiny mass. By virtue of their enormous number in the universe, they can account for 90 per cent of the total mass of the universe, which seems to be missing. If this is a fact, this so-called missing mass would be required to halt the expansion of the universe and cause a contraction.

The tauon has so far been the last lepton to have been discovered. In 1976, Martin Perl, an experimental physicist at Stanford, suggested the existence of a new lepton. In 1977-78, Perl's suggestion was confirmed by further experimental evidence obtained at Hamburg, Germany. This new lepton which was named as tau has a huge mass, 3,500 times the electron mass. The tau is supposed to have a chargeless, left-handed neutrino associated with it, although direct evidence for it has so far been lacking.

Muon decays into an electron, a neutrino and an antineutrino. The tau also can decay into lots of other lighter particles plus its associated neutrino. Notwithstanding this process of decay, the muon and the tau are just as fundamental as the electron. Mass is the only distinguishing feature among electron, muon and tau. The muon is a fat electron and the tau is a fat muon. Some characteristic features of the leptons have been furnished in Table 2.6.

Table 2.6: Some Characteristics of Leptons

Name	Symbol	Mass in units of electron mass	Electric charge in units of proton charge
Electron	e^-	1	-1
Electron neutrino	ν_e	Less than 0.00012	0
Muon	μ^-	207	-1
Muon neutrino	ν_μ	less than 1.1	0
Tauon	t^-	3491	-1
Tau neutrino	ν_τ	Less than 500	0

On the subject of particle physics, so far we have talked about hadrons (baryons and mesons) and leptons. In this connection, a question arises: "How are these particles glued together?" Instead of sticking together, the components of the atom can fly off; the planets can run away from their stars; the stars can leave their galaxy; and the galaxies can recede away. This is not happening. Matter, planets, satellites, stars and galaxies do exist in the universe. There must be some cementing and binding force or forces without which the micro- and the macro-world would not have existed as such.

There are only four fundamental quantum interactions which bind the universe. In order of their increasing strength they are: the gravitational interaction, the weak interaction, the electromagnetic interaction and the strong interaction.

How is the interaction brought about? What is the exact mechanism? A particle known as gluon is associated with each type of interaction. The particle is constantly exchanged between the interacting bodies. This phenomenon may be compared with the to-and-fro movement of a tennis ball between two players. The hydrogen atom may be taken as an example to explain this. Three quanta, viz., the proton and the electron of the hydrogen atom and a photon which is the gluon are involved in the game here. The game is played by two players—the proton and the electron. The photon acts as the tennis ball. By constant exchange of the photon, the proton and the electron of the hydrogen atom are bound together.

The gravitational interaction is the weakest of all the fundamental interactions. It is a long-range interaction. Any two entities with mass attract each other due to this gravitational interaction. In principle the interaction is operative both in the micro- and the macro-world. The proton and the electron of the hydrogen atom do experience this gravitational interaction like the Sun and the Earth. But at the atomic or the subatomic level the gravitational force is extremely weak. The gravitational attraction between the proton and the electron of the hydrogen atom is over a billion billion billion billion (10^{36}) times smaller than the electromagnetic force. This is, however, not the case with large bodies like planets and stars where there are large concentrations of matter. The feeble force between two quanta multiplied by a huge number becomes a significant force. The planets, satellites, stars and galaxies would not have been bound with one another but for this gravitational interaction.

Graviton is the gluon that is exchanged between any two bodies. The gravity field is quantized into innumerable gravitons. The graviton particle has been theorized, but so far it has not been directly detected. Whether there is an antigraviton is a subject of speculation for the present.

The weak interaction is extremely short-range. The disintegration of many quantum particles is brought about through this interaction. Radioactivity which involves disintegration of atomic nuclei operates through it. It is mediated by particles known as 'weak gluons' (W boson and Z boson). These mediator particles are extremely massive unlike the graviton and the photon. They are so massive that the energy of the existing accelerators cannot create them.

It has already been said that the weak gluons bring about disintegration of some quantum particles and the nuclei of the atoms of the radioactive elements. Only a few quantum particles, viz., the electron, photon, proton and neutrino, are stable. On the other hand, other particles such as neutrons, muons and other hadrons disintegrate rapidly into the stable ones. In the second category of disintegration, the radioactivity of some elements such as radium, uranium, thorium and others may be discussed. The nuclei of these atoms are unstable. They disintegrate, emitting alpha and beta particles and gamma rays. In both these types of interactions, the weak gluons change the flavour of quarks and thus make hadrons disintegrate.

The electromagnetic interaction is long-range like gravity. It operates between moving electrically charged particles, either positive or negative. This electromagnetic force is attractive between unlike charged particles and repulsive between like charged particles. Photon is the gluon that mediates the electromagnetic interaction. This particle was postulated as the particle of light by Einstein in 1905. It was experimentally detected in 1923. Photon is so far the only gluon whose existence has been directly confirmed by experimentation.

The macro-world is not affected by electromagnetic interaction since macro-matter is ordinarily electrically uncharged. This is, however, not the case with the individual particles in the atom. Electrons and protons of all atoms show electromagnetic interaction.

Inside the nucleus of every atom, protons and neutrons stay together. Neutrons are neutral electrically. But protons, being positively charged, are repelled from one another by the electromagnetic interaction. There must be some other greater force that is responsible for the binding of the nucleons inside the atomic nucleus. Even for the neutrons, it is not the weak gravitational force that binds them together inside the nucleus. This strong nuclear force is the strong interaction.

Inside the hadron (both baryon and meson), quarks are glued together. The quark structure of the proton is uud (up, up, down); that of neutron is udd. The quark structures of positive, neutral and negative pie meson are $\bar{d}u$, $\bar{u}u/\bar{d}d$ and $\bar{u}d$, respectively ($\bar{u}$= antiup; $\bar{d}$=antidown). The quark structures of negative and neutral K meson are $\bar{u}s$ and $\bar{d}s$, respectively (s=strange). Like this, all the hadrons have got internal structure. They are made of quarks. These quarks are glued together by a set of gluons called the 'coloured gluons'. These coloured gluons are so supersticky that the quarks can never be unglued. The strong interaction is the strongest of all the four fundamental interactions in Nature.

Some distinguishing features of the four types of gluons have been furnished in Table 2.7.

Study of Table 2.7 will clearly indicate that all these four types of gluons are different. Each type of particle mediates one type of fundamental quantum interaction. The question is: "Are these four types of quantum interactions fundamental?" Abdus Salam, Sheldon Glashow and Steven Weinberg shared the 1979 Nobel Prize in physics. It was proved that the electromagnetic and weak

Table 2.7: Some Characteristics of Gluons and Fundamental Forces

Name of interaction	*Gluon with symbol*	*Mass of gluon*	*Comparative strength of force*	*Range of force*	*Couples to*	*Role in quantum interactions*
Strong	coloured gluons	None	1	10^{-13} cm	coloured charges	Binds nucleons in atomic nuclei; binds quarks inside hadrons
Electromagnetic	photon (γ)	None	10^{-2}	Infinite	Electric charge	Binds orbital electrons to nuclear protons; acts between any two charged particles
Weak	weak gluons W^+, W^-, Z^0	W boson: 80 GeV Z boson : 90 GeV	10^{-10}	10^{-16} cm	Weak, flavour charges	Mediates in radioactive decay of hadrons and leptons
Gravity	graviton	None	10^{38}	Infinite	Mass	Functions in star and planet formation; binds planets to the Sun and stars to galaxies

interactions, instead of being two different ones, are one and the same. Does this unified theory account for four particles, viz., the two W particles, the Z particle and the photon? The answer is 'Yes'. Now we have got three types of fundamental quantum interactions instead of four. Even these three types are fundamentally one.

We are studying the interactions of quarks and leptons at relatively low energies available in our laboratory. At much higher energy, there would be only one fundamental force instead of three or four; the distinctions which we now observe among the four would vanish. The unified theory says that the four types of interactions which we see at present are the asymmetrical remnant of a once perfectly symmetrical world and that at ultra-high energies this world was symmetrical with only a single type of universal interaction. During the first few nano seconds after the big bang, such ultra-high energies existed and in that superheated condition there was only a single type of interaction.

After describing the different types of particles—the hadrons (baryons and meson), the leptons and the gluons—we come back to our original question, "What is the ultimate stuff of the universe and what is the size of this primary particle which has got no composite internal structure?"

It is better to dissolve this problem than to solve it. No single particle is the building unit of the universe. Several particles appear and disappear. Matter is a packet of energy. According to Einstein's mass-energy equation ($E=mc^2$), not only matter is equivalent to energy, but also matter is energy and vice versa. Again, energy is both wave and corpuscular, continuous and discrete. The substratum of energy is field which is unmanifested to our senses. Field gets manifested either as energy or as matter-particles. There is a unified field which is the canvas on which energy and matter appear as paintings. This unified field is also not fundamental, primary or basic. It has got a substratum. Anything that is mutable has got phenomenal existence. Anything that is immutable is the noumena. It may not be proper to use the words 'basic', 'primary', 'fundamental' and 'ultimate' for anything that has got a relative, phenomenal and empirical existence. The concept of fundamentality may be reserved for the Absolute only—the attributeless, functionless, partless, immutable One.

CHAPTER III

RELATIVITY

> As regards metaphysics...I experienced the delight of believing that the sensible world is real. Bit by bit, chiefly under the influence of physics, this delight has faded, and I have been driven to a position not unlike that of Berkeley, without his God...I find myself involved in a vast mist of solitude both emotional and metaphysical, from which I can find no issue.
>
> *Bertrand Russell*

BEFORE 1905, Newtonian absolutism held sway in the realm of physics. Space and time, as independently existing entities, were absolutes for Newton. He considered atoms to be the elementary building blocks of the universe; they were presumed to be absolutely solid, impenetrable, indestructible and unchangeable. He believed in the strictly causal nature of physical phenomena. He was sure that Nature could be described objectively.

Newtonian absolutism was discarded in the early part of the twentieth century. It may not be correct to say that Newtonian model is wrong. Newton's concepts are still useful and are made use of by physicists. It is not the question of right or wrong. The same concept is right in one referential context and wrong in another. Newtonian model is still valid in the macro-world where objects consist of large numbers of atoms. On the other hand, it does not hold good for the micro-world where subatomic microparticles behave in ways that can be explained by quantum mechanics. Newtonian model is valid for velocities which are small compared to the speed of light. When the velocities of particles approach the speed of light, relativity theory is applicable instead of Newton's theory. These apparently exclusive and contradictory models are approximations whose validity can be tested in a certain range of phenomena.

Einstein's Discoveries

At the age of twenty-six, in 1905, Albert Einstein published five papers of major importance. Three of these papers played pivotal role in the development of physics. He declared the quantum nature of light in one paper. This discovery won him a Nobel Prize in 1921. His second paper described molecular motion. The special theory of relativity was described in his third paper.

Prior to the development of the relativity concept by Einstein, two major discoveries by other scientists prepared the seed-bed for the concept of relativity to germinate. These were: (1) Ether could not be detected. (2) The speed of light in vacuum was found to be constant.

The Story of Ether

Sound travels as waves. It needs a medium. In the atmosphere, air works as a medium for sound to travel. Light also travels as a wave. It was thought that something had to be waving for light to be propagated as a wave. That something was postulated to be ether.

Never was there any experimental evidence for the existence of ether. For light wave to travel, there was need of a medium and so ether was a product of sheer imagination. There was a great deal of metaphysics in the 'physics' of ether. The metaphysical abstractions were: The entire universe lies in ether. It is pervaded by ether. But this all-permeating substance is invisible. It is devoid of properties and functions. It is tasteless and odourless. It simply exists. It exists everywhere and in everything. The sea of ether in which the universe exists is absolutely motionless. Every substance, the hardest one we can think of, is permeable to ether, that does not recognize any closed door anywhere.

Albert Michelson and Edward Morley conducted an experiment in 1887 to prove or disprove the existence of ether. They could not detect it. Their findings gave a verdict of death to the theory of the ether.

Einstein recognized the finding of Michelson and Morley. He declared the non-existence of ether. He asserted that electromagnetic fields were physical entities which could travel through empty space without the assistance of a waving medium and that the movement of such fields could not be explained mechanically.

Einstein's arguments were clear and decisive. It is a fact that light propagation can be envisioned either as a disturbance in the ether medium or as the propagation of energy through *empty space* (Vacuo). Since Michelson-Morley experiment failed utterly to indicate the presence of ether, it was logical for Einstein to accept the second alternative. In this regard, he was very much influenced by Maxwell, who was the discoverer of the electromagnetic field. Maxwell worked out some field equations that could convince Einstein to discard the ether.

According to Maxwell, electromagnetic fields "are not states of a medium (the ether) and are not bound down to any bearer, but they are independent realities which are not reducible to anything else."

Contrary to the concepts of classical mechanics that deals with objects and forces between them, Einstein could recognize electromagnetic fields unconcerned with objects whatsoever. He declared that electromagnetic fields are "ultimate, irreducible realities in themselves". Thus Einstein gave a death blow to the old concept of the imaginary ether.

The Constancy of the Speed of Light

Michelson and Morley had another significant finding that could influence Einstein's formulation of the special theory of relativity. They were to show experimentally that the speed of light in vacuum is constant, irrespective of the state of motion of the observer.

The classical transformation laws and common sense are at variance with the concept of the constancy of the speed of light. The speed of light is supposed to be its velocity as it is emitted from the source plus or minus the velocity of the observer, depending upon the movement of the observer towards the source or away from the source. But experimental findings of Michelson and Morley indicated that the speed of light remains constant, regardless of whether the observer is in motion or at rest relative to the light source. The velocity of light in vacuum remains the same in all frames of reference. Of course the speed of light changes in matter depending upon the index of refraction of the matter. In vacuum, the speed of light is invariably about 3×10^{10} cm per second or exactly $(2.997930 \pm 0.000003) \times 10^{10}$ cm per second (186,000 miles per second).

Galileo's Principle of Relativity

Galileo postulated the principle of relativity. According to this principle, the laws of mechanics that are valid in one frame of reference are valid in all frames of reference that move uniformly in relation to it. By saying this, Galileo recognized that it is impossible to determine experimentally whether one frame of reference is moving or at rest in relation to another frame of reference when the laws of mechanics are valid in both the frames.

This Galilean principle of relativity influenced Einstein considerably in formulating his theory of relativity.

Einstein expanded the Galilean principle of relativity. Instead of confining the principle to the laws of classical mechanics only, he applied it to all the laws of physics. Thus, according to Einstein, all the laws of physics are exactly identical in all frames of references that move uniformly relative to each other. This being a fact, it is not possible to distinguish absolute uniform motion or non-motion.

Einstein dismissed the idea of absolute non-motion and thereby accepted the concept of relativity.

FitzGerald-Lorentz Contraction

In 1892, George Francis FitzGerald proposed a hypothesis. He postulated one-dimensional contraction of any object in the direction of its motion, which contraction increased with the increase of its velocity. In 1893, Hendrik Antoon Lorentz independently worked out the same hypothesis, but he expressed his postulates in rigorous mathematical framework. Both FitzGerald and Lorentz imagined that compression of the rigid rods in motion was brought about under the pressure of the ether wind. Lorentz's mathematical formulations of the FitzGerald-Lorentz contraction were known as the Lorentz transformations.

Einstein dismissed the existence of ether and did not accept the explanation of FitzGerald and Lorentz. According to him, motion itself causes contraction and also time dilation. In spite of this difference, Lorentz transformations could stimulate Einstein for the formulation of his special theory of relativity.

Einstein's Special Theory of Relativity

Einstein formulated his special theory of relativity in 1905. This theory says: (1) Space is relative; (2) time is relative; (3) space is not three-dimensional; (4) time does not flow unidirectionally from the past to the present and from the present to the future;

(5) time is not an independent entity separate from space; there is no such thing as space *and* time; there is only space-time; (6) space and time are inextricably connected and form a four-dimensional continuum called space-time continuum; (7) mass is nothing but a form of energy.

A few simple mathematical equations in connection with the Special Theory of Relativity may be given here for better elucidation of the concept.

Effect of motion on mass. When an object moves relative to an observer, it appears to the observer that the mass of the object increases with the increase in its velocity, although the moving object itself does not become aware of the increase in its mass. This phenomenon is quantified by the following mathematical equation:

$$m' = \frac{m}{\sqrt{1 - \frac{v^2}{c^2}}}$$

Here m′ stands for relative mass, m for the mass of the object when it is at rest, v for the velocity of the object and c for the speed of light (3×10^{10} cm/sec). When v=c, m′ becomes equal to m/o or infinity.

Effect of motion on visibility. An object, moving relative to an observer, appears to the observer as if the moving object is shrinking in the direction of motion, although the moving object itself does not notice any such change in its own size. This phenomenon is quantified by the following mathematical equation:

$$L' = L\sqrt{1 - \frac{v^2}{c^2}}$$

Here L′ stands for relative length, L for length of the object when it is at rest, v for the velocity of the object and c for the speed of light. According to this equation, L′ becomes zero when the object moves at the speed of light. Thus an object travelling at the speed of light becomes invisible to the observer.

Effect of motion on time. Einstein conceives of time as only a product of motion. Time for an observer who observes an object moving dilates with the increase in the velocity of the object although the moving object or person does not experience any dilatation of time. This phenomenon is quantified by the following mathematical equation:

$$t' = t\sqrt{1 - \frac{v^2}{c^2}}$$

Here t′ stands for relative time, t for the time elapsed on Earth, v for the velocity of the object and c for the speed of light. As per the equation, t′ becomes zero when the object moves at the speed of light. Thus any person who moves at the speed of light becomes immortal. The twin paradox may be stated here briefly. A and B are twin brothers. When they are twenty years old, A climbs a spaceship and travels at 9/10ths the speed of light. He returns to Earth at the age of forty-six years while his twin brother B has attained the age of eighty years.

Newtonian space was absolute. It had three dimensions, viz., length, breadth and height. Newtonian time was also absolute. It was an independent entity separate from space. It flowed unidirectionally from the past to the future through the present. These ideas about space and time were discarded by Einstein. In relativity theory, one cannot talk about space without talking about time and vice versa. There is nothing like universal time. If different observers moving with different velocities relative to the observed events are asked to order the events in time, their fixation of temporal sequences will be different. One observer may see two events occurring simultaneously; but other observers who move with different velocities may see these two 'simultaneous' events occurring in different temporal sequences. All measurements involving space and time are devoid of any absolute significance. They are merely elements of descriptive language with special reference to the observer who describes the phenomenon as he observes it. If other observers in other frames of reference describe the same phenomenon or phenomena, their descriptive language involving measurements of space and time will be different. Thus all space and time measurements are relative.

A moving object appears to undergo contraction in its direction of motion. With the increase in its velocity, it becomes smaller in the direction in which it moves. When it acquires the speed of light, it disappears altogether.

The mass of a moving body measures more as its velocity

increases. This increase in mass continues until, at the speed of light, the mass becomes infinite.

A moving clock runs more slowly as its velocity increases. If the velocity continues to increase, the running of the clock becomes slower and slower until, at the speed of light, the clock stops running altogether.

An outside observer for whom the object is moving with high velocity sees the object being smaller and more massive, with its total duration of time becoming shorter. If an observer travels in a spaceship with high velocity, nothing of this sort happens for him. His ship and he himself do not become smaller or more massive and his watch keeps perfect time. The "twin paradox" becomes paradoxically perplexing when one twin remains on Earth and the other goes on a space voyage. When the space traveller returns, he sees his twin brother on Earth to have grown older than he. But if both twin brothers go on a space voyage, no one will be younger or older than the other.

We may use two adjectives—relative and proper—with reference to measurement of space and time. If a stationary observer measures a rod moving with high velocity relative to the observer, the observed length is the relative length. The relative length is always shorter than the proper length. If a 'stationary' observer sees a clock moving with high velocity relative to the observer, the observed time is the relative time. The relative time is always slower than the proper time.

Temporal words like 'now', 'sooner', 'later' and 'simultaneous' have relative meanings only. They all depend upon the state of motion of the observer relative to that of the observed object. In one frame of reference an event E_1 may be 'sooner' than an event E_2; in a second frame of reference event E_1 may be 'later' than event E_2; and in a third frame of reference both the events may be 'simultaneous'. Thus these words, 'sooner', 'later' and 'simultaneous', without mention of any specific frame of reference, are non-sensical in the universe at large.

In our gross observations of the day-to-day world, the special theory of relativity is not detected. We do not observe increase in the mass of the moving train or decrease in its length. We also do not observe the moving watch of the train-traveller to have slowed down. These phenomena are noticeable at very high velocities approaching the speed of light (3×10^{10} cm/sec).

It has already been said that space and time form a four-dimensional continuum. An event cannot occur in space without reference to any time; it cannot occur at any time without reference to any space. Space and time are not separate entities. In the space-time continuum, time is the fourth dimension. We live, breathe and exist in the space-time continuum.

Newton's space was unmoving. But his time was an ever-flowing stream from the past to the future through the present. Particles and objects are in motion in the unmoving space of Newton. Events develop with the passage of time. Because of the 'forward movement' of time, Newton viewed space and time as a dynamic one. In the special theory of relativity, it is more appropriate to think of the space-time continuum as a static one. On the static canvas of space-time continuum events do not develop; the paintings we see are just there. What appear to unfold now and then on the canvas of space-time continuum, what appear to have been projected, as being projected or to be projected on the space-time screen are already painted. The whole picture is static, although it appears to be dynamic. All the events of the past, present and future do not develop; all of them already exist *in toto*. It is mathematically possible to view the 'past', the 'present' and the 'future' events painted on the space-time continuum.

In addition to space-time continuum, interconversion of matter and energy is another topic on which light is thrown by the special theory of relativity. Einstein's mass-energy equation is given below:

$$E=mc^2$$

Here, E is energy in ergs, m is mass in grams and c is velocity of light, i.e., 3×10^{10} cm/sec. According to this equation mass is nothing but a form of energy. Mass can be converted into energy and *vice versa*.

In the micro-world, there is a continuous transmutation of particles. One type of particle is changed to other type or types. The daughter particles, in turn, change to others. Particles are created from energy; they again vanish into energy. There seems to be an ocean of energy from which particles appear and into which particles disappear. The ocean is to be one and continuous. Thus there is no object which is isolated, no substance which is material and no particle which is elementary.

The mass of an object changes with its velocity. With increase in the velocity, the mass of an object increases. With decrease in the velocity, the mass of an object decreases.

Kinetic energy is the energy of motion. An object that moves acquires kinetic energy and hence acquires additional mass.

The 'real' mass of an object is its mass when the object is not moving. But no object in the universe is at rest. Hence actual determination of 'real' mass cannot be a practicable proposition.

Subatomic particles have got relative masses. Most subatomic particles travel at different velocities. Hence a single subatomic particle, e.g., electron, possessing more than one velocity, has more than one relativistic mass. For this reason, the rest mass of any subatomic particle is *calculated.* This provides a uniform method for comparing the masses of particles.

Existence and Activity of Matter are Inseparable

Matter does not exist without activity. According to the relativity theory, the activity of matter is the very essence of its being. Being, as far as matter is concerned, is an activity, is a process. The existence of matter and its activity cannot be separated. They are one and the same.

At the macroscopic level, we get a notion that matter is substantial. At the microscopic level, the substantiality of matter disappears. Matter is made of molecules and atoms. Atoms consist of subatomic particles. The subatomic particles are energy bundles that are not made of any material stuff. The existence of these energy bundles can be recognized by virtue of their activity. There cannot be any static aspect of the existence of matter. The existence of matter is its activity and hence matter can be understood only in a dynamic context. It is always in movement and in a state of flux of interaction and transformation.

Atoms are too small. The atomic nuclei are still smaller. They are a hundred thousand times smaller than atoms. The nuclear particles, being confined to very small dimensions, move almost at the speed of light. At this high speed they can be described adequately in the framework of the special theory of relativity. Being micro-particles, their behaviour can be described by quantum theory. Hence the dynamic nature of the micro-world can be understood in the light of both relativity theory and quantum theory.

The idea of matter of classical physics has thus vanished. We no longer recognize any indestructible material substance with 'stuff' of which all things are made. Relativity theory proved that matter is energy and that it has nothing to do with material substance.

The question is then asked: "What is energy?" That which gives ability to do work is energy. Any change, either physical or chemical, cannot occur without expenditure of energy. Thus energy cannot be defined in terms of any physical existence. Its existence can be known only by its activity. It is an entity which is never static, but ever dynamic. It is nonsensical to think of a motionless universe, a changeless universe and an activity-less universe.

Particles, Binding Forces and Field

All the objects of the universe are made of atoms and atoms are made of subatomic particles. Are the particles isolated points in void? How are they bound together? What are forces? Is the so-called 'void' nothing? Is the 'void' another aspect of matter or energy? These questions may be answered in the framework of relativity theory.

The particles are bound together by forces. Not only different particles, but also the component parts of the same particles are glued by forces. Particles like proton and neutron are made of sub-particles that move faster than the parent particles. The sub-particles in a proton or a neutron are held together by forces. So also particles are bound by forces inside the atomic nuclei and the orbital electrons in atom are bound to the nucleus by forces. The same principle holds good to molecules and compounds.

Are these forces fundamentally different from particles they bind? It is not really so. What we call forces are practically exchange of particles. The mutual attraction or repulsion of particles is otherwise known as force and this involves exchange of other types of particles among particles. Thus in a relativistic description of particle-interactions, forces and particles belong to the same category. Matter and force were two different concepts before knowledge was acquired on particle-interaction. Now the concepts of matter and force are unified. Particles and forces being unified and the dynamic patterns of particles and forces being established, particles are no longer considered as isolated entities, but are understood as integral parts of the whole.

The subatomic world is an unbroken whole. It cannot be decomposed into constituent parts. The old concept of particles as separate points and the intervening spaces among them as void is no longer valid. That particles interact through forces and the forces are exchange of other particles leads to the conclusion that the whole fabric is one and the same. Being one and unbroken, it has got no component parts.

The Newtonian concept of space as empty or void has been discarded. There is nothing like a void in the universe. The 'void' or space is another aspect of matter or energy. For a better comprehension of the fullness of space, the concept of field may be introduced.

The field concept is not new. Faraday and Maxwell introduced the field concept in the nineteenth century. They conceived of field for describing the forces between electric charges and currents. Charged bodies create electric fields whose effects can be felt by charged bodies only. When charges are in motion, they create magnetic fields. Other moving charges can feel the magnetic forces resulting from them. It was later realized that the electric field and the magnetic field were not separate. In the relativistic formulation of electrodynamics, these two fields were unified into a single electromagnetic field.

There will be further discussion on gravitational field and quantum field theories. Whatever term we may use for field while describing different activities of matter, we really talk about one field only. This unified field is continuous. Einstein believed in a single unified field and he spent the last years of his life in search of this single field. With this field concept, the distinction between particles and the space surrounding them has totally vanished, and space is no longer considered as void.

If we recognize a continuous unified field, we may not accept the existence of matter as separate from that of field. When field takes form to be directly or indirectly perceived by our senses, we call it matter. The whole universe seems to be field only which is continuous and unbroken.

What is Really Relative?

After studying the relativity theory, we come to realize that there is nothing which is not relative. Deeper analysis of the concept of relativity really reveals that *appearances* are relative. It is a question of cognitive limitation. We know what appear to us. What appear to us are relative. Thus our total knowledge is relative only.

The special theory of relativity describes the ways in which knowledge about the universe is relative depending upon the state of motion of the observer relative to that of the observed. From this it may not be misconstrued that the special theory of relativity categorically proves that there is nothing absolute. In describing the relative world, the theory takes cognizance of the Being that is non-changing and absolute.

The field is not relative. Our knowledge about the field is relative. An example may be taken. If the velocity of a moving object increases, it continues to contract in the direction of its motion. When it travels at the speed of light, its dimension in the direction of motion becomes zero. Does the moving rod really vanish? No, not at all. It *appears* to us to have vanished. This is a visual illusion as demonstrated mathematically by James Terrell, a noted physicist.

We do not and cannot know the universe as it is. Our total knowledge about the world is relative. When one says that our known world is an illusion, one does not say thereby that the world does not exist. One says this much that we do not know the world as it is.

Space is relative. Time is relative. Space and time are interpenetrating. These things have been told again and again. It may be significant to say here that the space-time interval between two events is absolute instead of being relative. Different observers in different states of motion observe the two events differently. But this is appearance only. The space-time interval between two events is always invariant.

There is no past and future. There is eternality, the *now*. There is no 'there'. It is *here* only. This concept was given by Hermann Minkowski who was Einstein's mathematics teacher. He was very much inspired by his student's special theory of relativity. He deduced a space-time diagram out of his mathematical explorations. In this diagram, the past, the present and the future are mathematically related. All the past and all the future for each individual meet, and ever meet, at one single point of *now* in the diagram. The *now* of each individual is specifically located *here* (wherever the observer is) and nowhere else. Minkowski's diagram has got much philosophical significance. In the relative world where knowledge is variable depending upon the states of the observers, there can also be the invariant concept of *now* and *here*.

Verification of the Special Theory of Relativity

Einstein did not experimentally prove any of his predictions. He worked out the mathematics of his theories. He never deduced his theories from any experimental observations.

Experimental verification of time-dilation came from high-energy particle physics. The life-spans of muons of two sources were compared. The muon that was created at the top of the Earth's atmosphere by the collision of proton of cosmic radiation with air molecules lived seven times longer lives than the ones created in the accelerators of the laboratory. The muons that were created at the top of the Earth's atmosphere travelled much faster (with velocity approximately 99 per cent of the speed of light) than the ones created in the laboratory. At a fast speed approaching that of light, time dilation is quite noticeable. What is true of muons is also true of almost all subatomic particles.

In 1972, a second type of verification of time-dilation was made by putting four atomic clocks of super accuracy aboard an aircraft that flew around the Earth. At the end of the trip, these clocks were compared with their stationary, Earth-bound counterparts. Although both the groups of clocks were synchronized before the flight, the clocks in flight were found to be slightly behind the ones that were stationary on the Earth.

General Theory of Relativity

Ten years after the formulation of the special theory of relativity, Einstein announced his general theory of relativity in 1915.

Wherever there is matter, there is gravity. The more massive is the object, the greater is the gravity. Matter warps the space-time continuum. The larger is the piece of matter, the more pronounced is the warp.

In an imginary universe of only space devoid of objects, the space-time continuum is like a sheet of unstretched rubber. Gravity distorts the space-time continuum in a manner analogous to the stretching of a sheet of rubber. In our hypothetical space devoid of objects, the undistorted space-time continuum provides an inertial coordinate system to which the special theory of relativity applies.

However, the universe is not space only. There are particles, atoms, molecules, planets, satellites, stars and galaxies in the universe. Matter distorts the space-time continuum. It causes a curvature of the space-time in its vicinity.

Since space and time are not separate entities, gravity curves not only space, but also time; it curves the space-time continuum. The degree of curvature depends upon the massiveness of the object. The space in the vicinity of a star and that away from it are not equally curved. The curvature of space-time in the vicinity of a massive body is more pronounced. Thus space is not homogeneous and flow of time is not uniform in different parts of the universe. The whole structure of space-time is inextricably linked to the distribution of matter in the universe. Space is curved in different degrees and time flows at different rates in different parts of the universe. Space is not empty; it is not nothing; it is something, a positive entity that is not unchangeable and unresponsive.

Euclidean geometry that holds good for plane surfaces cannot be applied to the curved surface of a sphere. And so Euclidean geometry is not applicable to the curvature of space-time continuum.

The curvature of a two-dimensional surface is clear to us. It is impossible for us to visualize the curvature of space with three-dimensions. It is still more impossible to think of the curvature of space-time continuum which is four-dimensional. We live in a three-dimensional space. We cannot look at the three-dimensional space or four-dimensional space-time from outside and hence we cannot imagine how it can be bent in some direction.

The laws of geometry in a curved space or space-time are different. They are bound to be non-Euclidean. Such a non-Euclidean geometry was introduced in the nineteenth century by Georg Friedrich Riemann. At that time it was purely a mathematical idea. When Einstein declared that the three-dimensional space or four-dimensional space-time is curved by the gravitational fields of massive objects, the importance of Riemann's geometry was soon realized.

Einstein's equations relating to curvature of space to the distribution of matter in that space are called field equations. By making use of these equations, one can determine the variations in the curvature in different localities of space in the neighbourhood of stars and planets. The field equations also predict that the whole space of the universe is curved and finite.

The most important finding of the general theory of relativity is that matter distorts or curves the space-time continuum in its vicinity. In the ultimate vision of Einstein, matter itself is a curvature of the space-time continuum. (He however did not demonstrate it mathematically). In the real world, there is no matter, since matter is only a curvature of space-time; there is also no energy, since energy is mass which itself is space-time curvature. According to Einstein, there is no such thing as gravity which is only a mental creation. According to one of the interpretations of the General Theory of Relativity, the Earth, the Sun, the stars and the galaxies do not exist as they appear to be. Whatever exists in the world, whether matter or energy, is space-time curvature in motion.

In the final analysis, the universe is only space-time and the universe is in motion. There is nothing like motionless space-time. The universe is space-time in motion.

Matter is always associated with gravitational field. There is no mass without field. All massive bodies create gravitational fields. They also feel the gravitational fields. The gravitational forces which are really the exchange of graviton particles between bodies are always forces of attraction. Both attractive and repulsive forces operate in the electromagnetic fields. Unless two bodies are charged, electromagnetic field is not created. Unlike charges attract and like charges repel. This is not the case with the gravitational field. (Antigravity is still a speculation.)

Einstein, in his General Theory of Relativity, associated the gravitational field with the geometry of space. The space surrounding any massive body is conditioned by its gravity in such a way that it is curved.

In the old Democritean and Newtonian physics, matter and empty space—the full and the void—were two fundamentally distinct concepts. In General Theory of Relativity, matter and space cannot be separated and space, instead of being empty, is full. A massive body is necessarily associated with a gravitational field, and this field manifests itself as the curvature of space in the vicinity of the body. Of course, the field and the space are not two different entities. They are one and the same thing. The space is not a container and the field does not fill the space as a content. The field, as an agent, does not curve the space. Field and space are indistinguishable. The field is the curved space.

In General Theory of Relativity, matter, field and space lose their separate identities. Einstein's field equations represent field and space by the same mathematical quantity. Matter is not separate from its field of gravity. The field of gravity is not separate from the curved space. Matter and space are thus not fundamentally different. They are two independent parts of a single whole.

It is interesting to discuss the effects of the curvature of space-time during the gravitational collapse of a massive star. In the life of a star it reaches a stage where it collapses due to the mutual gravitational attraction of its particles. When it starts collapsing, the distance between its particles decreases and hence the mutual attraction rapidly increases. As a result, the collapse accelerates. If the star is more than twice as massive as the Sun, the collapse goes on indefinitely.

With continuing collapse, the star becomes denser and denser and the force of gravity on its surface becomes stronger and stronger. As a result, the space-time around the star becomes more and more curved. In this process, comes a stage where nothing, not even light, can escape from the star's surface. This is the stage of 'event horizon'. We cannot see such a star since light from this star cannot come out. Such a star is called a 'black hole'. One year after the announcement of the General Theory of Relativity, i.e., in 1916, the existence of black holes was predicted on the basis of this theory, although the term 'black hole' was not coined at that time.

When the star starts collapsing, the space around it is drastically affected and the flow of time also changes. It is more accurate to say that the space-time of the collapsing star is tremendously influenced. If a clock flashing its signals to us is placed on such a star, the signals slow down with the progressive collapse of the star. When the collapse reaches the event-horizon, or in other words, when the star becomes a black hole, particles, objects, light and all signals cannot escape the star and the slowing clock stops altogether. One may ask the question: "How long will the collapse of the black hole take?" The answer seems to be very simple. "To complete the collapse, the star will take infinite time". This answer is, however, not correct. Flow of time in the black hole is normal and the collapse will be completed in a finite period of time. The lifetime of a collapsing star is finite for somebody who is sitting there. It is infinite for somebody else who is observing from elsewhere. For different frames of reference the observation is relative. Without mentioning any frame of reference, if somebody asks the question whether the collapse of the black hole is finite or infinite, it may be said that the question does not make any sense.

There have been many speculations about the invisible black hole. Is the black hole rotating or not? If it is not rotating, the objects that will be sucked into it will be pulled to its centre to a point called the singularity. There it will be squeezed out of existence. Its volume will be zero. At the black hole singularity, space and time disappear.

If the black hole is rotating, things may happen in some other way. The objects that are sucked into the event horizon may miss the black hole singularity. If this universe is considered to have wormholes, the objects that are sucked into the black hole may emerge into different place and different time of this universe. There is also chance for the devoured objects to emerge into another universe through Einstein-Rosen bridges.

Things that are sucked into the black hole singularity and are squeezed out of existence do not really lose their existence. Things that disappear into the black hole appear somewhere else.

The general theory of relativity has so far been verified in four ways. Mercury's moving perihelion (the part of its orbit closest to the Sun) was the first verification.

The second verification was made by observing the bending of starlight in the vicinity of the Sun. Einstein predicted the bending of light beams by gravitational fields. This prediction was first verified on 29th May, 1919 when a total eclipse of the Sun occurred. Deflection of starlight in the vicinity of the Sun was experimentally observed on this occasion. The gravitational field of the Sun caused bending of the starlight.

The third verification of the General Theory of Relativity was made by observing gravitational red-shift. According to Einstein's prediction, any periodic process in an atom on the Sun takes place at a slightly slower rate than that on the Earth due to the stronger gravity of the Sun. The wavelength of the radiation of any given element as found in sunlight and that found in the laboratory on the Earth were compared and it was observed that the former was longer.

The phenomenon of the black hole is the fourth verification of the General Theory of Relativity. In 1958, David Finkelstein theorized a phenomenon on the basis of Einstein's General Theory of Relativity. He named it 'one-way-membrane'. In 1959, Roger

Penrose expanded Finkelstein's discovery and developed it into the modern theory of black hole.

Black holes cannot be seen since light cannot come from them. We indirectly get the proof of the existence of black holes. All the particles and objects that are sucked into a black hole are accelerated through its gravitational field, move at a speed that approaches the velocity of light and throw out tremendous amounts of electromagnetic radiation. Secondly, a visible star that is located near a black hole revolves around the latter.

Scientists became busy in search of these two phenomena in order to locate the invisible black hole. In 1970, one black hole named as Cygnus X-1, very close to a visible blue-hot supergiant star, was discovered. This black hole and this star form a binary system. Cygnus X-1 which is a black hole emits a million times more energy than the Sun.

Thus, both the theories of relativity which Einstein worked out on paper through mathematical deductions were later proved by experimental observations.

The meaning of eternality in relation to the General Theory of Relativity may be mentioned here. Time is elastic; it can stretch, shrink and warp. It stops altogether at a singularity as in a black hole. The word 'eternal' has got two meanings. It means everlasting or existing without beginning and end. It also means 'timeless'. There is no time without motion or change. If change is universal in matter and energy, if A cannot remain as A, but becomes non-A such as B, C or D, it cannot be said that matter and energy are eternal or everlasting. In order to be timeless, something must be changeless; and in order to be changeless, it must be actionless and attributeless.

The concept of relativity, both special and general, has profoundly influenced mankind's notion about the universe.

CHAPTER IV

QUANTUM PHYSICS

Anyone who is not shocked by quantum theory has not understood it.

Niels Bohr

I don't like it, and I am sorry I ever had anything to do with it.

Erwin Schrödinger

I think it is safe to say that no one understands quantum mechanics. Do not keep saying to yourself, if you can possibly avoid it, 'But how it be like that?' because you will go 'down the drain' into a blind alley from which nobody has yet escaped.

Richard Feynman

It seems hard to look in God's cards. But I cannot for a moment believe that He plays dice and makes use of 'telepathic' means (as the current quantum theory alleges He does).

Albert Einstein

Clash of doctrines is not a disaster, it is an opportunity.

A.N. Whitehead

IT IS DIFFICULT to comprehend quantum physics. It is obvious from the opinions of some famous scientists who have been quoted here. In another context, *Kena Upaniṣad* says: "It (Brahman) is known to him who thinks he does not know it. He who thinks it is known to him does not know it. It is not understood by those who understand it. It is understood by those who do not understand it."[1]

Planck's Equation

The year 1900 is the dividing line between classical (Newtonian) physics and modern physics. The physics discovered during the period from the time of Newton to 1900 is classical. Max Planck

(1858-1947), a German physicist, was the first actor to enter upon the stage of quantum physics. Theorists were working on black-body radiation. They imagined a body that could absorb or emit radiation 'perfectly'. It was a theoretically idealized one called blackbody. For solving the riddle of the blackbody spectrum, Max Planck combined thermodynamics and electrodynamics (both were classical theories) and came forward, in 1900, with an equation which is now known as Planck's equation. This equation is:

$$E = h\nu$$

Here E is energy, $h = 6.6256 \times 10^{-27}$ erg seconds and ν is frequency of radiation. The h in the equation is known as Planck's constant. In 1918, Planck received Nobel Prize for this work.

Planck invented the quantum. Quantum is a quantity of something. It is a specific amount. "Nature comes in bits and pieces." These bits or 'atoms of energy' were termed as quanta (singular, quantum) by Planck. 'Quantum' is a Latin word which means 'how much?' The equivalent word in Sanskrit is *katama*.

Ever since the time of Newton, physicists have been thinking that energy flows continuously. But Planck thought it otherwise. He assumed energy to be given off in discrete quantities or quanta. The atoms of energy are always given off in whole number(s). A radiating body can give off one, two, three or any number of atoms of energy; but this number is never fractional such as one and a half or one and a quarter. In other words, Planck imagined that the number of the atoms of energy radiated by any radiating body is always an integer.

Planck's equation establishes the relationship between the energy content of the quanta of radiation and the frequency of radiation. The energy content of the quantum varies directly with the frequency of radiation. In this relationship, h which is commonly known as Planck's constant is the proportionality constant.

Light Quanta

Anything that is in the form of a wave is continuous. Anything that is particulate or corpuscular is discontinuous or discrete. In the historical development of the concept of the form of light, it was sometimes regarded in terms of particles and some other times in terms of waves. Finally, it was concluded that light is in both forms—that of particle and wave. A brief mention of this historical development is made here.

Isaac Newton (1642-1727) considered light as a stream of particles. Christiaan Huygens (1629-95), a Dutch physicist, was a contemporary of Newton. He developed the idea of light as a wave. He visualized this light-wave propagating through a medium which he termed 'luminiferous ether'. Both the corpuscular theory of Newton and the wave theory of Huygens could adequately explain the reflection and refraction of light.

Thomas Young (1773-1829), an English physicist, declared the results of his experimental research in 1801. In his experimental set-up, he had, in succession, a source of light, barrier I with one narrow slit, barrier II with two narrow slits and a screen. Light coming from the source passed through the single slit in barrier I. Beyond barrier I, parallel semicircular waves of light moved in steps or in phases. These waves passed through the double slits in barrier II. Each slit in barrier II acted like a new source of semicircular waves. Both these sets of parallel semicircular waves fell on the screen. Young observed alternate light and dark bands on the screen. His experiments has been illustrated in Fig. 4.1.

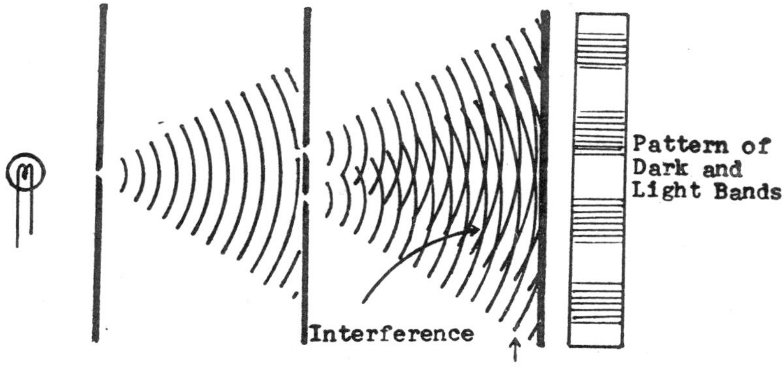

Fig. 4.1 Young's Double-Slit Experiment for proving the wave nature of light.

Why did Young observe alternate bands of light and darkness on the screen? He ascribed this phenomenon to the destructive interference of light waves. The interference may be constructive or destructive. When the crest of one wave of a series superimposes on that of another wave of a second series, the band of light becomes brighter. This is constructive interference. When the crest of one wave of a series superimposes on the trough of another wave of a second series, the band becomes dark due to destructive interference. Only waves can produce interferences. And hence Young proved that light is in the form of a wave.

Augustin Jean Fresnel (1788-1827), a French physicist, worked further on Young's idea and established the wave nature of light. In the 1860s and 70s, James Clerk Maxwell (1831-79), a Scottish physicist, established the existence of electromagnetic waves. According to him, electromagnetic radiation involves patterns of stronger and weaker electric and magnetic fields. This is like the crests and troughs of water waves. In 1887, Heinrich Hertz (1857-94) could transmit and receive electromagnetic radiation in the form of radio waves. Thus scientists, as a result of these findings, came to establish that light is a form of wave motion propagated through the ether.

After Max Planck, Albert Einstein (1879-1955) was the second actor to enter the quantum mechanical stage. He was twenty-one years old in March, 1900. He got a Clerk's job in Swiss patent office in the summer of 1902. In 1905, he published three papers in the same volume of the *Annalen der Physik*. One of these papers was on photoelectric effect; the second was on special theory of relativity and the third was on Brownian movement. Einstein got his Ph.D. degree in January, 1906. He received Nobel Prize in 1921 for his work on photoelectric effect. He applied Planck's equation ($E=h\nu$) to the electromagnetic radiation and re-established the corpuscular nature of light. Light comes in definite packets or quanta. This discovery of Einstein about the interaction of light with electrons was the first scientific work dealing with quantum mechanics.

Although Einstein became more famous for his theory of relativity, he got Nobel Prize for his work on the photoelectric effect and made his contribution to quantum physics through this work. The background of this work needs brief mention here.

In the last two decades of the nineteenth century, a peculiar behaviour of some metals was discovered. When light fell on such metal surfaces, electricity was given off by them. Physicists were beginning to understand at that time that the flow of electricity involved the movement of electrons. They could explain the photoelectric effect by the hypothesis that light could bring about ejection of the subatomic particle, electron, from the metal surface.

Philipp Lenard (1862-1947), a German physicist, conducted a number of experiments to study the photoelectric effect. He could not get emission of electrons at all from the metal surface by radiating intense red light on it. Intense orange light could bring about emission of many low-energy electrons, whereas few high-energy electrons could be emitted by a feeble violet light. This effect also varied from metal to metal. Lenard, in 1902, announced that, for each metal surface that showed the photoelectric effect, there was a limiting threshold frequency. The photoelectric effect was observed when light fell on these metal surfaces only when the frequency of light was above the threshold level.

Lenard's observation could not be explained by the physical theories of the nineteenth century. Einstein made use of Planck's quantum concept and advanced an explanation for this phenomenon in 1905.

Planck discovered that light is radiated in quanta. Einstein said that light is radiated in quanta and also absorbed in quanta. When light falls on a metal surface, it is absorbed by the electrons bound to the surface. But this absorption takes place at the rate of one quantum at a time. If the energy of that quantum is greater than the forces that hold the electrons to the surface, the electron is set free. In the reverse case, the electron cannot be ejected although the metal surface absorbs the light.

The size of the quantum is dependent on the frequency of radiation. The higher the frequency, the larger is the size of the quantum. At the threshold frequency, the quantum size is equal to the forces that bind the electron to the surface. At this level, electrons would barely be released since they would not possess any kinetic energy. At frequency beyond the threshold level, more and more energy is left over to act as kinetic energy for the ejection of the electron from the metal surface.

The threshold energy does not remain the same for all substances. Each substance has a characteristic threshold level of energy and this depends upon how strongly the electrons are bound to the particular surface. Einstein gave the following equation to express the relationship:

$$\frac{1}{2} mv^2 = h\nu - w$$

Here $\frac{1}{2}mv^2$ is the kinetic energy of the emitted electron, $h\nu$

(Planck's constant times frequency) is the energy content of the quanta absorbed by the surface, and w is the energy required to counteract the forces that bind the electron to the surface.

When Einstein could explain the photoelectric effect, the significance of quantum theory was better appreciated. Planck originally developed the quantum concept for explaining the emission of radiated energy. Einstein said that, not only emission, but also absorption of radiated energy takes place in quanta. The concept of quanta of energy was thus concerned with emission and absorption of radiation. When Einstein explained quite a different phenomenon, e.g., the photoelectric effect, through the help of the quantum concept, the newly born quantum theory became very impressive in the world of post-Newtonian physics.

In 1916, an American physicist, Robert Andrews Millikan (1868-1953) conducted experiments to measure the energy of the electrons that were ejected from metal surface as a result of absorption of light of different frequencies. His observations could provide an experimental verification of the equation predicted by Einstein. He calculated the value of h (Planck's constant) by fitting the values of the energy of the electrons ($\frac{1}{2}mv^2$), the frequency of the light (ν) and the threshold frequency for the surface (w) in Einstein's equation. The value of h, obtained by Millikan, was close to that obtained by Planck from his radiation equation.

Quantum theory was suggested by Planck in 1900. It got further support from the work of Einstein on photoelectric effect in 1905. Millikan's experimental verification in 1916 gave a strong basis to the theory. Since 1916, the theory has been universally accepted by the scientific world. Energy of any form was no longer considered as continuous entity. Both emission and absorption of energy takes place in whole numbers of quanta.

The particle-like property of light was clearly demonstrated in 1922 by the American physicist Arthur Holly Compton (1892-1962). He allowed X-ray to penetrate matter. In this process electrons were ejected by the pressure exerted by X-ray, which was itself deflected. The frequency of the deflected X-ray was slightly decreased, showing loss of energy by the X-ray. The ejected electron recoiled by gaining the same amount of energy which was lost by the X-ray. This phenomenon is known as the *Compton effect.* In 1927, Compton received the Nobel Prize for this discovery. The deflection of X-ray and the energy-transfer from the X-ray to the electron which recoils in the process of being ejected cannot be explained by the wave theory. Thus it is established that light consists of particles. The particle of light energy was termed 'photon' (the Greek word for light).

Law of Conservation of Action

The law of conservation of mass and the law of conservation of energy belong to classical physics. The law of conservation of action is a law of quantum physics. A constant action is absolutely constant; its size is the same for all observers in space and time.

The constant h in Planck's equation is expressed in the unit of erg seconds. Energy in ergs is multiplied by time in seconds. Such units are called 'actions'. Planck's constant is four-dimensional.

Action is a product of energy and time. The size of the energy does not remain constant for all observers; so also is the size of the time. But action remains the same for all observers. This is the law of conservation of action.

The law of conservation of action is inherent in special theory of relativity. This theory treats the three dimensions of space and one of time as a four-dimensional space-time continuum. The length, breadth and height of a solid are not the same for different observers moving at different speeds. For this purpose a moving train may be taken as an example of a solid. The train moves through time and thus exists in four dimensions, the fourth dimension being time. Time through which the train moves from one spot to another is not the same for different observers moving at different speeds. As the train moves, it traces out a hyper-rectangle. The height of this rectangle is the length of the train; the breadth of this rectangle is the time that has passed. The area of the rectangle remains constant. Different observers moving at different speeds observe different dimensions of the train and the time it takes, but they observe the same area of the rectangle. The same analogy holds good for the Planck's constant. Action, being product of energy and time, is a four-dimensional equivalent of energy. The action remains constant for all observers moving at different speeds.

Quantum Theory Applied to Atomic Model

In the atomic model of Ernest Rutherford (1871-1937), a small central nucleus was surrounded by a cloud of electrons. The classical physicists were very much puzzled since they could not explain the stability of Rutherford's atom. According to the classical laws of electrodynamics, the nucleus with positive charge could drag the electrons with negative charge. How could this be prevented? This was the question which had been irritating the physicists before 1913.

Niels Bohr (1885-1962), a Danish physicist, had been working with Rutherford in Manchester since 1912. He suggested an atomic model in 1913. He brought about a fusion of classical mechanics and quantum mechanics in his atomic model. He imagined the atom in the form of a miniature solar system. The nucleus was compared with the Sun and the electrons with the planets, encircling the nucleus in orbits. The idea of an orbit comes from classical physics. The orbiting of electrons around the nucleus is in accordance with the laws of classical mechanics and electromagnetism. The idea of energy levels, electron states and electron jump comes from quantum physics. The latter idea did not allow the electrons to spiral inward out of their orbits with continuous radiation since they could only emit whole quanta of energy.

Bohr published his theory of the atom in 1913. He introduced the quantum into this theory. He used Planck's constant, h, in the equations describing the atom. By doing this, he could explain the atomic spectra. A very sharp spectral line is produced by an atom by either emitting or absorbing energy with a very precise frequency, ν. According to Bohr's theory, electrons stay in an energy level or shell around the nucleus of an atom because they do not radiate energy continuously and they emit or absorb whole quantum of energy. An electron may jump from a lower level to a higher one by absorbing a quantum ($h\nu$) of energy. It may jump from a higher level to a lower one by emitting a quantum of energy. Thus the jump can occur in either direction, up or down the ladder of energy. There may be long jumps of electrons by absorption or emission of multiples of integers of quanta.

For discussion of Bohr's model of the atom, hydrogen atom, which is the simplest, may be taken as an example. In its nucleus it has got a single proton. Only one electron revolves round the nucleus. This electron does not spiral into the nucleus, but goes on circling and gives off radiation. The wavelengths of this radiation are highly specific. It was a puzzle for the scientists to account for the specificity of the wavelengths of this radiation. Bohr postulated that the electron converts its kinetic energy into radiation. In that process, the energy radiated must be in whole quanta.

Bohr could visualize a number of orbits for the electron to circle around the nucleus. The orbit closest to the nucleus is the one in which the electron possesses minimum energy and is said to be in the ground state. In the ground state the electron cannot radiate energy at all. Outside the orbit of the ground state there are a series of orbits which are situated farther and farther away from the nucleus. These orbits except the innermost one are said to be in excited states. In order to be lifted to any outer orbit, the electron has to absorb definite quanta of energy. When the electron from any of the excited states emits definite quanta of energy, it drops down from the exterior to the interior orbit. The size of the quantum of energy absorbed or emitted decides the orbit to which the electron is lifted or dropped.

In the arrangement of the orbits about the nucleus of the hydrogen atom, Bohr gave a series of particular values to the angular momentum of the electron. The size of the quanta of energy to be absorbed or emitted by the electron was the deciding factor for the position of the electron and hence the momentum of the electron involved Planck's constant. Bohr gave the following equation:

$$p=\frac{nh}{2\pi}$$

Here p is the angular momentum of the electron, n is a whole number, h is Planck's constant and π is the ratio of the circumference of a circle to its diameter.

After solving the equation given here, it may be expressed in another form as follows:

$$p=n\ (1.0545 \times 10^{-27})$$

The symbol n may assume any value in whole number such as 1, 2, 3, 4, and so on. It is called quantum number. Since there are other types of quantum numbers, it is often called the principal quantum number. When n equals 1, it refers to the ground state. When n takes value such as 2, 3, 4 and higher ones, it refers to the increasingly higher states that are said to be excited.

The single electron present in a hydrogen atom may occupy position in any one of possible orbits. If the electron in orbit 1 (ground state) absorbs a quantum of energy of fixed size, it rises from orbit 1 to orbit 2. This phenomenon of energy absorption is exhibited by a dark line against a bright background in a certain position in the spectral picture. The electron from orbit 2 may drop to orbit 1 by emitting a quantum of energy of the same fixed size. The emission of energy involves a bit of radiation of fixed frequency. This produces a bright spectral line in a fixed position. If the size of the quantum of energy absorbed or emitted is larger, say twice, three times or any other multiple of the quantum, the jump of the electron may be through more than one orbit at a time. As for example, the electron may directly jump from orbit 1 to orbit 3, 4, 5 or others and *vice versa* as a single step.

The quantum number that has been discussed here is Bohr's quantum number. There are other types of quantum numbers also. Bohr could visualize the orbits to be circular. But Sommerfeld thought of elliptical orbits in addition to the circular ones. He introduced a second type of quantum number which he called 'orbital quantum number'. A third type is the magnetic quantum number. The fourth type is the 'spin quantum number'. The spin is either clockwise or anticlockwise. For any value of n, there can be only two values of spin(s), viz., $\frac{1}{2}$ and $-\frac{1}{2}$.

Statistical Behaviour of Atoms

Early in the 1900s, Ernest Rutherford (1871-1937) and his colleague Frederick Soddy (1877-1956) conducted investigation to find out the nature of radioactivity. Atoms of a radioactive substance disintegrate. Every radioactive element has got a characteristic half life. During the half-life, exactly half of the atoms in a sample decay. The half-life of radium is 1,600 years; that of C^{14} (a radioactive form of carbon) is a little under 6,000 years; and that of radioactive potassium is 1,300 million years. All atoms in a radioactive sample do not decay simultaneously. In a vast array of atoms, one atom disintegrates now while its neighbours do not. One of its neighbouring atoms may disintegrate 2,000 years after. What causes atom X to disintegrate now and atom Y five minutes hereafter? Rutherford and Soddy could not answer this question. They made a statistical theory of radioactive decay. They believed that the decay process was accurately caused, that it had a specific reason and that the cause was hidden from them. They expected that eventually someone would find out exactly what made an individual atom decay.

Einstein ceased to be a patent clerk in 1909 and took up his first academic post as an Associate Professor in Zürich. In 1916, at the peak of the First World War, he introduced the notion of probability into atomic theory. To account for the details of the atomic spectra, he applied the statistical techniques to Bohr's model of atom. In an atom, an electron at a higher energy level jumps down to a lower energy level. Einstein thought that this process was very similar to the radioactive decay of an atom. He used the statistical techniques developed by Ludwig Boltzmann (1844-1906) to describe the quantum jumps of electrons from one energy state to another. Boltzmann developed this technique for dealing with the behaviour of collections of atoms.

Thus Einstein realized that atomic actions are random events. Chance plays role in the movement of an electron from a higher energy level to a lower one. In spite of this introduction of probability into quantum physics by Einstein himself, he too anticipated that later discoveries would remove the need for chance.

In classical physics, every effect is considered to have been caused, and every cause is also caused. This notion of strict causality was rejected in quantum physics as soon as radioactive chance-decay worked out by Rutherford and Soddy and probabilities of atomic transitions described by Einstein were recognized. The lower energy level is more desirable for the electron. The ground state is the most desirable one. The electron makes an attempt to reach the desirable state sooner or later. The likelihood of any specific electron to attain the desirable state is based on statistical probability. Its chance can be predicted. But, which electron will attain what state at what time cannot be ascertained before the event occurs. According to quantum physics, this event happens for no particular reason; it just happens; the electron jumps without the pushing of any outside agency; there is no internal clockwork that times the electron-jump. This break with strict causality came in 1916. It is ironical that Einstein who disowned the notion of chance of quantum physics was the first scientist who introduced the notion of chance into atomic theory in 1916. The idea that everything happens in the universe without necessarily having cause could not be accepted by Einstein. In this connection, his famous comment may be noted here—"God does not play dice".

Pauli's Exclusion Principle

Hydrogen atom contains a single proton in the nucleus and a single electron in the orbits. The single electron in hydrogen atom occupies the ground state energy level unless excited by absorption of quanta of energy. But this does not hold true for atoms of other elements containing more than one electron. Carbon atom, for example, contains six electrons. How are these electrons distributed among the orbits? Can a single orbit accommodate indefinite number of electrons? Physicists were trying to get answers to these questions. Bohr thought of system of filling up the orbits. In his atomic model, electrons are 'shells' around the nucleus. 'New' electrons go into the shell with the least energy until it is full, and then into the next shell, and so on. Bohr, however, could not explain how or why a shell becomes full.

In 1924, Wolfgang Pauli (1900-1958), an Austrian physicist, assigned four separate quantum numbers to the electron. One number described the angular momentum of the electron; the second one described the shape of its orbit; the third one described its orientation; and the fourth one described the electron's spin.

Ralph Kronig was the first scientist to propose 'spin'. He suggested that the electron had an instrinsic spin of one-half in the natural units ($h/2\pi$, written as $\hbar$) and that this spin could line up either parallel or antiparallel to the magnetic field of the atom.

In 1925, Pauli suggested that no two electrons in a given atom can have all the four quantum numbers identical. This means that in any orbit two electrons at the most may be present; and of these two, one must spin clockwise and the other anticlockwise. Thus, the presence of two electrons of opposite spin excludes other electrons, and this is called Pauli's *exclusion principle.*

Filling of the orbits with electrons starts from the one closest to the nucleus. When the innermost orbit is filled up with two electrons, the third and fourth electron go to occupy the second orbit which is outside the innermost one. This process of filling the orbits with electrons goes on systematically from inner to the outer orbits, with the maximum of two electrons in each orbit. Any atom with odd number of electrons must have one electron only in the outermost orbit among the orbits filled up.

The Pauli exclusion principle applies to *all* particles that have a half-integral amount of spin—$(\frac{1}{2})\hbar$, $(3/2)\hbar$, $(5/2)\hbar$, and so on. The neutrino, electron, muon, proton and neutron, together with their anti-particles, have spins of $\frac{1}{2}$. These particles with non-integral spins behave according to Fermi-Dirac statistics, worked out by the Italian physicist Enrico Fermi (1901-54) and the English physicist Paul Dirac (1902-84) in 1925 and 1926. These particles are called *fermions*.

Full-spin particles (with integral spin such as $\hbar$, $2\hbar$, $3\hbar$, and so on) and spinless particles behave, according to Bose-Einstein statistics, developed during 1924 and 1925. Such particles are called *bosons* after the name of the Indian physicist Satyendra Nath Bose. Pauli exclusion principle does not hold for the bosons. The Bose-Einstein statistics was Einstein's last great contribution to quantum theory.

Without the exclusion principle, the variety of the chemical elements and all the features that make up the physical world would not be possible. In recognition of the importance of the exclusion principle, Pauli was awarded the Nobel Prize in 1945.

Particle-Wave Duality

In the early twentieth century the physicists could realize that light behaves both as a wave and as a particle. Light is one type of electromagnetic wave. The physicists were convinced that, not only light, but also electromagnetic wave in general, demonstrates both wave-like and particle-like properties.

In 1905, Einstein re-established the concept that light is corpuscular. But he did not rule out the wave nature of light. He remained busy with this dual idea until 1911. He pointed out to the then unreceptive scientific world that the way to a better understanding of light would involve a fusion of the wave and the particle theories. In 1909, Einstein said:

> It is my opinion that the next phase in the development of theoretical physics will bring us a theory of light that can be interpreted as a kind of fusion of the wave and the emission theory.[2]

Scientists were still questioning: Is the wave-particle dualism confined to electromagnetic radiation only? If waves are particles, are particles also waves? If there is wave-matter, is there also matter-wave?

In 1923, the French physicist Louis Victor de Broglie (1892-1987) published three papers on the nature of light quanta in the French journal *Comptes Rendus*. Its English summary was published in 1924. He used his findings for his doctoral thesis in 1924. This thesis was published in 1925 in the *Annales de Physique*. He derived his equation in the following way:

$$\lambda = c/\nu \qquad \text{... (1)}$$

Here λ is the wavelength, c is the velocity of the wave and ν is the number of waves per second (frequency).

If we divide both sides of Planck's equation ($E=h\nu$) by h, we find the value of ν.

$$\frac{E}{h} = \frac{h\nu}{h}, \text{ or } \nu = E/h \qquad \text{... (2)}$$

The value of λ in the first equation may be expressed by replacing the value of ν, as obtained in the second equation.

$$\lambda = c/\nu = ch/E \qquad \text{... (3)}$$

According to Einstein's special theory of relativity, mass-energy relationship is expressed by the equation $E=mc^2$. The following equation is obtained by substituting this value of E in the third equation.

$$\lambda = ch/E = ch/mc^2 = h/mc \qquad \text{... (4)}$$

Mass times velocity (mc) is equivalent to momentum (p). A particle cannot travel as fast as light. De Broglie suggested to use the actual velocity (v) of the particle instead of c (speed of light) in equation 4. Thus, de Broglie's equation is given as follows:

$$\lambda = h/mv = h/p$$

$$\text{or,} \quad p\lambda = h \qquad \text{... (5)}$$

To express de Broglie's equation in words, momentum multiplied by wavelength is equal to Planck's constant. From this it is deduced that the smaller the wavelength, the bigger the momentum of the corresponding particle.

Through this equation, de Broglie declared the wave properties of matter. For his work he received a Nobel Prize in 1929. He established the particle-wave duality. Thus electron, being matter, is both particle and wave; and light, being energy, is both particle and wave.

The equation of de Broglie is not confined to the micro-particles only; it is theoretically applicable to any moving body from the electron to the giant star. As the momentum increases, the wavelength decreases. The wavelength of a massive body is too small to be detected by any existing known method. On the other hand, the wavelength of an electron is as large as that of an X-ray. The matter wave of electron could be detected independently in 1927 by two groups of scientists, viz., two American physicists Clinton Joseph Davisson (1881-1958) and Lester Halbert Germer (1896-1971) and two British physicists George Paget Thomson (1892-1975) and Alexander Reid. In their diffraction experiments, electrons were diffracted by crystal lattices like waves. This conclusively proved that de Broglie was correct. In 1937, Davisson and Thomson shared the Nobel Prize. In 1906, J.J. Thomson had received the Nobel Prize for proving that electrons are particles. In 1937, he saw his son (George Thomson) being awarded the Nobel Prize for proving that electrons are waves. Both the father and the son were correct.

From 1928 onwards, more experimental evidences were forthcoming for the detection of the wave properties of particles such as proton and neutron that are more massive than the electron. Now it is an established fact that wave-particle duality is a universal phenomenon in Nature. There is no entity that exhibits particle properties only without possessing wave properties, and vice versa.

Principle of Complementarity

Niels Bohr (1885-1962), the famous Danish physicist, was associated with Rutherford's group in Manchester until 1916. In this year he returned to Denmark to become Professor of Theoretical Physics in Copenhagen. He played a very prominent role in establishing the fundamentals of quantum theory. In the 1920s quantum physicists were busy with wave-particle duality and uncertainty principle. Light is both particle and wave. Electron is both particle and wave. Can something be X and not-X? Is this concept comprehensible? Is it logically compatible? These questions were puzzling scientists. During this period of confusion, Bohr cleared the fog by his 'principle of complementarity'. Light is particle; light is wave; but the particle and the wave properties of light are not mutually exclusive; they are complementary. Both the apparently contradictory concepts are necessary to provide a complete description.

What is said here of light is universally true. Particle physics and wave physics are equally valid; they are complementary descriptions of the same reality. When we say, "X is wave", we are correct; when we say, "X is particle", we are also correct. But neither description is complete in itself. It depends upon the circumstances in which one is more appropriate than the other. The particle concept may be more appropriate in one setting whereas the wave concept may be more appropriate in another setting. An entity such as an electron is neither a particle nor a wave. Under some circumstances it behaves as if it were a particle; under some other circumstances it behaves as if it were a wave. We get a complete understanding of the entity by knowing both the apparently contradictory properties. There is no way for us to observe both the opposite characters simultaneously. Under no circumstances can we invent an experiment to detect both the opposite behaviours at once. We observe one behaviour at a time in one experimental condition; we observe the opposite behaviour at some other time in a separate experimental condition. In reality, the so-called opposite behaviours are complementary to each other for a complete description and better comprehension.

Matrix Mechanics

In 1925, Werner Heisenberg (1901-1976) attempted to avoid use of Bohr's 'orbit' in the atomic model. He preferred 'state' to 'orbit'. He conceived of an electron jumping from one state to another. With reference to the change of state of an electron, he made a table representing all possible states and frequencies. Both rows and columns of states were provided in the table. Each square in the chessboard table represented one possible frequency of radiation, corresponding to the row and column states. For example, when an electron goes from S_1 (state 1) to S_2 (state 2), it produces light of frequency ν_{2-1}.

The concept of matrix was totally alien to physics in 1925. It was also unknown to Heisenberg himself. But this was in vogue in mathematics. Sixty-six years earlier, an Irish mathematician, W.R. Hamilton, had developed a system of arranging data into arrays, or mathematical tables called matrices. No use of these matrices was known before Heisenberg, Born and Jordan developed their matrix mechanics.

Heisenberg constructed equations describing the tables of frequencies, amplitudes, positions and momenta. He called them quantum-mechanical series. In the process of calculation of his quantum-mechanical series, he was distressed to observe an asymmetry. His new quantum theory seemed to violate the commutative law of mathematics. According to the commutative law, $A \times B$ is always equal to $B \times A$; the order in which two numbers are multiplied does not affect the result. But, quantum-mechanical series A multiplied by quantum-mechanical series B was not equal to quantum-mechanical series B multiplied by quantum-mechanical series A. To express it in mathematical symbols, $A \times B \neq B \times A$.

Max Born (1882-1970), who was Professor of Theoretical Physics since 1921 in Göttingen, was the supervisor of Heisenberg. Max Born went through the paper of Heisenberg and realized that the quantum-mechanical series were, in fact, what mathematicians call matrices. In 1925, matrices were totally unfamiliar to most mathematicians and physicists. Max Born was then one of the few European physicists (perhaps the only one) with a good knowledge of matrix mechanics. Today's rectangular form of writing matrices was introduced, for the first time, by Augustin Cauchy, a French mathematician. Heisenberg's equations were rewritten by Born as matrices. He wrote out the energy levels of atoms as a set of numbers. These numbers were arranged on rectangular arrays called 'matrices'. Manipulation of these matrices could be done by the help of matrix algebra. By such mathematical manipulation of the matrix mechanics, the spectral lines of individual atoms could be calculated. This system dispenses with any picture of the atom—either Bohr's planetary model or Schrödinger's standing waves.

By rewriting Heisenberg's equations as matrices, Max Born was surprised at some unusual observation. He noticed that matrix q for position and matrix p for momentum are noncommutative in a peculiar way. Firstly, pq and qp are not equal. Secondly, the difference between pq and qp is always the same irrespective of whatever p and q are chosen. Born, in his joint paper with Pascual Jordan (1902-), gave the following mathematical equation:

$$pq - qp = \hbar/i$$

Here $\hbar$, as usual, is Planck's constant divided by 2π and i is the square root of minus one.

Born requested his pupil, Pascual Jordan, to help him in the development of the matrix mechanics. This was in the summer of 1925. Jordan took up the work and concluded it. The paper of Born, Jordan and Heisenberg was published in *Zeitschrift für Physik* in 1926. This is the famous 'three-man paper'. The Göttingen team stressed that this is the fundamental quantum mechanical relation. Although matrix mechanics is an important part of quantum physics, it includes Newtonian mechanics in itself.

Wave Mechanics

The Austrian physicist Erwin Schrödinger (1887-1961) brought the matter-waves of de Broglie into the realm of atomic theory. He interpreted the structure of atoms in terms of particle waves rather than of particles alone. The analysis of the details in atomic behaviour on the basis of the Schrödinger model is termed wave mechanics.

In March 1926, Schrödinger published a single equation that successfully explained almost all aspects of the behaviour of electrons in terms of de Broglie waves, rather than that of matrices. In the same year, he published a series of papers to establish his concept of wave mechanics.

Schrödinger had a picture of the atom in which the electron circles the nucleus as a wave form. The electron exists only in orbits of such size that its wave form occupies it in a whole number of wavelengths. The wave form repeats itself as it goes round, falling exactly on itself. This picture of the electron is termed *standing wave*.

When the electron gains or loses energy, its wavelength changes. With gain of energy, its wavelength decreases; with loss of energy, its wavelength increases. When the wavelength of the electron increases or decreases slightly, the orbit no longer contains a whole number of wavelengths and in such a situation the wavelengths cannot fit the orbit. The gain or loss of energy must be just enough to decrease or increase the wavelength to such a degree that an integral number of wavelengths can fit the orbit. Thus, the different energy levels represent different standing waves.

There was intense controversy over matrix mechanics versus wave mechanics. Heisenberg was not in favour of Schrödinger's wave mechanics. But, Max Born, who had helped develop matrix mechanics, was attracted towards the continuum physics of Schrödinger. Some physicists, in favour of matrix mechanics, asked the question: "What is waving in the wave equation?" Schrödinger had answer to his critics' question. In his opinion, a particle is in reality a group of waves of relatively small dimensions in every direction; with reference to the micro-world, one must proceed from the *wave equation,* and not from the fundamental equation of mechanics. Heisenberg did recognize this implicit attack on the matrix mechanics. He reacted in a fury. He berated Born for deserting matrices.

Psychologically, Schrödinger's wave mechanics seemed superior to Heisenberg's matrix mechanics. The former offered a picture of wave forms, whereas the latter presented an array of pictureless numbers that lacked anything concrete for the image-seeking mind to grasp.

Schrödinger was a gentle, sober and decent man. He tried to avoid dogma. He mentioned his hope that wave mechanics and matrix mechanics would not fight against each other and that, on the contrary, they would supplement each other.

On April 12, 1926, Pauli communicated to Jordan through a lengthy letter in which he proved that both wave mechanics and matrix mechanics were identical. A month later, Schrödinger published his third wave paper in which he himself proved the same thing.

In 1944, the Hungarian-American mathematician John von Neumann (1903-57) could logically prove the equivalence of wave mechanics and matrix mechanics. He could show that whatever could be demonstrated by wave mechanics could be equally well demonstrated by matrix mechanics.

The English physicist Paul Adrien Maurice Dirac (1902-84) raised his doubts in Neumann's arguments in 1964. In his opinion, matrix mechanics and wave mechanics are not mathematically equivalent, and matrix mechanics fits reality more accurately.

Heisenberg's matrix mechanics applies to high-energy particles. When high-energy particles collide, collision results in scattering of particles. Hence matrix mechanics is otherwise known as Scattering Matrix or S Matrix. The Schrödinger wave equation works at lower energies. Being non-relativistic, it does not work for high energies.

The American chemist Linus Pauling made use of wave mechanics in explaining the covalent bonds in molecules. In a molecule where two atoms are linked together by contributing one electron each and sharing both the electrons, the bond so formed becomes more stable than what would have been done separately. In this model, the two shared electrons become two wave forms that resonate with each other. Such a model of the atom is known as Lewis-Langmuir model. Pauling expounded this theory of resonance in greater detail in his book, *The Nature of the Chemical Bond*, published in 1939.

Schrödinger was honoured by the award of the Nobel Prize for his work on wave mechanics. He shared the physics Nobel Prize with Dirac in 1933.

The Göttingen team, busy in establishing the matrix mechanics, was against the wave mechanics of Schrödinger. But, surprisingly, Max Born of the Göttingen team made a major contribution to the concept of Schrödinger in finding out a new way of interpreting the wave mechanics.

The important thing in Schrödinger's equation is the wave function psi (ψ). That this ψ corresponded to a 'real' electron wave could not be accepted by Max Born. He tried to find a way of associating this wave function with the existence of particles. He argued like this: The particles are real, but in some way they are guided by the wave. The strength of the wave (the value of ψ^2) at a point in space is a measure of the probability of finding the particle at that particular point. It is not possible for us to be sure about the position of a particle like electron. But the wave function enables us to work out the probability of its location. Born received the Nobel Prize in 1954 for his work on the probabilistic interpretation of quantum mechanics.

Heisenberg's Principle of Indeterminacy

Late in 1926, Werner Heisenberg discovered uncertainty inherent in the equations of quantum mechanics. The equation of quantum mechanics, $pq-qp=\hbar/i$, has already been mentioned. It has further been mentioned that quantum physics has recognized the non-commutative relation $pq \neq pq$. Here p stands for momentum and q for position; $\hbar$ is Planck's constant divided by 2π and i is the square root of minus one.

We can measure either p or q very accurately. But Heisenberg proved that it is impossible to determine, with absolute precision, both the position (q) and momentum (p) of a particle simultaneously. When the position of the particle is determined with accuracy its velocity is automatically altered. Consequently the momentum of the particle is changed. As a result, the value of the momentum of the particle becomes uncertain at the time of the accurate determination of its position. Conversely, when attempt is made to determine the momentum of the particle accurately, its position is automatically altered, and consequently the value of its position becomes uncertain. The degree of uncertainty of one bears an inverse relationship with the level of accuracy of determination of the other. The more accurate is the determination of one, the greater is the uncertainty of the other. We can know *approximately* both the position and the momentum of the particle simultaneously. The more we know about one, the less we know about the other. When we know the one with absolute precision, we know nothing about the other.

The equation of Heisenberg that mathematically expresses the principle of indeterminacy (the uncertainty principle) is given below.

$$\Delta p \Delta q \geqslant \hbar$$

The amount of 'error' in our measurement of position is Δq; similarly, the amount of 'error' in our measurement of momentum is Δp. Heisenberg says that Δp times Δq must always be bigger than $\hbar$, Planck's constant divided by 2π. If the error in the position (Δq) is very small, the error in the momentum (Δp) must increase so that the product, $\Delta q \times \Delta p$, is larger than $\hbar$. If the position (q) of a particle is measured with absolute precision and zero error, the corresponding error in the momentum becomes infinite; or in other words, the momentum is completely indeterminate.

The uncertainty principle is not restricted to position and momentum only. It applies to any pair of conjugate variables. These variables, when multiplied, give product in units of action (energy multiplied by time).

On March 23, 1927, Heisenberg's article, "On the Visualizable Content of Quantum Theoretical Kinematics and Mechanics" reached the Editor of the Journal *Zeitschrift für Physik*. It was published at the end of May, 1927.

For the work on the principle of indeterminacy, Heisenberg received the physics Nobel Prize for 1932. Throughout his scientific career, he was hostile and unkind to Schrödinger who was a kind and honourble person. It so happened that both the famous physicists were honoured simultaneously by the Swedish Academy in December, 1933. To receive the Nobel Prize in physics, Heisenberg was the delayed awardee for 1932 and Schrödinger was the co-winner (with Dirac) for 1933.

Heisenberg's uncertainty principle became a big blow to the ego of scientists. Both scientists and non-scientists had strong faith in the precision of scientific knowledge ever since the time of Newton. Now Heisenberg came forward with a doctrine that gave a big jolt to this faith. This type of uncertainty is not particular to the particles; this is a general phenomenon inherent in the nature of the universe itself.

Einstein was very much upset psychologically when he could neither accept nor reject the principle of uncertainty. He could not reject, because he had no valid scientific arguments against it. He was reluctant to accept it since it violated the 'strict' law of causality. If this principle is accepted, everything in Nature may be considered to take place randomly rather than orderly and the law of cause and effect may not be binding to the natural phenomena. "I can't believe", said Einstein, "that God would choose to play dice with the world".[3] But, in spite of this unwillingness of Einstein, he had to go with the principle of uncertainty. It had become an established principle in modern physics.

Philosophers took up the implications of the uncertainty principle in the 1930s and afterwards. They no longer accepted the law of causality. The concept infiltrated to literature where absurdity was accepted and strict causality was rejected. It had confrontation with some religions which uphold the concept of strict causality. Thus, the principle of indeterminacy has not only shaken the backbone of classical physics but also has revolutionized human thought altogether.

Heisenberg says at the end of his paper of May, 1927: "We *cannot* know, as a matter of principle, the present in all its details." The uncertainty principle tells us that the future cannot be predicted. Simultaneous and precisive determination of both position and momentum of a particle is impossible and hence the future is inherently unpredictable and uncertain. In this regard quantum physics is at variance with Newtonian physics. Newton believed in strict causality. He cherished the idea that the entire course of the future is predictable with the possible accurate knowledge of the position and momentum of every particle in the universe. The quantum physicist rejects such an idea of perfect prediction since he cannot know accurately and simultaneously the position and momentum of even a *single* particle.

What has been said with reference to the present and future does not, however, hold good for the past. Heisenberg has said:

"We *can* know, as a matter of principle, the past in all its details." Although the future is inherently uncertain, the past is clearly defined. In principle, an experiment can be designed to calculate backward and determine accurately what were the position and momentum of a particle at some time in the past. The determination of the past is possible in principle within the rules of quantum mechanics.

The Copenhagen Interpretation

From July 1925 until September 1927, Niels Bohr published hardly anything on quantum theory. In September 1927, he addressed a conference (Salvay Conference) in Tomo, Italy. He presented a group of ideas such as uncertainty, complementarity, probability, disturbance of the observed system by the observer, and so on. These ideas are collectively referred to as the 'Copenhagen interpretation' of quantum mechanics. There was no meeting at Copenhagen. There were no discussions and no consensus of opinions of physicists. However, the deliberations of Bohr at a public conference in Tomo, Italy were classically known as the Copenhagen interpretation.

The four cardinal points propounded by Niels Bohr in the Tomo conference have influenced twentieth-century thought, in a profound way. Bohr's complementarity and Heisenberg's uncertainty principle are two of these points that have already been discussed. The probability concept which is a key ingredient in the Copenhagen interpretation came from Max Born, the physicist of Göttingen, who gave the statistical interpretation of the wave function. The fourth point in the Copenhagen interpretation is the component of subjectivity in the act of observation.

It is a universal phenomenon that every entity in Nature possesses pairs of contradictory characters such as corpuscular property and wave property. The contradictory characters are not exclusive of each other, but are complementary. For an integral comprehension of the entity as a whole, it is necessary to know both the contradictory characters c and not-c. Although both c and not-c cannot be detected simultaneously by any single experiment, separate experiments with separate designs can be devised to detect a single character at a time. But knowledge of both the characters c and not-c are necessary for a better comprehension of the entity. This is Bohr's principle of complementarity.

There is no absolute truth at the quantum level. We cannot know the entirety of Nature with certainty. We can know Nature only approximately. The more precisely do we know the position of a particle, the less precise does its momentum become, and vice versa. When we know the position with absolute accuracy, we don't know anything at all about its momentum, and vice versa. This phenomenon is universally true for any pair of conjugate variables. All of the present cannot be known with precision. The future cannot be predicted precisely. Uncertainty is an inbuilt phenomenon in Nature. In contrast to this concept of uncertainty in quantum physics, Newtonian physics had a notion of certainty. Had all the initial conditions been known, it would be possible, according to classical physics, to predict the total course of the universe with absolute precision. Knowledge of science was considered to be certain by the classical physicists.

Everything happens by chance in quantum physics. The micro-world of quantum physics is chaotic. Micro-particles move randomly, collide with one another randomly, act randomly and appear and disappear randomly. There is no order in the micro-world. Disorder or chaos is the rule and not the exception in the micro-world. Chaos is a universal phenomenon. The cause-and-effect relationship does not function in the micro-world. Thus the causal law is rejected. Notwithstanding what has been said here, amid utter chaos, the trend of Nature can be predicted. It is not possible to predict that an individual entity X will be Y. The probability of X being Y in a population of a huge number of entities can be predicted. The total behaviour of a large population of micro-particles can be statistically predicted. There is no way for us to say that an individual event shall occur before its actual occurrence. In contrast to this concept of causality and chance phenomenon in quantum physics, classical physics had adherence to strict causality and precise predictability.

Quantum physics does not recognize an objective world independent of the subject who observes. The observer, in the act of observation, influences the thing observed and substantially alters it. We cannot observe anything in Nature without influencing and altering it. We observe a property which we want to observe and in this sense we create that property. By choosing to measure position of a particle precisely, the quantum physicist forces the particle to develop more uncertainty in its momentum, and vice versa. He eliminates the corpuscular feature by choosing to observe the wave properties while designing an experiment, and vice versa. In quantum physics, the observer is in a real sense part of the experiment.

In Newtonian physics, the objective world exists and functions with or without the existence of an observer; the world is a *machine* which functions precisely by the universal law of causation. The 'I' in the observer is the subject; the world outside this 'I' is the object. The object is there when the subject observes or does not observe. The subject and his act of observation do not influence the object in any way, according to the concept of classical physics.

Some quantum physicists are extreme subjectivists. They do not believe that an object exists when the subject does not observe it. Some others do not commit the non-existence of an object at the time of non-observation; they assert that we cannot say anything about any object at the time of our non-observation. At time t_1 we observe an electron in an atom in energy state A. At time t_2 we observe an electron in energy state B. We generally say that electron e was in energy state A and that the same electron jumped from energy state A to state B. The quantum physicist asserts that we cannot say that we observed the *same* electron at time t_1 and t_2. Further, he states that we cannot say that the electron *jumped* from energy state A to B. No statement can be made, says the quantum physicist, about the electron when we are not looking at it. We observed an electron at time t_1 in energy state A; we observed an electron at time t_2 in energy state B. Only this much that we observe can be said. We cannot say if there was an electron when we were not observing; we cannot say if electron at energy state B was the same one at energy state A; and we cannot say if the same electron jumped from energy state A to energy state B.

The Copenhagen interpretation does not make any differentiation among the observed (object), the act of observation (action) and the observer (subject). The person who observes is therefore part of the reality that he is probing. Some physicists believe that the picture of the observed phenomenon must include the mind of the observer. Thus the Copenhagen interpretation puts much emphasis on the consciousness of the observer.

Einstein was a bitter critic of the Copenhagen interpretation of

Niels Bohr. He himself was the first proponent of the statistical interpretation of the subatomic phenomena. But he opposed the concept of probability of the Copenhagen interpretation. He said: "Quantum mechanics is very impressive....but I am convinced that God does not play dice."[4] The rejection of cause by the quantum physicist was not appreciated by Einstein. He did recognize the random or chance phenomena in Nature; but he believed that beneath the surface of chance actions there is some fundamental reality at the deeper level that regulates on some rational ground. According to the Copenhagen interpretation, reality cannot be comprehended in its entirety. Einstein did not agree to this. He said: "The most incomprehensible thing about the world is that it is comprehensible."[5] In the opinion of Einstein, a physical theory is not complete unless it has one-to-one correspondence with phenomena. He said: "Whatever meaning assigned to the term *complete*, the following requirement for a complete theory seems to be a necessary one: *every element of the physical reality must* have a counterpart in the physical theory."[6] Quantum theory does not accept this one-to-one correspondence between theory and reality. And hence it seemed to Einstein that quantum theory was incomplete. The Copenhagen interpretation denies the objectivity of the world. Bohr says that reality is created by the observer. The fuzzy and nebulous micro-world sharpens into concrete reality only when an observation is made. In the absence of an observation, the atom or the subatomic particle is a ghost. The ghost materializes only when the observer looks for it. Einstein did not accept this notion of quantum theory. He assumed that the physical world exists independently of the human observer. Heisenberg criticized this notion of Einstein and called it 'dogmatic' or 'metaphysical' realism. He said: "Quantum theory does not allow a completely objective description of nature."[7] And he added further: "The ontology of materialism rested upon the illusion that the kind of existence, the direct 'actuality' of the world around us, can be extrapolated into the atomic range. The extrapolation is impossible, however."[8] Einstein could never accept this sort of subjectivism of quantum mechanics.

The Copenhagen interpretation of quantum mechanics, having accepted the physical world as idea of the observer, does not consider it as non-material, however. We perceive the physical world. We describe it as we perceive. But we cannot be sure that our description conforms to the 'suchness' of the world. The world in reality may or may not be different from what we perceive. The world in our mind is actually the cognitive construction of the world in whatever form it is. Our cognitive construction of the physical world appears to be substantive. But there is no way to be sure that what appears to us is the real nature of the physical world. In a nutshell, we express this by saying that what we observe is itself unknowable.

Some quantum physicists become agnostic. They predict something and calculate equations to describe it. When one goes through the precise mathematical equations, one gets the feeling that knowledge about that something is exact. But the quantum physicist who is the father of the equation about that something does not know what he is talking about.

Mathematics gives us a false notion of exactitude and preciseness. As the mathematician-philosopher Bertrand Russell puts it :

> Mathematics may be defined as the subject in which we never know what we are talking about, nor whether what we are saying is true.[9]

Werner Heisenberg was a supporter of agnosticism in quantum physics. In his view, man can never know what actually goes on in the invisible, subatomic world. He advises us to "abandon all attempts to construct perceptual models of atomic processes".[10] In such a situation his approach is pragmatic. What we see at the beginning of the experiment and at the end are our observables. What happens in between the beginning and the end of the experiment are unknowable and hence anything we say about the unknowable is speculation only.

What we observe, according to the agnostic quantum physicist, is itself unknowable. But our observation is our experience. Quantum mechanics correlates our experiences. Although Einstein was not agnostic, his tone in the following words of his own is so :

> Physical concepts are free creations of the human mind, and are not, however it may seem, uniquely determined by the external world. In our endeavour to understand reality we are somewhat like a man trying to understand the mechanism of

a closed watch. He sees the face and the moving hands, even hears its ticking, but he has no way of opening the case. If he is ingenious, he may form some picture of a mechanism which could be responsible for all the things he observes, but he may never be quite sure his picture is the only one which could explain his observations. He will never be able to compare his picture with the real mechanism and he cannot even imagine the possibility of the meaning of such a comparison.[11]

Einstein was very much distressed with the Copenhagen interpretation. It is, however, surprising that even some strong advocates of quantum mechanics were not very comfortable. The philosophical implications of quantum mechanics seemed to them absurd or paradoxical. Werner Heisenberg writes:

> I remember discussions with Bohr (in 1927) which went through many hours till very late at night and ended almost in despair; and when at the end of the discussion I went alone for a walk in the neighbouring park I repeated to myself again and again the question: Can Nature possibly be as absurd as it seemed to us in these atomic experiments?[12]

The concept of interaction is a fundamental assumption in the complementarity theory of Niels Bohr. In this concept, the subject and the object, the 'I' and the 'you', or the 'I' and the 'that' are not separately considered. We never experience the external reality as it is. As a matter of fact, there is nothing 'external' and 'internal', 'I' and 'that'. What we experience is our *interaction* with the physical world.

The wave-particle duality is not specific to light. It is a characteristic of everything in the physical world. Thus the theory of complementarity of Niels Bohr has a philosophical implication which has a profound influence on metaphysics. The conclusion derived from complementarity leads us to think that the world consists of interactions instead of things. In this connection, the following statement of Bohr is significant:

> ....an independent reality in the ordinary physical sense can be ascribed neither to the phenomena nor to the agencies of observation.[13]

The mathematical equation given by Louis de Broglie and that by Schrödinger exerted significant impact on the thoughts of the quantum physicists. De Broglie's equation said that waves are particles and that particles are waves. Schrödinger's equation described the electrons as spread out over their wave patterns in the form of tenuous cloud. The questions that are posed in this connection are: Do these equations, either of Schrödinger or of de Broglie, represent real things? Are they not mere mathematical abstractions?

Schrödinger believed that his equations were not mathematical abstractions, but that they described real things. What are these real things? Nobody knows. Schrödinger declared the electrons to be standing waves. But scientists were not sure what was waving. Schrödinger gave a name, psi, to that something that was waving.

In this connection, Max Born thought differently. In his opinion, these waves are probability waves, but are not real things.

He wrote:

> ...the whole course of events is determined by the laws of probability; to a state in space there corresponds a definite probability, which is given by the de Broglie wave associated with the state.[14]

Born could think it impossible for a real thing to exist in more than three dimensions. He wrote:

> We have two possibilities. Either we use waves in spaces of more than three dimensions...or we remain in three-dimensional space but give up the simple picture of the wave amplitude as an ordinary physical magnitude, and replace it by a purely abstract mathematical concept...into which we cannot enter.[15]

The real things in Nature seem to be indeterminate. But Schrödinger's and de Broglie's equations describe these indeterminate things. In this connection Born wrote: "Physics is in the nature of the case indeterminate, and therefore the affair of statistics."[16]

In this light of quantum mechanics, the atom and the subatomic particles may be ideas of the physicists to correlate their experiences. It may not be meaningful to visualize any definite picture of the atom. Bohr's planetary model of the atom was discarded. But the new picture which replaced the planetary model is hardly any picture at all. A wave function is an abstract mathematical concept. It is hard to say whether a wave function actually exists. Electron clouds are also unvisualizable abstractions. Hydrogen atom which contains one electron has an electron cloud that exists in three dimensions. All other atoms contain more than one electron and hence their electron clouds exist in more than three dimensions. Oxygen atom with eight electrons has an electron cloud which exists in twenty-four dimensions. Uranium atom, with ninety-two electrons, has an electron cloud of two hundred and seventy-six dimensions. Similar is the situation with wave function. Schrödinger's equation generates an endlessly proliferating number of possibilities. A wave function contains three dimensions for each possibility that it represents. The mind that can have a mental picture of three dimensions only is totally lost in the jungle of multitudes of dimensions.

The quantum physicists have been asking the question, "Do particles really exist?" If we call something a particle, we can safely infer that it has a determinate position. There is no particle at rest. A particle, for its own existence, has to remain in constant motion. The moving particle has definitely a momentum. Of these two properties of the particle, we have got the choice to precisely observe one at a time. We cannot observe both the properties of the particle, with absolute precision, simultaneously. Thus the particle is never discernible to us as it "really is". It appears to us in a way as we choose to see it. As Heisenberg himself wrote: "What we observe is not Nature itself, but Nature exposed to our method of questioning."[17]

All particles have *always* both position and momentum. We can accurately determine either the position or the momentum at a time, but cannot do both simultaneously. The question is: "Are we justified to call anything a 'particle' if we cannot determine both these properties simultaneously? In this connection Max Born wrote:

> ...if we can never actually determine more than one of these two properties (possession of a definite position and a definite momentum), and if when one is determined we can make no assertion at all about the other property for the same moment,

so far our experiment goes, then we are not justified in concluding that the 'thing' under examination can actually be described as a particle in the usual sense of the term.[18]

Einstein did not contradict the equations of quantum mechanics. But he vehemently argued against some of the philosophical implications accrued from the Copenhagen interpretation. He was very much distressed with the acausal concept of quantum mechanics. Quantum mechanics in general and its uncertainty principle in particular renounces the idea of a causal universe. That quantum mechanics entails "the necessity of a final renunciation of the classical ideal of causality and radical revision of our attitude towards the problem of physical reality"[19] has been written by Niels Bohr.

Quantum Electrodynamics

Paul Adrien Maurice Dirac (1902–1984) was a renowned physicist who contributed significantly to quantum physics. He completed his Ph.D. in the spring of 1926. For working out his theory during the last months of 1926 and the first week of 1927, he used an old idea, that of a *field* as his principal tool. By using Heisenberg's matrix mechanics, Dirac developed a Hamiltonian (Sir William Hamilton, famous British mathematician of the nineteenth century, developed equations that were used by the quantum physicists) for the field. He found Hamiltonian for the entire process by adding up the separate Hamiltonians for the atom, the field and the interaction. By such mathematical exercises, Dirac gave the first real quantum field theory. In this theory both quantum mechanics and the dynamics of electromagnetic fields were linked. Hence Dirac called it *quantum electrodynamics*. He submitted his paper to the *Proceedings of the Royal Society* in the last days of January of 1927.

Einstein's mass-energy equation is given below:

$$E^2 = m^2c^4 + p^2c^2$$

When the momentum (p) is zero, the equation becomes $E = mc^2$. Dirac was a genius. He took the square root in a strict sense. As the square root of 4 is ± 2, Dirac expressed the equation as $E = \pm mc^2$. He did not ignore the alternative relation, $E = -mc^2$. He was puzzled over the implications of this relationship.

Dirac considered the energy levels in the relativistic version of quantum mechanics. He could think of two sets of energy levels—positive energy state corresponding to $+mc^2$ and negative energy state corresponding to $-mc^2$.

According to this theory electrons ought to fall into the lowest unoccupied energy state. In spite of this, all electrons do not fall into the negative levels and disappear. Dirac could account for it by saying that electrons are fermions and that only one electron can go into each possible state (two per energy level, one with each spin). When all the negative energy states are already full, there is no scope for the electrons to fall into them.

Dirac compared the so-called 'empty space' with a sea of negative energy electrons. If energy is supplied to the negative energy electron, it can jump up the ladder of energy states. To get from the state of $-mc^2$ to the state of $+mc^2$, an input of energy of $2mc^2$ is necessary. In consideration of the mass of an electron, about 1 MeV of energy is to be supplied for the electron in the negative energy sea to jump up into the real world and become visible as an ordinary electron. The input of this amount of energy is feasible through atomic processes or collision of particles.

When the negative energy electron is promoted into the real world as a positive energy electron, it leaves behind a *hole* in the negative energy sea. The absence of a negatively charged electron has been symbolized as a hole. Dirac could visualize the hole to behave like a positively charged electron. At first thought, he assigned the same mass to both the negatively charged and positively charged electrons on the ground of maintenance of symmetry. But he changed his idea in a moment of weakness at the time of writing his paper for publication. In the late 1920s, only two particles, viz., electron and proton were known. Dirac suggested that the positively charged particle might be the proton. Here he was wrong.

Dirac won the physics Nobel Prize in 1933. James Chadwick discovered neutron in 1932 and received the Nobel Prize in 1935. Carl D. Anderson discovered the 'hole' particle of Dirac in cosmic ray in 1932 and for this work he won the Nobel Prize in 1936.

In 1930, Robert Millikan who was Head of the physics laboratory at the California Institute of Technology, asked Carl D. Anderson to build a new cloud chamber to be used for study of cosmic rays. On August 2, 1932, Anderson discovered the positively charged electron in cosmic ray. He gave the name 'positron' to it. This was the first discovery of antimatter.

Dirac's theory allows the production of any particle and its anti-particle counterpart provided enough energy is supplied in consideration of the mass of the particle (the energy input being $2mc^2$ and c being constant, the amount of energy would decide the mass of the particle to be generated). Whenever a particle and its anti-particle counterpart meet, they fall into the 'hole' and disappear, with liberation of energy ($2mc^2$).

Schrödinger's Cat

The cat paradox of Schrödinger has been widely discussed in quantum physics. He was as upset as Einstein about the implications of quantum theory. He wanted to show the absurdity of these implications. He imagined an experiment to establish the flaw in the strict Copenhagen interpretation. His cat-in-the-box paradox first appeared in print[20] in 1935.

In the imaginary experiment of Schrödinger, a closed box contains a live cat, a phial of poison and a lump of radioactive material. There is a precise 50:50 chance that one of the atoms of the radioactive material will decay in a certain time. If the decay does happen, it will be registered by a detector, say a Geiger counter. Occurrence of the radioactive decay will break the poison-container and the cat will die.

A person, unacquainted with quantum physics, can say, without looking into the box, that the cat inside is either dead or alive. There is a fifty-fifty chance for the decay to occur and consequently the cat is either dead or alive.

A quantum physicist who accepts the Copenhagen interpretation has to reject this 'either-or' business. For him, nothing is real unless it is observed. He has not opened the box; he has not observed inside; and hence neither of the two possibilities open to the radioactive material, and therefore to the cat, has any reality. Without his actual observation, the atomic decay has neither happened nor not happened and the cat has neither been killed nor not killed. The radioactive material may be in a superposition of states, and so is the cat. Once the quantum physicist looks into the box, the atom is forced into one state or the other, either decayed or not decayed; and the cat is forced to be dead or alive. The cat in the box exists in some indeterminate state, neither dead nor alive, until an observer observes how things are getting on. Schrödinger could not accept this conclusion of the strict version of Copenhagen interpretation.

The EPR Paradox

The EPR paradox refers to a thought experiment[21] that was published in 1935. Amid turmoil in his life during the early 1930s, Einstein continued to feel puzzled over the interpretation of quantum theory. Due to the threat of persecution by the Nazi regime he left Germany. By 1935 he was settled in Princeton, U.S.A. His second wife, Elsa, suffered from a protracted illness and died in 1936. In spite of these setbacks in life, he was mentally occupied with the 'incomplete' Copenhagen interpretation. He worked in Princeton with Boris Podolsky and Nathan Rosen on the thought experiment which was published in 1935.

In order to test the quantum rules, Einstein thought of an imaginary experiment. Heisenberg's uncertainty principle says that we cannot precisely determine both the position and momentum of a particle simultaneously. Einstein used experimental information about one particle to deduce the position and momentum of a second particle. By this approach he tried to show that Heisenberg's principle of indeterminacy was violated.

Einstein and his collaborators imagined two particles, p^+ and p^-. These particles interacted with each other and then flew apart. In their sojourn in opposite directions, they did not interact with anything else until the experimenter investigated one of them. When the particles were close together, their total momentum and the distance between them were determined. The precise determination of the total momentum of the two particles, added together, could be done without violating the quantum rules. This total momentum of the particle-pair remained constant even if they were far apart. When they were away from each other, the momentum of one of them (say, p^+) was accurately determined. Simply by deduction, the momentum of the other particle (p^-) was derived. After finishing the measurement of momentum, the accurate position of particle p^+ was determined. This measurement of position of p^+ disturbed its momentum, but *presumably* did not disturb the momentum of particle p^- which was far away from p^+. The position of particle p^+ was used to derive the position of particle p^-, with the availability of the momentum of p^- and the original separation of the particles. Thus both the position and momentum of the distant particle p^- could be accurately deduced.

Two alternative interpretations of the EPR thought experiment were made. Since both the position and momentum of the distant particle p^- could be deduced precisely, Heisenberg's uncertainty principle was violated. Alternatively, in violation of causality, action at a distance could take place, an instantaneous communication travelled across space from p^+ to p^- and the latter was affected in prompt response to the former's disturbance. When the momentum of particle p^+ was disturbed consequent to the precise determination of its position, the momentum of particle p^- was instantaneously disturbed. Einstein and his colleagues rejected the notion of action at a distance. They could not accept the idea that disturbance in the properties of particle p^+ affected instantaneously the properties of particle p^- which is present at billions of light years away. They said: "No reasonable definition of reality could be expected to permit this."[22]

Unbroken Whole

The EPR thought experiment puzzled the quantum physicists for many decades. Particle p^+ and p^- appear from one source and then are separated. They go in opposite directions to a distance of billions of light years. In spite of this separation they are constantly in communication with each other and respond to each other's actions and reactions. How does it happen? What is the mechanism through which this happens?

Physicists tried to obtain direct, experimental proof of the outcomes of the EPR thought experiment. They did not measure the position and momentum of particles in the modern experiments. They used spin and polarization as parameters in their real experiments. The idea of spin measurements in the newer designing of EPR experiments was suggested in 1952 by David Bohm of Birkbeck College in London. John Bell, an Irish physicist at the European Organization for Nuclear Research (CERN) in Switzerland, utilized this concept and published a paper[23] in 1964. The technicality of Bell's paper is not presented here for the purpose of simplification. The main idea has been discussed here for focusing the cardinal points.

Bell wanted to test the fundamental premise of the 'local realistic' view of the world. According to this view, real things exist regardless of the existence of any observer; information cannot be propagated faster than the speed of light; and general conclusions can be drawn from consistent observations or experimental findings. The two assumptions—objectivity and local causality—are key ones in the local realistic view of the world.

Bell calculated the spin of proton. The three components of the spin are called X, Y and Z. The experimenter can never know the three components of spin for the same particle. When X spin of a proton is +1, the X spin of its counterpart is −1. The experimenter can measure the X spin of a proton and the Y (or Z, but not both) of its counterpart. By working in this way, one can get information about both the X and Y spins of each of the pair. By following this technique, one can identify pairs of spins for pairs of protons such as XY, XZ and YZ. If the local realistic view of the world is correct, the number of pairs for which both the X and Y components have positive spins must always be less than the combined total of the pairs in which all the XZ and YZ measurements show positive values of spin. Bell derived a mathematical formula, an inequality. He showed this inequality in his classic paper of 1964. If 'Bell's inequality' is violated, the local realistic view of the world is false and the Copenhagen interpretation of quantum theory is right.

Bell's inequality can be checked experimentally. If the inequality is violated, the two assumptions viz., objectivity and local causality, of the local realistic view of the world is rejected.

Bell's inequality applies to any correlated measurement on two correlated systems. It is equally applicable to spin measurements of material particles and measurements of the polarization of photons. The latter, though difficult, is relatively easier than the former. Hence, most of the tests of Bell's inequality have involved measurements of the polarization of photons.

The correlations which Bell used were calculated. His theorem was based on statistical predictions. What he said in 1964 was still a hypothetical construct. In 1972, Bell's inequality was experimentally tested[24] by John Clauser and Stuart Freedman at the Lawrence Berkeley Laboratory of the University of California. They used photons and actually performed experiments to confirm or disprove the predictions of Bell. Their results confirmed Bell's theorem.

In 1976, a team of physicists at the Saclay Nuclear Research

Centre in France reported the results of an experiment in which proton was used. Shooting of low-energy protons was done at a target that contained a lot of hydrogen atoms. Two protons interacted through the singlet state. Their spin components could be measured. The results clearly demonstrated that the local realistic view of the world was false.

In the mid-1970s, experimenters used photons in the form of gamma rays produced as a result of annihilation of an electron and a positron. In such a case, the polarizations of the two photons must be correlated. The results of the measurements of the polarizations in such experiments showed that Bell's inequality was violated.

Experimental test of Bell's inequality using time-varying analyzers was done by Alain Aspect, Jean Dalibard and Gerard Roger at the University of Paris-South. They published[25] their results on 20th December, 1982. In the experimental design Alain Aspect's team closed the last loophole for the local realistic theory. They used photons from a cascade process. They changed the structure of the experiment while the photons were in flight. They found that Bell's inequality was violated. The results were in good agreement with quantum mechanical predictions.

Bell's theorem and the tests conducted to verify the EPR thought experiment conclusively prove that the Copenhagen interpretation of Niels Bohr was correct and Einstein's criticism of it was wrong.

Thus the controversy that started in 1935 over the EPR thought experiment was over in 1982 after the publication of the results of Alain Aspect's team. It was settled that Bohr was right and Einstein was wrong with regard to the Copenhagen interpretation of quantum physics. However, the riddle remained unsolved. How does action-at-a-distance take place? How is the information transmitted from particle p^+ to particle p^-? The spin may be taken as an example. If the spin of p^+ is $+1$, that of p^- must be -1, and the total of the spins of the particle-pair must be zero. If, by some device, the spin of p^+ is changed, simultaneously the spin of p^- is correspondingly changed so that the total is zero. The pair of particles may be separated to a distance of billions of light-years. Still p^+ and p^- act in unison. How does information reach from one particle to another? According to Einstein's relativity theory nothing can travel faster than light. Superluminal (faster-than-light) communication is impossible because communication requires a signal to go from one place to another and no signal can travel faster than light. Then how can one explain the propagation of message from one particle to its counterpart at speed faster than that of light?

Jack Sarfatti, a noted physicist, put forward his postulate of superluminal transfer of negentropy without signals.[26] According to this postulate, each quantum jump is a space-like superluminal transfer of negentropy. This process does not involve any transport of energy. Nothing travels from particle p^+ to particle p^-. Nonetheless, there is an instantaneous change in the quality of the energy in both the particles located at area A and B. Sarfatti's postulate has not yet been elevated to a theory since it has not yet been supported by any sound theoretical foundation or experimental evidence.

Theorists such as Bernard d'Espagnat and David Bohm do not recognize the separation of area A and B and the propagation of any signal between these two areas. They say that non-separability is one of the most certain general concepts in modern physics. They are strongly in favour of the view that everything is connected to everything else and only a holistic approach to the universe can explain the synchronistic behaviours of the particle-pair separated superficially but connected at the deeper level.[27]

The universe is an unbroken whole. Nothing is separated from this whole. Everything is connected with one another to form this whole. Separation is only apparent. At the surface, the stars, planets and galaxies are separate. At the surface, the molecules, atoms, protons, electrons, neutrons, neutrinos and photons are separate. Superficially, galaxies, stars and planets are widely separated and micro-particles are quantized. But, at the deeper level, *all* is a homogeneous, single entity which is partless and undifferentiated. The deeper one is *the* Reality, the unbroken whole, the nondual one without a second.

Double-Slit Experiments and Conscious Particles

The classical double-slit experiment was performed by Thomas Young in 1801 to prove the wave nature of light. When both the slits were open, alternate bright and dark bands were observed on the white screen. In the twentieth century physicists have performed double-slit experiments to test some notions of quantum mechanics. In the opinion of Richard Feynman (1918-1988), the basic element of quantum theory is presented by the double-slit experiment. It is impossible for classical physics to explain the phenomenon of this experiment.

The experimental design is simple. There is a source of photon or electron. In the former case, it may be light of a lamp, and in the latter case it may be an electron-gun. Photon or electron passes through a small longitudinal slit or a round hole. A screen with two slits or holes is located on the way. The photon or the electron has the choice of passing through any one slit or hole. After passing through either of the two holes (or both the holes), it falls on a detector screen which may be a white surface or may have a photographic plate for detection of light or which may have an electron-detector for the detection of electrons. The experiment is illustrated in Fig. 4.2. When one hole is blocked and another is open, we observe the biggest waves nearest the open hole, across the shortest distance, the amplitude of the waves being less on either side. The pattern is the same with either of the two holes open. The intensity of the wave which is a measure of the amount of energy carried by the wave is proportional to the square of the height or amplitude (H^2). The pattern of the H^2 is similar for either of the hole. But when both holes are open, the pattern is different and complex. When both the holes are open, a single wave can diffract through the two holes. On the other side of the screen, one wave from one hole interferes with another wave from the other hole. The crest of one wave being positive and the trough of the other wave being negative, the two waves interfere with each other. This interference pattern is reflected on amplitude pattern observed on the detector screen.

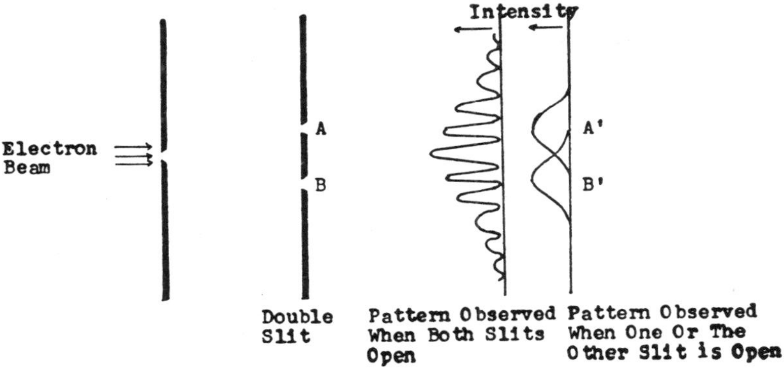

Fig. 4.2 Pattern observed in double-slit experiment with electron or photon when one or two slits are open.

The diffraction of waves through the two open holes and the interference of waves have so far been described. But the photon or the electron is both particle and wave. How can we say that the particle passes through both the open holes at a time? When we slow down our electron gun so as to allow one electron to go at a time through the whole setup, we still get the pattern for interference by waves. One particle goes through only one hole and arrives at the detector screen. Then a second particle goes; after that a third one and so on. After enough electrons pass through, the pattern that is built up through the detector screen is the diffraction pattern for wave. The pattern obtained by the passage of a thousand electrons one after another and that obtained by the passage of a thousand electrons simultaneously are similar. How does a single photon or a single electron, on its way through one hole in the wall, obey the statistical laws? It can obey the law if it 'knows' whether or not the other hole is open. How does it know that? This mystery of quantum physics is still unsolved.

In the two-hole experiment, physicists have tried to cheat the particle. They have shut or opened one of the holes quickly after the particle has left the source and while it is in transit through the apparatus. Surprisingly, the particle has not been cheated. The pattern on the detector screen has been the one expected for the state of the holes at the instant of the particle's transit.

The particle 'sees' the experimenter, who observes the hole through which the particle passes, and 'behaves' accordingly. The experimenter always sees a particle passing through one hole or the other, never both at once. If an arrangement is made to record the specific hole through which the particle passes, the pattern that builds up on the detector screen does not show any trace of interference. This means that the particle has passed through one hole or the other but not through both the holes. The particles are conscious of two things. They know whether or not both holes are open. They also know whether or not any observer is watching them. They not only know, but also adjust their behaviour accordingly. This provides the clearest example of the interaction of the observer with the experiment.

Schrödinger's wave mechanics and Born's probabilistic interpretation of the wave mechanics may explain this strange phenomenon of the wave-particle duality. When the experimenter looks at the spread-out wave, it collapses into a definite particle. When he does not watch, the wave-particle entity keeps its options open. To interpret this phenomenon by Born's probabilities, the wave-particle entity is being forced by our measurement to choose one course of action out of an array of possibilities.

Schrödinger's function ψ is the variable in his wave equation. When a wave diffracts through the two open holes in the screen, an interference pattern is produced. Here ψ acts like the amplitude of the wave and ψ^2 acts like the intensity. The diffraction pattern of the two-hole experiment is a pattern of ψ^2. Thousands of electrons are present in the electron beam. They rush through the two holes and reach the detector screen. Can we locate a particular electron at a particular spot A or B on the detector screen? We cannot do that. We can assess only the probability of finding an electron in some particular place, and ψ^2 represents that probability. The location of the electron can be predicted on a statistical basis by using Born's interpretation of the ψ wave.

From the two-hole experiment, we get an important deduction. The object observed, the subject or the observer and the apparatus are all inalienable parts of the whole experiment. When the electron leaves the electron-gun, passes through the apparatus and reaches the detector screen, it knows whether one or two holes are open and whether or not the observer is looking at it. The experimenter cannot say whether the electron has passed through hole A or B without looking at the holes at the instant of the actual passing. The observer, the observed and the apparatus through which observation is made constitute a holistic whole, in which the parts are in some way in touch with the whole.

According to one interpretation, the electron vanishes after it leaves the gun and is out of sight. On its vanishing, it is replaced by an array of ghost electrons. Each ghost electron follows a different path to the detector screen. The ghosts interfere with one another. This interference of ghosts is detected on the detector screen even if only one electron is ejected by the electron gun. The array of ghost electrons exist and function when we are not looking at them. When we look, all of the ghosts except one vanish. One ghost that does not vanish materializes as a real electron for us. All that has been described here with reference to the double-slit experiment is interpreted in terms of Schrödinger's waves and Born's probabilities of the waves. Each 'ghost' corresponds to a wave, or rather a packet of waves. Born interpreted these waves as a measure of probability. All the probable waves exist and function when they are not observed. The act of observation makes all but one packet of waves disappear. This is called 'collapse of the wave function'. On observation, only one packet of waves crystallizes into reality.

In the double-slit experiment, there are many paths that an electron or photon can choose through each of the two holes. For the purpose of simplification, we may recognize only two paths, A and B. Each path may represent a different world. The world we experience is a hybrid world of A and B. Our experienced world is not a world, purely A or purely B; it is a hybridized picture which is real for us.

One important implication of the two-hole experiment is that the particles are not insentient and that they are contained on some substratum that is consciousness itself. In this connection, Eugene Paul Wigner, a Nobel-Laureate in physics, has said:

> It was not possible to formulate the laws of quantum mechanics in a fully consistent way without reference to the consciousness (of the observer)........(Remarkably,) the very study of the external world led to the conclusion that the content of the consciousness is the ultimate reality.[28]

Many-Worlds Interpretation of Quantum Mechanics

The Copenhagen interpretation requires the wave functions to collapse on observation. According to it, the act of observation crystallizes reality out of the web of quantum possibilities. Without observation, the probable worlds are infinite in number; when observation is made, only one world crystallizes to be real and all the rest vanish. In contrast to this notion of 'collapse of wave function', the many-worlds interpretation of quantum mechanics does not accept collapse of the wave functions which are considered to be real.

Hugh Everett was a graduate student in the 1950s in Princeton University—working for his Ph.D. degree. His many-worlds interpretation of quantum mechanics was first published[29] in 1957. John Wheeler published[30] a paper in the same volume of the journal and in his paper he drew attention to the importance of Everett's work.

Everett's multi-world theory claims that the wave functions are real things and that all of them happen. All possibilities that the wave functions represent actualize in different worlds that coexist with ours. The development of the Schrödinger wave equation generates an endlessly proliferating number of different branches of reality.

Everett's paper was ignored by the scientific community until Bryce DeWitt took up the idea in the late 1960s. He himself wrote about the concept and encouraged his student Neill Graham to develop the idea of Everett further. Graham extended Everett's work for his own Ph.D. thesis. In a paper published by DeWitt in 1970, he explained that the Everett interpretation had an immediate appeal to the paradox of Schrödinger's cat. The many-worlds interpretation of quantum mechanics was further established by the publications of DeWitt and DeWitt and Graham[31] in the early 1970s.

The parallel universe theory proposed by Everett was championed by DeWitt in his publication of 1971. All the possible alternative quantum worlds are equally real. They exist in parallel with one another as illustrated in Figure 4.3. In this connection, DeWitt writes:

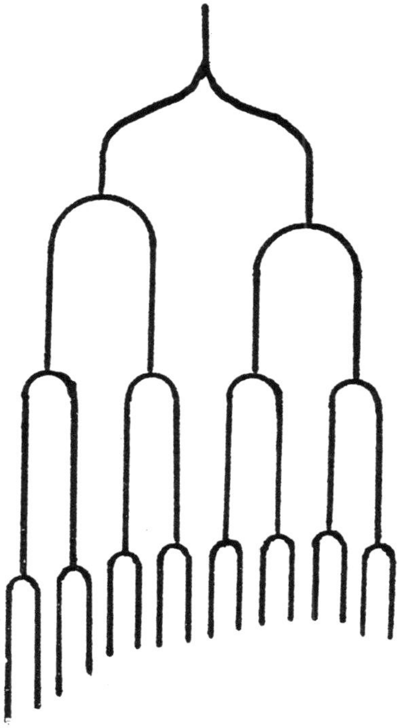

Fig 4.3: Parallel worlds in super-space-time.

> Every quantum transition taking place on every star, in every galaxy, in every remote corner of the universe is splitting our local world on earth into myriads of copies of itself.........Here is schizophrenia with a vengeance.[32]

Thus a multifoliate reality is generated. The universe continually branches into myriads of parallel universes. These universes are physically disconnected. But all of them are real.

Another version of the parallel universe theory is the constantly branching universe. The universe constantly splits like a branching tree. The splitting process is endless. Such a model is illustrated in Figure 4.4.

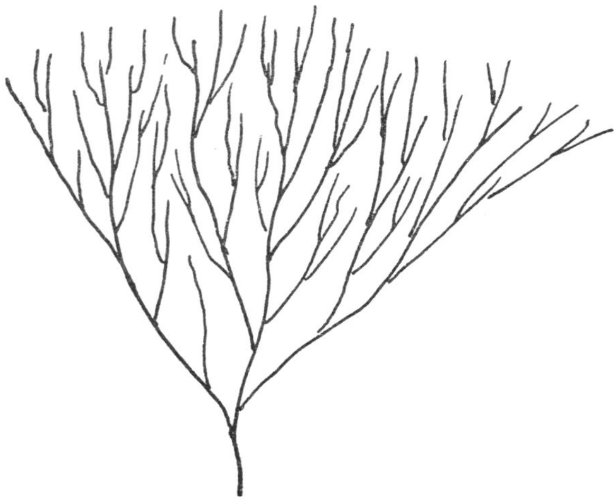

Fig. 4.4: Constantly splitting universe in super-space-time.

Everett presents the idea of super-space and super-time. The overlapping wave functions do not collapse, since none of them are ghosts and all of them are real. All the wave functions (all the worlds) exist in their own parts of superspace-supertime. When an experimenter makes a measurement at the quantum level, he is forced by the process of observation to select one of the innumerable alternatives. This selected one becomes the real world for the experimenter. The act of observation severs the bond that keeps all the alternative worlds together and projects one 'real' world for a particular observer. At the same time, the other alternative worlds go to their own separate ways through superspace-super-time. Each of the alternative worlds has got the potentiality of being a 'real' world for some other observer. Thus, according to the many-worlds interpretation of Everett, each individual observer's world is a unique one of his own and may or may not be identical with the world of any other observer.

Einstein, in his general theory of relativity, has presented a picture of the finite and closed universe. Everett's idea of endlessly branching and ever proliferating worlds contradicts Einstein's theory. Many physicists do not agree with Everett and think that the multi-world interpretation is highly speculative. John Wheeler who was a strong supporter of Everett's many-worlds interpretation has expressed doubts. In response to a questioner at a symposium held in Princeton in 1979 to mark the centenary of Einstein's birth, he expressed his revised views on the many-worlds theory as follows:

> I confess that I have reluctantly had to give up my support of that point of view in the end—much I have advocated it in the beginning—because I am afraid it carries too great a load of metaphysical baggage.[33]

Participatory Universe

The two-hole experiment has demonstrated that the 'real' world actualizes only when it is observed by an observer. Without observation, multiple 'ghost' worlds exist. The ghosts are probable wave functions. It is a fundamental axiom of quantum theory that no elementary phenomenon is a phenomenon until it is a recorded one. John Wheeler (1911-) pondered over this question: "Who has observed the big bang? Who has observed the early universe? How has the past of the universe actualized?"

Wheeler devised a delayed-choice experiment. It is a variation of the double-slit experiment. But it is another thought experiment. The experimental setup has been illustrated in Figure 4.5.

Light from a source passes through a small hole in a screen. It falls on a lens which combines two slits. The screen, with two slits, of the standard double-slit experiment is replaced by the lens here. This lens focuses light on a second lens that diverges the rays. The photon is deflected by the second lens off to a detector shown at the bottom of the diagram. By locating the photon

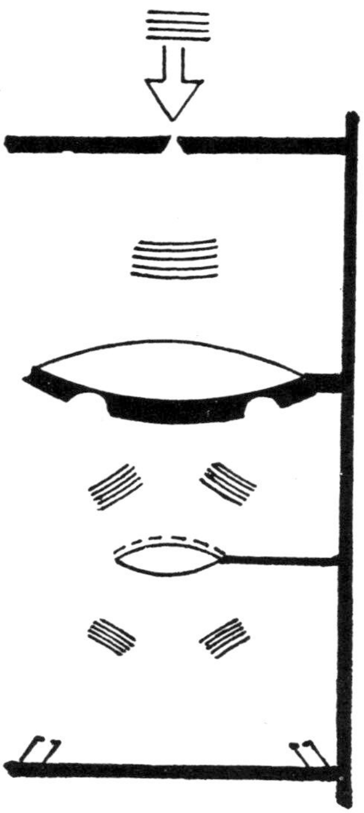

Fig. 4.5: Wheeler's delayed-choice double-slit experiment.

on the left or the right of the detector, one can know which slit each photon went through. If one photon is allowed at a time to pass through the apparatus, the path it follows can be unambiguously identified. In such a situation, there is no interference because there is no superposition of states.

The apparatus may be modified by covering the second lens with a photographic film arranged in strips like a venetian blind. When the strips are closed, photons cannot pass through the second lens. The closed strips on the second lens serve as the detector screen of the classic double-slit experiment. With the strips closed, we cannot know the specific hole through which a photon passes and we have interference pattern caused by the passage of each individual photon through both the holes at once.

We may open the strips after the photon has already passed the two holes. Now we create an experiment to know whether the photon has gone through one hole alone or through both the holes at once. This is Wheeler's modification of Young's two-slit experiment. This delayed choice experiment reveals that an observer today can be partially responsible for generating the reality of the remote past. Something a participator does now has an irretrievable influence on the past. The past history of a photon is decided now, basing upon how the participator chooses to make a measurement. John Wheeler's delayed-choice experiment has been described in his article 'Beyond the Black Hole' presented at the centennial symposium to celebrate the birth centenary of Einstein.[34]

Wheeler prefers the term 'participator' to 'observer'. He introduces a strong holistic element into our world view. In this holistic approach, the distinction between subject and object is demolished. An observer-subject does not observe an observed-object. Both the subject and the object are component parts of a holistic unit and both are participators. The universe is brought into being by the act of participation. Mind is responsible for the retroactive creation of reality.

Quantum physicist like John Wheeler becomes a sceptic. The photon does not exist until it is registered. Or, it may be better to state that we cannot say anything about the existence and functioning of the photon until it is registered. Some mind is necessary to create reality. But who observes the observer? Does the observer exist without anybody observing him? Is solipsism to be accepted in order to avoid nihilism? The particle does not exist without an observer. Does the galaxy made of particles exist without an observer? Does the Earth made of particles exist without an observer? Does man made of particles exist without an observer? Does the existence of an individual man depend upon the method of measurement done by an observer? Every macroscopic object in the universe is made of particles that obey the quantum rules. Every perceivable object called 'real' is made of particles regarded by the quantum physicist as 'unreal'. Then how can the observable object be called real? John Wheeler says: "What choice do we have but to say that in some way, yet to be discovered, they all must be built upon the statistics of billions upon billions of such acts of observer-participation?" In Wheeler's view, the whole universe is a participatory, self-excited circuit.

Quantum Field

The term 'quantum field' seems to be self-contradictory. 'Field' is continuous and 'quantum' is discrete or discontinuous. Field refers to the pervasive nature of some unmanifested entity. A field is not directly sense-perceptible. Quanta are particulate and are manifested micro-entities. They are not pervasive. In spite of these opposite characters of quanta and field, 'quantum field' is a meaningful concept in quantum physics. The evolution of the field concept will be described in chapter V. Particles appear in a field wherever the latter becomes intense. Particles originate from field. They also dissolve into field. The field concept of Faraday and Maxwell was later refined in the twentieth century by the quantum physicists. Paul Dirac's discovery of 'hole' in space in 1927 changed the idea of physicists about the 'empty' space. No longer space could be considered as void.

The Japanese physicist Hideki Yukawa (1907-1981) suggested in 1935 that space is occupied with 'subtle energy' that is the source of virtual particles. This 'subtle energy' of Yukawa is the field. Yukawa's theory is an extension of Heisenberg's uncertainty principle. This principle states that position and momentum cannot be simultaneously determined with complete accuracy. The uncertainty in the determination of position ($\triangle q$) multiplied by the uncertainty in the determination of momentum ($\triangle p$) is approximately equal to Planck's constant. Time and energy can be substituted in place of position and momentum. Thus the precise energy content of a system cannot be determined at an exact moment of time. There is always a small time interval during which the energy content is uncertain. The uncertainty in energy content ($\triangle E$) multiplied by the uncertainty in time ($\triangle t$) is approximately equal to Planck's constant. During the short interval of time in which energy content is uncertain, the law of conservation of energy fails in the realm of particle and field physics. The particle which is emitted and reabsorbed during this short and indiscernible interval of time is a virtual particle.

Richard Feynman has contributed significantly to quantum electrodynamics that explains the electromagnetic interaction in quantum terms. This branch of quantum physics flowered in the 1940s. It obeyed both the principles of quantum theory and relativity theory. The interactions of virtual photons with electrons were worked out by both theoretical and experimental physicists.

The agreement was remarkable. For the theory of the existence of virtual particles, the work done in the 1940s by Julian Schwinger, Richard Feynman (both were American physicists) and Sin-itiro Tomonaga (Japanese physicist) was recognized. For their contributions to quantum electrodynamics, these three physicists were jointly awarded the Nobel Prize for physics in 1965.

The theoretical physicists were very much encouraged by the triumph of the quantum field theory applied to electron and virtual photons. They tried to find a similar theory for the strongly interacting quanta, the hadrons. During the 1950s and 60s they did not know that the hadrons were made of quarks. For a number of reasons they could not get success when they applied the field theory to the hadrons.

Many theoretical physicists thought of abandoning field theory and replacing it with S-matrix (S for 'scattering') theory. They were not much interested in the unending race for search of newer and newer particles. Secondly, they gave much emphasis on the dance, but not on the dancer. The events were important for them. The unobserved entity that might have produced that event was a speculative one and they abhorred speculation. They were in favour of experimental verification. The fundamental fields were beyond the reach of experiment. By contrast, the S-matrix theory was applied to experimentally observable quantities only.

The philosophy of Ernst Mach (1836-1916) exerted profound influence on the proponents of S-matrix theory. Mach was an Austrian physicist and philosopher. He exerted influence on the Vienna Circle of Logical Positivists. He exercised an influence over Einstein through his operational approach to the world. He was in favour of getting rid of unobservables. Any concept without reference to sense-experience was rejected by him. He went so far as to say that the world consists only of our sensations. Although young Einstein was inspired by Mach, he could not accept Machism during his later career.

In the programme of Mach, physics should be got rid of all theoretical concepts which are not concerned with observable entities. The field theory was not Machian and hence was not favoured by the physicists who were pleading for the S-Matrix theory.

In the mid-1970s, field theory could be extended to the hadrons. The fundamental fields of the strong interactions corresponded not to the hadronic quanta but rather to the quarks and gluons that bound them together. After the discovery of the quarks and gluons, physicists could build up a successful field theory of the strong interaction. This was known as quantum chromodynamics.

The concept of symmetry has to be comprehended for an understanding of the development of theoretical physics in quantum chromodynamics. Chen Ning Yang, a Chinese-American physicist and Robert Mills, an American, initiated work back in 1954 to develop the gauge field theory. After the early 1970s, the gauge field theory could bring about a conceptual revolution in physics. Today physicists believe that all the four fundamental interactions, viz. gravitational, weak, electromagnetic and strong, are based on gauge fields. The gluons of these interactions are the quanta associated with the gauge fields.

Virtual particles associated with weak interactions were theorized. These were bosons W^+ and W^-, that carried charge and neutral Z boson that did not carry any charge. Sheldon Glashow of Harvard University, in 1960, worked out the correct mathematical symmetries involving the weak interaction and the particles, W^+, W^- and Z. He published his findings in 1961.

Physicists discovered around the mid-1960s that the Yang-Mills symmetry could be broken spontaneously. Steven Weinberg and Abdus Salam used this idea of a spontaneously broken symmetry to construct their 1967 gauge field theory of the unified electromagnetic and weak interactions. In 1979, Glashow, Weinberg and Salam shared the Nobel Prize for their work.

The four fundamental fields for the four types of fundamental interactions were unified within a few nanoseconds after the big bang explosion. The gauge symmetry was unbroken in that fireball stage. At that time there was one field only.

Nihilism and Vacuum Fluctuation

Some quantum physicists are in favour of Vedānta. They do recognize a substratum which is one alone without a second, which is consciousness and which is the support of all the phenomena that are transitory and unreal. In contrast, there are many quantum physicists who do not accept anything as real. John Lennon (1940-80) has said, "Nothing is real"[35]. In the prologue of John Gribbin's book "*In Search of Schrödinger's Cat*", he has given the title "Nothing is Real".[36] In the epilogue of the same book he has discussed the topic, "Is the Universe a Vacuum Fluctuation?"[37] He writes:

> ....the universe and everything in it may be no more, and no less, than one of those vacuum fluctuations that allow collections of particles to burst forth out of nothing, live for a while, and then be reabsorbed into the vacuum. The idea ties in very closely with the possibility that the universe may be gravitationally closed. A universe that is born in the fireball of a Big Bang, expands for a time and then contracts back into a fireball and disappears, *is* a vacuum fluctuation, but on a very grand scale.[38]

In 1971, John Gribbin gave the idea of the possibility of the universe being born in fire, expanding, and then recollapsing into nothing.[39] In 1973, Edward Tryon, of the City University of New York, published his idea of the Big Bang as a vacuum fluctuation.[40]

Alan H. Guth, a famous cosmologist of the Massachusetts Institute of Technology, has suggested that the universe appeared from a 'false vacuum'. His initial version of the inflationary universe did not explain the origin of the initial tiny bubble. Perhaps this concept had similarity with the vacuum fluctuation of Tryon. In the cosmological model of Guth the bubble of space-time appeared from false vacuum. There was perfect symmetry at this time in the very hot, very dense phase of the bubble universe. As the universe began to cool, the symmetry was broken and the fundamental interactions went their separate ways. The broken symmetry was the driving force that burst the bubble of space-time. With this, the universe entered into its expanding phase. Thus, the breaking of symmetry in the early universe generated an overwhelmingly large repulsive gravitational force, that resulted in the big bang explosion.

It is generally accepted that the void (*śūnya*[41]) of the Buddhists and the vacuum of the quantum physicists are identical. Everything of the phenomenal universe is impermanent (*anitya*[42]) and not-self (*anātman*[43]). *Ātman* (Self) is the concept in Vedānta that is permanent, everlasting and absolute entity, which is unchanging behind the changing phenomenal world. Some schools of Buddhism do not recognize any such reality that is unchanging, permanent and absolute. Everything of the phenomenal world is impermanent and momentary (*kṣaṇika*[44]) in these schools of Buddhist philosophy and there is nothing like noumena behind the phenomena. The analytical method (*vibhajja-vāda*[45]) of Buddhist philosophy maintains that there does not exist a unity like 'substance' and that 'one' is always expressed in 'many'. There does not exist a chariot apart from its wheels, axles and other parts; there does not exist an action apart from the multiple movements to bring about that action; there does not exist a unitary consciousness that is not composite of multiple psychic factors; and there does not exist an 'individual' that is not composed of aggregates (*skandha*).

Conditioned co-production (*pratītyasamutpāda*[46]) is the concept of the dynamic state of flux in Buddhism. Everything in the phenomenal world has a dependent origination. The *Hīnayānists* show that all constituted things have a preceding cause and condition and hence they are without any substantiality. The *Mahāyānists* use this to formulate a concept of the world which, being relatively existent, is unreal like things perceived in a dream.

'*Nirvāṇa*' literally means 'to be extinguished'. According to some interpreters, something, by attaining *nirvāṇa,* becomes nothing. This is the nihilistic view. According to this view, *nirvāṇa* is absolute void; it is not an entity; it is pure nothingness.

In the *Abhidharma Piṭaka,*[47] *nirvāṇa* has been described as a state of complete and final liberation from *vāna* or desire. It has got three modes, viz., void, distinctionless and desireless. It is unconditioned; it is not subject to conditioned co-production. It is inexpressible; it is unconstituted; it has no origin, no decay and no change. Individuality ceases in *nirvāṇa*. Still it is not absence of everything (*abhāva*). It is to be realized only within one's own self.

According to some schools of Buddhism,[48] *nirvāṇa* is existence, eternal, blissful and pure. For some other schools like the Mādhyamikas and the Yogācāras, *nirvāṇa* is beyond all predications and hence cannot be stated as eternal or non-eternal, blissful or not blissful and pure or impure. The Mādhyamikas hold that *nirvāṇa* is the impersonal absolute immanent in nature and is the only reality, all others being thought-constructions and illusory. For them, *nirvāṇa* is non-dual, without any subject and object, is neither of the nature of being nor non-being.

Nirvāṇa is that which is neither existence nor non-existence. It is both *śūnyatā* (void) and *Tathatā* (suchness of THAT). As void, all phenomenal things have only a semblance of existence; they are like mirage without any substantiality whatsoever. As *Tathatā*, it is the Reality, the unconditioned absolute. If Reality is considered to have a positive and a negative aspect, *Tathatā* represents the positive one and *śūnyatā* the negative one.

Buddha's *nirvāṇa* is not eternal death. It is not nihil, not absolute void. It is not of the nature of being either. It is void in a special sense in consideration of being imperceptible to our senses and indescribable in language. The void (*śūnya*) is full (*pūrṇa*). It is the Reality.

There are some quantum physicists who, being nihilists, do not recognize anything as reality. They would prefer the nihilistic interpretation of Buddhist philosophy and find similarity between Buddhism and quantum physics. The other quantum physicists who recognize Reality as the substratum of the phenomenal universe would consider *nirvāṇa* as a positive entity which is the substratum of the phenomenal universe.

The world of particles and waves, matter particles and energy particles, matter waves and energy waves is illusory and unreal for the non-dualist philosopher of Vedānta. The world of quanta has got relative existence; it exists, does not exist and exists and does not exist. Every micro-entity of the phenomenal world appears, stays for a moment and disappears. But, below the surface of the phenomena, there is a substratum, the noumena. It is Pure Consciousness, unconditioned and absolute. It is eternal, timeless, unbroken whole, beginningless, endless, actionless, attributeless and changeless. It is the Reality, the non-dual one. It is unobservable and hence beyond the scope of physics, especially the experimental physics. It is, however, realizable, not through any mediation, but directly.

NOTES

1. Ken, II.3.
2. Einstein, A., Quoted by Gribbin, J. in "*In Search of Schrődinger's Cat*", Wildwood House, London, 1984, p. 82.
3. Einstein, A., Quoted by Frank, P. in "*Einstein: His Life and Times*", Alfred A. Knopf, New York, 1947, p. 342.
4. Einstein, A., *The Born-Einstein Letters*, McMillan, London, 1971, p. 91.
5. Einstein, A., "On Physical Reality", Franklin Institute Journal, 1936, vol. 221, p. 349.

6. Einstein, A., Podolsky, B. and Rosen, N., "Can Quantum Mechanical Description of Physical Reality Be Considered Complete?", Physical Review, 1935, vol. 47, pp. 777-80.
7. Heisenberg, W., *Physics and Philosophy*, Allen & Unwin, London, 1959, p. 96.
8. *Ibid.*, p. 128.
9. Russell, B., Quoted by Heisenberg, W., *Across the Frontiers*, Harper & Row, New York, 1974, p. 75.
10. Heisenberg, W., *Physics and Beyond*, Allen & Unwin, London, 1971, p. 76.
11. Einstein, A. and Infeld, L., *The Evolution of Physics*, Cambridge University Press, Cambridge, 1971, p. 31.
12. Heisenberg, W., *Physics and Philosophy*, Harper & Row, New York, 1958, p. 42.
13. Bohr, N., *Atomic Theory and the Description of Nature*, Cambridge University Press, Cambridge, 1934, p. 53.
14. Born, M., *Atomic Physics*, Blackie & Son, Glasgow, 1969, p. 95.
15. *Ibid.*, p. 96.
16. *Ibid.*, p. 102.
17. Heisenberg, W., *Physics and Philosophy*, Harper & Row, New York, 1958, p. 58.
18. Born, M., *Atomic Physics*, Blackie & Son, Glasgow, 1969, p. 97.
19. Bohr, N., *Atomic Theory and Human Knowledge*, John Wiley, New York, 1958, p. 60.
20. Naturwissenschaften, 1935, vol. 23, p. 812.
21. As [6].
22. Pais, A., *Subtle is the Lord*, Oxford University Press, London, 1982, p. 456.
23. Bell, J.S., Physics, 1964, vol. 1, p. 195.
24. Freedman, S. and Clauser, J., "Experimental Test of Local Hidden Variable Theories", Physical Review Letters, 1972, vol. 28, p. 938.
25. Aspect, A., Dalibard, J. and Roger, G., "Experimental Test of Bell's Inequalities Using Time-Varying Analyzers", Physical Review Letters, 1982, vol. 49 (no. 25), pp. 1804-7.
26. Sarfatti, J., "The Case for Superluminal Information Transfer", MIT Technology Review, 1977, vol. 79 (no. 5), p. 3.
27. Gribbin, J., "*In Search of Schrödinger's Cat*", Wildwood House, London, 1984, pp. 228-30.
28. Wigner, E.P. in Wigner, E.P., ed, *Symmetries and Reflections*, Indiana University Press, Indiana, 1967, p. 172.
29. Everett, H., " 'Relative State' Formulation of Quantum Mechanics", Review of Modern Physics, 1957, vol. 29 (no. 3), pp. 454-62.
30. Wheeler, J., Review of Modern Physics, 1957, vol. 29 (no. 3), p. 463.
31. DeWitt, B.S. and Graham, N., ed, *The Many Worlds Interpretation of Quantum Mechanics*, Princeton University Press, 1973.
32. DeWitt, B.S., "The Many-Universes Interpretation of Quantum Mechanics", *Foundations of Quantum Mechanics*, ed, B. d'Espagnat, Academic Press, 1971.

33. Wheeler, J., "Some Strangeness in the Proportion", ed, Harry Woolf, Addison-Wesley, Reading, Massachusetts, 1980, pp. 385-6.
34. Wheeler, J., "Beyond the Black Hole" in "*Some Strangeness in the Proportion*", Chap. 22, ed, Harry Woolf, Addison-Wesley, Reading, Massachusetts, 1980.
35. Lennon, J., Quoted by Gribbin, J. in "*In Search of Schrödinger's Cat*", Wildwood House, London, 1984, p. v.
36. Gribbin, J., *In Search of Schrödinger's Cat*, Wildwood House, London, 1984, pp. 1-4.
37. *Ibid.*, pp. 270-2.
38. *Ibid.*, p. 271.
39. Gribbin, J., Nature, 1971, vol. 232, p. 440.
40. Tryon, E., Nature, 1973, vol. 246, p. 396.
41. (a) Kashyap, B.J., *Abhidhamma Philosophy*, Bharatiya Vidya Prakashan, Delhi, 1982, Book I, p. 189.
(b) Śūnyatāsaptati of Nāgārjuna.
42. Conze, E., *Buddhist Thought in India*, George Allen & Unwin, London, 1983, pp. 134-44.
43. *Ibid.*, pp. 36-9.
44. *Ibid.*, pp. 134-7.
45. Kashyap's *Abhidhamma Philosophy*, Book II, pp. 19-22.
46. (a) Kashyap's *Abhidhamma Philosophy*, Book I, pp. 211-21.
(b) Conze's *Buddhist Thought in India*, pp. 156-8.
(c) Dutt, N., *Mahāyāna Buddhism*, Firma KLM, Calcutta, 1976, p. 258.
47. Kashyap's *Abhidhamma Philosophy*, Book I, p. 189.
48. (a) Suzuki, B.L., *Mahāyāna Buddhism*, George Allen & Unwin, London, 1981, pp. 39-48.
(b) Dutt's *Mahāyāna Buddhism*, pp. 178-254.

CHAPTER V

COSMIC DANCE

> Still there are moments when one feels free from one's own identification with human limitations and inadequacies. At such moments, one imagines that one stands on some spot of a small planet, gazing in amazement at the cold yet profoundly moving beauty of the eternal, the unfathomable: life and death flow into one, and there is neither evolution nor destiny, only being.
>
> *Albert Einstein*

> Space has devoured ether and time; it seems to be on the point of swallowing up also the field and corpuscles, so that it alone remains as the vehicle of reality.
>
> *Albert Einstein*

> Nothing can be created out of nothing.
>
> *Lucretius*

IN THE WORLD, there are both movable and immovable objects. Animals are capable of locomotion. Plants are generally immobile. Locomotives, spaceships and machines that acquire motion use external source of fuel. When this external energy-source which may cause a nonliving thing to move is not considered, lifeless objects are generally regarded as motionless. The stone, the mountain, the building and myriads of such things appear to be motionless.

It is not incorrect to say that the Himalayas are unmoving and still, that a building is motionless and that a piece of rock is at rest. Motion is a relative term; X moves in relation to Y. In this sense, the majority of things of the world are motionless.

In reality, there is nothing (except Brahman) which is motionless. Without motion, no entity can maintain a form and a position. It is universally true that motion is necessary for the existence of everything with form and position.

Every object in the macro-world is in motion. The Earth is

rotating around its own axis and revolving in an elliptical orbit around the Sun. The Sun also moves, but very slowly. The stars, including the Sun, move in vast elliptical orbits around the core of the Milky Way galaxy. All the galaxies are receding. They are moving away from one another. The whole world is expanding.

The Sanskrit word for the universe is *jagat* (*gam*+*kvip*). Etymologically it means "that which is in motion". That everything in the world, both micro- and macro-, is ever in motion has been given in the Ṛgveda[1], Yajurveda[2] and Īśopaniṣad.[3] The electron may be taken as an example from the micro-world. It spins on its own axis and orbits around the nucleus of the atom. It cannot maintain its individuality unless it is in motion. The nucleus of the atom has got proton(s) with positive charge. The electron carries negative charge. The electron is too small in comparison with the proton. But for the motion, the electron would crash into the nucleus due to electromagnetic attraction. The velocity of the electron is variable depending upon its distance from the nucleus. Its orbit around the nucleus is elliptical instead of being circular. When it is nearer the nucleus, it increases its velocity; when it moves away from the nucleus, it decreases its velocity. This regulation of the speed of the electron is purposeful. Whether it is mechanical or volitional may be a matter for dispute. But the fact remains that it is mathematically precisive. Any deviation from this precision would be disastrous for the existence of the electron. That tiny particle is both a particle and a wave for man. It is not a particle and a wave simultaneously. Its precisive determination of position and momentum at the same time is also not possible for man. In spite of this uncertainty, the electron regulates its velocity very *intelligently* without allowing any chance for any disaster to occur. Such a manoeuvre of the electron becomes an inevitability for the very existence of its individuality.

What happens in the micro-world with reference to the electron also applies in principle to the macro-world with reference to the planets, stars and galaxies. All the planets of the Sun increase their speed when they are nearer the Sun and decrease when they are farther away. This they do for their very existence. The Earth would disastrously crash into the Sun if, due to some reason, the speed at which the Earth orbits the Sun were suddenly to decrease. The regulation of the speed of the planets around the Sun with reference to their respective distances from the Sun is necessary to counteract the attractive force of gravity.

The phenomenon of duality of motion is universal. It is not restricted to the atom or the solar system. One motion of every entity is on its own axis, and the other is around a central nucleus. As the planets orbit the Sun, the Sun also does likewise. It spins on its axis and moves in the general direction of the constellation Sagittarius at approximately 77,248 kilometers per hour, carrying the entire solar system with it.

In the universe there is no matter that does not exert gravitational pull on others. All bodies attract one another. But in spite of this universal gravitational pull, planets, satellites, stars and galaxies are situated in space far apart. How does this happen? This question baffled physicists for millennia. The answer was obtained when the expanding universe was discovered. The kinetic energy of the original big bang explosion is still functional. The universe is expanding, although the present receding speed is much slower than what it was in the beginning. This receding force is still greater than the gravitational force. This prevents the total collapse of the universe. The reverse phenomenon will take place sometime in the future when the gravitational force will be greater than the receding force.

What has been described so far in this chapter is regarding the motion of particles or larger bodies. This chapter, however, purports to describe the cosmic dance which is not exactly motion, although it involves motion. The micro-world is not stationary for any single moment. Everything is constantly dancing. The resting condition of a piece of stone is only apparent. All the micro-particles in the so-called immobile stone are appearing, dancing and disappearing. The dance is vigorous. Particles appear to dance; they change their forms while dancing; they procreate newer particles; in this act of procreation, very often they are replaced by newer particles; and the particles die a cruel death; they disappear. The stone stays for hundreds and thousands of years. But the particles of which the stone is made live momentarily, for a billionth or a trillionth of a second. This phenomenon of cosmic dance is not restricted to the non-living world only; it operates in the living world also, in man, cow, tiger, snake, amoeba, bacteria and virus. When we talk about the subatomic world, we deal with not only micro-particles of matter, but also energy and field. The micro-world is constantly beaming with activity. The micro-cosmos is perpetually dancing. Nothing in the world (except Brahman) is absolutely calm and quiet.

Dancing of Unstable Particles

Particles are many in number. Out of them, proton, electron, photon and neutrino are stable particles. They live for ever (the proton's disintegration has been discovered; but the proton has a life-span of at least 10^{30} years) unless they are involved in a collision process where they can be annihilated. On the other hand, all the other particles are unstable. They live for a moment only. This 'moment' is variable depending upon the nature of the particle. It is less than a billion-billionth of second. A 'particle second' is a time unit which is equivalent to 10^{-23} human seconds. The unstable particle decays into other particles after a very short time of existence. The daughter particles may decay again until a combination of stable particles remains. Thus the unstable particles are constantly dancing, appearing, living transiently and disappearing.

One may ask the question: "How do we detect the dancing of the unstable particles?" Among the great number of unstable particles, the tracks of only a few can be detected in bubble chamber pictures. Most of the unstable particles live for a considerable shorter duration and decay after a few 'particle seconds'. They cannot travel farther than a few times their size. Hence they cannot be detected in the bubble chamber. Their dancing has neither been photographically recorded nor visually perceived. That the micro-cosmos is perpetually dancing has been mathematically deduced. May be there is dance without a dancer, or, the dance and the dancer may be identical.

The neutron may be taken here as an example of dancing unstable particles. It disintegrates spontaneously. One particle of neutron decays into three particles, viz., a proton, an electron and an antineutrino (electron-antineutrino). Neutron decay has been shown in Figure 5.1.

Dancing to Die

Every particle has an antiparticle. When particles are produced out of energy, they appear in pairs. When a particle and its corresponding antiparticle meet each other, they get annihilated with

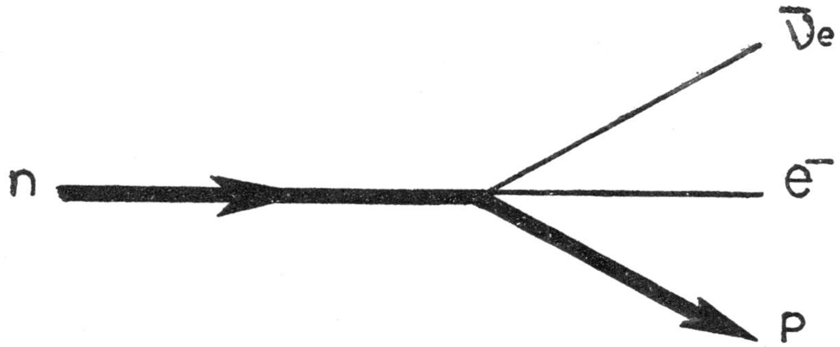

Fig. 5.1: Neutron decay.

consequent production of energy. Figure 5.2 shows the annihilation of an electron and antielectron (positron). A negative electron comes from the left. A positive electron comes from the right. Both meet at the point indicated by the dot and annihilate each other. Two photons are created at the spot of annihilation and depart in opposite directions at the speed of light.

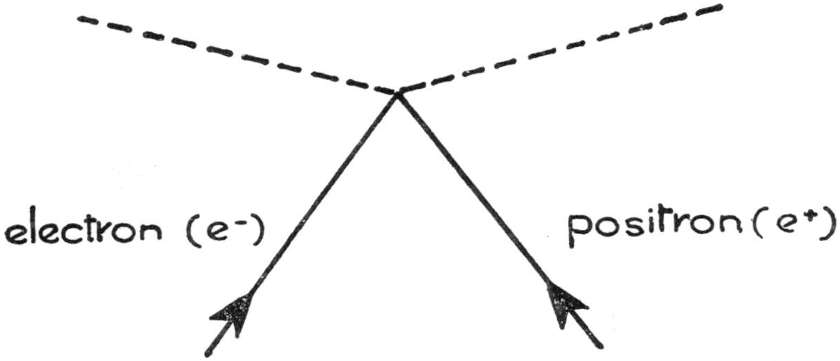

Fig. 5.2: Electron-positron annihilation with the production of two photons (photons are marked by broken lines).

This type of diagram is called Feynman diagram. Richard Feynman (1918-1988) is one of the founders of the theory of quantum electrodynamics. He made important contributions to particle physics. In 1949, he worked on the space-time maps of particle interactions. This work of Feynman was an extension of

Dirac's theory propounded in 1928. The X-axis in the map stands for space and the Y-axis for time. 'Event' which is a happening in the subatomic world is indicated in Feynman diagram by a dot. Wherever there is a dot in the diagram, it indicates the annihilation of the initial particles and the creation of the new ones.

Virtual Particles

Virtual particles were discovered by three physicists, viz., J. Schwinger and Richard P. Feynman of U.S.A. and S. Tomonaga of Japan. The theory of the existence of virtual particles was worked out in the 1940s. But the three discoverers were jointly awarded the Nobel Prize in 1964.

What are these virtual particles and how are they different from the real particles? A virtual particle is a would-be particle. It has no definite mass and exists for only a short time. It exists in a tiny region of space. Subatomic particles like electron, proton and neutron emit particles and immediately reabsorb them. These particles that are emitted and immediately reabsorbed are called virtual particles. They are virtual, because they are particles in effect or essence, but not in actual fact. All electrons, protons and neutrons, without exception, are surrounded by clouds of virtual particles. They are beehives of activity. They never sit tight. Never for a moment do they remain in a constant condition.

As an example, a real photon and a virtual photon may be compared and contrasted. Both are photons. But a real photon, like electrons, has an infinite life, provided it does not interact with other particles. On the other hand, a virtual photon has a very brief life-span, a transient existence. The real photon is massless. But the virtual photon need not be massless. The Heisenberg's uncertainty principle permits the virtual photon to possess variable mass. The briefer the existence of the photon, the larger can be its mass.

Charged particles, both protons and electrons, are surrounded by clouds of virtual photons. The mother particle (proton or electron) constantly emits and absorbs virtual photons. The virtual photons cannot fly off. They are re-absorbed by the mother particle as soon as they are emitted.

The emission and the re-absorption of the virtual photon may be mathematically expressed. At moment m_1, the electron is e^-. At the next moment m_2, which is $m_1+\delta m$, e^- emits a virtual photon, gamma, i.e., e^- becomes $e^- + \nu$. In the third moment, m_3, which is $m_2 + \delta m$, ν disappears and e^- alone remains. Originally it was electron. Then it became electron and photon. Again it became electron only. This is the puzzle. How does e^- become $e^- + \nu$ and again e^-? Can we explain this phenomenon in terms of the conservation law of mass-energy? Can we say that something is created out of nothing and something is converted to nothing? This much we can say here that Heisenberg's uncertainty principle allows it without self-contradiction. The full and satisfactory answer we get when we discuss the concept of quantum field.

The concept of virtual particle is the free creation of the human mind. No such virtual particles have been perceived directly or indirectly. Even if a virtual particle is charged, it cannot be visible in a bubble chamber due to its extremely short life. The existence of virtual particle is inferred mathematically. The concept that particles exert force on each other by exchange of particles has to be explained. In order to explain this phenomenon, virtual particles become necessary and hence they are freely created by the human mind. The scientist does not necessarily know how Nature 'really is'; he makes an attempt to explain the behaviour of Nature in an integral way free from contradictions. There may be more than one way to explain the same thing. It is not important to know whether the theory is 'really right'; it is, however, important to be satisfied, in a convincing way, with the explanation of the working of Nature. In this connection, the view of Albert Einstein, given in 1938, may be quoted here:

> Physical concepts are free creations of the human mind, and are not, however it may seem, uniquely determined by the external world. In our endeavour to understand reality we are somewhat like a man trying to understand the mechanism of a closed watch. He sees the face and the moving hands, even hears its ticking, but he has no way of opening the case. If he is ingenious he may form some picture of a mechanism which could be responsible for all the things he observes, but he may never be quite sure his picture is the only one which could explain his observations. He will never be able to compare his picture with the real mechanism and he cannot even imagine the possibility of the meaning of such a comparison.[4]

The seers of the Ṛgveda have said: "Reality is one only: the wise men describe it in many ways."[5] This corroborates the views of Einstein. If the reality-watch cannot be opened, the observers of the exterior of the watch may describe their respective mental pictures regarding the interior mechanism. But we cannot be sure of the fact that the mental picture really corresponds with the actual mechanism.

Virtual particles are not real particles. They have not been experimentally detected. Their existence has been mathematically derived. There are not only virtual photons, but also others like virtual electrons and positrons. It is also not a fact that only electrons, protons and neutrons have got virtual particles. Virtual particles emit virtual particles that emit virtual particles in diminishing sequence. No particle, p, in Nature constantly remains as p. Particle-becoming is an illusory activity of being something-nothing-something which is a perpetual process. Each particle exists potentially. Each one has a certain probability of existence. Each particle, without exception, is more than one combinations of other particles.

Fundamental Forces and Particle Interaction

The universe, both macro and micro, is held together by cementing forces. There are four types of forces or glue, viz., strong force, electromagnetic force, weak force and gravitational force. In the age of classical physics, it was postulated that the forces act at a distance. However, this concept of instantaneous action at a distance was in vogue one without any basis of scientific explanation. In the twentieth-century physics, the concept of action-at-a-distance has been discarded. Now 'force' is better expressed by 'interaction'. Everything in the universe is glued together by particles called gluons. In this process of particle-interaction, exchange of particles takes place between any two particles. The exchange particles are called gluons.

Electromagnetic interaction takes place between charged particles. It is a force seen in the form of electric and magnetic fields. It is a long-range force. It can be either attractive (between unlike-charged particles) or repulsive (between like-charged particles).

Electromagnetic force binds atoms in molecules. It also binds, inside an atom, the nuclear proton(s) and the orbital electron(s).

It acts as a repelling force between any two protons inside the atomic nucleus.

The gluon associated with the electromagnetic interaction is the photon. Einstein, in 1905, postulated photon to be the particle of light. In 1923, experimental evidence was obtained in favour of the existence of photon. This was, however, the real photon. The virtual photon is the gluon that works in electromagnetic interaction.

Very precise experiments were devised for the measurements of the electromagnetic interactions of photons and electrons. The photon was described by the quantized electromagnetic field and the electron by the quantized electron field. This aspect of quantum physics is called quantum electrodynamics. It was invented in the 1920s by Werner Heisenberg, Wolfgang Pauli, Pascual Jordan and Paul Dirac. In the late 1940's, quantum electrodynamics was given a definite shape by the mathematical work of Richard Feynman, Julian Schwinger and Sin-itiro Tomonaga, who were jointly awarded the Nobel Prize for this work in 1964.

The interaction between two electrons, two protons, or a proton and an electron is mediated by exchange of virtual photon. Figure 5.3 is a Feynman diagram showing the repulsion of two electrons due to exchange of virtual photon quanta.

Electrons are ever surrounded by a swarm of virtual photons. When two electrons come close enough so that their virtual photon clouds overlap, it becomes probable for the virtual photon emitted by one electron to be absorbed by the other and *vice-versa*. This is exactly what has been demonstrated in Figure 5.3.

The closer the electrons come, the more virtual photons they exchange. The more virtual photons they exchange, the more sharply their paths are deflected. This explains the 'repulsive force' existing between two electrons.

The concept that the virtual photon is the exchange particle for electromagnetic interaction was accepted by all physicists. This was the grand success of quantum electrodynamics. But this was not the final solution of the problem. Physicists wanted to explain the action of the other fundamental forces in a similar way. They used the virtual photon concept as a paradigm in their search for other gluons associated with other fundamental forces.

The particles, both proton and neutron, located inside the nu-

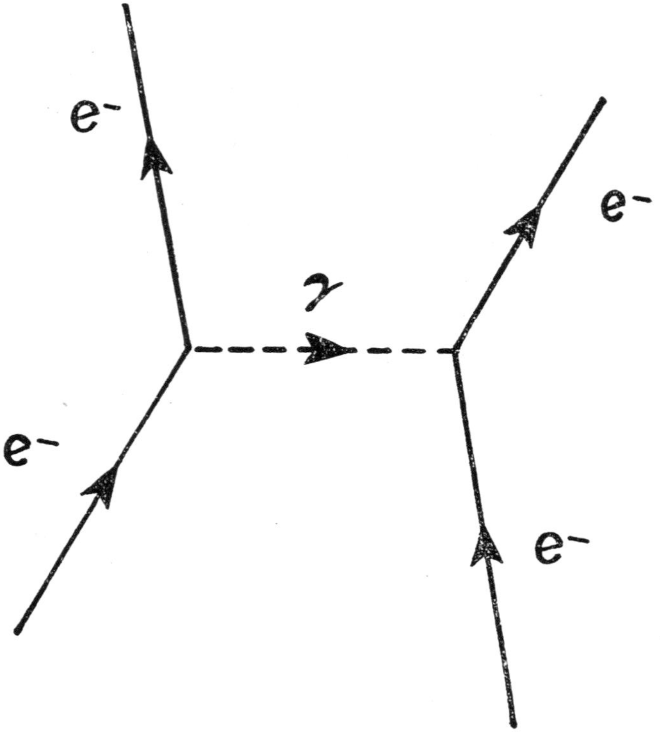

Fig. 5.3: Electromagnetic interaction between two electrons.

cleus of an atom are called nucleons. The nucleons are packed very closely in the nucleus. They are close to each other at a distance which is 10^{-13} cm or less. This is not possible without a binding force, especially when we consider the like-charged particles, protons. We know that the nuclear protons, carrying positive charges are repelled by the electromagnetic force. But, in spite of this repelling force, protons are bound together in the nucleus. Hence the force that binds the protons in the nucleus must be a strong force, stronger than the electromagnetic force, which works against it. That force is at least one hundred times stronger than the electromagnetic force. It is the strongest force in Nature. It works in the shortest range which is 10^{-13} cm.

In 1935, Hideki Yukawa, a Japanese graduate student in physics, could think of applying the new virtual particle theory to the strong force. He proposed that the strong interaction is mediated by exchange of virtual quanta called mesons between nucleons. Yukawa determined the mass of the hypothetical meson. It was estimated by him to be 100 MeV, i.e., about one-tenth the mass of the proton. The pi-meson or pion that was theoretically postulated by Yukawa was experimentally discovered in cosmic rays in 1946. Pions could be artificially created in the laboratory in 1948, when new cyclotrons were built. The mass of the experimentally produced pion was determined and it was 140 MeV. There are three pi-mesons, viz., π^+ (positive pion), π^- (negative pion) and π° (neutral pion). Positive pion is the antiparticle of negative pion. The neutral pion is its own antiparticle.

Figure 5.4 is a Feynman diagram which shows strong interaction between two nucleons via the exchange of virtual meson quanta.

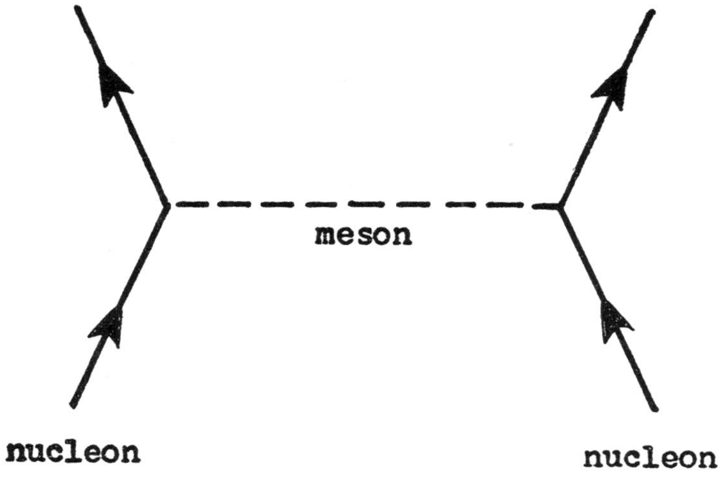

Fig. 5.4: Strong interaction between two nucleons through the exchange of virtual meson quanta.

Every nucleon constantly emits and re-absorbs virtual pions and thus is surrounded by a cloud of virtual pions. If two nucleons come close enough so that their virtual pion clouds overlap, some of the virtual pions are exchanged by the two nucleons. The two nucleons may be compared with two tennis-players and the virtual meson with the tennis ball, hopping back and forth. The whole process of strong interaction is a multiple exchange of virtual pions between nucleons. The strength of the force is directly proportional to the number of exchanges, which increases as the distance decreases.

What has been described for the electromagnetic and strong interactions applies in principle to the weak and the gravitational interactions. Of course, for each type of interaction, the virtual particles that are exchanged are specific. But the exchange of virtual particles in the working of the four fundamental forces is a common phenomenon.

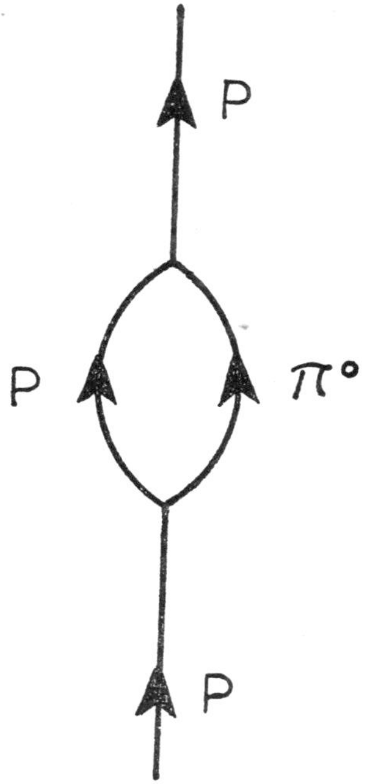

Fig. 5.5: Self-interaction of a proton, that momentarily becomes p and π° in the intermediate stage.

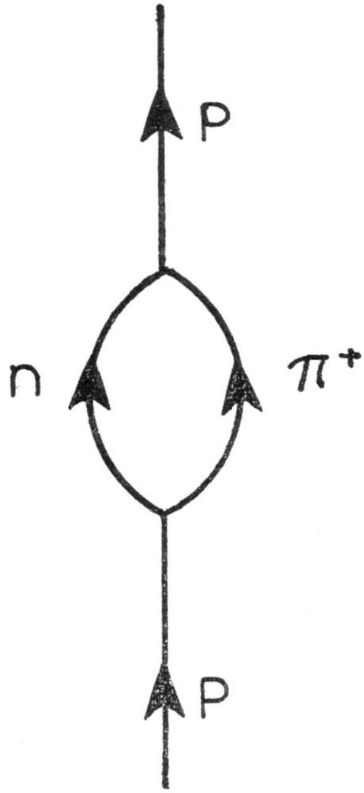

Fig. 5.6: Self-interaction of a proton, that momentarily becomes n and π^{+} in the intermediate stage.

Solo Dances

Every micro-particle dances alone or with other partners. The former type of dance, which is a solo dance, is scientifically termed self-interaction.

An electron constantly interacts with itself by emission and immediate re-absorption of photon. The photon emitted by the electron is a virtual particle. It cannot fly off. It has a transient span of life. It appears and disappears. It originates from the electron; it merges into the electron. An electron becomes electron and photon and immediately becomes electron again. The whole dance is transient and is imperceptible.

Figure 5.5 is a Feynman diagram showing the simplest type of the self-interaction of a proton. One proton suddenly ceases to exist. At the same point in space and time, another proton and a neutral pion come into existence abruptly. Immediately these new particles merge together and annihilate each other. Corresponding to their annihilation, one particle of proton is created. Originally it was a proton; finally it became a proton. In the intermediate stage which was transient, it became a proton and a neutral pion.

Another way of the self-interaction of a proton is presented in Figure 5.6. The proton suddenly ceases to exist and, corresponding to its disappearance, a neutron and a positive pion appear. Immediately these two new particles merge and annihilate each other. With the disappearance of the neutron and the positive pion, the original proton reappears.

How a proton dances in a flicker of moment, permitted by Heisenberg's uncertainty principle, is given in Figure 5.7. The original particle is proton. The final particle is proton. The virtual particles that appear in the intermediate, transient phase are eleven in number. The emission of virtual particles by virtual particles has been shown in the diagram.

Figure 5.8 is a Feynman diagram which depicts the self-interaction of a negative pion, a virtual particle. The negative pion momentarily transforms itself into two virtual particles, a neutron and an anti-proton. Immediately these two particles disappear with the reappearance of the negative pion.

Like protons, neutrons also emit and reabsorb virtual pions.

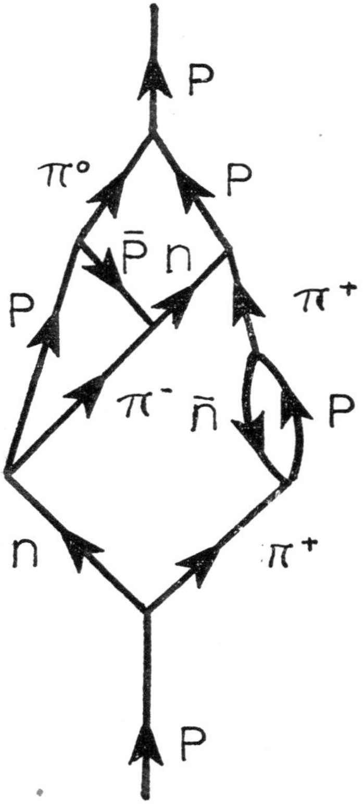

Fig. 5.7: Solo magic dance of a proton.

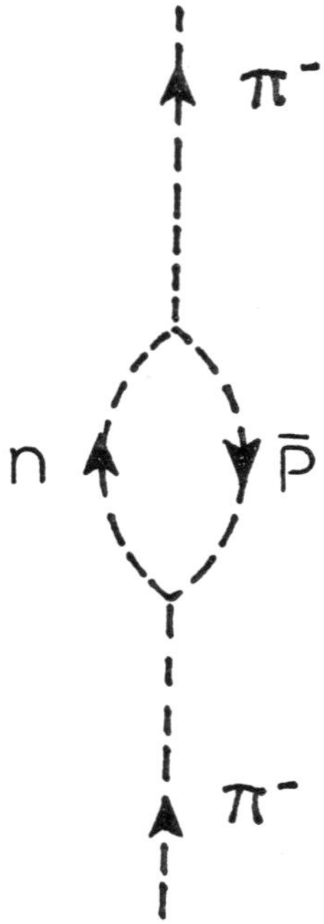

Fig. 5.8: Self-interaction of negative pion—a virtual particle.

Figure 5.9 is a Feynman diagram which shows the self-interaction of a neutron. In this case, the neutron emits and reabsorbs neutral pion.

A neutron can emit a negative pion as a virtual particle. When this occurs, momentarily the neutron disappears and in its place appear a proton and a negative pion. These two new particles immediately merge and annihilate, resulting in the reappearance of a neutron. The Feynman diagram of this process is presented in Figure 5.10.

Dancing with Partner

Solo dance of the micro-particles has been described in the foregoing paragraphs. But not only do they dance alone, they also dance with partners. Inside the atomic nucleus, every nucleon is constantly surrounded by a cloud of virtual pions. The mother nucleon emits and immediately reabsorbs the pion. If a nucleon comes close enough to another nucleon so that their virtual pion-clouds overlap, the virtual pion emitted by one nucleon may be

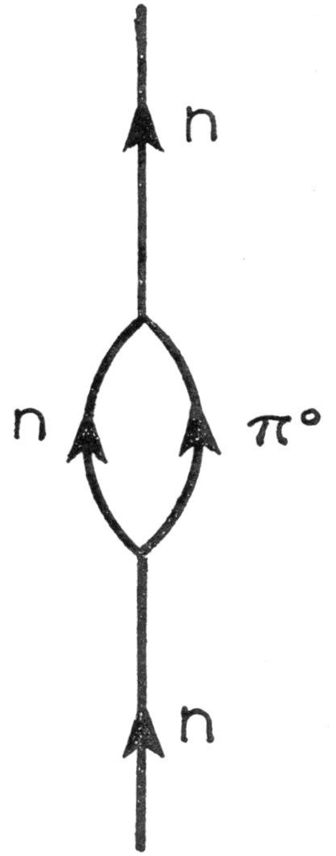

Fig. 5.9: Self-interaction of a neutron emitting π° as virtual particle.

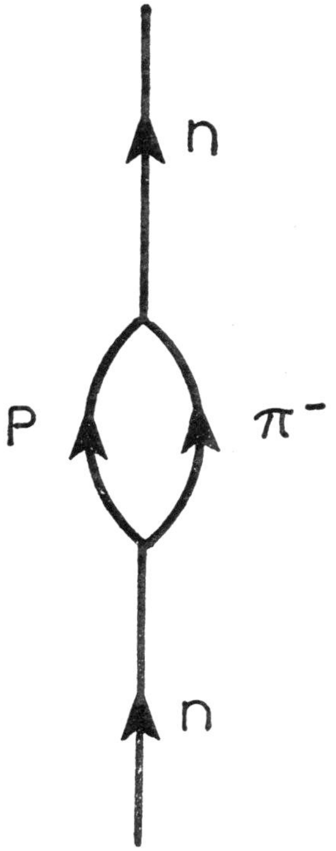

Fig. 5.10: Self-interaction of a neutron, that momentarily becomes p and π^{-} in the intermediate stage.

absorbed by a neighbouring nucleon and *vice versa*. Figure 5.11 is a Feynman diagram showing the exchange of positive pion between proton and neutron. The proton that emits the virtual particle becomes a neutron and the neutron that absorbs the virtual particle becomes a proton.

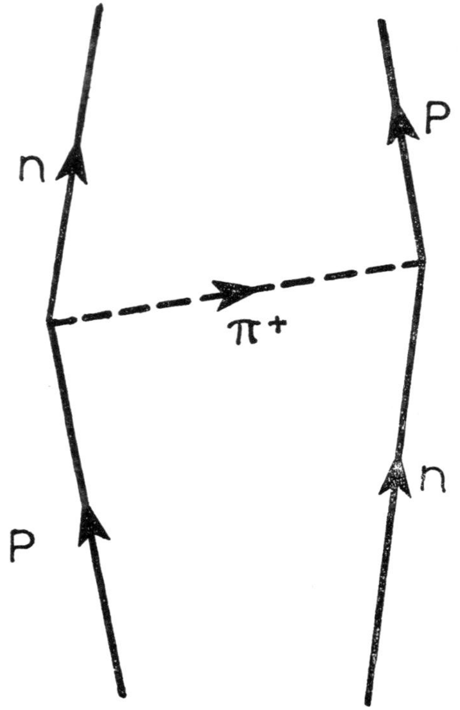

Fig. 5.11: Interaction between proton and neutron by exchange of positive pion.

When a neutron emits a negative pion at a distance close enough to a proton so that their clouds of virtual particles overlap, the negative pion is absorbed by the neighbouring proton, resulting in the transformation of the neutron to a proton and the proton to a neutron. The Feynman diagram of this exchange is presented in Figure 5.12.

Unlawful Dance

The law of conservation of mass and energy clearly states that something cannot be created out of nothing and something cannot be converted into nothing. This law is contravened by the cosmic dance. Of course, this contravention is not real, but apparent. One can get a convincing solution of this riddle when one refers to the 'field' concept that will be discussed in this chapter.

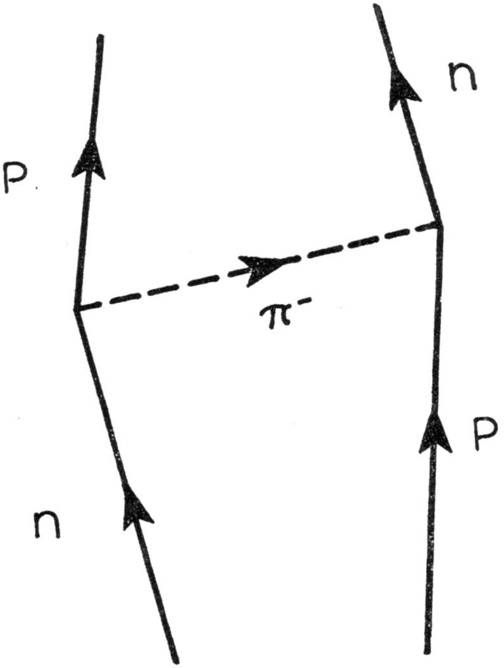

Fig. 5.12: Interaction of a neutron, emitting negative pion, with a proton.

An interaction involving the contravention of the law of conservation of mass and energy is being described here as one example. A negative pi meson and a proton collide and annihilate. Two new particles, viz., a neutral K meson and a lambda particle, are created. These two new particles are unstable. They live less than a billionth of a second. The neutral meson decays into a positive pi meson and a negative pi meson. The lambda particle decays into a negative pi meson and a proton. It is interesting to note that these two were the initial particles. From particle p_1 and p_2, finally we got particles p_1, p_2, p_3 and p_4. The Feynman diagram of this interaction is given in Figure 5.13.

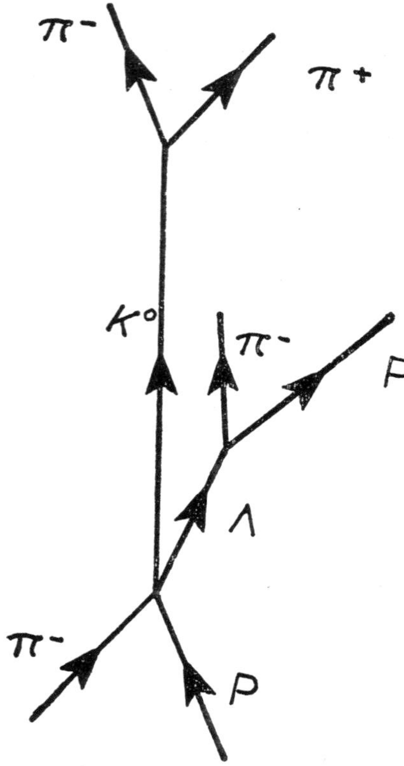

Fig. 5.13: Particle interaction involving contravention of conservation rule.

Vacuum Diagrams

A vacuum diagram is a special type of Feynman diagram. In this diagram, no world line leads to the interaction and no world line leaves it. From vacuum some things appear and again they disappear into that vacuum.

In reality, there is no such thing as vacuum. There is nothing like empty space. The vacuum which we mentally construct as the empty space is really a plenum, a full reservoir of infinite energy. As waves appear on the surface of ocean-water and again disappear, so also particles appear from the so-called vacuum and again dissolve into it. The void is not non-being; it is not a nothing; it is a positive entity and it is also full.

Figure 5.14 is a vacuum diagram of a three-particle interaction. A proton, a negative pion and an antineutron appear from *nowhere* and immediately disappear, leaving no trace at all.

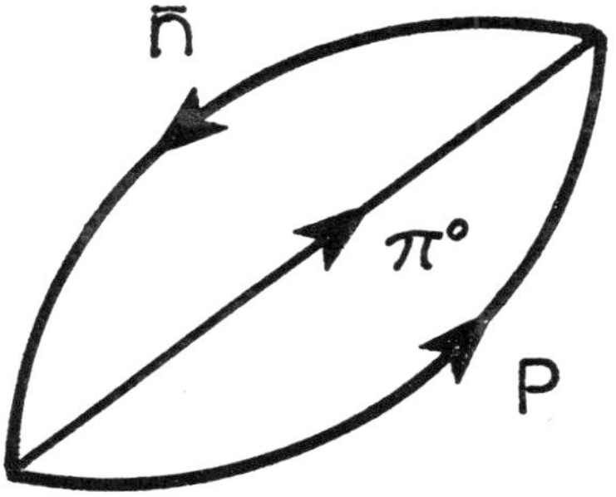

Fig. 5.14: Vacuum diagram of a three-particle interaction.

Another vacuum diagram of a six-particle interaction is presented in Figure 5.15. It depicts an exquisite dance of the formless becoming form and *vice versa*.

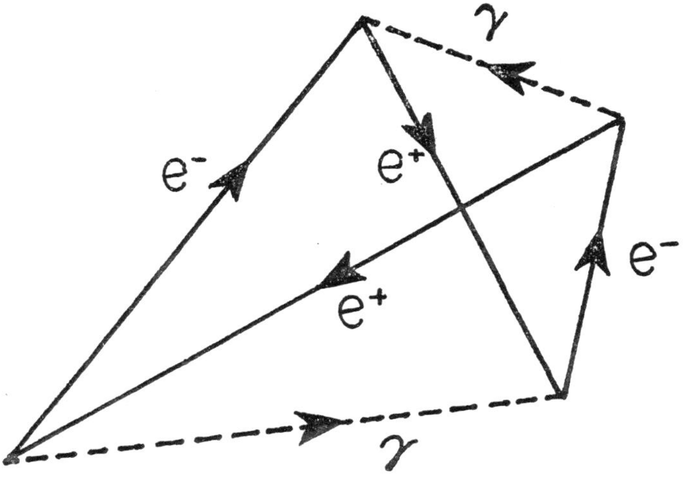

Fig. 5.15 Vacuum diagram of a six-particle interaction.

What has been described here by two examples of vacuum diagram are only two spots in the entire cross-section of the microcosmos. In the subatomic realm, this sort of dance is universal and perpetual. Particles are formed from the energy of being and the energy of motion. Particles are formed from the vacuum or empty space that is really something positive but formless. The formless assumes forms which again become formless as stated in the Bhagavadgītā.[6]

S-Matrix

The full form of S-Matrix is Scattering Matrix. The key concept of this theory was originally proposed by Werner Heisenberg in 1943. When particles collide, they scatter. This is represented in the form of a matrix that is a type of mathematical table. The S-Matrix is a collection of probabilities for all possible reactions involving hadrons. In any collision of particles, there are various probabilities of outcomes. By study of S-Matrix, one can predict the various probabilities.

Physicists were unceasingly busy with their unending search for the ultimate particle. This was a sort of syndrome that was diagnosed by the S-Matrix theory. There was attempt not to solve this problem, but to dissolve it. According to the S-Matrix theory, it is not at all meaningful to ask the question, "Which particles are elementary?" That any particle is elementary is not recognized by S-Matrix theory. This theory is based upon *events*, not upon things; it recognizes the dance, and not the dancer. The dances are the interactions. Particles are intermediate states in a network of interactions. All of the particles represented in an S-Matrix diagram are defined in terms of each other. Particles do not stand apart as significant entities.

S-Matrix theory gives a symbolic presentation of the cosmic dance. In this presentation, the dance is primarily important; there is no emphasis on the dancer. The interactions are the events and they are important. The interacting particles are the intermediate appearances only.

Figure 5.16 is an S-Matrix diagram. A proton and an antiproton collide; they annihilate each other. Consequent upon their annihilation, two new particles, viz., a negative pion and a positive pion are created. In this diagram, the collision area is the circle. The proton and the antiproton go into the collision area. The

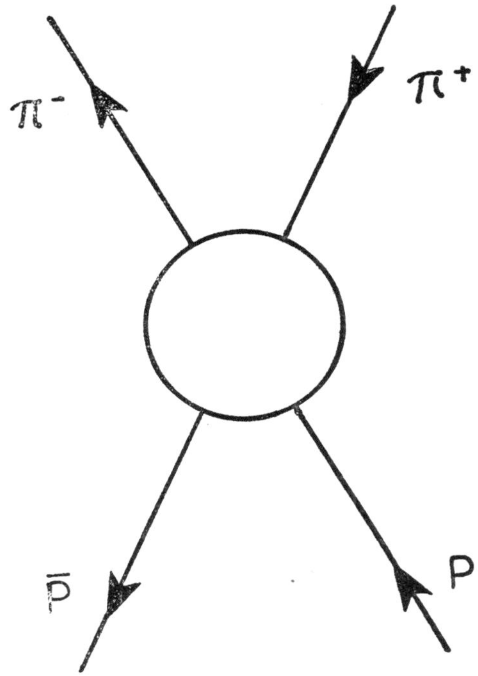

Fig. 5.16: S-Matrix diagram showing proton-antiproton interaction.

negative pion and the positive pion come out of the collision area. Nothing is told by the diagram about the happening, if any, at the point of collision. This much the diagram tells that certain particles went into the interaction and certain particles came out of the interaction. It also does not show the positions of the particles in space or time.

The particles resulting from one interaction may be involved in a second interaction. One such case has been represented in Figure 5.17.

The lines drawn in S-Matrix diagram are not the world lines of particles unlike in Feynman diagrams. The lines connecting the circles in interaction network are reaction channels through which energy flows. The 'neutron' in Figure 5.17 is a reaction channel. S Matrix theory considers 'particles' as intermediate states in a network of interactions.

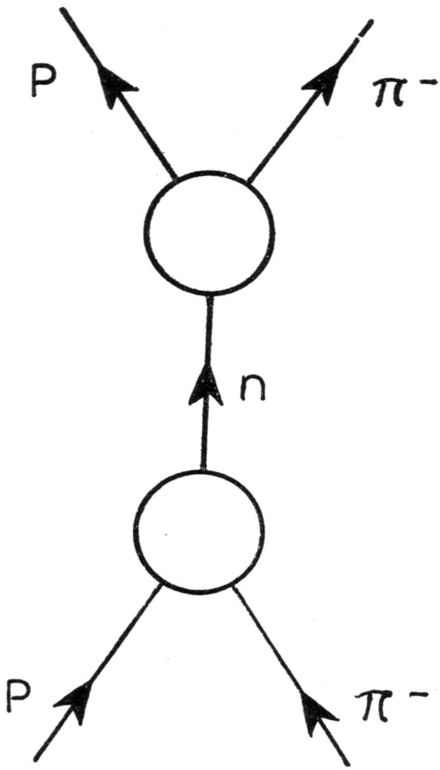

Fig. 5.17: S-Matrix diagram showing a network of two interactions.

The dance is important in S-Matrix theory. It does not put emphasis on the dancers. A network of two interactions with neutron as the reaction channel has been shown in Figure 5.17. If more energy is available, the same channel can be created by other particles. As for example, a lambda particle and a neutral kaon can do it. Its S-Matrix diagram has been presented in Figure 5.18.

We can observe the input and the output channels in S-Matrix diagrams. But our vision is totally blurred or even blocked to know anything in the interaction region inside the circle. The philosophy of S-Matrix theory is that Nature is unanalyzable in detail. The dance is visible, not the dancer(s). Is there really any dancer? The S-Matrix diagram refuses to answer this question.

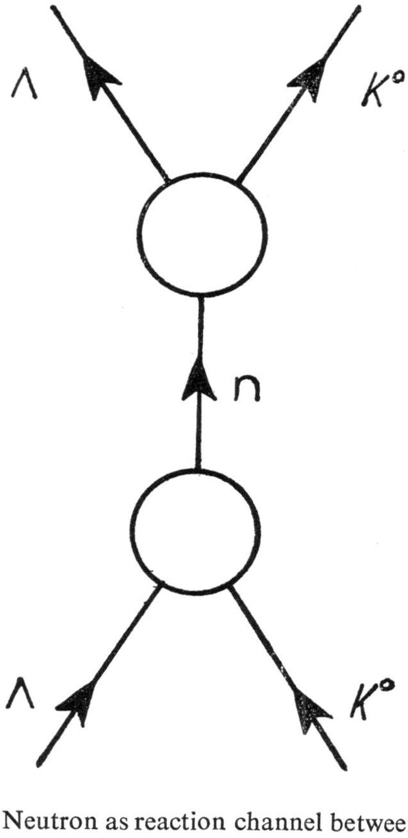

Fig. 5.18: Neutron as reaction channel between two interactions of a lambda particle and a neutral kaon.

Field Concept

The perpetual dance of the microcosmos has been presented in a nutshell in this chapter. The cosmic dance *apparently* shows that quanta are created out of void and that they again become void. It *apparently* shows that larger mass can be produced out of smaller mass and that larger mass can be converted to smaller mass. Can we deduce from the appearance of the dance that something can be nothing and nothing can be something? A number of scientists, after observing the cosmic dance, accepted *ex nihilo* creation as a fact. A deeper analysis shows that the law of conservation of being is a formal truth and cannot be refuted in any circumstances. In any chemical reaction, if A and B react to produce C, D and energy, we mathematically express it as $A+B=C+D+(E)$. Similarly, if something becomes nothing and nothing becomes something, we mathematically express as "something=nothing" and "nothing=something". This may be expressed in propositional form as (1) Something is nothing and (2) Nothing is something. Linguistic and concept analysis will show that such propositions, equations and concepts are self-contradictory and hence not valid. The law of conservation of being is well formulated in the *Bhagavadgītā*. "That which does not exist cannot be something (*nāsataḥ vidyate bhāvaḥ*); that which exists cannot be nothing (*nābhāvo vidyate sataḥ*).[7] This law of conservation is formal. The statements given in the *Gītā* are not synthetic. Being analytic, they are *a priori* truths. This law does not refer to matter and energy. It does not limit itself to manifested entity and form. It says that being remains as being without gain and loss, although becoming permits transformation from one form to another, and from form to formlessness and *vice versa.*

In the domain of science, the existence of the unmanifested, the formless being was not accepted before the discovery of quantum physics. The field concept took a crude shape in the nineteenth century. Michael Faraday, in England, while working on electricity and magnetism, could visualize the physical existence of electric and magnetic fields. Intuitively, he thought of the field to be essentially the physical object. In his opinion, an electrically charged particle is a point at which the field becomes infinitely large. To him, the field was primary and the particle was secondary. Particle is a manifested expression of the field. Faraday postulated the 'field' in a non-mathematical way. This speculative field of Faraday became a physical reality when James Maxwell propounded his electromagnetic theory of light. In the 1860's, Maxwell developed the idea of Faraday by mathematical analysis of the interrelationship of electricity and magnetism. In 1864, Maxwell devised a set of four equations. The nature of interrelationships of electricity and magnetism is deduced from these Maxwell's equations. As per these equations, the electric field and the magnetic field cannot be considered in isolation. The two are invariably present together, at right angles to each other. In reality, it is a single electro-magnetic field instead of two separate fields. According to Maxwell's electro-magnetic theory, light is a wave of oscillating electric and magnetic fields that propagate in space and carry energy and momentum.

Light is particulate. Light is wave. This wave-particle dualism was a persistent irritant to scientific thought for a long time. Newton considered light as particles. Up to the eighteenth century, scientists had confidence in the existence of light-particles. In 1801, Young could experimentally prove the wave nature of light. This gave a blow to the particle theory of light. But this blow was only temporary. In 1905, Einstein proved the particle nature of light and he gave the name 'photon' to this particle. This created a troublesome puzzle. How can light be both particle and wave? Light is an electromagnetic wave field as in Maxwell's theory. In Einstein's explanation of the photoelectric effect, light is required to be of the nature of a particle. Does it contradict the logical law of the excluded middle? Can A and not-A be both correct? This was a great puzzle before the advent of quantum theory. Before quantum physics was known, physicists had a notion that particles and fields are distinct entities. At that time, the birth and the extinction of particles could not be conceived of. Particles were thought to be immutable and eternal. Fields were recognized after Faraday and Maxwell; but they were considered to emanate from particles and be responsible for the forces between them. The suggestion of de Broglie that particles like electrons have associated wave fields became an important step towards resolving the problem of wave-particle dualism. The quantum-physicists soon realized that particles behave like wave fields and wave fields like particles. In the late 1920s, the dualism of fields and particles was rejected. In this connection, Steven Weinberg remarks:

> In 1926, Born, Heisenberg and Jordan turned their attention to the electromagnetic field in empty space and........were able to show that the energy of each mode of oscillation of an electromagnetic field is quantized.........Thus the applica-

> tion of quantum mechanics to the electromagnetic field at last put Einstein's idea of the photon on a firm mathematical foundation.......... However, the world was still conceived to be composed of two very different ingredients—particles and fields—which were both to be described in terms of quantum mechanics, but in very different ways. Material particles, like electrons and protons, were conceived to be eternal........ On the other hand, photons were supposed to be merely a manifestation of an underlying entity, the quantized electromagnetic field, and could be freely created and destroyed. It was not long before a way was found out of this distasteful dualism, toward a truly unified view of nature. Essential steps were taken in a 1928 paper of Jordan and Eugene Wigner, and in a pair of long papers in 1929-30 by Heisenberg and Pauli. They showed that material particles could be understood as the quanta of various fields, in just the same way as the photon is the quantum of the electromagnetic field. There was supposed to be one field for each type of elementary particle. Thus the inhabitants of the universe were conceived to be a set of fields—an electron field, a proton field, an electromagnetic field—and particles were reduced to mere epiphenomena. In its essentials, this point of view has survived to the present day, and forms the central dogma of quantum field theory: *the essential reality is a set of fields*, subject to the rules of special relativity and quantum mechanics; all else is derived as a consequence of the quantum dynamics of these fields.[8]

These ideas of some great physicists laid the foundation of relativistic quantum field theory which brings about fusion of relativity theory and quantum theory. In order to understand atomic and subatomic particles, one has to transcend the old idea of matter as a 'material stuff'. According to the relativistic quantum field theory, particle and field are complementary manifestations of one and the same thing.

The primacy of field over particle may be comprehended from the following statements of Capek:

> The ultimate material reality that physics can apprehend is the 'field' and in the aspect of the quantum field, it is both a continuum and a discontinuum, the discontinuities being

> temporary condensations of space-time where the field is unusually intense, giving rise to corpuscular matter.[9]

In this connection, Capek has quoted the words of Albert Einstein as follows:

> We may therefore regard matter as being constituted by the regions of space in which the field is extremely intense........ There is no place in this new kind of physics both for the field and matter, for the field is the only reality.[10]

According to the relativistic quantum field theory, what we mean by reality is the transformation and organization of field quanta; there is nothing else other than this. Thus reality is a set of fields that give rise to the probabilities for finding their associated quanta. The field is invisible. We cannot perceive it. But we can infer its existence from our determination of its effects.

Paul Dirac, who laid some major corner stones of the quantum field theory in 1928, visualized a separate field for each type of particle. Three types of particles, viz., electron, proton and neutron, were known in 1928 and hence three different fields were recognized. We no longer accept a separate field for each type of particle. There is really one unified field that is the source of the manifestation of a set of fields.

As a matter of fact, particles are interactions between fields. When two fields interact, they do it instantaneously and locally at a single point in space. These interactions are the particles. Thus physical reality is essentially nonmaterial. According to the quantum field theory, the universe is not made of matter; it is made of fields that alone are real. Matter is made of particles that are the momentary manifestations of interacting fields. However, particles are never substantial. They appear to us as substantial as a result of the interactions of fields.

Even the term 'quantum field' is an outrageous contradiction. A 'field' is a term which refers to a pervading area with homogeneity and continuity. A 'quantum' is a term which refers to a spatial point with a separate individuality and discontinuity. These are two incompatible concepts that are brought together for juxtaposition. In terms of classical logic, it is a paradox. Either A or not-A is correct in classical logic. But in quantum logic, both A and not-A can be correct and hence quantum field theory has been accepted to explain the apparent contradictions of Nature.

Physicists who believe in a single unified field have got an idea that space is an empty container and that the field permeates all space. Hideki Yukawa, a Japanese physicist, first suggested that space is occupied with subtle energy that is the source of virtual particles that apparently appear from nowhere and that is again the receptacle of virtual particles that apparently disappear into nowhere. This 'subtle energy' of Yukawa is the field. In his concept, field occupies space. Such a notion, however, is not correct. It is a fact that field is all-pervading; it is also a fact that space (*ākāśa*) is all-pervading. But these two are not two separate entities. Field and space are one and the same thing. A great genius like Einstein was himself confused by thinking that field and space are two different entities. We have already quoted Einstein who has said that field is the only reality. Here we again quote him who says that space is the only reality. Shortly before his death, Einstein formulated the quintessence of his world-view in the following words:

> Space has devoured ether and time; it seems to be on the point of swallowing up also the field and corpuscles, so that it alone remains as the vehicle of reality.[11]

It will be discussed in Part III of this book that space has not really devoured ether and field. If we establish their identity, there is no question of devouring. If we maintain their distinctions, we commit conceptual error. Hence it is not correct to say that field pervades space; in reality, field and space are one and the same thing.

While discussing the cosmic dance of micro-particles, we have given few vacuum diagrams. Particles appear from the so-called vacuum, void, nothing or *śūnya*; in a billionth of a second or even earlier, they disappear into that void. We also know that there is loss of mass in the decaying processes. It always happens when some particle decays. The total rest mass of the new particles is always less than the rest mass of the original particle. We may take one example here. A negative omega (Ω^-) has a rest mass of 1,636 MeV. When it changes to a neutral xi (Ξ°) with a rest mass of 1,286.5 MeV and a negative pion (π^-) with a rest mass of 136.5 MeV, there is loss of rest mass equivalent to 213 MeV approximately. How can we explain these phenomena without accepting the existence of a field that is all-pervasive?

Before Yukawa conceived of the appearance and disappearance of virtual particles from and into the so-called 'void', Paul Dirac, in 1928, could visualize a non-energy electron field that permeates the entire universe. Dirac could predict the existence of an anti-electron (positron). According to his theory, electron-positron pair can be generated from this electron field and absorbed into it. Dirac's theory brought about merger of quantum theory and relativity and thus gave birth to relativistic quantum field theory.

It we accept the so-called vacuum, void, *śūnya* or space (*ākāśa*) as field, which is really a plenum, we can explain the appearance and disappearance of the virtual particle-pairs. Electron-positron pair cited here is only an example. As a matter of fact, all types of virtual particle-pairs are constantly generated by the field and after a moment, short enough to be permissible as per Heisenberg's uncertainty principle, are absorbed by the same field. This dance of all possible virtual particles, their appearance from vacuum, transient living and disappearance into the vacuum, may be regarded as the fundamental activity of Nature. Thus what was considered to be *śūnya*, void, vacuum, or nothingness before the discovery of relativistic quantum field is now accepted as *pūrṇa* (full or plenum) by the quantum physicists. The field-interactions resulting in vacuum fluctuations and appearance of virtual particle-pairs occur at micro-distances in space and micro-duration in time. In micro-physics, the vacuum-ocean is a positive entity, has small ripples and larger waves, has fluctuations everywhere and always. In macro-physics, the vacuum-ocean is nothing, absolute void, inactive, calm and free from fluctuations. The virtual particles can be real particles if energy from outside is supplied to the vacuum. The present world is a much cooler world compared to the world within a few nanoseconds after the big bang explosion. That ultra-high energy prevalent during the moments immediately after the big bang explosion cannot be artificially created by man. At that high temperature, the new-born world was perfectly symmetrical and there was only a single unified field. Particles were spontaneously generated from the field at that extremely high temperature. With the progressive drop in temperature of that fire-ball world, symmetry broke down and instead of a single field, multiple fields appeared. The gravitational field was the first to appear. Later on, strong field, electromagnetic field and weak field functioned as separate fields. The generation of particles from vacuum in the new-born universe took place at ultra-high energy. Now if we desire to create real particles from vacuum, we can do so provided we supply energy to vacuum from external source. When energized, the virtual particles will jump out as real particles.

In order to understand the cosmic dance of the micro-world, one has to make a thorough comprehension of the relativistic quantum field theory. If field is taken as a positive entity, there would be no place for confusion regarding questions of *ex nihilo* creation and violation of law of conservation of mass and energy. Unmanifested *Prakṛti* or *Māyā* manifests itself and again goes to unmanifested condition.

Tāṇḍava as Symbol of Cosmic Dance

The concept of the cosmic dance is very old in Indian mythology and philosophy. The Ṛgveda[12] describes, in categorical terms, the vigorous dance of the particles on the stage of the cosmic field. The *Brahma-Sūtra*[13] speaks of the cosmic vibration. The Upaniṣadic[14] description of the *prāṇa* corresponds to the unified field of the quantum-physicists.

The cosmic dance of the quantum physicist and the *tāṇḍava* dance of the Hindu god Rudra-Śiva may be correlated here. Banerji writes about this dancing god as follows:

> Śiva's dance is *tāṇḍava*, energetic and virile.........The *damaru* or drum in his upper right hand stands for creative sound, the fire in the upper left hand for destruction, the '*pātaka*' hand which depicts the pose of *Abhaya Mudrā* is for boon, peace, content and maintenance. The foot held aloft gives release. The cosmic process of creation and destruction, manifestation and non-manifestation, the worldly evolution and change are fundamentals in Hindu theology and Śiva's dance is the depiction of the same.[15]

Carl Sagan has given a description of the symbolic significance of the tenth-century Chola bronze sculpture of India (Figure 5.19).

Fig. 5.19: Cosmic dance of Natarāja.

"In his manifestation as Lord of the Dance, the Hindu god Shiva dances the dance of creation. In this tenth-century Chola bronze, Shiva's aureole of fire (the *prabhāmaṇḍala*) represents the rhythm of the universe and emanates from a lotus pedestal, the Hindu symbol of enlightenment. Shiva dances on the prostrate form of the *Apasmārapuruṣa*, a symbol of human ignorance. The back right hand carries the *damaru*, a small drum symbolizing creation. The back left hand holds *agni*, the fire of destruction. The front left hand is in the *gajahasta* ("elephant trunk") position. The front right hand is held in the *abhaya-mudrā* pose (literally, "do not be afraid")."[16]

The words '*Śiva*' and '*Śaṅkara*' mean 'auspicious' or 'one whose actions are good'. Thus the deity Śiva is auspicious and benevolent. He is worshipped in the form of phallus that symbolises the 'Divine Father'. The phallus symbol penetrates into *Śakti* (Energy) which is symbolized as the generative organ of the 'Divine Mother'. Śiva is a fertility god. His dancing symbolizes creation. But the same Śiva is *Rudra*. The word '*rudra*' means 'ferocious', 'one with terrorizing cry'. Rudra's actions are destructive. He dances for the annihilation of everything. Thus Śiva and Rudra are two concepts that are antagonistic to each other and are mutually exclusive. Notwithstanding the contradictory aspects of these two words, the Hindus bring about a fusion of two contradictory concepts to synthesize an integral concept of *Rudra-Śiva*. Such a concept is apparently paradoxical. But, in reality, this is a bipolar concept, in which both the opposite poles are indispensable to each other and one cannot exist without the other.

Many scholars are also very much confused on this issue. The Hindus recognize one and only one God Who is formless. This one God is conceived in many forms. As a coin has two faces, so also one single God has three phases with reference to actions and attributes. These three phases constitute the Trinity (*trimūrti*) of the Hindus. They are Brahmā, Viṣṇu and Maheśvara. Brahmā possesses the attribute of *rajas* (mode of activity) and is responsible for the creation of the universe. Viṣṇu possesses the attribute of *sattva* (mode of purity) and is responsible for the sustenance of the universe. Maheśvara or the Great Controller possesses the attribute of *tamas* (mode of inertia) and is responsible for the dissolution of the universe. According to this Trinity concept,

Maheśvara or Rudra-Śiva is destructive in nature. If this is a fact, we find difficulty in associating creative activity with *Rudra-Śiva*. But the *Natarāja* concept contains mixture of creative, destructive and supporting activities. The question is: "Is it a justifiable concept?"

Natarāja concept is religiously, philosophically and scientifically justifiable. The *Natarāja Mūrti* belongs to the *Śaiva* cult, in which the Trinity is fused into One. Śiva creates, sustains and destroys. He Himself does not do anything. *Śakti* (Energy), the Consort of Śiva, does everything; Śiva remains as the substratum (*adhiṣṭhāna*) of all the events that happen in the universe.

The concepts of creation and dissolution with special reference to the Trinity need some elaboration here. The Viṣṇu-Purāṇa[17] describes three types of creation, viz., *prākṛta* (the original creation of *Prakṛti* or Nature), *dainandina* (the creation done by Brahmā on each day of his) and *nitya* (the creation taking place every moment). There are fourfold dissolutions,[18] viz., *nitya* (destruction taking place every moment), *prākṛta* (total dissolution of *vyakta Prakṛti* or the manifested universe along with the death of Brahmā), *naimittika* (occasional dissolution on the end of a day of Brahmā) and *ātyantika* (the dissolution of *jīva* or individual soul in Brahman).

The creation and dissolution that are taking place every moment in the universe are symbolized in the *tāṇḍava*-dance of *Rudra-Śiva*. The Master Dancer is *Natarāja* who goes on dancing. In this supreme Cosmic Dance, particles and antiparticles appear from *ākāśa* (space); these micro-particles may generate newer particles; the particles dance vigorously; suddenly they appear, transiently they live, for a billionth or a trillionth part of a second they dance, and then they disappear. When they disappear, they apparently vanish; but they don't become nothing. They originate from space; they are dissolved into space. In the beginning they were unmanifested (*avyakta*); in the middle they became manifested (*vyakta*); and in the end they became again unmanifested (*avyakta*). There is no gain and no loss in this whole process. Really there is neither generation nor annihilation. We are talking about coarse (*sthūla*) existence or subtle (*sūkṣma*) existence; and again we are concerned with different degrees of subtleties.

Neutron, proton and electron are particles. Pions, photons and gravitons are particles. Although they are all particles, in size, mass and penetrability, all of them are not the same. A neutrino is not the same as a proton. Neutrino has neither rest mass nor charge. It continuously moves at a speed approaching the velocity of light. It has an extremely high penetrating power. If two hundred and fifty Earths were placed in series, a neutrino could fly through them without reacting with any of their constituents. This shows that a neutrino, being a particle, is too subtle in its existence of perpetual race. This is an example of the existence of subtle entities. Space (*ākāśa*) which looks like void or vacuum (*śūnya*) is not nothing. It is a form of matter (including energy). It is too subtle to be perceptible to our senses. That's why it is *asat* (non-existent to our senses, but really existent). When something is generated from this very subtle substance (*asat*) and becomes perceptible to our senses either directly or indirectly, we say that the generated entity is *sat* or existent. But, as a matter of fact, both the *asat* and *sat* are existent. *Sat* is generated from *asat* and is again reconverted to *asat*. This is exactly what happens in the appearance of particles from space and their disappearance into the same space.

In Vedic terminology, *Apāṁ Napāt* or *Prāṇa* or *Dakṣa* or *Nāra* is the primeval subtle essence (*arka* or *apraketa salila*) that was the unified field during the first nanoseconds after the bursting of the cosmic egg. Space or *ākāśa* or *aditi* is a product of this *Prāṇa*. The dancing of *reṇus* (particles), their appearance in opposite pairs and subsequent disappearance have been described in symbolic form in the Vedic literature.[19] Our comprehension of Reality would be much better if we make a comparative study of the Vedic literature and quantum physics.

Notes

1. ṚV, I.164.14.
2. YV, 40.1.
3. Īśa, 1.
4. Einstein, A. and Infeld, L., *The Evolution of Physics*, Cambridge University Press, Cambridge, 1971, p. 31.
5. ṚV, I.164.46.
6. BG, II.28.
7. BG, II.16.
8. Weinberg, S., Quoted by Pagels, H.R. in '*The Cosmic Code*', Penguin Books, Harmondsworth, 1984, pp. 247-8.

9. Capek, M., *Philosophical Impact of Contemporary Physics*, D. Van Nostrand, Princeton, New Jersey, 1961, p. 319.
10. Einstein, A., Quoted by Capek, M. in [9], p. 319.
11. Quoted by Thiel, R., *And There was Light*, 1958, p. 345.
12. ṚV, X.72.6.
13. BS, I.3.39.
14. Kaṭ, II.3.2.
15. Banerji, P., *Natarāja, the Dancing God*, Cosmo Publications, New Delhi, 1985, p. 99.
16. Sagan, C., *Cosmos*, Macdonald, London, 1981, p. 244.
17. VP, I.7.44-5.
18. VPDA, Ch. VII.
19. ṚV, II.35.2 & 8; X.72.2-6; AĀ, II.1.8.6-7.

CHAPTER VI

ASTROPHYSICS

> The known is finite, the unknown infinite; intellectually we stand on an islet in the midst of an illimitable ocean of inexplicability. Our business in every generation is to reclaim a little more land.
>
> *T.H. Huxley*, 1887

> We do not ask for what useful purpose the birds do sing, for song is their pleasure since they were created for singing. Similarly, we ought not to ask why the human mind troubles to fathom the secrets of the heavens........The diversity of the phenomena of Nature is so great, and the treasures hidden in the heavens so rich, precisely in order that the human mind shall never be lacking in fresh nourishment.
>
> Johannes Kepler, *Mysterium Cosmographicum*

THE EARTH, THE HEAVEN AND THE UNIVERSE

Early Western Concept

Man has been cherishing the idea of anthropocentrism and geocentrism. "God has created man and created everything else for the pleasure of man. The centre of the universe is man. Earth is the place where man lives. Hence the anthropocentric universe is bound to be geocentric. Earth is the centre of the universe. It is stationary and every thing else is moving around it. The sky is a dome-shaped blue canopy hanging over the Earth. The Sun and the Moon are very small objects wandering in the sky. The stars are insignificant specks of light glued to the sky for decorative purpose only." This was the anthropocentric and geocentric concept of the Western man.

'The world', 'the universe', 'the cosmos' and 'the Earth' were synonymous terms in the geocentric concept. Such an idea has now been discarded. It has been realized that the Earth occupies an insignificant dot in the illimitable universe.

For Aristotle (384-322 B.C.), the Greek philosopher, it was the law of Nature for the heavens to be perfect and changeless. Hipparchus (190-120 B.C.) was a Greek astronomer. Claudius Ptolemaus (A.D. 100-170), who was another Greek astronomer, summarized Hipparchian system and his own in the form of a book. Both these astronomers could visualize epicyclic motion of planets. Ptolemy gave the idea of a geocentric universe. In the Ptolemaic system, the Earth is pictured as the centre of the universe, with all other astronomical bodies circling around it. The Bible supported the idea of the geocentric universe.

Pliny (A.D. 23-79), a Roman scholar, wrote in his encyclopedia two centuries after Hipparchus about the star catalogue prepared by the latter, who was astonished by observing a 'new star' in Scorpio. But how could it be possible? If it violated the concept of the 'perfect and changeless heavens', could it be correct? Is it not sacrilegious to report a change in the heavens? The medieval astronomers in Greece and the Middle East might have observed changing stars in the heavens; but they might not have reported their findings, on religious grounds, and might have explained them away as their observational errors. The astronomer of that age, whether Christian or Muslim, saw in the perfection of the heavens a symbol of the perfection of God. He could not dare to find a flaw in the perfection of the created objects of God. There cannot be a flaw in the workmanship of a perfect God. Hence a devout astronomers could ascribe a flaw only to his sense-perception when he observed a changing star in the heaven. For him, the Earth also would have been perfect, had not Adam and Eve committed the first sin. They ate the forbidden fruit in the Garden of Eden. That was the reason of the Earth being imperfect. But nothing like that happened for the heavens. And so the heavens were perfect and changeless.

In the sixteenth century, there was a conceptual change in the Western world, and hence the old idea of the changelessness of the heavens was discarded. In 1543, Nicholas Copernicus (1473-1543), a Polish astronomer, published a book that contained the heliocentric theory of the universe. A freshly printed copy of this book was handed to him on his deathbed. Copernicus proved that the Sun was the centre of the universe and that all the planets including the Earth revolved around the Sun. The Christian world revolted against this theory, which aroused intense controversy. But Copernicus was no more on the Earth to be punished.

Giordano Bruno (1548-1600), an Italian philosopher, was a disciple of Copernicus. He expanded and supported the Copernican heliocentric theory. He also popularized his own theory. It was a revolutionary doctrine for that period. According to this doctrine, each star is a sun attended by a retinue of planets. This was originally the doctrine of Nicholas of Cusa (1401-1464), a German cleric. This may be presented in a nutshell.

> Infinite number of stars are spread through infinite space. Each star is really a sun; it seems to be only a faint dot of light because of its situation at enormous distance. Stars have planets that revolve around their respective star. At least some of the planets are inhabited by intelligent beings.

These notions of Nicholas were adopted by Bruno a century and a half later. At that time, no one believed the fact that there are stars too dim to see. People questioned. "Why should such invisible stars exist? Why did God create them? Is it not sacrilegious to suggest that God's creation is purposeless?" Bruno was declared to be a heretic and burned at the stake.

On November 11, 1572, Tycho Brahe (1546-1601), an astronomer of Sweden, observed a new star. He reported this in 1573 in his book *De Nova Stella* ('Concerning the New Star'). This was the first observation of the changing heavens in the Western world. Of course, the vague tale of Hipparchus' new star was considered as an ancient fable and this was dismissed since Ptolemy said nothing about it.

The word 'nova' means 'new'. But 'nova' in the title of the book of Tycho carried a new meaning. It meant 'new star'. Tycho's book was the cause of the end of a long period of Greek astronomy. The notion of the permanent and perfect heavens prevalent in the Western world for millennia was thus abandoned.

Copernicus had a notion that the planets were revolving around the Sun in circular orbits. Johannes Kepler (1571-1630), a German astronomer, proved that the planetary orbits were elliptical instead of circular.

Western astronomy laid its scientific foundation in the sixteenth and the seventeenth centuries with the discoveries of Copernicus,

Kepler and Galileo. In 1609, Galileo Galilei (1564-1642), an Italian scholar, heard about the telescope. A tube with lenses at each end, which had been invented in the Netherlands, was able to make objects appear larger and closer. After hearing this, Galileo started working on the construction of a telescope. He got success at once in making his telescope.

Galileo was the first astronomer who observed the heavenly bodies with the telescope. His observations strengthened the Copernican view of the solar system. This got him into trouble with the Inquisition. Galileo was forced to deny the Copernican view. In order to save his life he did deny his own observations, although he tenaciously held his view within himself. Of course, Galileo's open denial of the Copernican view did not help the conservative religious forces. The scientific community of Europe quickly accepted Copernicus' heliocentric picture of the solar system and Kepler's ellipses.

In the heliocentric view of Copernicus, the Sun was taken as the centre of the universe; it was thought to be at rest while the Earth and other planets revolved round it.

The heliocentric concept was in vogue until Harlow Shapley (1885-1972), an American astronomer, gave a big blow to it. He showed that the Sun was not the centre of our galaxy and that it was far on the outskirts of the galaxy. According to him, our position in our galaxy (Milky Way) and the then supposed universe was eccentric.

Our galaxy, the Milky Way, was then considered as *the* universe. Now it is known that there are innumerable galaxies. It is further known that no galaxy, no star in any galaxy, and in general no celestial body is at rest. Our Sun moves; our Milky Way moves; all galaxies move. In our present concept, the universe has no centre. We live in an acentric universe.

Early Indian Concept

To quote Carl Sagan, "*The Cosmos is all that is or ever was or ever will be*".[1] The Sanskrit word for 'universe' is '*viśva*', meaning 'all'. Thus the universe may be defined as that which includes everything. '*Jagat*' is another word in Sanskrit, used in the sense of the universe. It is derived from the Sanskrit verb root *gam* (*gam*+*kvip*), which means 'to go'. Everything in *jagat* is in motion, everything is changeable, mutable. Anything which is at rest, which is motionless and immutable is not concerned with *jagat*. There is another word '*saṁsāra*' (*sam+sṛ+ghañ*) in Sanskrit. It is also used for the universe. According to this concept, everything in the universe moves with others in harmony. It is akin to the word 'cosmos' involving order instead of disorder or chaos. *Pṛthivī* is the Sanskrit word for the planet Earth. In Indian astronomy, philosophy and literature, the concept of *Pṛthivī* was never equivalent to that of the universe.

Study of Vedic literature of ancient India reveals that a few astrophysical concepts prevalent at that time have close resemblances with those of modern science. The cosmic egg, the excessive heat produced in the cosmic egg and the bursting of the egg have been mentioned in unambiguous language.[2] After the explosion of the primordial egg, the universe expanded.[3] The stars were formed out of clouds of gases and dust.[4] The Earth had its origin from the Sun. All the planets of our solar system and the moons of the planets originated primarily from the Sun.[5] The Earth is spherical in shape.[6] The Sun, the Earth, the Moon, the other planets and the space are all spherical in shape.[7] The interior of the Earth is full of hot, molten mass.[8] The Earth and the other planets of the solar system rotate round their respective axis and revolve round the Sun.[9] It is not known how the Vedic Indians arrived at these conclusions at a time when the inhabitants of this Earth were primitive and barbarous. Whatever may be the source of their knowledge and the methodology of their investigation, their inferences are correct.

Our Solar System

Planetary Motion

The Sun with its planets constitutes the solar system. Each planet rotates about its axis and revolves round the Sun. A satellite like the moon revolves round its planet. Why does the satellite revolve round the planet? Why do the planets revolve round the Sun? Such questions have puzzled astronomers in the past. Johannes Kepler (1571-1630) declared that the planets moved in elliptical orbits with the Sun at one of the foci. Kepler, however, did not give the reason for the planetary motion. Isaac Newton (1643-1727) used Kepler pattern for finding out the cause of the planetary motion. He discovered the inverse square law of gravitation. This law is mathematically expressed as follows:

$$F = G \frac{m_1 m_2}{r^2}$$

Here, F is the force of attraction, m_1 and m_2 are the masses of the two bodies, r is the distance between the two bodies and G is the constant of gravitation. Newton could show that the planetary motion in elliptical orbits round the Sun was due to this gravitational attraction. The gravitational attraction is universal. Wherever there are masses, there is gravitation without exception.

Distances of Planets from the Sun

The average distances of the planets from the Sun are presented in Table 6.1. The average distance of the Sun from the Earth is considered as an astronomic unit. One astronomic unit is equal to 149,588,000 kilometers, or roughly 150,000,000 kilometers. By expressing the distances of the planets from the Sun in astronomic units (abbreviated A.U.), we can avoid expression by million kilometers. Secondly, we may express the distance in terms of the time taken by light to traverse. Light travels in vacuum at a velocity of 299,792.5 kilometers per second (roughly 3×10^{10} cm/sec or 300,000 km/sec). A distance of approximately 300,000 kilometers may be termed as one light-second. One light-minute, i.e., distance travelled by light in one minute, is sixty times this (300,000km $\times$ 60 = 18,000,000 km). Sixty times one light-minute, i.e., 1,080,000,000 kilometers (approximately one billion kilometers) is one light hour.

Table 6.1 : Distances of Planets from the Sun

Planet	*Average distance from the Sun*		
	Million kilometers	*Astronomic units*	*Light-hour*
Mercury	57.9	0.387	0.0535
Venus	108.2	0.723	0.1020
Earth	149.5	1.000	0.1370
Mars	227.9	1.524	0.2110
Jupiter	778.3	5.203	0.7220
Saturn	1,428.0	9.539	1.3210
Uranus	2,872.0	19.182	2.6600
Neptune	4,498.0	30.058	4.2600
Pluto	5,910.0	39.518	5.4700

It is interesting to note that the distances of the planets from the Sun maintain a regular pattern. This was first discovered in 1776 by the German astronomer Johann Daniel Titus. The same pattern was later confirmed by another German astronomer, Johann Elert Bode (1747-1826) who was not aware of Titus' discovery. This Bode-Titus relationship is a numerical rule that is presented in Table 6.2. In this Table the mean distances of the planets from the Sun are expressed in terms of the Earth's mean distance (astronomical unit taken as one).

Table 6.2 : Bode-Titus Relationship

Planet	*Mean distance from Sun (astronomical units)*
Mercury	0.4
Venus	0.4×0.3
Earth	$0.4 \times 2(0.3)$
Mars	$0.4 \times 4(0.3)$
Asteroids	$0.4 \times 8(0.3)$
Jupiter	$0.4 \times 16(0.3)$
Saturn	$0.4 \times 32(0.3)$
Uranus	$0.4 \times 64(0.3)$
Neptune	$0.4 \times 128(0.3)$

Planetary Sizes and Masses

The sizes and masses of each member of our solar system are given in Table 6.3. The mass of our Earth is six billion trillion tonnes, nearly 6×10^{24} kg. Its density is 5.52 grams per cubic centimetre.

Table 6.3: Sizes and Masses of the Sun and its Planets

	Equatorial diameter in km	*Equatorial diameter in units of Earth's dia*	*Mass in units of Earth's mass*	*Mass in tonnes*
Mercury	5,101	0.40	0.056	3.346×10^{20}
Venus	12,753	1.00	0.8	4.781×10^{21}
Earth	12,753	1.00	1.0	5.976×10^{21}
Mars	6,376	0.50	0.11	6.574×10^{20}
Jupiter	143,000	11.20	317.9	1.9×10^{24}

Saturn	121,000	9.50	95.0	5.677×10^{23}
Uranus	47,000	3.68	14.5	8.665×10^{22}
Neptune	44,600	3.50	17.0	1.016×10^{23}
Pluto	6,376	0.50	0.1	5.976×10^{20}
Sun	1,392,000	109.00	324,000	1.936×10^{27}

If the mass of the Sun is denoted by the symbol $M_{\odot}$, the mass of our Galaxy (Milky Way) is about 10^{11} $M_{\odot}$. Taking the symbol $M_{\odot}$ as the astronomical mass unit, the total amount of matter in the observable universe has been estimated to be at least 3×10^{20} $M_{\odot}$. This gives a rough idea about the relative masses of our Sun, our Galaxy and the observable universe.

Spin and Revolution of Planets

All the planets are ever in motion. Each one spins about its axis. The Sun also spins slowly on its axis—once every twenty-six Earth days. In addition to the rotation, each planet revolves round the Sun. The Earth rotates on its own axis every 23 hours 56 minutes 4.09 seconds and revolves round the Sun once in every 365.25 days. Taking the period of rotation of the Earth as one unit and its period of revolution around the Sun as one unit, the periods of rotation and revolution of the planets of the solar system are given in Table 6.4.

Table 6.4: Relative Periods of Rotation and Revolution of the Planets of the Solar System

Planet	*Period of rotation or spin*	*Period of revolution*
Mercury	59.00	0.24
Venus	243.00	0.62
Earth	1.00	1.00
Mars	1.03	1.88
Jupiter	0.41	12.00
Saturn	0.43	29.50
Uranus	0.45	84.00
Neptune	0.66	164.00
Pluto	0.27	247.00

Distances of Neighbouring Stars

Our Sun is one of the innumerable stars we see and don't see in the sky. Like our Sun some other stars have also got their planetary systems. How far is our Sun from some of its neighbouring stars has drawn the attention of astronomers. They have furnished reliable estimates of the distances of some relatively near stars. They had to devise special units for measuring such distances. Kilometer is a unit too small for astrophysical dimensions. The unit of light-year is preferred to kilometer for convenience in astrophysics. A light-year is the distance travelled by light during a period of one year. The speed of light in vacuum is 299,792.5 kilometers per second. In a year's time it travels a distance of $365 \times 24 \times 60 \times 60 \times 299{,}792.5$ km or 9,460,563,614,000 km, or 9.46×10^{12} km (9.46 trillion kilometers).

About nine and a half trillion kilometers is, for us, a staggeringly long distance. In spite of this, a light-year is too small a unit to express astronomical distances. For galactic distances, astronomers use another unit known as 'parsec'. A parsec (Parallax-second) is the distance at which a star would have a parallax of one second of arc (3600th part of a degree). One parsec is equal to 3.26 light-years or 31 trillion (1 trillion $= 1 \times 10^{12}$) kilometers. The parsec (pc) and the kiloparsec (kpc) are the units used for measurements of stellar distances in our Milky Way galaxy, while the unit mega-parsec (Mpc = a million parsec) is used to express extragalactic distances.

Table 6.5 contains the distances from us to some of the relatively near stars.

Table 6.5: Distances to Some of the Nearer Stars

Star	*trillion km*	*Distance*	
		light-years	*parsecs*
Alpha Centauri	40.58	4.29	1.32
Barnard's star	56.48	5.97	1.84
Wolf 359	73.22	7.74	2.38
Sirius	82.30	8.70	2.65
61 Cygni	105.95	11.20	3.42
Procyon	106.90	11.30	3.48
Kapteyn's star	120.14	12.70	3.87
Van Maanen's star	124.87	13.20	4.06
Altair	148.52	15.70	4.82
Vega	255.42	27.00	8.28

The star, Altair, is situated at a distance of 15.70 light-years from us. Light which reaches our eyes now from Altair source left the source 15.7 years ago. The star might have been out of existence during this time; still we continue to see it.

The Fuel Source of the Sun

The Sun has been shining since 4.6 billion years. Every moment it has been burning with the production of tremendous quantity of heat. The question is: What is that which is burning in it? Is it coal or oil? What is the nature of this fuel? Had it been coal, the Sun would have been dead ash in 1,500 years after its birth. Thus the question of chemical burning in the Sun is ruled out. In 1854, the German physicist Hermann L.F. von Helmholtz (1821-1894) thought that it was the energy that came from the contraction of the Sun itself. But this could not be correct, since at the present level of the Sun's energy output it would take only 9.25 million years for its present size to shrink to zero volume.

Radioactivity was known towards the last part of the 19th century. In 1896, the French physicist Antoine-Henri Becquerel (1852-1908) discovered the disintegration of the atoms of uranium into other, smaller atoms at a very slow but quite steady rate. This was what we later called radioactivity. In 1901, it was shown by Pierre Curie (1859-1906), another French physicist, that small quantity of heat was produced in the process of radioactivity. In 1906, Ernest Rutherford (1871-1937), the New-Zealand-born physicist, showed that atom was composed of subatomic particles, viz., protons, neutrons and electrons, and that energy was released from the atomic nucleus that underwent changes during radioactivity.

Scientists were still puzzled about the source of solar energy. The law of conservation of energy was worked out in 1847 by Helmholtz. According to this law, energy cannot be created or destroyed but can only be transformed. This law must hold good for the Sun or any other star. Scientists started asking the questions: "Does the Sun shine because of nuclear energy? Is the Sun a huge ball of uranium or thorium? Experimental evidence obtained in the 1900s did not help to answer these questions positively. From the studies of solar spectrum, it was known that the Sun contained uranium and thorium in traces only. Hence it could not be proved that nuclear energy was the source of the solar energy.

In 1915, William Draper Harkins (1873-1951), an American chemist, could give theoretical explanation for the generation of nuclear energy through processes other than radioactivity. That nuclear energy can be liberated due to nuclear rearrangement was his discovery. He pointed out that four hydrogen nuclei, when fused to form one helium nucleus, can yield unusually high quantities of energy. He suggested that this hydrogen-fusion was the source of the solar energy.

Hydrogen-fusion does not take place at ordinary temperatures. It requires enormously high temperatures. Even the temperature at the glowing surface of the Sun is not enough for hydrogen nuclei to fuse into helium nucleus.

In the 1920s, Eddington was trying to know why the Sun had not already collapsed and contracted into a tiny sphere under the pull of its own gravity. He estimated the temperature at the central core of the Sun to be 15 million degrees Centigrade. He suggested that this heat generated in the core of the Sun was the force that could keep it expanded against its gravity.

In 1929, the American astronomer Norris Russell (1877-1957) analysed the solar spectrum and found out the constitution of the Sun in greater detail. About one per cent of the mass of the Sun was made of complex atoms. Of the remaining 99 per cent, about 75 per cent of it was hydrogen and 25 per cent helium.

In 1938, the German-American physicist Hans Albrecht Bethe (1906–) confirmed the suggestion of Harkins that solar energy was derived from nuclear energy due to the fusion of four nuclei of hydrogen into one nucleus of helium. To arrive at this conclusion, Bethe took into account the Sun's composition and its central temperature. Hydrogen-fusion takes place at enormously high temperature available at the core of the Sun.

What has been described here to explain the mechanism of the heat production of the Sun holds equally good for other stars.

Death of the Sun

Since 4.6 billion years the Sun has been pouring out energy into space at enormous rate. Eon after eon, year after year, moment after moment, the Sun has been losing energy. How long will this process continue? Will it continue for ever? It is not possible.

When one helium nucleus is formed as a result of fusion of four nuclei of hydrogen, it involves 0.71 per cent loss of mass. This mass which is lost is converted into energy. Every second 588 billion kilograms of hydrogen is converted into helium in order that the Sun radiates energy at the present rate. This quantity of hydrogen represents three quintillionths (3×10^{-18}) of the mass of the Sun. If this is the case, how can we suppose that the Sun will continue to shine for ever? Helmholtz was the first to realize this. He argued: The energy of the Sun has to come from somewhere and the supply shall have to be totally consumed some day, whatever may be the source of the energy supply.

Thus we come to the conclusion that one day the Sun's energy-source will be fully exhausted. If it is assumed that the Sun started its life as a ball of pure hydrogen, one-twentieth of its hydrogen could have been consumed by the 4.6 billion years of its existence at the present rate of hydrogen-fusion. This estimate enables us to predict the remaining life of the Sun, which is about eighty-seven eons (1 eon$=1 \times 10^9$ years).

Of course, the Sun did not begin as a ball of pure hydrogen. Firstly, the big bang formed a universe that contained appreciable quantity of helium to begin with. Secondly, the Sun was formed ten eons after the big bang, and by that time some more quantities of helium was formed. The newly born Sun contained 80 per cent hydrogen and 20 per cent helium. The present percentages of hydrogen and helium in the Sun are 75 and 25, respectively. If the present stock of hydrogen were to be consumed at the present rate till all of it exhausted, the Sun would continue to shine for sixty-eight eons more.

Even this estimate of sixty eight eons is not likely to be correct. The future life of the Sun will depend upon the nature of the thermonuclear reactions at its core. As hydrogen-fusion continues, the Sun's core becomes richer in helium in comparison with its body. As a result, the core, becoming denser and denser, contracts and becomes hotter and hotter. Elevation of the core temperature to still higher levels will force helium to fuse into more massive forms of matter. The excessive quantity of heat thus produced will force the Sun to expand enormously.

The Sun will expand a million times its present volume. The expanded Sun will have a much larger surface. The surface will cool down to a mere red heat. However, the total radiation given off by the larger surface of the expanded Sun will be enormous. At this stage, the Sun will be called a 'red giant' just like the ones, viz., Betelgeuse, Antares and Mira, that have already been detected.

The expanded red-giant Sun will devour and destroy the Earth. The Earth can remain as a habitable planet only when the Sun is on the main sequence, i.e., during the time when hydrogen-fusion is the chief source of energy. The Sun is about middle-aged. It will continue to shine five or six billion years more.

Cosmology and Cosmogony in Science

Newtonian Static Universe

In the Newtonian concept of the universe, space and time were absolute and the universe was static. Both space and time were beginningless and endless. Space was the receptacle of matter and energy. Time was the playground where events occurred.

The Newtonian universe was based on the laws of motion and the laws of gravitation. Of course, the Newtonian static model of the universe could not explain the functioning of these laws satisfactorily. If it was supposed that all the constituents of the universe were held at rest at any starting moment, it could not explain the gravitational phenomenon. Due to the gravitational force, every constituent of the universe would attract every other constituent, resulting in the movement of all constituents towards one another. This would violate the concept of the static model of the universe. If some initial explosion could be conceived of, all the constituents of the universe would fly away from one another. In that case, it would be a receding universe for all times to come. There is an alternative to the eternal recession of the constituents of the universe. The receding universe would stop moving away, come to a momentary rest and then would start contracting. Both these probabilities contravene the concept of a static universe. But, in spite of these self-contradictions inherent in the Newtonian static model, most astronomers of the nineteenth century and those of the early twentieth century believed in a static universe.

Einstein's Static Universe

Einstein also believed that the universe *as a whole* was static. But, in spite of his belief, his gravitational theory, like Newton's, failed to explain such a model. To get rid of this difficulty, Einstein conceived of a force of repulsion, which was opposite to the force of gravitation. He introduced 'λ-term' into his equation to describe this repulsive force. The force of repulsion could counteract the force of gravitation, thus holding the universe in a static condition. In 1917, Einstein proposed his cosmological model from the point of view of general relativity. 'Einstein' universe is finite in volume but unbounded. It presents a static, timeless view of the universe.

Big Bang Model of Lemaître and Eddington

The notion of an expanding universe from zero volume was first given in 1922 by the Russian mathematician Alexander Alexandrovich Friedmann (1888-1925). He died soon afterwards and could not develop it further. The Belgian mathematician Abbé Georges Edouard Lemaître (1894-1966) independently advanced similar notion in 1927. This had been done even before Hubble announced his law. Lemaître suggested that in the far distant past the universe had all its mass compressed into a small volume which was named by him as 'cosmic egg'. This egg had tremendous density and internal pressure, as a result of which it exploded in an enormous cataclysmic outburst. The energy locked up within the cosmic egg was suddenly released consequent to the explosion. Later, particles interacted in space and condensed to form stars of galaxies, planets of stars and satellites of planets.

Abbé Lemaître and Sir Arthur Eddington (1882-1944) jointly gave this model. The Russia-born American physicist George Gamow (1904-1968) gave the name 'big bang' to the explosion of the cosmic egg. Thus this model is popular as the big bang model. In this model, the universe starts with a big bang, slows down for a period and then expands to infinity.

Hubble's Observation of the Expanding Universe

In 1842, Christian Johann Doppler (1803-1853), an Austrian physicist, showed a peculiar behaviour of the pitch of sound. When the source of sound recedes relative to the observer, the pitch is lowered; when the source approaches relative to the observer, the pitch is raised.

In this respect, what is true for sound is also true for light, which is also a wave phenomenon. Armand H.L. Fizeau (1819-1896), a French physicist, worked on light and proved, in 1848 the same truth about light, viz., when a source of light recedes from an observer, the light emitted by it is shifted towards the long-wave red; when it approaches the observer, the light it emits is shifted towards the short-wave violet.

The Doppler effect works at any distance. Hence it is reasonable to expect that it should work with a star. In 1868, the English astronomer William Huggins (1824-1910) could observe a distinct, although small, red shift in the spectral lines of the star Sirius.

Vesto Melvin Slipher (1875-1969), an American astronomer, observed the spectral lines of light coming from other galaxies. In 1912, he declared that the Andromeda galaxy was approaching our solar system at the speed of about 200 kilometers per second. He studied the spectra of other galaxies and noted to his surprise that all but two of the galaxies he studied were receding from us.

Studies of spectra of light coming from stars and galaxies were continued by other American astronomers, viz., Edwin Powell Hubble (1889-1953) and Milton La Salle Humason (1891-1972). They found that galaxies were receding. The dimmer the galaxies, the faster were they receding.

Hubble's law was announced in 1929. This law states: The rate of recession is proportional to the distance of a galaxy from us. Hubble, by working with the 100-inch telescope at Mt. Wilson in Southern California, observed the expanding universe during the period from 1928 to 1931. He observed 'red-shift' of light coming from distant galaxies. The entire spectrum, including the continuum and the absorption lines, was observed to shift towards the long-wavelength end. This phenomenon was named as 'red-shift' since the shifting was towards the red end. The magnitude of shifting was directly proportional to the distances of the galaxies. Hubble could take the help of the Doppler effect to explain the phenomenon of red-shift and propounded the theory of the expanding universe. The space in which the galaxies are embedded is itself expanding. All the galaxies of the universe move away from one another.

Einstein's general theory of relativity predicted that such an expansion would take place. According to this theory, gravity stretches or distorts space and time. The Sun stretches space; the stars stretch space; and so do the galaxies. As the galaxies move apart, the intergalactic space is stretched or inflated. Thus, with the expansion of the galaxies, more and more space is simultaneously created. By this process, the universe expands into the expanding space instead of into the so-called external void.

Gamow's Big Bang

The explosion of the primordial egg or the cosmic egg was given the name 'big bang' by George Gamow. Opinions differ regarding the exact time when the big bang explosion took place. By measuring the temperature, the luminosity and the mass of certain stars, astronomers have arrived at an estimate of sixteen to eighteen billion ($10^9=1$ billion) years. A second technique involves the expansion theory. The galaxies have been receding away from one another since the big bang. By using the rate of recession and the present positions of the galaxies, an estimate ranging between ten and twenty billion years has been made. Even a larger range of the age of the universe has been estimated by measurement of the presence of radioactive elements in meteorites. Most astronomers have now tentatively accepted that the big bang took place fifteen billion years ago. Some other astronomers have presented evidence that favours nine-eon (1 eon = 1 billion years) age of the universe. A third opinion is in favour of an age longer than fifteen eons. Until more reliable evidences are obtained, it may be wise to stick to the age of fifteen eons. Thus time began fifteen eons ago. At $t=0$, the universe exploded into existence. Prior to this, there was no space, no time, no universe, no observers, no object to be observed, no subject to observe, no physical laws to be observed.

Scientists use the word 'singularity' to describe the primordial state of the universe. Only the 'singularity' existed without space and time, without particles and antiparticles; there was no becoming at all.

The cosmic egg was shrunken to 'singularity'. It was not an 'egg' surrounded by a void; it was not an egg that floated in infinite space. There was no space before the explosion of the cosmic egg. Einstein holds that space and time are finite and that both had beginning. According to this concept, neither space nor time can be extended back through the initial singularity. Both time and space began at the big bang.

The present hyperspherical cosmos of Einstein has neither

centre nor edge. He imagines this hypersphere shrivelling away to nothing. As one can imagine the surface of a sphere being shrunk to zero radius, so does Einstein make a mental picture of the volume of the cosmic hypersphere vanishing. This primordial state of the universe, otherwise called the cosmic egg, had zero radius. Physicists call such a boundary a 'singularity'.

The 'standard big bang model' of the universe is now accepted by most scientists. According to this model, everything of the universe was confined within the cosmic egg which was a singularity. Everything was concentrated into a superhot and superdense primordial matter soup. The cosmic egg suddenly exploded and the matter soup rapidly expanded.

What was the primal substance present in the primordial egg? Gamow postulated that this primal substance was 'Ylem', a word coined by him to denote a substance of compressed or fused neutrons. This 'Ylem' of Gamow was known as 'neutronium' in scientific circles. According to the suggestion of Gamow, neutrons appeared from Ylem after the cosmic explosion; the neutron split into electron and proton; and electron and proton formed hydrogen atom.

Gamow is credited for his substantial contribution to the big bang cosmological model. But his concept of Ylem or neutronium did not prove to be exactly true. There was nothing like Ylem or neutronium, and hence there was no occasion of the generation of neutron from neutronium. At about one-hundredth of a second after the big bang explosion, the temperature of the universe was about 10^{11} degrees Centigrade. At this high temperature, it was not possible to hold together the components of molecules, atoms, atomic nuclei or even protons and electrons bound together in the form of neutrons. Light or photon particles formed the dominant constituent of the universe at this time. George Gamow could visualize the early universe to be largely made of high-intensity radiation rather than matter. Of course, the present state of the universe is matter-dominated. In the early universe, whatever matter was present was made of electrons, positrons and neutrinos. Electrons and anti-electrons (positrons) were present in large numbers in almost equal quantities. There were also roughly similar numbers of various kinds of neutrinos. These particles—photons, neutrinos, electrons and positrons—were continually being created out of pure energy and, after short lives, were annihilated again.

Gamow's prediction about the radiation of the early universe and the residual background radiation still existing in the present universe has come out to be true. In the 1940s, he pointed out that immediately after the big bang explosion, the tiny and unimaginably hot universe must have emitted radiation that was extremely short-wave and energetic. With the expansion and consequent cooling of the universe, the radiation would grow steadily long-wave. This radiation would be of microwave length in the present universe in consideration of its expansion and consequent cooling from zero time to the present.

The reduction in the intensity of radiation was not strictly proportional to the rate of expansion of the universe. With the expansion of the universe, the intensity of radiation was reduced much more rapidly in relation to the reduction in the density of matter, and hence is the present state of the universe. In 1949, Gamow could predict the present existence of a very faint background of radiation as the relic of the big bang. He put forward his thesis that the initial radiation released after the big bang should have by now simmered down to the level of radio waves spread evenly through space.

Was Gamow's prediction correct? Astronomers wanted to verify it. They were anxiously waiting for the detection of a dim background of microwave radiation in all directions equally. At that time, astronomers had no instruments capable of such a detection. But the techniques of radio astronomy rapidly developed and experimental verification of Gamow's prediction was done in the mid-sixties of the twentieth century.

In 1965, Arno A. Penzias (1933-) and Robert W. Wilson (1936-), two American physicists at Bell Telephone Laboratories, published a paper in the *Astrophysical Journal* with the title 'A Measurement of Excess Antennae Temperature at 4080 MHz'. It had a companion paper in which the American astrophysicists Robert H. Dicke, P.J.E. Peebles, Peter G. Roll and David T. Wilkinson gave an explanation of the importance of such measurements for cosmology. Penzias and Wilson could detect a weak background radio signal that came equally from all directions in space at a wavelength of 7.35 centimeters. For doing this, they used the large radio horn antenna at Holmdel,

New Jersey. They couldn't explain their finding and hence sought the help of Dicke and his colleagues who were working at Princeton. The Princeton group was building a special radio telescope to look for the residual background thermal radiation. Dicke was busy in the experimental verification of George Gamow's prediction. If the universe had evolved from a fireball state with a temperature of 100 billion degrees or more, the very intense, high-frequency (short wavelength) gamma radiation would still be present in an enormously red-shifted form, due to the expansion of the universe. This was the prediction of George Gamow in the late 1940s and it was also the prediction of Dicke and his colleagues in 1965. The finding of Penzias and Wilson could be appropriately explained by Dicke and his colleagues in the companion paper published in the *Astrophysical Journal.* Calculations could show that the expansion of the universe increased the wavelength of the initial hot radiation by about a factor of 1,500. The thermal radiation that filled the universe initially had short wavelength; that has been red-shifted owing to the expansion of the universe; what Penzias and Wilson discovered is the homogeneous, isotropic background microwave radiation which is the altered form of the initial gamma radiation. With this discovery of Penzias and Wilson, the big bang model of the universe was finally accepted by the scientific community as a fact rather than fiction.

Standard Big Bang Model

We do not know the temperature of the 'cosmic egg' before the big bang explosion. We are not sure just how high the temperature of the universe was at the moment of the big bang. The initial universe was superheated; it was homogeneously hot; it was in a state of thermal equilibrium. At ten-thousandth of a second before the zero moment, the universe was hotter than one trillion degree Kelvin (the absolute or Kelvin degree is the same as the centigrade degree, but the zero of Kelvin scale is 273° below 0°C). At still earlier period, the universe must have been too hot for protons and neutrons to exist. If protons and neutrons were placed in such superheated condition, they would be torn apart into their constituent particles, viz., quarks and antiquarks. At very high temperatures unfavourable to the existence of protons and neutrons, and still favourable to the existence of matter, quarks and antiquarks were in equilibrium with the very hot protons, electrons, positrons, neutrinos and antineutrinos.

According to the 'standard big bang model', the temperature of the primordial soup was one hundred billion degrees Kelvin at the first one-hundredth of a second after the big bang explosion. At this time, the soup consisted mostly of photons, electrons, positrons, neutrinos and antineutrinos. In the radiation-dominated early universe, these particles were continually being created and annihilated. In addition to these particles, the soup contained a tiny contamination of protons and neutrons. Of course, at the first millionth of a second, this contamination did not exist. The soup, in the first millionth of a second, consisted of leptons, quarks and gluons, that were interacting with one another. At still higher temperature and earlier times there might have been transmutation of the quarks and leptons. At the highest temperature and earliest time, the universe had perfect symmetry. The creation of asymmetry of the universe took place at the first one-hundredth of a second after the big bang.

After the first tenth of a second, the universe cooled down to about ten billion degrees Kelvin. At this temperature, all that remained was electrons, neutrinos and photons.

During the first three seconds after the explosion, temperature dropped from one trillion degrees to about five billion degrees. It was a short period of rapid cooling. During this period, the muons and antimuons annihilated themselves and the electron-positron pairs began to annihilate. The universe was still dominated by intense radiation. It consisted of almost entirely photons (gamma radiation), neutrinos and antineutrinos, with a trace of electrons, neutrons and protons. Most of the neutrons changed to protons, resulting in a neutron-proton ratio of 1 : 5. The electrons that were present were released from the neutrons that changed into protons. The protons and electrons were equal in number at this time.

During three minutes after the big bang explosion, the universe cooled off to a temperature of about one billion degrees. At this temperature, neutrons began to fuse with protons to form helium and possibly elements like lithium, beryllium and boron. At the end of three minutes or some more, the universe consisted by weight of 25 per cent ionized helium (alpha particles) and 75 per cent ionized hydrogen (free protons and electrons) with some traces of deuterium, lithium, beryllium, boron, and possibly carbon. With further expansion of the universe and consequent reduction of temperature below one billion degrees, there was beginning of shifting of dominance of radiation to that of matter. The temperature dropped to a few thousand degrees after about a billion years, when the universe became matter-dominated instead of radiation-dominated. Formation of atoms took place at this time. The free protons and alpha particles (helium nuclei) combined with free electrons to form hydrogen and helium, respectively. The first stars, otherwise called population-II stars, were formed from these primordial hydrogen and helium.

Formation of heavy elements such as carbon, oxygen, neon, sodium, etc. did not materialize appreciably during the early life of the universe. In order to build up heavy elements from hydrogen, very high temperature is necessary, and this was available in the early universe. But a long time is necessary so that heavy elements are formed from hydrogen by thermonuclear fusion.

There had been no such time since the high-temperature phase of the early universe was over in a matter of hours. Alternatively, carbon build up would have been possible in the early universe if the concentration of helium were incredibly high. It was not so and hence carbon build up took place when the stars were formed. For a billion years or more, the deep interiors of the stars had very high temperatures and high density that were conducive to the thermonuclear fusion of helium into carbon via the triple alpha process.

Steady-State Universe

An alternative to the big bang model of the universe was put forward in 1948 by three astronomers, viz., Herman Bondi, Thomas Gold and Fred Hoyle. Their model is known as the steady-state model.

Einstein's 'cosmological principle' states: The universe in the large looks the same to all observers no matter where they are and in what direction they are looking. According to this principle, the universe is homogeneous and isotropic *at a given cosmic time*. With change in time, there may be change in the universe, and this is allowed by the cosmological principle.

In 1948, Herman Bondi and Thomas Gold proposed the steady-state model of the universe. They modified the concept of the cosmological principle and said that the universe remains the same at all cosmic times. They imagined uniformity of structure of the universe not only in space but also in time. This was named by them as the 'perfect cosmological principle' (PCP). Such an unchanging universe is called the 'steady-state universe'.

The model of the steady-state universe was criticized by many scientists. It is an observed fact that the universe expands, that the galaxies move away from one another and that the volume of the universe ever increases due to expansion of space. Accepting the expanding universe as an observational truth, one is bound to conclude that the material density of the universe would gradually fall with progress of time. Thus the steady-state theory is refuted.

The perfect cosmological principle can be saved by assuming the continuous creation of matter, thereby making up for the depletion produced by the expansion. The critics questioned about the source of the continuous creation of matter. Does it not mean that the law of conservation of matter and energy is violated if *de novo* creation of matter out of nothing is accepted as a fact? Bondi and Gold could not answer to the critics' question.

Fred Hoyle, a British astronomer, made an attempt to substantiate the steady-state model by adding a term to Einstein's gravitational field equation. Hoyle's 'perfect cosmological principle' states that the universe looks the same at all times—past, present and future. He imagined a reservoir of negative energy. He called it C-field. This C-field was supposed to have no mass, no charge and no spin. Whenever a particle with certain energy is created, a C-field of equal but negative energy is also created, thereby conserving the overall energy. Hoyle says that matter is being created continuously, although at a very slow rate, to compensate the loss of density of the universe owing to the expansion.

Hoyle's concept of C-field is to be critically analysed. Is it a fact or is it a fiction created for overcoming the difficulty? Nobody has experimentally detected the existence of C-field. There is also no theoretical indispensability for postulating a negative reservoir like this. In such a situation there is need for conceptual analysis of the negative reservoir. Conceptually, a reservoir is always positive unless it is totally empty. The water-content of a water-reservoir is always a positive quantity unless the reservoir is completely dried up. A dry reservoir is a big receptacle and should not be called a reservoir. A reservoir reserves something and that something is positive. A positive quantity, howsoever big it may be, is bound to be zero some time, if positive quantity is continuously deducted from it. However, this is not the case with negative quantity. When positive quantities are deducted from the negative quantities, we never get zero even if infinite number of deductions are made. Hoyle has taken advantage of this principle of mathematics of deducting positive quantities from a negative quantity. But closer scrutiny reveals that this is untenable in the present case. There can never be creation out of non-existence. An example may be taken here to clarify the point. A person X has got minus one hundred rupees. If he lends to others, he can lend any amount, to any number of persons and any number of times without rendering his account zero. If he lends one thousand rupees, his own account will be minus rupees one thousand and one hundred. He may go on lending to any number of persons, but his account will never be zero. But the question may be asked here: Can X lend rupees if there is no rupee anywhere? Rupee is a positive thing. There is no entity like negative rupee. When we say "X has got minus one hundred rupees", we mean thereby that this 'minus' is a relative term with reference to X. He has borrowed Rs. 100.00 from Y. He will further borrow Rs. 1,000.00 from Z in order to lend. But the fact remains that the rupee is somewhere. Hence, the concept of the continuous creation of matter out of a negative reservoir or C-field, as postulated by Hoyle, is erroneous conceptually.

In the controversy of evolving versus steady-state universe, most astronomers (if not all) have made their opinion in favour of the former. They have got enough evidence to justify the acceptance of the former and the rejection of the latter.

It has been known from counts of galaxies by optical telescope and detection of radio signals emitted by radio galaxies through radio telescopes that the concentration of galaxies was greater a few billion years ago than it is now. It is deduced from such observations that the universe is not in a steady-state but is evolving. With the continual expansion of the universe, matter in it is thinning out. The volume of the universe goes on increasing with its age; no new matter is created to keep the density of the universe constant; hence the density falls.

A third type of evidence has been obtained from quasars (quasi-stellar object or QSO). These objects were discovered quite accidentally in the early 1960's. On photographic plates, they look like ordinary stars, but they differ in a number of ways. They are powerful sources of radio waves. They emit ultraviolet and infrared radiation. They have exceedingly large red-shifts, from which it is concluded that they are farther away than the most distant galaxies known. By application of Hubble's law (the greater the red-shift, the greater the distance), the distances of some quasars may be estimated even up to ten billion light-years. From this it must be concluded that the quasars present a very early stage in the evolution of the universe (somewhere between four to seven billion years ago). Quasar-counts show quite conclusively that the universe was much more compact in the past than it is now.

The evidence from the cosmic background radiation, obtained in 1965 by Arno A. Penzias and Robert W. Wilson, strongly supports the evolving model of the universe and rejects the steady-state model.

Oscillating or Pulsating Universe

The universe has been expanding since the big bang explosion. It is still expanding, although the present rate of expansion is less than what it was in the beginning. The kinetic energy of the big bang is the driving force for this expansion. The retardation in the rate of expansion is brought about by the gravitational force of the total matter of the universe. Thus the kinetic energy of the original explosion is pushing the universe outward and gravity is pulling it inward. So far the former is greater than the latter and hence the universe is expanding.

How long will the universe continue to expand? Will it expand *ad infinitum* or will it halt at some time? This question has been puzzling astronomers for many decades.

If the deceleration of the expansion of the universe, brought about by gravity, is strong enough, the expansion will be brought to a halt; otherwise it will go on expanding for ever. An example may be taken here for illustration. If an object is shot into space from the Earth at a speed greater than its speed of escape, it will never return to the Earth, even though its speed decreases constantly as it moves away. On the other hand, it will rise to a certain height and then fall back to the Earth if its speed is less than its speed of escape. What is described here applies to the whole universe. If the galaxies or clusters of galaxies are rushing away from one another with speed larger than the speed of escape, the universe is open and infinite and will go on expanding for ever. If the reverse is true, the universe is closed and finite and will stop expanding some day.

The American astronomer Allan R. Sandage, among others, has determined the deceleration parameter. This is a number which expresses the rate at which the Hubble constant is decreasing. Measurement of the deceleration parameter, done by Sandage, provides evidence to show that the galaxies are receding at speeds less than the speed of escape. From this it is concluded that the expansion of the universe must ultimately stop. This means that the universe is closed and finite.

Astro-physicists have been concerned with another related question. What should be the average density of matter in the universe so that the observed value of Hubble's constant may be explained and the halting of the expansion of the universe may be justified? It has been calculated that the average density of matter in the universe should be, for this purpose, equal to or larger than one gram of matter spread uniformly throughout a cube each of whose dimensions is about 35,000 kilometers. The universe will halt its expansion and start contraction if it has got an average density like this. The actual measurement of density of the mass of the universe has been made, basing on the known number of stars and the estimated matter between the stars. This is 100 times smaller than what it should be. How is this to be interpreted? The observed value of the deceleration shows that the universe will halt its expansion some day. In order that it would happen, the density of matter in the universe should be about 100 times greater than that deduced from the presently known amount of matter in the observable universe. It is concluded from this that there must be some 'missing matter'. Physicists have been searching for this missing matter. So far they have been unsuccessful. Some scientists believe that the 'missing matter' may be present as neutrinos, black holes and gravity waves.

The rate of expansion of the universe is steadily falling. The universe will one day come to a halt. But it will not remain static in that position. The gravitating power of the universe will not allow it to remain in a static condition, and hence it will start to contract. At first the contraction will be slow, and then will accelerate over billions of years. Galaxies that fly away at present will rush towards one another at that time. The rate of contraction will accelerate with passage of time. The universe will fall back on itself in a monstrous cataclysm known as the 'big crunch'.

We may try to visualize the condition of the universe when it shrinks to one hundredth its present size. The compression effects will elevate the temperature to the boiling point of water. The galaxies will lose their individuality by merging with one another. There will be no intergalactic space.

When the universe shrinks further, the temperature will be raised to still higher level. The sky will glow like a furnace. The stars will boil and then explode.

Shrinkage will be still more quickened. Temperature will be still higher. All structures will be vapourized. Molecules will break up and atoms will be dispersed. In a few hundred thousand years from this time, there will be no atoms. Atoms will disintegrate in the escalating temperatures and their nuclei will be smashed to pieces. As the volume of the universe becomes smaller and smaller, gravity becomes greater and greater, temperature becomes higher and higher; consequently, the pace of cosmic contraction is hastened into an uncontrolled implosion. This is the 'big crunch'.

A few microseconds before the death of the universe, nuclear particles break apart into quarks. For a fleeting instant, subnuclear particles are smashed to still smaller particles, and there is a dynamic state of flux of whatever forms of entities exist at that time. Finally, in a twinkling of an eye, the entire universe shrivels into less than the space of an atom. This is what the physicists call 'singularity', whereupon space-time itself disintegrates. The big crunch is just the reverse of the big bang.

The highly compressed cosmos implodes to oblivion at a space time singularity. Is this the total annihilation? Nothing will be left. No space, no time, no things. All space, time and matter came into existence in a big bang; they will go out of existence in a big crunch. There is a final 'singularity'. Nobody knows whether this 'singularity' is a positivity or an absolute negativity. All existence vanishes; nothing is left; there is no space, no time, no matter, no energy, no universe.

Scientists are human beings first and scientists next. Many of them are not prepared for the sad demise of the universe which they love so much. "The universe came into existence out of nothing in a big bang; it will go out of existence and will be nothing in a big crunch." The logic of this 'nothing-something-nothing' concept is not convincing for many scientists. They believe that unknown physical forces will cause the big crunch to halt at some fantastic density, whence the universe will 'bounce' back to come out again. Thereafter it will embark on a new cycle of expansion and contraction. The cycles of expansion and contraction will be repeated *ad infinitum*. This is the concept of the oscillating universe. In 1956, Allan R. Sandage suggested a period of 82 billion years for each oscillation. Many astronomers, notably W.B. Bonner of England, agree that the universe has gone through an unending series of such oscillating cycles.

Birth of Galaxies and Stars

The universe was born in the big bang some fifteen billion years ago. In the beginning, its volume was unimaginably tiny and its temperature was inestimably high.

The newly born universe rapidly expanded and cooled. First, it consisted of photons, quarks, electrons and neutrinos. Protons and neutrons were formed later. As the expansion and cooling of the universe continued further, hydrogen and helium nuclei were formed. All these processes took place within a few minutes. Our baby universe was chemically predominated by nuclei of hydrogen and helium gases.

Further expansion of the universe took place. In about 700,000 years, the temperature drop was just enough for the formation of hydrogen and helium atoms. Negatively charged electrons were aligned to positively charged protons by means of electromagnetic forces and thus atoms were formed. With lowering of temperature, hydrogen atoms combined to form hydrogen molecules.

Formation of Galaxies

With the expansion of the universe, hydrogen and helium gases diffused in all directions. In this way, we could have got a universe with a thin and uniform cloud of hydrogen and helium gases. As the universe expanded, the density of the gases could have been less and less without affecting the homogeneity.

But the density of the cloud did not remain uniform. The homogeneity of the gas-mixture was disturbed. There were random fluctuations in the gas-cloud with consequent turbulence, certain regions of slowly rotating gas-clouds of greater than normal density were formed and these regions were separated by regions of gas-clouds of less than normal density.

The gas-clouds of high-density regions developed gravitational field of higher intensity. This gravity prevented the spreading out of the randomly moving atoms. Rather it could capture atoms from the low-density regions. By this process, rotating clusters of gas-clouds were formed in different regions of space and each cluster was separated by near-vacuum regions.

Each vast gas-cloud, thus formed, was a protogalaxy. Within each protogalaxy, further heterogeneity developed due to random movement of atoms. As a result, billions of smaller gas clouds were formed within a protogalaxy. Each protogalaxy rotated and each smaller component of the protogalaxy rotated.

Each gas-cloud had its own gravitational field. It contracted under the influence of this gravity. The contracting gas-cloud became steadily denser and denser; its gravitational field became more and more intense, thus the rate of contraction of the gas-cloud quickened.

The pressure and temperature at the centre of each gas-cloud increased. The gas-cloud became hot enough to radiate light. Its pressure and temperature at its core became high enough to initiate nuclear fusion. At this stage, each gas-cloud became a star and the protogalaxy with a huge number of stars formed a vast star-group called a galaxy. It took about a billion years after the big bang for the galaxies to form.

All galaxies are not similar in shape and size. Following the classification of Hubble, astronomers have divided the galaxies into four categories, viz., ellipticals, normal spirals, barred spirals and irregulars. The elliptical galaxies have symmetrical structures. They are devoid of dust and spiral arms. They are spherical or ellipsoidal in shape. The stars in them are red or yellow. They do not contain blue or blue-white stars. A spiral galaxy is a flattened, disc-like structure. Its core is luminous, reddish and bulging. Generally two well-defined spiral arms emerge from this core. Each spiral arm contains dust and very luminous blue-white stars. It spirals the core once or twice. A barred spiral galaxy has a small luminous core. In some cases, the core has a small spiral structure. The galaxy has a long bar that cuts right across the core. There are two spiral arms—one from each end of the bar. These arms encircle the galaxy. As the name indicates, the irregular galaxies have no definite shape. They are aggregates of dust, gas and stars distributed without any definite pattern.

Our solar system is situated in the Milky Way galaxy. It is a spiral galaxy. It has a concentrated core in which the very oldest stars are situated. Three spiral arms originate from the core. Young and middle aged stars are situated in the spiral arms. The diameter of the core is about 30,000 light-years. The thickness of the core at its centre is about 15,000 light-years. The concentration of stars in the core is 100,000 to one million times greater than in the spiral arms. Each spiral arm is about 1,000 light-years thick (the dimension perpendicular to the galactic disc) and 3,000 to 4,000 light-years wide (the dimension in the plane of the galaxy measured radially). The intervening space between any two spiral arms is few thousand light-years wide. The distance between neighbouring stars in the arms is about 4 to 5 light-years. The core is free from dust whereas the arms contain dust in the interstellar space. The presence of this dust in the spiral arm obscures the centre of the galaxy from direct view. The gases (hydrogen and helium) and the dust (ice particles, large organic molecules, and the like) present in the spiral arms are the raw materials from which new stars are born.

The three spiral arms of our Milky Way galaxy are named. They are the Orion arm, the Sagittarius arm and the Perseus arm. They are named so for the location of the constellation Orion, Sagittarius and Perseus in the respective arms. The Sagittarius arm is the closest to the core of the galaxy. The Perseus arm is the outermost. The Orion arm is situated in the middle between the other two spiral arms. Our solar system is located in the inner edge of the Orion arm. The Milky Way galaxy consisting of the core and the three spiral arms has a diameter of about 80,000 light-years. It contains about 300 billion (3×10^{11}) stars. The stars located at the core of the galaxy are 8 to 9 billion years old. The stars located in the spiral arms are a few million years old. The core of the galaxy is surrounded by a halo of globular clusters. Each globular cluster contains 100,000 to one million stars. The stars in the globular clusters are very old like the ones in the core.

We do not exactly know how many galaxies are there in the universe. It is estimated from the visible universe that there may be about 100 billion (1×10^{11}) galaxies.

Formation of Stars

The galaxies, in the beginning, were composed of hydrogen and helium (mostly hydrogen). The stars that formed out of gas-clouds made of hydrogen/helium are 'first-generation stars'. They are small and quiet. They can remain on the main sequence (period for the hydrogen-fuel to be used up) for fourteen billion years. When they collapse after the nuclear fuel is exhausted, they do so relatively quietly to be converted into white dwarfs. There are galaxies in which virtually all the stars are of first generation. They have very little dust and gas-clouds left. During their protogalaxy period, the distribution of gas-clouds in them was even and the gas-clouds themselves were of relatively uniform size.

Stars that are formed out of interstellar clouds with appreciable content of massive atoms are 'second-generation stars'. They are made of mainly hydrogen/helium. Nevertheless, a small but a measurable component of their structure has come from the core of other stars that are already dead and gone or are no longer on the main sequence.

In some galaxies, including our own Milky Way, the clouds of gas were uneven in size due to some reason or the other. The larger clouds developed more intense gravitational field and hence condensed more quickly. The smaller clouds took more time to condense. More massive stars were formed out of the larger clouds whereas less massive stars were formed out of the smaller clouds. The more massive stars are short-lived and explode as supernovas.

In the supernova explosion, material formed inside the massive star is thrown into space. That mixes with gas-clouds that have not yet condensed into stars. This injection of supernova debris into gas-clouds serves two functions. Firstly, the energetic supernova particles, by mixing with gas-clouds, would have heating effect. The gas-clouds would thereby be hotter and their atoms would have faster random motion. Atoms, with more rapid movement, would move outward for wider dissipation. The gravitational field of a hotter gas-cloud would be weaker in intensity and the condensation of such a gas-cloud into star would be prevented or delayed. Secondly, the supernova material would inject the gas-cloud with nuclei more massive than helium. These massive nuclei would combine with hydrogen or with each other to form heavier atoms and molecules which are called dust particles in astrophysics. Thus the clouds consist of gas and dust.

We observe some galaxies with no more than 2 per cent of their total mass in the form of interstellar clouds of gas. Such galaxies have not been appreciably affected by supernova explosions. On the other hand, there are galaxies with 25 per cent of their total mass in the form of interstellar clouds of gas and dust. These galaxies have been heavily injected with supernova debris.

The spiral galaxies are generally cloud-rich. Clouds are not evenly distributed in such galaxies. Clouds of gas and dust are more concentrated in the spiral arms. Our own galaxy, the Milky Way, is a typical example. About half of the mass of the three spiral arms of our galaxy constitutes interstellar clouds of gas and dust.

The interstellar clouds present in our galaxy have been mixed with energetic materials of millions of supernova explosions for fourteen billion years. As a result, massive atoms beyond helium constitute about 1 per cent of the atoms of the interstellar clouds present in our galaxy or 3 per cent of their mass. Once in a while, such interstellar clouds containing some heavy atomic detritus begin to undergo contraction. They contract to form one or several new stars or a cluster of stars.

Our Sun is a second-generation star. It was formed 4.6 billion years ago when our Milky Way galaxy was about ten billion years old. The cloud which was the precursor of our Sun had continued to be mixed with the incoming debris of supernova explosions for a vast length of period covering about ten billion years. That explains the presence of atoms heavier than helium in the Sun which has predominantly a hydrogen/helium structure. About 1.5 per cent of the Sun's mass is made of atoms other than hydrogen and helium. These heavier atoms could not be formed soon after the big bang. They were formed in the core of massive stars that underwent supernova explosions and threw materials into space. This happened before the Sun and its planets were formed. The Earth contains a small quantity of hydrogen and a trace of helium. All of the Earth, except the hydrogen and helium, was once formed at the core of the stars that had existed before our Sun was born. About 10 per cent of the living tissues of plants and animals on the Earth are made of hydrogen. The rest 90 per cent came from the core of some stars that underwent supernova explosions.

Our Sun is a star. Many stars had been dead before our Sun was born. It was born about ten billion years after the big bang. Are there not stars younger than the Sun? Are stars born at present? Will stars be born in future? Stars have been born after the Sun came into being. Star-formation is taking place at present. Stars will be formed in the future. Hence it is not a fact that all stars were formed at a definite period in the past and that no new stars were and are formed or will be formed.

The raw material for the formation of a new star is provided by clouds of gas and dust existent here and there in the universe. The elliptical galaxies are practically devoid of gas and dust. The spiral galaxies are rich in interstellar clouds of gas and dust and this richness is confined to their spiral arms. The core of our galaxy and the globular clusters present around its core contain very little gas and dust.

It has been estimated that about ten billion (1×10^{10}) stars are yet to be formed in our galaxy. This seems to be a large number. Again, in the universe, there are other galaxies where star formation will take place. The number of all these stars that are to be formed is too small in comparison with that of stars already formed in the past and in existence today.

Of course, an already formed star can be converted into gas and dust. This can be achieved through supernova explosion. Supernovas are important to star-formation in two ways. They throw gas and dust and thereby add to the raw material necessary for star-formation. Secondly, any cloud of gas and dust, present not very far away from a supernova, may undergo compression, initiated by the shock wave of the explosion. Thus the process of star-formation may set in.

Another question may be posed here. Stars that have been too old have been dead. Stars that are young now will be old and will be dead. Stars are now being formed and will be formed in future. Old and massive stars are undergoing supernova explosions and providing gas and dust that add to the raw material for star-formation. Would it be correct to assume that the process of star-formation continues for ever? Or, would there ever be a dark universe without a single luminous star?

The more massive a star, the less life it has. Basing on this principle, we may consider the longevity of stars in our galaxy and in the universe. Only about 4 per cent of the stars in the Milky Way galaxy are more massive than the Sun. Another 9 per cent are roughly as massive as the Sun. This amounts to the fact that about 87 per cent of the stars in our galaxy are less massive than the Sun. It may be presumed that the mass distribution of stars in other galaxies may follow a similar pattern. All the stars that are less massive than our Sun will remain in the main sequence for a period much longer than 12 eons (1 eon = 1 billion years). The least massive stars may remain on their main sequence for as long as 200 eons.

The stock of clouds of gas and dust is not unlimited. This will be used up in course of time through formation of stars. Supernovas are not unlimited in number. Less than 1 per cent of the stars in the universe are massive enough to undergo spectacular explosion to add to the dust and gas of the universe. Moreover, the debris they throw into space is poor in hydrogen and rich in more massive nuclei. These more massive nuclei may be important to the development of planets like our Earth and evolution of life. But they are not important fusion-fuel. Hydrogen which is important as a fusion-fuel is constantly being used up. The universe is becoming poorer and poorer in hydrogen. The stars formed in an older universe would contain less hydrogen than those formed in a younger universe. Thus, all galaxies will gradually dim and, after about 400 eons, the universe would be dark. New star-formation shall not be a continual phenomenon.

Birth of the Solar System

According to the Biblical view, the universe was formed six thousand years ago, about four thousand years before the birth of Christ. The Bible rejects the evolutionary origin of the universe and upholds its *ex nihilo* theory of genesis. The entire universe—the Earth, the Sun and all its planets, the moon and the stars—were created by God out of nothing in six days only.

Scientists narrate a different history on the origin of the solar system. Our solar system is 4.6 billion years old. The Sun, its planets and satellites are almost of equal age. The Sun was formed from a fragment of an interstellar cloud.

The scientific theories of planet formation may be grouped in two categories, viz. catastrophic and quiescent. The first modern scholar to give a theory of planet formation was the French naturalist Georges L.L. de Buffon (1707-1788). In 1778, he published his catastrophic theory on the development of the Earth. He suggested that the Earth was formed from the Sun by a catastrophic collision of the Sun with another heavenly body (a comet). This tidal interaction of a passing body with the Sun ripped off the materials which eventually formed planets. There is a second version of this catastrophic theory. According to this version, the Sun was a member of a binary star system, the binary companion exploded and left behind a wisp of material, and this material went to form the planets of the Sun.

The catastrophic theories have been discarded by scientists due to various valid reasons. The essential feature of most of the quiescent theories dates back to the French astronomer and mathematician Pierre Simon de Laplace (1749-1827). Laplace's nebular hypothesis originated from the notion of the German philosopher Immanuel Kant (1724-1804). Kant postulated that all the matter of the Sun and its planets was originally spread out as a vast, rarefied cloud of gas. The gas-cloud contracted and rotated more rapidly. In this process, rings of matter separated from it. In 1796, Laplace developed the idea of Kant. He suggested that the entire solar system, including the Sun, had originated from a nebula (from the Latin word for cloud). This nebula was a vast swirling cloud of dust and gas. The rotating prestellar gas-cloud was collapsing under the pull of its own gravitation. As it did so, its rate of rotation increased according to the law of conservation of angular momentum. The cloud spun too rapidly. The centrifugal force at the periphery of the rotating nebular cloud became too large at a certain point of its contraction. An equatorial bulge developed. As a result, a ring of matter was torn away from its equator. This ring then contracted gravitationally to form the most distant planet first. After this, the central cloud contracted still further and rotated even faster. Due to the centrifugal force, a second ring of matter broke away from the central cloud. This second ring of matter contracted to form the second most distant planet. This happened over and over again. Thus, all the planets were formed. Finally what was left of the cloud became the Sun.

Laplace's nebular hypothesis was very popular throughout the nineteenth century. But, in the second half of the same century, scientists started questioning it and raised a number of objections to it. The most serious objection to this hypothesis was the discrepancy in the conservation of angular momentum. The rotational motion or angular momentum for a single body of mass is expressed mathematically by a product of three terms, viz., $m \times v \times r$, where m is the mass of the body, v is its velocity and r is the radius of its orbit. The Sun moves in a very small orbit around a fixed point very close to its own centre. This movement is due to the gravitational pull of its planets, especially Jupiter. But this motion of the Sun contributes little to its angular momentum. The Sun rotates about its own axis. Almost all the angular momentum of the Sun is due to this rotation. The Sun rotates only once every twenty-five days of the Earth. Due to this slow rate of rotation, the total angular momentum of the Sun is only a small fraction of that of the planets. The Sun contains 99.9 per cent of the mass of the solar system. In spite of this, it contains only two per cent of the total angular momentum. How could 98 per cent of the angular momentum in the solar system be concentrated in about 0.1 per cent of the total mass? This was a great puzzle for the scientists. And this was the main reason for casting doubt in Laplace's nebular hypothesis.

The collision hypothesis of Buffon was revived in 1900 by the American geologist Thomas Chowder Chamberlin (1843-1928). It was also proposed by the American astronomer Forest Ray Moulton (1872-1952) and independently by the English physicist James Jeans (1877-1946). According to this theory, in the distant past, an approaching star came very close to the Sun and gravitational influence of each on the other tore large chunks of matter out of the two. This extracted matter was later fragmented and became the various planets of the Sun by gravitational contraction.

Related to the collision hypothesis, a tidal hypothesis was proposed by Sir Harold Jeffreys. Both these hypotheses could not account for the large amount of angular momentum concentrated in the planets. There were also other serious and unanswerable objections. Having gained popularity for about thirty years, the collision hypothesis and other related ones had to be abandoned due to insuperable difficulties.

The nebular hypothesis regained popularity. This was possible due to the findings of the German astronomer Carl Friedrich von Weizsäcker (1912-) in 1944. In 1943, he got the first clue as to how the planets obtained their present disproportionate share of the total electromagnetic field. As the Sun condensed from the nebula, its electromagnetic field could serve to transfer angular momentum to the planets. Thus the riddle was solved and the nebular hypothesis could be re-established. It was Weizsäcker who showed that the entire solar system—the Sun, its planets and the satellites of the planets—would form more or less simultaneously. Thus the solar system, 'including the Sun and the Earth, was formed about 4.6 eons ago, i.e., 4,600,000,000 years ago.

The Fate of a Star

A star, once formed, does not continue as such for ever. It changes in size, luminosity, temperature and other characteristics. It may be converted into a 'red giant', a 'white dwarf', a 'neutron star' or a 'black hole'. It may die; it may disappear from the space which it once occupied.

There are various types of stars. In mass, they range widely. There are stars with a fraction of the solar mass; there are others that are 10-100 times more massive than our Sun. Stars differ in sizes, chemical composition, temperatures, and so on.

A star is on the 'main sequence' when its main production of energy is through hydrogen-fusion. Our Sun, which is intermediate in mass among the stars, is now on the main sequence. It has already existed for 4.6 billion years. It has still got a hydrogen supply that will last ten to twelve billion years more. Nearly 85 per cent of the stars we see in the sky are on the main sequence.

The more massive a star, the more hydrogen it contains. But, the more massive a star, the more gravitational pull it has and hence more heat is required to keep it expanded against the greater gravitational contraction. The large store of hydrogen-fuel of a more massive star is used up more quickly than the small store of hydrogen-fuel of a less massive star. Therefore, the greater the mass of a star, the shorter its lifetime.

Red Giants

Red giants are stars that have already passed the main sequence stage. They are too big in size and hence are called giants. They look red in colour, because their surfaces are cool, or at least not more than red-hot. The surface temperatures of red giants may be about 2,000°C.

Over millions and billions of years hydrogen-fusion takes place at the core of a star and helium is produced. Helium, being denser than hydrogen, collects at the very centre of the star. Thus, a helium-ball is formed at the centre and, around this ball, hydrogen-fusion continues.

The helium ball condenses; it becomes smaller and denser due to contraction. Its temperature rises. Eventually, the high temperature and pressure of the helium ball allow helium-fusion to begin. More complex nuclei like those of carbon, nitrogen and oxygen are formed as a result of fusion of helium nuclei.

Heat is already produced through the hydrogen-fusion at the outer edge of the helium core. The heat produced inside the helium core due to helium-fusion is added to it. Due to the excessive heat production, the outer layers of the star are overheated and expand enormously. The expanding star leaves the main sequence at this point.

With the expansion of the outer layers of the star, it cools to a mere red heat. But, despite its cool surface, the total amount of heat radiated by the red giant is much more than that of a normal star. This becomes possible due to the increase in the surface area of the star. If its diameter increases by 100 times, its surface area increases by 100×100 or 10,000 times.

The red giant stage does not continue for a very long time from the stellar view point. It may last one or two million years. Helium fusion supplies far less energy than hydrogen-fusion. The products of helium-fusion can also fuse further. But the energy produced by hydrogen-fusion is twenty times more than that produced by helium fusion. In spite of the low rate of energy availability from helium-fusion, the red giant continues to emit heat at a fearsome rate. As a result, the helium supply is exhausted much earlier than what would have happened with the hydrogen supply. Since red giants do not live for eons, few red giants are detected in the sky. Only about one per cent (two and a half billions in number) of the stars in our galaxy are red giants.

It has already been said that the nuclei of the products of helium-fusion further fuse at the centre of the red giant. In very massive stars, the temperature rise at the centre is too high and this allows such fusion of nuclei for some period. But there comes a point when the temperature at the stellar core is not high enough to allow nuclei fusion. Whatever may be the case, fusion can proceed until iron nuclei are formed. After that, iron nuclei may fuse to produce larger nuclei (fusion), or may break to produce smaller nuclei (fission). In both these processes, energy is not produced and rather energy-supply is necessary. Thus, iron nuclei are the last products of fusion reactions that are responsible for production of nuclear energy.

After the nuclear fire of the red giant is extinguished, it stops expanding and starts contracting itself. Now the heat inside is not sufficient to keep the star expanded against its own gravity. It shrinks by its own gravitational pull. It collapses and does so very rapidly.

White Dwarf

The mass of our Sun is used as a mass-unit for expressing the other stellar masses. This unit is written by the symbol $1\,M_{\odot}$ Stars that have mass less than $1.44\,M_{\odot}$ become white dwarfs when they have exhausted all their nuclear fuel.

This $1.4\,M_{\odot}$ is known as the 'Chandrasekhar limit'. The India-born American Nobel-Laureate astronomer Subrahmanyan Chandrasekhar (1910-) first obtained this result in 1935. According to his calculations, no star more than 1.4 times the mass of our Sun could become a white dwarf in the 'normal' process.

When the star with mass less than $1.4\,M_{\odot}$ has exhausted all its nuclear fuel, it collapses due to its own gravity and becomes a white dwarf. Chandrasekhar showed that what kept a white dwarf distended was its content of electrons. The electrons inside a white dwarf do not exist as components of atoms. Due to excessive compression of matter inside the star, the electrons become quantum-mechanically 'degenerate'. They move about randomly and form a kind of electron gas. Electrons in the electron gas repel one another since they carry negative charge. This repulsive force of the electrons in the electron gas may be termed 'degenerate-electron pressure' and this resists the further compression of the white dwarf that has a tendency to shrink further due its intense gravitational field.

The strong gravitational field of the white dwarf compresses the electron gas, but it fails to do so beyond a certain point. The more massive the white dwarf, the more intense the gravitational field; the more intense the gravitational field, the more compressed the electron gas. It follows that the more massive the white dwarf, the smaller its diameter.

When the mass of the star is equal to 1.44 times the mass of the Sun, the ability of the electron gas to resist compression brought about by the gravitational field of the star itself breaks down, and in such case the white dwarf would collapse. This calculation was made by Chandrasekhar.

Over 95 per cent of the stars that exist have masses below Chandrasekhar limit. Up to about 15 per cent (45 billions in number) of the stars in our Milky Way galaxy may be white dwarfs. Even for the small minority of the stars that have masses above the Chandrasekhar limit, there may be a device for them to end up as white dwarfs. Before collapsing, a star with mass more than 1.4 $M_\odot$ may explode to drive off the outer layers and thus may lose mass to be on the lower side of Chandrasekhar limit. The more massive the star, the more forceful the explosion and the greater the loss of mass. If this explosion hypothesis is accepted, the chance of any massive star with mass beyond the Chandrasekhar limit to end up finally as a white dwarf is to be recognized. Through explosion, the excess mass would be blown off and the left out core would be a white dwarf.

Neutron Star

Chandrasekhar did not rule out the possibility of the non-explosion of a massive star. There is no unavoidable necessity of a massive star to explode and leave an intact core with mass less than 1.44 times the mass of the Sun.

A star with mass in the range of 1.44 to 3 $M_\odot$, after using up its thermonuclear fuel, is converted into a neutron star. Such a star starts shrinking under the influence of its gravitation. With the increase in the intensity of the gravitational field, the electrons are pushed closer to the protons inside the atoms, and at a certain point of compression the electrons are forced to combine with the protons to form neutrons. For this to occur, the matter density must be about 100 times higher than that in a white dwarf.

Such a collapsing star consists of neutrons only. Earlier its atoms consisted of neutrons, protons and electrons. Its protons and electrons combined to form neutrons that were additional to the already existing neutrons. After this process is over, the star contains nothing but neutrons. The neutrons do not carry any charge and hence there is no repelling force among them. By gravitational contraction the star shrinks until the neutrons come in close contact with one another. At this stage we get a neutron star. In the visual field, a neutron star may be a million or more times fainter than the Sun. This is the reason for our failure of detecting a neutron star although we have been able to detect white dwarfs. However, we have already detected pulsars that may be associated with rotating neutron stars.

Pulsars are astronomical objects characterized by the extreme regularity and short period of their pulses. It is now believed that pulsars are associated with rotating neutron stars. The pulses originate from their plasma (charged particles) moving in magnetic fields. In 1968, the Cambridge radio-astronomers discovered a pulsar for the first time. After that dozens of pulsars have been discovered.

The mass of a neutron star is not higher than about 3 $M_\odot$. The question may be asked: "What is the fate of a star that has got mass more than $3M_\odot$? "There are two paths open for such a massive star. It may undergo continuous gravitational contraction and finally it becomes a black hole. Alternatively, after the end of its nuclear fuel, it may become a 'supernova'.

Supernova

A massive star, after using up its nuclear fuel, undergoes an implosion and an explosion. Its core collapses under its own gravitational attraction and thus releases energy which causes the outer envelope to explode. Depending upon the mass of the imploding core, it may form a white dwarf or a neutron star. The exploding envelope throws enormous quantities of energy outwards in the form of electrons, protons, nuclei and electromagnetic radiation. It has been suggested that supernova explosions are sources of cosmic rays that reach our Earth's atmosphere.

As per an estimate, one supernova explodes, on the average, every fifty years in any given galaxy. For every 1,250 ordinary novas, there is eruption of one supernova. On 4th July, 1054, the Crab Nebula supernova explosion was seen from the Earth. It emits radio waves, X-rays and high-energy cosmic ray particles. It is the seat of a pulsar. This pulsar was discovered in October, 1968. A pulsation emanates from it in every 0.033099 second. It means that microwave bursts emerge from it about thirty times a second. It has been considered that the central star of a supernova remnant is a pulsar. A rotating neutron star pulses. The faster the rotation, the faster the pulse. The rotating neutron stars steadily lose their energy and the rate of rotation slowly decreases. As a result, the interval between pulses increases. A pulsar may remain as a detectable object for three or four million years, however.

Black Holes

Black holes are invisible holes in space. The terminology is not very scientific and precise. But we do not get a better term and this term, through use, has already conveyed definite meaning to us. The American physicist John Archibald Wheeler (1911-) used this term and since that time it has been in vogue.

When we discuss black holes, we really talk about gravitation. Sir Isaac Newton invented the modern concept of gravity. To him it was a force. The concept of black hole does not find a place in Newton's scheme of gravity. The black hole is a child of Einstein's general theory of relativity, which too is a theory of gravitation. Unlike Newton, Einstein did not consider gravity as a force. Gravity is a distortion of the very nature of space and time, as conceptualized by Einstein. He worked out some gravitational field equations that describe the gravitational field produced by any body and every body. But Einstein did not find an exact solution to these equations. Karl Schwarzschild (1873-1916), a German astronomer, gave correct solution to the gravitational field equations of Einstein. His paper was published in the 1916 edition of the *Journal of the Royal Prussian Academy of Sciences.* It was entitled 'On the Field of Gravity of a Point Mass in the Theory of Einstein'. This paper described the black hole, although Schwarzschild did not use this term and was not aware of the existence of any black hole. The real significance of this paper was not appreciated even upto the mid-sixties of the twentieth century.

In 1939, the American physicist J. Robert Oppenheimer (1904-1967) was working out the mathematical details of neutron stars. He was concerned with the possible consequences of increase in the mass of a star. With the increase in the mass of a star, the intensity of its gravitational field increases. When the mass exceeds 3.2 times the mass of our Sun, the intensity of the gravitational field becomes so great that even the neutrons in contact fail to withstand the compression induced by the field. As a result, the neutrons collapse and the neutron star contracts. Oppenheimer predicted that this contraction would continue indefinitely until the star approached zero volume and infinite density.

Schwarzschild radius of any spherical body may be calculated from the following equation:

$$R_S = \frac{2\ GM}{c^2}$$

Here, R_S is Schwarzschild radius, G is the gravitational constant, M is the mass of the spherical body and c is the velocity of light in vacuum (300,000 kilometers per second). If calculated as per this equation, the Schwarzschild radius for our Sun is 3 kilometers. If the Sun shrinks from its present radius of 700,000 kilometers to 3 kilometers, it is changed into a black hole.

The Schwarzschild radius is a critical radius of a spherical body. With the attainment of this radius, the escape velocity from the surface of the body equals the velocity of light. When the body shrinks to radius smaller than the Schwarzschild radius, nothing can escape from it. Light cannot escape from its surface. Any light directed to the collapsed surface of this sphere from any outside source cannot get reflected out. Any matter or radiation will be trapped in the curved space-time geometry of the sphere once it reaches it within its Schwarzschild radius. Such a collapsed body does not emit anything and devours everything. Since it does not emit light, it cannot be seen. Hence, it is designated as a black hole.

Schwarzschild surface is the surface of a sphere whose radius is its Schwarzschild radius. Since nothing escapes from the Schwarzschild surface, such a surface is called the horizon of the black hole.

In black hole matter collapses. With increasing pressures and densities and rising gravitational intensities, approaching the infinite, matter inside the black hole loses its identity.

A black hole cannot be seen. It does not emit light. It does not reflect light directed towards it from an outside source. It does not emit any form of radiation. Hence, not only it cannot be seen, but also it cannot be directly detected. If one partner of a binary star system is converted into a black hole and the other partner is visible, the black hole can be detected indirectly since it continues to exert gravitational pull on its partner. The presence of a black hole can be felt through its gravitational field. An isolated black hole could be detected by us if it affected us gravitationally through its huge mass or close proximity or both. There could be millions of black holes, with the mass of ordinary stars, randomly scattered throughout our galaxy and we could be unaware of their presence.

The story of the detection of a black hole may be interesting here. This was possible due to the black hole being a partner of a binary-star system. The binary stars are so close to each other that each one is held in the other's gravitational field and each circles the centre of gravity of the other. Up to 70 per cent of the stars are part of binary systems or systems that are still more complicated. Our Sun is a single star and such single stars are in a minority.

In 1971, a strong X-ray source was detected in the constellation Cygnus by the X-ray detecting satellite Uhuru. The X-ray emission varied irregularly. The source of microwave emission was very close to a visible star, listed in the catalogue as HD-226868. This visible star is bluish and is thirty times as massive as our Sun. This star is a member of a binary system. It circles its partner which is five to eight times as massive as the Sun. The companion star is an intense source of X-rays and still is invisible. This invisible object is a black hole.

The visible star is expanding to enter into the red-giant stage. Its matter may be spilled over into the black hole companion. The accretion disc about the black hole may be producing the X-rays.

Shattered Dogma

We started with the idea of geocentric-cum-anthropocentric universe with an unchangeable heaven. The stars, the sun and the moon were thought to be immutable and eternally existent. We had dichotomy of opinion regarding cosmogonical processes. Many theologians accepted the versions of the sacred texts as final and inviolable. They considered the universe to have been created *ex nihilo* by an eternal, omnipresent, omniscient and omnipotent God within a few days. Whatever God created was in a finished form. Some philosophers and scientists accepted the eternality of the universe that ever existed and will ever exist. They recognized changes in Nature; but these changes are transformations that are ever in dynamic state of flux. They did not feel the need of any Creator.

In the twentieth century, astronomers and astrophysicists have discarded some old knowledge, revised some others and added much new knowledge. Their discoveries have revolutionized our thought regarding the vastness of the universe, the changeable stars, the origin and the death of the universe and the insignificant place the Earth occupies in the unfathomable universe.

NOTES

1. Sagan, C., *Cosmos*, Macdonald, London, 1981, p. 4.
2. TdBrā, VII.10.1; JBrā, I.145; III.72; KS, XIII.12; ŚBrā, VI.1.2.3.
3. Mu, I.1.8.
4. ṚV, V.47.3; X.121.5; YV, XIII.30; TBrā, 1.5.2.5; ŚBrā, VII.5.1.8; X.6.5.2; JBrā, II.45 and 62; ABrā, IV.20.
5. TS, III.4.3; VII.3.10; ŚBrā, I.4.1.22; JBrā, I.87; Vāp, 50.99.53.
6. ŚBrā, VII.1.1.37.
7. JBrā, I.257; II.62; ŚBrā, VII.1.1.37.
8. YV, XI.57; ŚBrā, XIV.9.4.21; TS, V.5.2.
9. YV, III.6; ABrā, III.4.6.

CHAPTER VII

THERMODYNAMICS

Whatever an enemy can do to his enemy,
Whatever a hater can do to the hated,
A thought erroneously directed could do still worse.

Dhammapada, III. IO.

OF ALL FORMS OF ENERGY, light and heat were the ones to which man was first exposed. Heat was the form of energy which was harnessed by man for the first time. F. Engels has said that man rubbed one stone against another and thus, by friction, generated fire which gave man control over one of the forces of Nature for the first time. This was not a simple discovery. It was so momentous that it separated man from the animal kingdom.

The early man could experience 'hot' and 'cold'. He could utilize fire for hunting animals; could utilize heat for cooking his food; he used fire for warming himself in cold weather. He could realize the usefulness of heat. He could see fire devouring all organic matter. He was terrified by the ferocious nature of fire. He could visualize a god in fire. He worshipped fire.

In spite of this old acquaintance of man with fire, the science of heat was not known to man until the advent of the nineteenth century.

There was some scientific work on temperature before the exact nature of heat was known. In 1603, Galileo invented a primitive device which may be called a crude type of thermometer. In 1654, the Grand Duke of Tuscany, Ferdinand II evolved a thermometer. At about the same time a similar thermometer was devised by the English physicist Robert Boyle. The French physicist Guillaume Amontons used mercury in thermometer. The German physicist Gabriel Daniel Fahrenheit invented his thermometer in 1714. In 1742, the Swedish astronomer Anders Celsius invented the centigrade thermometer.

Heat and temperature are not synonymous. Heat is the total energy contained in the molecular motions of a given quantity of matter, whereas temperature is the average energy of motion per molecule in that matter. A burning match-stick is at higher temperature than a bucket of lukewarm water. But the former has got less heat than the latter. Heat flows from higher to lower temperature. If the burning match-stick is immersed in the warm water in the bucket, the match-stick will lose heat and the water will gain heat. The question is "What is it that flows from the match-stick to water?" This question has troubled the minds of scientists for many centuries.

Heat Conceived as Matter

Heat was speculated to be a form of matter. It was perhaps Lavoisier who used the term 'thermogen' for the heat-matter. It was further postulated that the thermogen particles repelled each other and that attractive forces acted between particles of thermogen and those of bodies to be heated. For matter that undergoes combustion, the concept of phlogiston was born. Metal was considered a combination of scale and phlogiston; in the process of combustion, phlogiston evaporated with scale remaining as residue.

Like any other material substance that can be poured or shifted from one substance to another, heat was considered as a substance known as 'caloric' (Latin word for heat). Wood is burned to boil water in a kettle. In this process, the caloric present in the wood passes into the flame; then it passes from the flame to the kettle above the flame; finally it passes from the kettle to the water in the kettle. When water is filled with caloric, it becomes steam. This was the speculated story of the invisible caloric.

The material theory of heat was supported by important scientists such as Galileo and Descartes. Scientists like Wolff, Wilke and Black played prominent role in spreading the notion that heat is a material substance.

Heat as a Form of Vibration

In 1798, Benjamin Thompson (Count Rumford) bored a cannon. He could notice the formation of great quantities of heat in this mechanical operation. He tried to rationalize this heat formation. He thought that heat could not be matter. The motion of the boring instrument against the metal of the cannon was transformed into the motion of the smaller particles of both the borer and the metal. Rumford thought that this internal motion was heat.

In 1799, Humphry Davy, a chemist, conducted an experiment to prove that heat must be a vibration and not a material. The idea of Rumford corroborated by the experimental evidence of Davy should have been conclusive for the rejection of the caloric theory, which nevertheless persisted to the middle of the nineteenth century. This was anticipated in 1800 which was before the discovery of the atomic theory. That objects are made of small particles and that these particles move internally and invisibly were incredible ideas at that time. Hence the vibrational theory of heat was disregarded for decades after its discovery.

In the 1840s, James Prescott Joule conducted series of experiments to convert work to heat. Joule's findings could strengthen the observations of Rumford. The development of the idea on the kinetic theory of gases could further elucidate the nature of heat as motion. The molecules composing a gas are in continual motion; they bounce off one another and off the walls of their container. Daniel Bernoulli, the Swiss mathematician, was the first man who investigated in 1738 the properties of gases from this standpoint. Finally in the 1860s, James Clerk Maxwell and Ludwig Boltzmann worked out the mathematics rigorously and established the kinetic theory of gases. This theory shows that heat is equivalent to the motion of molecules. Thus the caloric theory of heat received its final death-blow. Heat is a vibrational phenomenon; it is a form of motion on the atomic scale. The movement of molecules in gases and liquids or the jittery to-and-fro movement of molecules in solids generates heat.

Transfer of Heat

The old concept of heat is no longer valid. It is not matter. It is not a fluid. It is a form of energy. The molecules, atoms, electrons and ions in all bodies are in a continual state of vibration. The kinetic energy acquired by these particles by virtue of their vibratory movement is called heat. These particles have relatively larger amounts of kinetic energy in hot bodies, and smaller amounts in cold bodies.

Heat was previously considered to flow like fluid. A volume of cold water, when added to a volume of hot water, gets warmed up until the whole mixture acquires a uniform temperature in between those of the cold and the hot water. In this case, the cold water gains heat and the hot water loses heat. There is an analogy between this exchange of heat and the exchange of water between two interconnected water-vessels one of which is placed at higher level than the other. Water flows from the higher level to the lower level until both the levels are the same. Does heat flow similarly like water or any other fluid? It was thought like that. No longer is it considered to be correct. Heat is transferred by convection in gas or liquid, conduction in solids and radiation across vacuum.

Convection. The word 'convection' has come from Latin source. It means 'to carry together'. The transfer of heat by currents of gas or liquid is done through a process known as convection. There is physical movement of matter in this case. The molecules of the hot fluid possess higher kinetic energy and those of the cold fluid possess lower kinetic energy. As a result of the physical intermingling of the molecules of both the hot and the cold fluids, the mixture as a whole acquires an average kinetic energy which is intermediate in value.

Conduction. The word 'conduction' is of Latin origin. It means 'to lead together'. The transfer of heat through the main body of a solid is done through a process known as conduction. If one end of a metallic rod is placed in fire, the other end gets slowly heated up. It is not a fact that the atoms or molecules in the metal move from the hot end to the cold end. As the end of the metal-rod in or near the fire grows hot, the atoms of the hot end gain kinetic energy. As long as the rod remains solid, its atoms do not have the freedom to move to a distance. The average position of each atom of the hot solid rod remains fixed, but each can and does vibrate about that position. With gain in energy, the vibrations of the atoms become more rapid and vigorous. The atoms in the hottest end of the rod vibrate most energetically and by that they jostle their neighbouring atoms. The impact which the neighbouring atoms get makes them vibrate more energetically with greater amplitude. Thus, kinetic energy jostles itself from atom to atom from the hot end of the rod to its cold end.

Radiation. There is a third process of transfer of heat known as radiation. Even if there is vacuum between the source of heat and the receiving body, heat is transferred. This is how the Earth gets heated by solar radiation and our finger gets heated up near a burning electric bulb. In both conduction and convection, there are actual impingements of energetic atoms or molecules upon less energetic atoms or molecules, and thereby energy is transferred by direct contact. There is no such direct contact in the case of radiation. In this process energy traverses from the source of heat to the receiving body through space. Heat radiation, like light radiation, is a wave. It also travels in straight lines. Both heat and light waves are commonly designated as electromagnetic waves. Infrared or heat waves are those which are longer than visible waves and shorter than radio waves. It is to be noted that the wave motion is not heat and that it produces heat when it gets absorbed.

Relation between Temperature and Volume of Gas

When anything—solid, liquid or gas—is heated, its volume expands. Quantitatively speaking, this is less in solid, more in liquid and most in gases. It has already been discussed that the molecules and atoms of an object, on being heated, gain kinetic energy and move more energetically. This explains the expansion in volume. The reverse process takes place when an object is cooled. Hence there is contraction in volume.

Guillaume Amontons, a French physicist, conducted experiments in 1699 on air. He made a quantitative study of the expansion of gases with temperature change. This was the first attempt on this topic. In 1802, the French chemist Joseph Louis Gay-Lussac determined the coefficient of cubical expansion of air and gases such as hydrogen, nitrogen and oxygen. The following equation is a mathematical generalization of his findings:

$$\triangle V = 0.00366V\ (\triangle t) = \frac{V\triangle t}{273}$$

Here V is the volume of gas, $\triangle V$ is the change in the volume of gas and $\triangle t$ is the change in the temperature from 0°C.

Jacques Alexandre César Charles, another French physicist, claimed that he had discovered the relationship between gas-volume and temperature in 1787, before Gay-Lussac made his conclusions public. For this reason, Gay-Lussac's law is often known as Charles' law. This is, however, contrary to the accepted norms in science, since Charles never published his results.

Gay-Lussac's or Charles' law may be expressed in a very simple way as follows:

$$\frac{V_2}{V_1} = \frac{T_2}{T_1}$$

Here V is volume and T is absolute temperature (degree Celsius +273°).

The mathematical relation given above may be expressed in common language in the following way: The volume of a given mass of gas is directly proportional to its absolute temperature, if the pressure on the gas is held constant.

By maintaining the constant pressure, one may observe the volume changes of a gas by varying the temperature recorded in the centigrade scale. The observed data may be plotted on a graph. A straight-line relationship of temperature-volume is obtained. This has been shown in Figure 7.1.

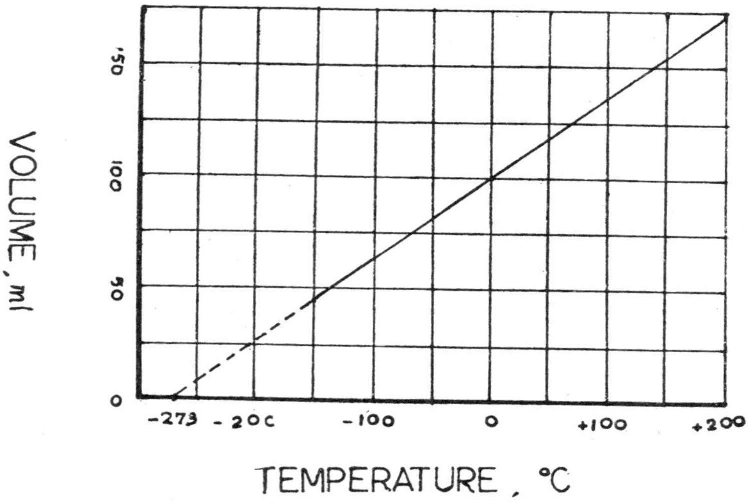

Fig. 7.1: Change in volume of a gas with change in temperature, at constant pressure.

Extrapolation of the straight line in Figure 7.1 shows that the line touches the abscissa at −273°C (more precisely −273.16°C). At this temperature the volume of the gas would fall to zero. The question is: "What would happen to the gas at −273.16°C?" That matter would ever have zero volume is inconceivable. If it were true, it would be equivalent to saying that matter vanishes at a temperature of −273.16°C. Some scientists dissolve this problem by two suppositions. Firstly, matter in gaseous form would be converted to liquid form before the temperature of −273.16°C was reached. The coefficient of cubical expansion of liquids is much smaller than that of gases. Secondly, it would not be unreasonable to think that Gay-Lussac's law might not be applicable strictly at very low temperature.

In 1848, William Thomson (who was later honoured by the title Lord Kelvin) pointed out that $-273°C$ might be the lowest temperature or the absolute zero. As the temperature increases, the molecules move faster, they acquire more 'elbow room' and the volume becomes greater. Conversely, as the temperature decreases the movement of molecules becomes slower, they occupy less room and the volume becomes smaller. Although this is generally true, Thomson did not say anything about the disappearance of volume at $-273°C$. He suggested that, for every degree of cooling, the average kinetic energy content of the molecules declines by 1/273. According to this rate of decline in the kinetic energy, the molecules will have zero kinetic energy at $-273°C$ ($-273.16°C$ precisely). The lowest possible temperature is that at which the kinetic energy of molecules or atoms is zero. Since $KE = \frac{1}{2} mv^2$, the velocity of the particles must be zero at the absolute zero temperature. At this lowest temperature matter is at absolute rest and no particles of it can move. There is nothing like motion at the absolute zero temperature. On the Kelvin scale, the absolute zero is designated as 0°K. The freezing point of water is 0°C or $(0+273.16=273.16)$ 273.16°K. The boiling point of water is 100°C or $(100+273.16=373.16)$ 373.16°K. A change of 1°K is equal in magnitude to that of 1°C.

Heat as a Form of Energy

The word 'energy' has Greek origin, 'en' meaning 'in' or 'content' and 'ergon' meaning 'work'. In 1807, the English scientist Thomas Young proposed the term 'energy' for the work-store. The literal meaning of this word is 'work-within'.

The most acceptable definition of 'energy' is *that* which has got the ability to do work. A physicist uses the word 'work' in a technical sense. Work is force multiplied by the distance through which a body moves in the direction of the force. Mathematically it is expressed as $w = fd$. In the cgs system, where f is force in dyne and d is distance in centimeter, w is work in dyne-centimeter, otherwise known as erg.

The definition of work, as given above, says nothing about the time taken. The rate at which work is done is 'power'. It is ergs per second in the cgs system.

Energy is a very important concept in science. But from its definition, it is almost impossible for anybody to identify it as an entity. Energy is *that* which has got the ability to do work. A singer has got the ability to sing. A player has got the ability to play. A cow has got the ability to yield milk. A tree has got the ability to bear fruit. A singer, a player, a cow or a tree can each be identified as an entity. But there is no such identification of energy as an entity. In the definition of energy given here, *that*, as an entity, cannot be identified.

The equivalent word of energy in Sanskrit is *śakti,* etymologically derived from the verb root *śak* (*śak+ktin*). This root means 'to be able to do'. *That* which is able to do is *śakti.* But what is *that*? Advaita Vedānta says that it is indefinable (*anirvacanīyā*[1]). It exists, does not exist and exists and does not exist (*sat, asat, sadasat*[2]). It is illusory (*bhrānti*[3]). For its existence and functioning, it depends upon a substratum[4] (*adhiṣṭhāna*) that is functionless and immutable.

Although energy is illusory and indefinable, the manifested universe (*jagat*) is nothing without it. There are different forms of energy. Heat, light, electricity, magnetism and motion are several forms of energy and all such forms can do work.

Mechanical energy constitutes two forms, viz., kinetic energy and potential energy. The energy associated with motion is called kinetic energy. The word 'kinetic' is from a Greek word meaning 'motion'. Lord Kelvin, an English physicist, introduced the term 'kinetic energy' in 1856. A force causes the movement of a body. According to Newton's second law, this force is equal to the mass of the moving body multiplied by its acceleration ($f=ma$). This mathematical relationship can be otherwise expressed as $w=\frac{1}{2}mv^2$, where w is work, m is mass of the body and v is its velocity. For our purpose here, $w=e_k=\frac{1}{2}mv^2$, where e_k is the kinetic energy.

When an object is thrown up, it acquires a certain velocity and therefore certain kinetic energy. The gravitational field of the Earth imposes acceleration upon it and its velocity decreases as it goes higher and higher. Consequently its kinetic energy decreases and becomes zero when the object reaches maximum height and comes to a halt.

Where does the kinetic energy go? How can it disappear and be converted into nothing? Really it does not disappear. The decrease in kinetic energy through the ascendance of the object is concurrent with the corresponding appearance of energy of position. At the maximum height all the kinetic energy of the object is converted into the energy of position, that is converted back into kinetic energy as the object falls once more. Thus the energy of position has the potentiality of becoming kinetic energy. Hence the Scottish engineer William J.M. Rankine suggested the term 'potential energy' in 1853.

The French chemist Antoine Laurent Lavoisier (1743-1794) established the law of conservation of matter. Scientists thought that the same principle may hold good for energy. James Prescott Joule spent thirty five years converting various kinds of work into heat. In the 1840s, he discovered the mechanical equivalent of heat. As per Joule's findings, a certain quantity of work, of any kind, invariably produced a certain quantity of heat. Work could be converted into heat and conversely heat could be converted into work. In 1847, the German physicist and biologist Hermann von Helmholtz enunciated the law of conservation of energy. Although a number of scientists have contributed to this concept, Helmholtz is accepted as the discoverer of this law. According to this law, energy can be converted from one form to another but cannot be created or destroyed.

Thermodynamics

Nicholas Léonard Sadi Carnot is the founder of the science of thermodynamics. He did his work in the 1820's. His study was focused on the movement of heat with particular attention to the workings of the steam engine. The term 'thermodynamics' has come from Latin, meaning 'motion of heat'. There are three laws of thermodynamics.

First Law of Thermodynamics

In the process of the motion of heat, heat does not arise out of nothing and does not vanish into nothing. This is the first law of thermodynamics. Extending this principle to all forms of energy, the law may be restated: The total energy content of a closed system is constant.

A closed system is one that exchanges no energy with the outside world. It does not take up and give off energy. Inside the closed system, heat flows from a hot object to a cool object and this flow continues until the different portions of the system attain the same temperature. By this, the total heat content of the closed system remains unchanged; but heat is distributed within the system, leading to an equalization of temperature. Heat flows 'downhill'. It flows from a locality of high temperature to one of low, irrespective of the heat content in each locality.

The first law of thermodynamics is mathematically represented by the following equation:

$$W = JH$$

Here W is work (measured in ergs) used in generating heat, H is heat developed (measured in calories), and J is mechanical equivalent of heat (its value is 4.18×10^7 ergs/cal).

If the mechanical energy and the heat energy are measured in the same units, the said law may be restated as follows: If heat is transformed into other forms of energy, or other form of energy is transformed into heat, the heat energy is equal to the amount of transformed energy.

The universe is a perfectly closed system. It is finite, as proved by Einstein. The Sanskrit word for the universe is '*viśva*', meaning 'all'. There is nothing beyond *all*. Everything is included in *all*. Advaita Vedānta says that space is created, that any created thing, howsoever large it may be, cannot be infinite, and that space has got birth and death. Einstein has said that the curved space is finite. Hence, it is meaningless to use such language as 'outside the universe'. There is nothing beyond the *boundary* of space. Since the universe is a perfectly closed system, it does not give off energy and does not take up energy. Its total energy content (considering matter as packets of energy) is constant. It is not possible to extract more energy from this closed system of the universe than the total energy present in the first place.

Second Law of Thermodynamics

Before introducing the second law of thermodynamics, a few generalizations are in order here. As has already been said, heat flows downhill. The spontaneous flow of heat is always unidirectional from the higher to the lower temperature. The term 'spontaneous' in this case means 'without the expenditure of energy'. Inversely speaking, the spontaneous flow of heat never occurs from a colder to a hotter body.

Continuous operation of any machinery by heat energy obtained from bodies with temperature equal to or lower than that of surrounding bodies is impossible. Heat energy can be converted to useful mechanical energy only when it is obtained from bodies warmer than their surroundings. This is with reference to heat engines. A temperature difference is a prerequisite for heat energy to be converted to work. But all work-producing devices are not heat engines. Work can be obtained from electric batteries without involvement of temperature differences. Here, of course, there must be difference in the electric potential. Work can be obtained from chemical reactions although the reactants and the products are at the same temperature. In this case, the difference in the chemical potentials would represent the available energy. Whatever may be the form of the energy, work can be obtained only if the energy is present in a state of greater intensity in one portion of the system against a state of lesser intensity in another portion. The difference between the higher and lower intensities represents the available energy. The total energy minus the available energy is the unavailable energy.

Work can be converted entirely into heat. But the reverse is not true. When heat is converted into work, all of the heat cannot be turned to work; some of it is bound to be unusable and is unavoidably wasted. This is true in the conversion of any form of energy. A part of it is wasted. The wasted part is not lost. It does not disappear. It is converted to heat, which gets dissipated in the environment. That part of the energy that is used for the performance of an act is 'free energy'; the unusable part of the energy that is lost as non-useful heat is reflected in the measurement of entropy.

The word 'entropy' was first introduced in 1850 by the German physicist Rudolf Julius Emmanuel Clausius. This is a word of Greek origin. The prefix 'en' means 'in' and 'trepein' means 'to turn, change'. Entropy is a measure of the degradation of energy. The more energy degrades, the higher the level of entropy.

Clausius was the discoverer of the second law of thermodynamics. His concepts of energy degradation, available energy and entropy laid the foundation of this second law. In any process involving flow of energy, there is always some loss. That part of the energy that is used for work production is the available energy or free energy. The total energy of the system minus its available energy is the unavailable or non-useful heat energy. Entropy is a measure of the unavailability of energy. Mathematically it is expressed by the following equation:

$$\text{Entropy} = k \log D,$$

where k is Boltzmann constant ($=3.2983.10^{-24}$ cal/°C) and D is a quantitative measure of the atomistic disorder of the body in question. The unit in which entropy is measured is calories per degree Celsius.

The entropy of a system can remain unchanged under ideal conditions, but always increases with time under actual conditions. The entropy of the universe is continually increasing. This is one version of the second law of thermodynamics.

To start with, the universe had a certain amount of energy. Even though the quantity was huge, still it was finite and not infinite. Continually disorder increases and more and more energy is degraded. With the increase in entropy, there is corresponding decrease in the amount of available energy, since the total energy (available+unavailable) is constant. The process of entropy increase will continue. When the entropy of the universe is maximum, its available energy will be zero. This condition is referred to as the 'running down of the universe', or the 'heat death of the universe'.

The 'heat death of the universe' needs some explanation. When the entropy of the universe is maximum, with zero available energy, heat will be evenly distributed throughout the universe. This would result in temperature equalization. Without temperature difference, there will be complete halt of all energy-transformations. That condition is the 'heat death of the universe'.

The second law of thermodynamics points out that work can be extracted from a heat engine only when there is temperature difference. It also maintains that it is impossible to extract more work from a system than the quantity of available energy present. The laws of thermodynamics apply to closed systems only. *In any closed system heat spontaneously flows from a hot region to cold region.* This is another version of the second law of thermodynamics.

Some scientists say that increase in entropy is the arrow of time. When the entropy of the universe is maximum with its maximum disorderliness, there will be equalization of temperature. In that condition, the whole universe will stop working. With zero available energy and isothermic conditions throughout the universe, no work is possible. Can the universe remain in that non-functional condition for eternity? No, that is also not possible. The molecules, atoms and subatomic particles cannot maintain their positions without expenditure of energy. The planets, stars and galaxies cannot remain in their positions without expenditure of energy. The existence of a non-functional universe is inconceivable. No change is conceived without work. No time is conceived without change. Hence 'eternity' is a meaningless term for the non-functional universe.

The 'heat death of the universe' has generated much heat among scientists and political thinkers. Many scientists are in favour of it whereas many others are opposed to it. The Marxists vehemently oppose the concept of the 'heat death'. Theologians were very much encouraged to know this scientific evidence for the death of the universe. They claim that the universe has got birth and death. They further maintain that God is the cause for the birth and the death of the universe. They are delighted with the notion that science confirms the existence of God. The non-Marxist and Marxist atheists show their strong reaction to the concept of the 'heat death of the universe'. One dogma fights against another dogma. It will be shown here that the dogma conceals clear vision and functions as strong hallucinogen.

The Marxists' debate against the 'heat death of the universe' is based on three suppositions. Firstly, they presume that the universe is infinite. Secondly, they derive from the first supposition that the universe, instead of being a closed system, is an open system. Thirdly, they speculate that entropy and negentropy cancel each other and thereby maintain the *eternal motion* of the universe. In this connection, it may be appropriate to quote here the reactions of some Marxist thinkers.

In connection with Clausius' idea Engels wrote:

> ....energy is lost if not quantitatively then qualitatively. *Entropy cannot be destroyed by natural means, but can certainly be created.* The world clock has to be wound up, then it goes on running until it arrives at a state of equilibrium from which only a miracle can set it going again. The energy expended in winding has disappeared, at least qualitatively, and can only be restored by an *impulse from outside*. Hence, an impulse from

> outside was necessary at the beginning also, hence, the momentum, or energy, existing in the universe was not always the same, hence, energy must have been created, i.e., it must be creatable, and therefore destructible. *Ad absurdum*![5]

Alekseev gives a note to Engels' statement in the following words: "In other words, attempts to apply the second law to the entire universe result in a disagreement with the principle of eternity of motion in the universe, which is expressed by the principle of conservation and conversion of energy."[6]

It would not be enough to say that Engels' arguments are weak. As a matter of fact, he has got no arguments and tries to defend his dogma in vain. "Matter and motion are eternal." This is one central dogma of Marxist philosophy. There are no facts, no evidences and no logical arguments in support of this dogma. This cannot be taken as an axiomatic truth, since all axioms are analytic statements and this dogma is a synthetic statement. The law of conservation of energy applies to closed systems and it does say that energy cannot be created or destroyed. If energy is converted to unavailable or non-useful heat, it is not destruction of energy. It is simply conversion of energy from utilizable form to non-utilizable form. Furthermore, the second law of thermodynamics says that it is impossible to have a machine of perpetual motion. That being so, it is unscientific to speculate a machine with eternality of motion.

Marx and Lenin have got another erroneous idea. They think that matter is real, that it has got objective existence independent of our consciousness and that the universe with matter in it is infinite. Their idea may be quoted here.

> Marxist-Leninist theory defines matter as an objective reality that exists independently of our consciousness while being reflected in it. This definition is clarified and supplemented by natural-science data about the structure and characteristics of matter. Cognition of these aspects means cognition of matter itself. Matter, which is inseparably linked with motion, space and time, is capable of self-development and is quantitatively and qualitatively infinite.[7]

Albert Einstein has shown that space is finite. The idea of an infinite universe is old and obsolete. Any physical entity has got finite dimensions and finite volume. We should not equate vastness with infinity, or 'dimensions unmeasured till to-date' with infinity. The universe is, of course, vast, but it is finite. The total amount of energy (energy+matter which is packet of energy) in the universe is constant. The entropy of the universe is always on the increase and will sometime be maximum. With the continual conversion of the available energy into the disordered form of energy, which we call unusable heat, there is continual depletion in the stockpile of the available energy in the universe. Since the total energy content of the universe is finite, the available energy will be zero when the entropy is maximum. The notion of infinity of the universe has enabled Marx and Engels to get over this difficulty; however, the concept of infinity has got no scientific support.

Alekseev makes use of infinity and negentropy to disprove the concept of the 'heat death of the universe'. He writes:

> Since all real processes are accompanied by friction and heat exchange, entropy continuously increases (naturally, only in those isolated systems which receive no energy from outside). Some scientists therefore concluded that eventually, perhaps after a very long time, all the energy available on this planet and in other parts of the universe would convert to heat. According to this theory, the even distribution of heat between terrestrial and universal bodies would result in temperature equalization and the complete halt of all energy transformations, i.e., to a 'heat death of the universe'.
>
> The theory did not take into consideration the infinity of the universe, however, where the processes of energy degradation and concentration alternate in time and space. The concept of infinity is necessary to account for stores of energy on the Earth and in the solar system. In fact, a natural process of energy concentration and entropy decrease is currently occurring on the Earth. In this process of photosynthesis the dissipated energy of solar radiation is transformed into the concentrated chemical energy in green plants. A further decrease in entropy occurs in animal and human organisms, the most sophisticated systems on Earth, during food digestion and assimilation.[8]

Negentropy (negative entropy) is a measure of the orderliness of a system. It is opposite to entropy. It is mathematically expressed by the following equation:

$$-(\text{entropy}) = k \log (1/D)$$

If D is a measure of disorder, its reciprocal, 1/D, may be regarded as a direct measure of order. There is decrease in entropy in the process of negentropy. That decrease in entropy is a natural process is recognized in science. The formation of any star from gas spheres involves decrease in entropy. The green plants utilize solar energy in the process of photosynthesis and in this process there is decrease in entropy. The animal system and the human system synthesize tissues and energy-rich molecules in anabolic processes and there is decrease in entropy in all anabolic processes. In the non-living world, many things are synthesized with decrease in entropy. The household refrigerator is a familiar example of negentropy. Whenever we detect an entropy decrease, it is invariably the case that we study part of a system and not an entire one. Again these are all open systems and not closed systems. In the refrigerator, for instance, heat is constantly pumped out from within and, for this, external energy is expended. If there is decrease in entropy in X, there is increase in entropy in Y, and if we consider the net effect in X and Y combined the entropy is greater than the negentropy. This is exactly what happens in the open systems. If the universe is considered to be consisting of systems S_1, S_2, S_3, ...S_{n-1}, S_n, none of which are isolated from one another, there are occurrences of both entropy and negentropy, with the net result of increase in entropy. If a system is isolated from its surroundings, the changes that occur within it must drive up the entropy until it becomes the maximum. At that stage, there shall be no further changes. No work is possible in a condition of thermodynamic equilibrium.

Erwin Schrödinger, while writing about negentropy in living organisms, has said:

> When a system that is not alive is isolated or placed in a uniform environment, all motions usually come to a standstill.............., temperature becomes uniform by heat conduction. After that the whole system fades away into a dead, inert lump of matter. A permanent state is reached in which no observable events occur. The physicist calls this the state of thermodynamical equilibrium, or of 'maximum entropy'.

> Living matter evades the decay to equilibrium.[9]

What Schrödinger has said holds good for the living system. But as far as the whole universe is concerned, there is no agency that can evade the final 'heat death of the universe'.

The universe is finite and is a perfectly isolated system. It has got no surrounding for exchange of energy. There is nothing outside it. It is ideally a closed system. In such a system, entropy is continually on the increase. The first law of thermodynamics says: "The total energy of the universe is constant." The second law of thermodynamics says: "The total entropy of the universe is continually increasing." Considering both these laws, one is bound to reach the conclusion that eventually the unavailable energy will reach a point where it is equal to the total energy. The unavailable energy cannot be more than the total energy and hence the entropy of the universe at this stage will be the maximum. With maximum entropy, available energy becomes zero. Without available energy, no processes involving energy transfer are possible. Thus no work can be done. The universe has 'run down'.

Two inferences follow from the thermodynamic equilibrium. The first is that the universe will eventually have a death. The physicists call it the 'heat death of the universe'. The second is that the universe must have been born and must not have been ever existent. Had the universe been birthless, it would have reached its thermodynamic equilibrium end state in the past. Thus we cannot avoid the two conclusions: (1) The universe did not always exist. (2) The universe will not always exist.

Notwithstanding the scientific laws stated in the foregoing paragraphs and the conclusions derived from them, N.G. Chernyshevski, a Russian writer, has said:

> The formula which predicts the end of motion in the universe contradicts the fact that motion exists presently. This formula is false.......... The very fact that the end has not yet come makes it clear that the process was interrupted a countless number of times by a reverse process transforming heat into motion.........On the whole, it is a succession of vibrations, which has no beginning and no end.[10]

There does not seem to be any basis for the arguments of Chernyshevski. The universe has not yet died and hence Chernyshevski infers that death has been prevented in the past, is being prevented at present and will be prevented in the future. In drawing such an inference, he presumes the birthlessness of the universe and is not prepared, against all proofs, to accept something that violates the *sacrosanct truth* of the Marxists that "matter and motion are eternal". The universe was born with birth of time. From perfect order (*ṛta*) it became disorder (*anṛta*). Some order prevailed from extreme chaos. Both processes of construction and destruction become operative in the cosmos. Wherever there is construction, there is more negentropy and less entropy. Wherever there is destruction, there is preponderance of entropy. The cosmic processes go on. The net effect is continual increase in entropy. This process will continue. If it continues so that entropy will be maximum and utilizable energy will be zero, motion of the universe will be bound to stop. We have to accept it. If we catch hold of a dogma, a *sacred* dogma that matter and motion are eternal, and then try to substantiate our predetermined conclusion, then all our exercises are futile. That is what happens with the Marxist scientists as far as the laws of thermodynamics are concerned.

The second law of thermodynamics is statistical. It is not applicable to a few objects. It does not work unless there are many entities in a given situation. Scientists worked out the kinetic theory of gases where a large number of molecules are in random motion. One of the earliest papers on this topic was prepared in 1845 by the English physicist Sir Charles Wheatstone. In 1850 and 1851 Rankine and Joule published their works. In 1856, the German physicist A. Kröning published a paper in which he introduced the notion of the chaotic motion of molecules and made application of the theory of probability. After this, Clausius published his results on the motion and collisions of gas particles. In 1859, the Scottish physicist James Clerk Maxwell, basing on the theory of probability, formulated his law for the distribution of molecular velocities. The Austrian physicist Ludwig Eduard Boltzmann, in 1872, published a major paper called 'A Further Study of the Thermal Equilibrium of Gas Molecules'. He calculated the probability of various states of a system and proved that the most probable state is that in which the system's entropy is maximum. In 1886, Boltzmann wrote: "...........each distribution of energy corresponds to a quantitatively determined probability. Inasmuch as it coincides in practically important cases with the value which Clausius has termed 'entropy', we think it must also be designated by this term."[11] Thus Boltzmann related entropy to probability.

In 1905, Albert Einstein formulated the relationship between Brownian motion and kinetic theory. Statistical thermodynamics (statistical mechanics for gases) was developed by Josiah Willard Gibbs, a scientist at the University of Yale. He did this more comprehensibly and completely, independently of Boltzmann and Maxwell.

The Marxist scientists have got a bias against Clausius and his concept of entropy. They are very much antagonistic to the notion of the 'heat death of the universe'. They take refuge in Boltzmann, Maxwell and Gibbs who talk about statistical thermodynamics. In this connection, Alekseev writes: "Hence, the second law is a statistical law inapplicable to the universe, the bodies of which do not move chaotically but are each subject to its own laws of motion. Moreover, the second law can be violated more often the fewer particles in the system and the slower the velocities."[12] He further writes: "Thus the hypothesis that the universe would suffer a heat death was defeated. In contrast to the universal law of nature, i.e., the conservation of energy, the second law turned out to be a statistical law that is only applicable to systems consisting of a large number of chaotically moving particles."[13]

It is not correct to say that the second law of thermodynamics is inapplicable to the whole universe. Heat production is concerned with atomistic motion. The microworld is chaotically in motion. The statistical law of probability is applicable to the microworld like quantum physics. If we consider number, the microparticles in all the objects of the universe are countless. Hence, there is no reason to think that the second law of thermodynamics is not applicable to the whole universe.

Preconceived ideas are prejudicial to search for truth. We should search for evidences, analyse facts and reach a conclusion which we may retain or give up in future basing upon further evidences. It is unscientific to be allergic to God if evidences for His existence are forthcoming. It is equally unscientific to explain everything by the miracle of God without any rationality. The Marxist reaction to the second law of thermodynamics seems to stem from political indoctrination and not from pure science.

It has already been discussed in chapter VI and will again be discussed in part III of this book that the 'heat death of the universe' is really avoided. The cosmic processes do not continue to that point. There will never be a time when entropy is maximum. The universe is now expanding due to the kinetic energy of the original big bang against its own gravitational force. At a certain stage, the universe will stop this phase of expansion and will start contracting itself. It will continue to contract with greater and greater force. Scientists are also speculating that it would be a big crunch. In the state of extreme contraction, the universe will dissolve into the unmanifested *Prakṛti*. The phase of expansion followed by the phase of contraction and final dissolution constitutes one Great Cosmic Phase (*mahākalpa*). This repeats in cycles. Thus, there is no such thing as the 'heat death' or the 'crunch death'. Instead, we talk of the emanation and the dissolution of the universe.

Third Law of Thermodynamics

On progressive cooling a gas first becomes liquid and then solid. In the cooling process, the order of location and motion of particles increases with decrease in entropy. On the grounds of such observations, the German physicist and chemist Walther Nernst formulated in 1906 his 'Heat Theorem'. This was not a theoretical discovery. Nernst investigated chemical reactions over a wide range of temperatures. He could not reach the absolute zero temperature (—273.16°C). He plotted his data on a graph. He got a straight-line relationship. He extrapolated the straight line to the abscissa. The point where the straight line touched the abscissa was the absolute zero temperature (—273°C approximately).

Temperature as low as 0.0000001°K has been attained, but absolute zero could not yet be attained. Nernst has said in his Nobel-Prize-winning treatment of the subject that absolute zero is unattainable. In his opinion, absolute zero lies at an infinite distance even though one approaches very close to it.

Nernst's famous 'Heat Theorem' is otherwise known as the 'third law of thermodynamics'. This law says: No change in entropy occurs in a chemical reaction, if it takes place between pure crystalline solids at absolute zero temperature, i.e., the entropy of the products equals that of the reactants. To express it in another form, entropy S tends to zero as temperature T approaches 0°K; at 0°K, which is practically unattainable, entropy is zero.

In Advaita Vedānta, the existence of any manifested entity of the universe (*jagat*) without moṭion is not acceptable. Absolute inaction and hence absolute zero entropy are applicable to only Brahman that is not sense-perceptible. This explains the unattainability of absolute zero temperature.

Notes

1. BSŚB, I.4.3; II.1.14; Śve ŚB, I.9; VC, 109.
2. BSŚB, I.4.3; Śve ŚB, I.9; Bhā, III.5.25; VC, 109.
3. BGŚB, VII.25; VS, 51-54; VC, 111, 113, 115.
4. BSŚB, I.2.22; I.4.3.
5. Engels, F., Quoted by Alekseev, G.N. in *Energy and Entropy*, Mir Publishers, Moscow, 1986, p. 174.
6. Alekseev, G.N. in 5, pp. 174-5.
7. *Ibid.*, p. 18.
8. *Ibid.*, pp. 11-2.
9. Schrödinger, E., *What is Life & Mind and Matter*, Cambridge University Press, Cambridge, 1980, p. 74.
10. Chernyshevski, N.G., Quoted by Alekseev, G.N. in 5, p. 175.
11. Boltzmann, L.E., Quoted by Alekseev, G.N. in 5, pp. 177-8.
12. Alekseev, G.N. in 5, p. 177.
13. *Ibid.*, pp. 179-80.

PART II

ADVAITA VEDĀNTA

CHAPTER VIII

REALITY VERSUS APPEARANCE

> This I have said to you, O Kālāmās, but you may accept it, not because it is a report, not because it is a tradition, not because it is so said in the past, not because it is given from the scripture, not for the sake of discussion, not for the sake of particular method, not for the sake of careful consideration, not for the sake of forbearing with wrong views, not because it appears to be suitable, not because your preceptor is a recluse, but if you yourselves understand that this is so meritorious and blameless, and, when accepted, is for benefit and happiness, then you may accept it.
>
> *Buddha's Advice in Aṅguttara Nikāya, III*.653.

IN ADVAITA VEDĀNTA, only Brahman is real and nothing else; the world we see and live in is an illusion. In this chapter, we shall discuss the fundamental concepts of reality versus appearance. The concepts of Brahman, *Māyā*, world, *jīva* (individual self) and God or *Īśvara* (Universal Self), that are vitally important to Advaita Vedānta, will be the subject matter of this discussion.

Brahman

Whatever exists is real; whatever is immutable is real. Existence (*satya*)[1] and immutability (*avikārya*)[2] are the two criteria of Reality in Advaita Vedānta. In modern linguistic philosophy, it is recognized that existence is not predicable. That does not contradict the statement that whatever exists is real. The word '*satya*' (*as*+*kyap*) in Sanskrit means 'that which exists'. The statement "Whatever exists is existent (*yadasti tat satyam*)" is an analytical statement. It does not say anything new. The subject and the predicate in the statement mean the same thing. All analytical statements are necessarily true. Hence the statement given here is true without any empirical verification. The statement does not categorize anything that exists. It does not qualify anything. It does not say whether it is matter or energy. It does not say anything about its shape, size, mass, consistency, density, colour, taste, odour, number, etc. It says only this much, "That which exists, exists." Unless somebody is a nihilist, unless someone discards the existence of everything including himself, total non-existence cannot be an acceptable proposition. A second statement which is relevant in connection with Brahman is given like this: "Whatever is existent is Brahman (*yat satyaṁ tad Brahma*)." A name, i.e., Brahman is given to whatever exists. We don't need a proof for this. A liquid substance, made of atoms of hydrogen and oxygen in the proportion of two to one, with freezing point of 0°C and boiling point of 100°C, is water. In Sanskrit it is *jalam*. A proof is not necessary for naming the substance as aqua, water or *jalam*.

The second criterion of Reality, i.e., immutability, is a condition for the concept of Brahman. Any changeable entity is bound to have beginning and end; it is bound to decay. If x changes to y and y changes to z and this changing process continues, the whole process cannot be eternal. In this example, y has got birth and death. The y is born the moment x disappears and in its place y appears. The y dies the moment y disappears and in its place z appears. There cannot be any change without expenditure of energy. The Sanskrit word for energy is *śakti*. It is that which has got the ability to do work. There is no other better definition of energy. Wherever there is change, there is work and wherever there is work, there is expenditure of energy. Expenditure of energy implies decay (*kṣaya*) of a body from which energy is used up. Marx, Lenin and others have argued that there is dynamic flux of energy in the whole universe that is unborn, unending and eternal. This concept has been discarded in chapter VII. There is degradation of energy; the entropy that is produced as a result of expenditure of energy is not reconverted into usable energy. In chapter VI, the cosmogony of science has been discussed. The cosmic egg starts with a 'singularity'; it explodes. The universe expands. Again it contracts, and finally it ends in a 'singularity'. The scientist has invented a positive word and named it 'singularity'. In real sense it is negative and nothing. Let us visualize a condition where there is no universe, no space, no time, no activity and no change. The changeable world shrinks and shrinks to nothing. What is there in this condition of nothing or singularity? Is it absolute nothing? Is it absolute nihil? Science does not answer this question. Again, the cosmic egg appears and the universe becomes active. Wherefrom does the universe appear? Is it ex-nihilo? Science does not answer. We don't get a solution by confining ourselves to the mutable world. We must go beyond the mutable world. That something beyond this material world is immutable. It is changeless and absolutely changeless.

The mutable world constantly undergoes changes. The duration of time for any specific state may be infinitesimally small; let it be δt. The world, W_1, at time t_1, does not remain as W_1 at time t_2 which is $t_1 + \delta t$; it becomes W_2 at time t_2. Moreover, at any particular time, any substance, s, is both s and not-s and many variables in the range of s and not-s. This has been discussed in Part I of this book in connection with the uncertainty principle of Heisenberg. Such uncertainty is not applicable to Brahman. Here, B (Brahman) is not contradicted by any method and in any circumstances whatsoever.[3]

Thus, B remains as B. It is ever B→B→B→B→B→........ ....→B. Whenever any entity undergoes modification, A changes to B, B changes to C and C changes to D; it has a beginning (*ādi*) and an end (*anta*) in each stage of existence. In the case of Brahman, B does not undergo any modification. Hence, it is beginningless (*anādi*)[4] and endless (*ananta*)[5].

Advaita Vedānta does not accept any concept that says that consciousness is a product of insentient matter. Consciousness (*caitanya*) is not a product, it is the Reality and the primary substratum of everything. Before the manifestation of the world, there was no matter (including energy). The world did not come out of nothing. That positive entity that ever exists and existed before the cosmic manifestation is not insentient. That positive sentient entity deliberated and the world was a product of that deliberation.[6] There is grand design[7] in the cosmic anatomy and physiology. For maintenance of the cosmic processes, intelligent co-ordination, control and execution are unavoidable.[8] Again, for the orderly dissolution and reabsorption of the cosmos, intelligent controller is necessary. The mutable is insentient and the immutable is sentient. So Advaita Vedānta says that Brahman is pure Consciousness.[9]

Is consciousness an attribute of Brahman? Redness is an attribute of the rose. Sweetness is an attribute of the grape. Is Brahman an object and is consciousness the attribute of that object? Advaita Vedānta does not accept such an idea. According to *Viśiṣṭādvaita* and *Nyāya-Vaiśeṣika* systems of philosophy, an attribute (*dharma*) is possessed by an object (*dharmī*) and there cannot be an attribute without an object. What has been said here is true for any product, but not true for the Reality that is primary and fundamental. Advaita Vedānta says that Brahman is pure Consciousness and that it is not an object[10] which possesses the attribute of consciousness.

The Upaniṣad declares that Brahman is existence (*satya*), Consciousness (*jñāna*) and endless (*ananta*).[11] It does not undergo any modification. It is changeless (*avikārya*). Because it is never modified and B remains as B, it has neither any precedent stage (*apūrvam*)[12] nor consequent stage (*anaparam*).[13] For this reason it is birthless (*ajam*),[14] deathless (*amaram*)[15] and eternal (*nityam*).[16] Any non-changing entity, ever free from modifications, is bound to be eternal. On the other hand, any entity that has a beginning must have an end (*yadārabdhaṁ tadanityam*).[17] To have a beginning implies that a product has been formed due to modification. Any product must spend energy for maintaining its form and position. Change occurs in any process where expenditure of energy is involved. Thus every product has to change. A product, p_1, becomes p_2, p_3, p_4,........., p_n, and it cannot continue to be p_1 for ever. Change and eternality of the same entity are incompatible concepts. So all products are changeable and no product is eternal. Brahman is not a product. It never undergoes any change. What was B in the past is B at present and will be B in future. Brahman, being no product of anything and itself having no product, is ever immutable and hence is eternal. It is not only eternal, it is also timeless and beyond the three periods of time, viz., past, present and future.[18] A *mahākalpa* is the period between the emanation and the subsequent dissolution of the universe. During a *mahākalpa*, space exists as an entity and time exists, not as an entity, but as a mental construct. After a world-cycle terminates and before the next world-cycle begins, there is no time and no space, but there is Brahman only. Thus Brahman is not only timeless, but also spaceless (*anākāśam.*).[19]

Brahman is formless (*arūpam, akāyam, nirākāram*).[20] It is attributeless (*nirguṇa*)[21] and actionless (*niṣkriya*).[22] Anything that maintains form and position spends energy. Anything that exhibits any quality spends energy. Exhibition of quality is an action and cannot be accomplished without involvement of energy-expenditure. Anything that spends energy undergoes modification.

Brahman, being immutable and eternal, has got no form, no qualities and no functions.

Brahman, being changeless, does not undergo decay (*avyaya*)[23] and is imperishable (*akṣara*).[24] It does not grow.[25] Decay, perishability and growth involve change.

Since Brahman is not a product, it has no precedent stage. Thus Brahman is uncaused. Not only it has got no cause, it is also not cause of anything else. It does not undergo any change. Hence it has not got any consequent stage. Thus Brahman is not the material cause (*upādāna kāraṇa*) of any product. Brahman, being attributeless and actionless, is not an agent (*kartā*) of any action. Thus Brahman cannot be the efficient cause (*nimitta kāraṇa*) of any product. And so the scriptures declare that the uncaused Brahman is not cause of anything.[26]

Brahman cannot be preceived by our five senses, viz., visual, auditory, olfactory, gustatory and tactile organs.[27] Anything that is formless, attributeless and actionless cannot be perceived by any of our senses. Anything that is sense-imperceptible (*avyakta*)[28] cannot be thought of in the mind. Thus Brahman is not only ungraspable, but also unthinkable (*acintya*).[29] It cannot be seen, heard, smelt, tasted and touched.

The epistemology of Advaita Vedānta is relevant to the present discussion. We see a red rose. Light of certain wavelength comes from the rose and falls on our eye. Photochemical changes take place in the retina of the eye. An electric impulse is transmitted through the optic nerve to the visual centre of the brain. This visual centre feels something and that something is the red colour of the rose. What has been described here for the visual perception holds good, in principle, for the auditory, olfactory, gustatory and tactile perceptions, although their modi operandi are different. In all such cases, sense organ receives stimuli from an object; the stimuli are processed and then transmitted through nervous pathway to a specific centre situated in the brain. The centre in the brain gets a feeling and that is our perception. What exactly happens in the brain centre is not known. The receptor sense-organ, the conducting nerve pathway and the brain centre are all insentient (*jaḍa*). In spite of this, we get knowledge through the instrumentation of the insentient organs. Advaita Vedānta says that knowledge is possible due to reflection of Consciousness on the insentient organs. By the help of Consciousness or Brahman, the visual organ is able to see, the auditory organ is able to hear, the olfactory organ is able to smell, the gustatory organ is able to taste, the tactile organ is able to touch and the mind is able to think.[30] In such a situation, how can we perceive Brahman by our five senses and think of Brahman by our mind? Divested of the light of pure Consciousness, our sense-organs are like wood or clods of earth. They cannot function if they are not inspired by the reflection of Brahman.[31] By the reflection of Brahman on our receptor sense-organs, conducting nerve-pathways, brain-centres and internal instrument of cognition (*antaḥkaraṇa*), our perceptions, conceptualization and cognition are possible. That being so, it is not possible on our part to perceive, conceptualize and cognize Brahman.[32]

Brahman is indeterminable (*aparimeya*).[33] The dimensions of a thing that has got form and size are measured. The intensity of a property of a thing such as hotness, colour, sound, odour, sweetness or bitterness may be determined. The working capacity of a thing may be measured in terms of dyne, watt, horse-power, etc. That which is formless, attributeless and actionless is immeasurable. Again, something that is not perceived by senses and is not cognized cannot be determined since determination is done only through the instrumentation of our senses.

There is Brahman and nothing else.[34] Brahman is the only Reality. It is non-dual, one without a second.[35] Hence it is non-relational.[36] Without a second, there is no question of Brahman perceiving anything else or anything else perceiving Brahman.[37] It does not see anything else and anything else does not see it. It does not hear anybody else and anybody else does not hear it. It does not smell anything else and anything else does not smell it. It does not taste anything else and anything else does not taste it. It does not touch anything else and anything else does not touch it. It does not think of anything else and anything else does not think of it.

Brahman is partless[38] (*niṣkala*, *niravayava*) and unbroken whole (*akhaṇḍa*).[39] It cannot be non-dual if it is broken. It cannot be broken if it is non-functional. Of course, it can have parts even if it is unbroken whole. A tree, being single, has got parts like trunk, branches, leaves, flowers, seeds, roots, etc. The body of an individual human being has got parts like head, chest, hands, legs, etc. Advaita Vedānta holds that Brahman is an undifferentiated (*avyākṛta*)[40], homogeneous whole of Consciousness (*prajñāna-ghana*).[41] Without work and expenditure of energy, there cannot be differentiation. Brahman is actionless and hence is bound to be undifferentiated.

Brahman is all-pervasive (*parivyāptam, tatam*).[42] It pervades all and nothing else pervades it.[43] It is both inside and outside everything. It is both inside and outside the whole universe. There is no space which is not pervaded by it.[44]

It has been said that there is Brahman and nothing else. Brahman is the only Reality without a second. If this is so, how does Brahman pervade everything? What is the meaning of 'everything' here?

There are three types of existence (*sattā*), viz., absolute (*pāramārthika*), relative (*vyāvahārika*) and illusory (*prātibhāsika*).[45] Brahman, that cannot be contradicted by any means and in any circumstances, is absolute existence. The existence of the world is dependent upon Brahman and even this existence is ever mutable. Such an existence is relative. When we see a snake which is really a rope, the snake which is illusory appears real for us for that moment. Such an existence is illusory.

When we say "Brahman pervades everything and the whole universe", we mean thereby that the empirical world is pervaded by Brahman. Due to our ignorance, we get manifold vision of the world against the substratum of the single Reality of Brahman. Although the apparent world is not real in the absolute sense, it is not nothing in the empirical sense. Recognizing the relative existence of the universe, we say that Brahman is all-pervasive (*vibhu, paribhu, sarvagata, sarvavyāpī*).

The empirical world, with its relative existence, appears to exist and function on the substratum (*adhiṣṭhāna*)[46] of Brahman. We see the waves, the ripples and the surf on the ocean-water. We hear the roaring of the beating waves. What we perceive on the surface of the ocean-water are names and forms of the water itself. The waves, the ripples and the surf do have existence for us; but none of them has existence independent of the substratum of water.

Brahman is self-effulgent, self-luminous (*svayaṁ-jyotiḥ*).[47] It illumines the whole universe; it is not illumined by anything else. The Sun illumines by the illumination of the Self; the moon and the stars illumine by the illumination of the Self; the fire and the lightning illumine by the reflection of the self-luminous Brahman. Whatever shines in the universe, whatever is dazzling and lustrous in the universe is effected by the reflection of the light of the self-luminous Brahman.[48]

Blissfulness (*ānanda*) is Brahman.[49] This is a word used in a special sense in Advaita Vedānta. It is not joyfulness, opposite of sorrowfulness. It is not happiness, opposite of unhappiness. It is not an attribute of Brahman. It is a state of quietude (*śānta*)[50] of ever-contentedness (*nitya-tṛpta*).[51] Brahman has got no need that is to be fulfilled. It has no sorrow to be removed. It is not joyous for having attained anything since it has nothing to attain. *Ānanda* is an ever-quiet and ever-contented state, uncontaminated with the opposites of joyfulness and sorrowfulness, and that is Brahman.

Brahman is motionless and ever-still (*sthāṇu, acala*).[52] Anything that moves spends energy. Motion is an action. Any type of motion is not possible without the expenditure of energy. Anything that moves and spends energy cannot be unchangeable, undecaying and eternal. Brahman, being eternal and timeless and free from modification, is immobile and still.

Brahman is pure, spotless and free from defects and blemishes (*śuddha, nirañjana*).[53] The qualities possessed by any object may be good or bad. The functions of any agent may be good or bad. The form of any object may or may not have defects. Any physical entity may be contaminated with something that may be unclean, dirty or impure. Brahman is formless, actionless, attributeless, non-dual and non-relational. Hence it has to be pure, uncontaminated and free from defects and blemishes.

Whatever happens in the insentient, empirical world is witnessed by Brahman that is pure Consciousness. The omniscient Brahman is the only witness (*sākṣī*).[54] After the dissolution of the universe, the relative existence disappears and only the absolute existence (Brahman) remains. When nothing else is there, and only pure Consciousness remains, it becomes the witness without any other thing remaining (*aśeṣasākṣī*).[55]

Any entity, living or non-living, is described by language. We use words for classes like cow, horse, man, etc. Any particular individual of a class such as Devadatta (the name of a person) may also be described by language. Adjectives such as 'tall', 'beautiful', and 'many' are used to qualify or quantify anything. Words such as 'reading', 'playing', 'cooking' and 'eating' are used for actions. To express relations, we use words such as 'son', 'daughter', 'parents', 'friends', 'enemies', etc. We use prepositions such as 'in', 'on', 'over', 'under', etc. for expressing positional relations. Conjunctions such as 'and', 'or', 'either or', 'neither nor', etc. are used to express conjunctions, disjunctions, etc.

We cannot use any language for Brahman. It is not an object. It is formless, actionless and attributeless. It is only one, without a second. It is non-relational. Hence Brahman cannot be described.[56] Language cannot be used for it. The word 'Brahman' is used to name Reality. But this word does not help us for cognitive purpose. We cannot conceptualize Reality by the use of the word 'Brahman'.

Very often scriptures make vain attempt to describe Brahman by use of contradictory language.[57] Brahman is smaller than the smallest and larger than the largest. It is stationary and mobile; it runs and runs not; it moves and moves not; it is far and near; it is inside and outside everything. The problem of the indescribability of Brahman is not solved at all by such use of contradictory language. This is one way of our confession in expressing our inability in describing Brahman by language.

Seers have also expressed their inability for describing Brahman by use of negative language.[58] It is not gross, not minute; not short, not long; not internal, not external; and so on. Brahman is not conscious of the internal world nor conscious of the external world, nor conscious of both the worlds, nor a mass of consciousness, nor simple consciousness, nor unconsciousness. After describing in negative language, the Upaniṣadic seer says: It is unseen, trans-empirical, ungraspable, uninferable, unthinkable and indescribable. It is to be experienced without any mediation with one-pointed concentration on Self alone, where there is cessation of the phenomenal world. It is quiet, auspicious and nondual. This Self is to be known (*vijñeya*).[59]

The Upaniṣadic seers refuse to describe Brahman and refute any description by saying, "It is not this (*neti*).[60]" Any way of description of Brahman is not correct. In whatever way the disciple tries to describe Brahman is not satisfactory to the teacher and so he says, "It is not this (*neti*)." When the disciple demands an answer in categorical language, the teacher answers by remaining silent. Brahman is to be pointed out, but not to be spoken of (*lakṣyate, na tu ucyate*).

Manu is of the opinion that the existence of Brahman cannot be proved by logic and that Brahman is unknowable (*avijñeya*).[61] Logic deals with language. For Brahman, language cannot be used. Hence logical method cannot be applicable to prove the existence of Brahman. For cognition and conceptualization, sense-perceptibility is a necessary condition. Brahman is sense-imperceptible and hence it is unknowable.

But the scriptures advise us to know Brahman.[62] How to know something which is unknowable seems to be self-contradictory. In reality, however, it is not.

The Self is Brahman. There is nothing else other than the Self. For everybody there is no difficulty in cognizing the 'I' and nobody has a feeling "I am not".[63] The Self is to be experienced directly, without any mediation. This process is called 'immediate experience' (*aparokṣānubhūti*). Brahman is Self to be experienced without any mediation (*pratyagātmā*).[64]

Śaṅkara says that Brahman is to be investigated, that it is to be known (*vijijñāsitavyam*).[65] Knowledge of Brahman does not need subjective intellectualization (*na puruṣabuddhyapekṣam*); it is objective (*vastutantram*).[66] Brahman is imperceptible to the senses. It is not describable by language. Hence it is what it is. It is *that* that exists (*tat sat*). It can be indicated without use of words. That is that (that = that). It is an identical statement. It is a necessary truth.

The Great Statements (*mahāvākya*) of the Vedic Scriptures may be analyzed here. "That thou art (*tattvamasi*)[67]." 'That' stands for Brahman. If one sublates 'thou', the statement becomes an identical one (*akhaṇḍārtha vākya*). One may remove the idea of the world and the body, may remove the idea of multiplicity and duality and may concentrate on one's identity with Brahman. By attaining knowledge and dispelling nescience, one becomes non-different from Brahman. One will have immediate experience of "I am Brahman (*ahaṁ brahmāsmi*)[68]", "This Self is Brahman (*ayamātmā brahma*)[69]", "All this is verily the Self (*ātmaivedaṁ sarvam*)[70]", "All this is verily Brahman (*brahmaivedaṁ sarvam*; *sarvaṁ khalvidaṁ brahma*; *brahma khalvidam vāva sarvam*).[71] With this realization, the difference between subject and object disappears; there is nothing like 'you' and 'I', 'seer' and 'object seen'.[72] The knower, the knowable and the knowledge become one and nondifferent. All is pure Consciousness and Consciousness only.

Māyā

Māyā is power (*śakti*)[73] of Brahman. It is otherwise known as *Prakṛti*[74], *Avyakta*[75] or *Avidyā*[76] (Nescience). It exists; but it does not exist as an independent entity second to Brahman; its existence depends upon the existence of Brahman.[77] Due to such dependent existence, it is different from Brahman, non-different from Brahman and neither different nor non-different from Brahman.[78] The President of a country is a person; he exists as an entity. The President has power and by virtue of that power he can do and does so many things. But the power of the President is not a separate entity; it has no independent existence. Likewise, the power of Brahman has no independent existence. Advaita Vedānta says that Māyā exists, does not exist, and exists and does not exist.[79] It exists in unmanifested form and hence is called *Avyakta*. As darkness is opposite of light, so Māyā is opposite of knowledge, and hence is called *Avidyā*. Brahman is eternal and timeless; it is beginningless and endless. Māyā, being power of Brahman, is beginningless[80] and endless.[81] It is eternal and timeless.[82] The original Māyā (*Mūlaprakṛti*)[83] is undifferentiated (*avyākṛta*).[84] It consists of three constituents,[85] viz., *sattva* (serenity), *rajas* (activity) and *tamas* (inertia), kept in equipoise. When Māyā is undifferentiated and still consists of three constituents, it is known as with, without, and with and without parts.[86] Such an entity called Māyā which is existent, non-existent and both existent and non-existent, with parts, without parts, and both with and without parts is indescribable (*anirvacanīyā*).[87]

By the help of the *tamas* (inertia) constituent, Māyā has the veiling or concealing power (*āvaraṇa śakti*)[88]. It acts as a cover. Truth is not revealed to us because of this cover. Our vision is blurred. Reality remains concealed to us.

But, instead of total non-perception, we perceive the world in various ways. Reality, R, is not perceived as R, but as A, B, C, D,........., X_1, X_2, X_3,.........$X\infty$. This phenomenon of R appearing as not-R is due to the projecting power (*vikṣepa śakti*)[89] of Māyā. This projecting power works through the *rajas* (activity) constituent. Māyā deludes[90] every being by this power.

Māyā, being the power of Brahman or *Īśvara*, takes shelter in

Reality (*brahmāśrayā, īśvarāśrayā*).[91] It may not be misconstrued that the locus of Māyā is Brahman or *Īśvara*. Māyā is not an existent entity to occupy a place in Brahman or *Īśvara*. Any object (*viṣaya*) with body or mass can be stained with impurity. Brahman or *Īśvara* is not an object. It is formless and without a body. Furthermore, Māyā is not a thing that is impure, dirty and staining. Hence Brahman or *Īśvara* is not stained or polluted with Māyā. Māyā is an indescribable power, belonging to Brahman or *Īśvara*. So it is said that Māyā takes shelter in Brahman or *Īśvara*.

Before the manifestation of the cosmos, the universe was potentially existent in Māyā in an unmanifested state.[92] As long as the three constituents (*guṇa*) were in equilibrium, there was no manifestation. God or *Īśvara* created a vibration in Māyā and, due to this vibration, the three constituents of Māyā lost their equilibrium. In the *rajas*-predominant stage, the dormant, potential, unmanifested universe became manifested. This was the emanation which was not creation *ex nihilo*. The preservation of the universe in the manifested state is effected in a stage that is *sattva*-predominant. During the *tamas*-predominant stage, the processes of dissolution, just the reverse of those of manifestation, become operative. The three processes of emanation (*sṛṣṭi*), preservation (*sthiti*) and dissolution (*pralaya*) cannot be operative when the three constituents of Māyā are in equilibrium.[93]

The first product that emanates from Māyā is space (*ākāśa*). Gaseous matter orginated from space. As a result of condensation and gravitational contraction of gases, heat was generated. The heated gaseous material was liquefied. In course of time, heat was dissipated from the exterior surface and thus solid matter was produced. Śaṅkarācarya has explained this genesis in *Tattvabodha*[94] and has categorically said that the Māyā of Brahman is the progenitor of the cosmic products. Not only Māyā is the source of the cosmos, it is also the final receptacle of the cosmos when the whole universe is dissolved in Māyā and stays in a latent, unmanifested condition.[95]

Māyā is the material cause (*upādāna kāraṇa*) of the universe.[96] Every product, without any exception, has some material cause. The chair is made of wood. Here chair is the product and wood is its material cause. The necklace is made of gold. Here necklace is the product and gold is its material cause. When we say, "X is a product", we state thereby that X is made out of some raw material. A product, P, has got preceding material status. A becomes B and B becomes C. A is the preceding stage of B and B is the preceding stage of C. B is the product and A is its material cause. C is the product and B is its material cause. In this sense we say that Māyā is the material cause of the universe.

Māyā is insentient and cannot be the Creator of the universe. The insentient wood does not make a chair. The carpenter makes a chair. The carpenter is the efficient cause (*nimitta kāraṇa*) of the chair. Whenever there is an action, there must be some doer of the action (*yat kāryaṁ tat sakartṛkam*). There cannot be verb without a subject, whether expressed or understood. The world-product has got an efficient cause that needs omniscience for designing and execution. Both Māyā and *jagat* (universe) are insentient (*jaḍa*) and lack in omniscience, and hence cannot be the efficient cause. God or *Īśvara* is the efficient cause of the universe. But, without the help of Māyā, God cannot work as the Creator.[97] God does not need an instrumental cause (*sahakārī kāraṇa*). Māyā may be considered as the instrument of God.[98] It works as material and it also works as instrument. By the manifold and wonderful power of God, He creates the multiple and wonderful products, all of which constitute the cosmos.[99]

Māyā is under the control of God.[100] Of course, the reverse is not true. By exercising supreme control on Māyā, God creates the universe, supports it and brings about dissolution of it.

Both Māyā and the product of Māyā, i.e., the universe, are not-self (*anātma*).[101] Māyā is not Reality; the universe is not Reality. The whole universe constitutes the appearances of a magic show. The magician is God Himself; He plays the magic by his power of Māyā.[102] In the whole magic show of the phenomenal cosmos, the magic appearances do not affect the magician. God is totally unaffected by the cosmic magic show.[103] He operates Māyā for effecting the magic show, but is Himself unaffected by Māyā.

The universe and everything and everybody of the universe are under the control of Māyā.[104] They are deluded by the influence of Māyā. They do not get the right knowledge due to the influence of Māyā. Unless the veil of Māyā is thrown out, experience of Reality will be impossible.

Māyā is the limiting adjunct (*upādhi*)[105] of God. Without this limiting adjunct, God or *Īśvara* ceases to be with attributes and becomes identical with attributeless Brahman.

After describing so many things about the indescribable Māyā, one may ask the question, "What are the justifications for recognizing Māyā?" Can't we explain the universe without Māyā? Is the Māyā concept unavoidable?

If we accept as a fact that Brahman is Reality and the only Reality, we reject the universe as an existing entity. But the empirical universe cannot be altogether rejected, since its existence is relative, although not absolute. The concept of Brahman is violated if the universe is considered as a second entity or a product of the immutable Brahman. The empirical world that we perceive is not Reality since it has no absolute existence and it is ever mutable. On finer analysis, it cannot be established that the micro-constituents of the macro-world are really existent. Since the relative existence of the empirical world has to be recognized and its absolute existence has to be rejected, the original source of the world has to be something which is not Brahman and which is not second to Brahman. The world which is a product is an empirical entity; hence the existence of its origin must be inferred.[106]

Universe

In Advaita Vedānta, Brahman is accepted as the only Reality, non-dual, one without a second, and the universe of plurality is rejected.[107] The universe is unreal (*mithyā*)[108] for a non-dualist. A very common statement often quoted from Advaita Vedānta is as follows: "Brahman is real; the universe is an illusion, and *jīva* (individual self) is verily Brahman, not other than Brahman (*brahma satyaṁ jaganmithyā, jīvo brahmaiva nāparaḥ*)".

Gauḍapāda, the grand-teacher of Śaṅkara, propounded the theory of the non-origination of the universe (*ajātivāda*).[109] According to him, the universe was never born. It has got no existence at all. It is empirical. We perceive the pluralistic world, although it does not exist. We see many things in a magic show, although they are not really so. We see multiple phenomena in dream without any trace of reality. In the dream, one can see a beautiful city in the sky. This city is empirically meaningful for us, although it has no real existence. Things are said to exist only from the standpoint of empirical truth (*saṁvṛtisatya*).[110] So Gauḍapāda admits the empirical existence of the universe and he explains this as activity of Māyā.[111] He does not recognize any *de novo* creation or transformation of the original stuff. The universe is of the nature of Māyā, illusory manifestation or transfiguration. The one, non-dual Brahman somehow appears as the pluralistic universe through its own Māyā.[112] What is real cannot be really born. Brahman is beginningless, endless and immutable and that's how it exists. It is not born from anything else and anything else is not born from it. The world of plurality is an illusory appearance and Gauḍapāda thinks that to be born and to exist as not-self (other than Brahman) mean to have illusory appearance. The Bṛhadāraṇyaka Upaniṣad[113] also says that the Lord, on account of Māyā, is perceived as manifold.

Gauḍapāda considers the universe as non-existent. Hence he says that the non-existent universe is not born through Māyā, but illusorily appears through Māyā. The son of a barren woman is born neither through Māyā nor in reality and so is the universe.[114]

Māṇḍukya Upaniṣad[115] describes four quarters of the non-dual Brahman. These are: *Viśva, Taijasa, Prājña* and *Turīya. Viśva* is the waking state (*jāgrata*);[116] it cognizes external objects and experiences gross material things. The sphere of activity of *Taijasa* is the dream state (*svapna*);[117] it cognizes internal objects and experiences things that are subtle. *Prājña* acts in the state of deep sleep (*suṣupti*);[118] at this state it is one and verily a mass of cognition; it experiences bliss and is full of bliss. This *Prājña* is the Lord of all, Omniscient, inner Controller of all, source of all and the place of origin and dissolution of all.[119] What has been said here as *Viśva, Taijasa* and *Prājña* are not three different entities. It is one and the same entity that has been thought of in three ways. The fourth is *Turīya* which is trans-empirical and nondual. The phenomenal universe of plurality does not exist in *Turīya.*[120]

In *Viśva* and *Taijasa,* there is consciousness of subject and object—knower and things known, experiencer and things experienced. The subject-object consciousness is absent in both *Prājña* and *Turīya*; but there is a subtle difference. Only the seed of duality is present in *Prājña* while it is totally absent in the *Turīya.*[121]

Both *Viśva* and *Taijasa* are conditioned by cause and effect. *Prājña* is itself uncaused, but is the efficient cause of everything in the universe. *Turīya* has no cause (*kāraṇa*) and no effect (*kārya*).[122]

Gauḍapāda says that nothing exists except the non-dual Brahman which exists in four states and that the non-existent, phenomenal universe (*prapañca*) is nothing but imagination of Brahman in its three states, viz., *Viśva, Taijasa* and *Prājña.* All this duality and multiplicity of the phenomenal world is nothing but Māyā.[123]

The concept of illusion was introduced by Gauḍapāda. In darkness a rope may be mistaken as a snake. But if one ascertains that what appears as snake is really a rope, the illusion disappears. Similarly, the nondual Brahman appears as the world due to illusion. The illusion is caused by ignorance (*avidyā*). Right knowledge dispels this illusion and with that the world of plurality disappears.[124]

Śaṅkara was very much influenced by Gauḍapāda's philosophy of non-dualism. But he did not accept all the concepts of Gauḍapāda in toto. For Gauḍapāda, the external world is non-existent; for Śaṅkara, it is existent.[125] This existence is not absolute; it is relative and empirical. The world does not exist as an independent entity. Brahman is its substratum and its existence is dependent on that of Brahman.[126] Without Brahman the world cannot exist. The world of plurality is an appearance of the non-dual Brahman. As a rope appears as a snake or nacre appears as silver, so does Brahman appear as the world.[127] Gauḍapāda says that the non-dual Brahman as Consciousness, which is unborn, non-moving and attributeless, appears as the world of plurality which seems to originate, move and change and possess attributes.[128]

Every entity of the phenomenal world, small and large, is ever moving and ever changing. The Sanskrit word for the universe is *jagat* (*gam*+*kvip*), which means 'that which is ever moving and ever changing'. Without motion and change, no entity of the universe can ever exist for a moment.[129] The supergalaxies are moving; the galaxies are moving; the whole universe is expanding. The stars are rotating; the planets are rotating; they are revolving. In the subatomic world, every micro-particle is ever in motion. Without motion, the electron cannot exist, the proton cannot exist. Over and above this type of physical motion, processes of transformations are ever operative in every micro- and macro-entity of the universe. Everything in the universe is in a dynamic state of flux. Everything is ever changing. A becomes B, B becomes C, C becomes D, D becomes B and B becomes A. Nothing in the universe does remain static; nothing in the universe does remain immutable.

In logic, there are contrary and contradictory terms. The Sanskrit word '*sat*' means 'existent', and '*asat*' means 'non-existent'. '*Asat*' is contradictory to '*sat*'; but '*mithyā*' is contrary to '*sat*'. Strictly speaking, the universe is not *asat* or non-existent, but is *mithyā*. It has got a dependent existence. It appears to exist on the substratum of Brahman. It is not eternal and timeless. At time t_1, any substance of the world is s_1 and at time t_2 it is s_2. The whole world is W_1 at time t_1 and W_2 at time t_2. Not only any specific entity changes, but also its relationship with the rest of the world undergoes change. In consideration of this type of relative and dependent existence and perpetual mutability of the universe, it is called *mithyā*.

The universe has got origin; it has also got termination. Time starts with the origin of the universe; time ends with the dissolution of the universe. Space is born with the origin of the universe; it expands; then it contracts; finally it is dissolved with the dissolution of the universe. Such a universe that has got origin, sustenance and termination, that is not eternal and timeless, is called *mithyā*.

The whole universe is an object (*viṣaya*); every entity of the universe is an object. Every object possesses attributes. These attributes are ever-changing. We cognize the object by virtue of its actions and manifestations of its attributes. The cognizer (*viṣayī*) is the Self or Consciousness. There is no way of ascertaining whether the cognitions are 'as they really are'. If A is cognized as A and never as not-A, the cognition is correct. There can never be such a correct cognition of the phenomenal world. And hence the world is *mithyā*.

Śaṅkara describes the cognition of the illusory world in an appropriate way. "Its form, as described here, cannot be determined with any degree of certainty. It is apparent like a dream, water of a mirage or a city in the sky. It is fugitive, its own form being evinced and not evinced. Therefore, it has no end, no fixity, no determinacy, it never stays as a particular form exclusive of other forms; it can never be determined conclusively. Similarly, it has no beginning; nobody can determine it as starting from something and becoming something definite. Nobody can determine it as having any definite existence or intermediate existence."[130] What Śaṅkara has said here is an ancient version of the indeterminacy of Heisenberg. If anything in the universe cannot be determined with certainty, and A can be A and not-A and anything in the range of A and not-A, such a universe is *mithyā*.

The greatest contribution of Śaṅkara to Advaita Vedānta is his doctrine of superimposition (*adhyāsa*). He has explained this doctrine in his introduction to the Brahma-Sūtra.[131] Superimposition is erroneous cognition, it is illusory appearance (*avabhāsa*). When A is cognized as not-A (*atasmiṅstadbuddhiḥ*), it is erroneous cognition (*mithyā-jñāna*). The rope is not a snake. The nacre is not silver. When rope is cognized as snake or nacre is cognized as silver, such cognition is erroneous. In superimposition, there is coupling of the real and the unreal (*satyānṛte mithunīkṛtya*). The unreal is superimposed on the real. The snake is superimposed on the real rope. The silver is superimposed on the real nacre. The universe which is unreal is superimposed on Brahman which is real. For elucidation of superimposition, the examples of rope-snake and nacre-silver have been classical. The real snake and real silver that have been seen before remain in the form of memory. The observer of the unreal snake in the place of the rope and the unreal silver in the place of the nacre does not see that experienced real snake or real silver. Nor is he conscious of it as a mere recollection. The locus of superimposition here is rope or nacre. What is superimposed is snake or silver. The superimposition has a nature which is like that of recollection; it itself is not recollection (*smṛtirūpaiḥ paratra pūrvadṛṣṭāvabhāṣaḥ*). In superimposition, one appears as having the attributes of another (*anyasya anyadharmāvabhāsaḥ*). The attributes of a rope are different from those of a snake. But due to superimposition, the rope appears as having the attributes of the snake. The content of erroneous cognition cannot be real, because once knowledge is obtained and the rope is cognized as rope, the snake-cognition is sublated. This content cannot be unreal because it appears. It cannot be real and unreal because that would involve contradiction. Thus it is indeterminable (*anirvacanīya*).

Nescience (Māyā or *Avidyā*) is the cause of superimposition. It is two-fold in its functioning. It has got veiling power and projecting power. It veils the nondual Brahman and projects pluralities of the world. Due to the functioning of Māyā, there is non-apprehension of the real (*tattva-pratibodha*). Brahman, B, is not apprehended as B. Māyā also functions by causing apprehension of one as another (*anyathāgrahaṇa*). Here B is not apprehended as B; moreover, it is apprehended as non-B, and C, D, E, F and others.

There is Brahman only; it is nondual and partless. It is Consciousness and the Self (*Ātman*). Its power is Māyā or *Avidyā* or nescience. It is beginningless and endless. There is nothing like the world. The world which does not exist in reality is the not-Self (*anātman*). The question is: "How is the world which does not exist superimposed on Brahman?" In the rope-snake or the nacre-silver case, both the entities in each example exist empirically. This is not the case with Brahman and the world. The former exists and the latter does not exist. Secondly, here the cognizer is Brahman alone which is Consciousness and that which is cognized is the non-Self. In Śaṅkara's language, the cognizer is *asmat* or the first person (*Ātmā*) and the not-Self is *yuṣmat* or the second person (thou). How can there be self-delusion of the omniscient Brahman?

In order to understand *saṁsāra* (metempsychosis), thorough comprehension of Māṇḍukyopaniṣad is necessary. There is no question of subject and object in Advaita Vedānta. There is only the subject (*viṣayī*); there is no object (*viṣaya*). In Śaṅkara's language in the Adhyāsa-Bhāṣya, the subject and the object are antagonistic to each other like light and darkness. Light exists; darkness does not exist; the absence of light is darkness. Although darkness does not exist in reality, it has got empirical existence. So does the world, which is not-self, empirically exist. Although Self alone exists, it exists as *Viśva, Taijasa* and *Prājña* in the waking, dream and deep sleep, respectively. These are three names of the same one Self in the three states. *Viśva* is conscious of the external world, enjoys what is gross and is satisfied therewith. *Taijasa* is conscious of what is within, enjoys what is subtle and is satisfied with it. *Prājña* is a mass of consciousness without the distinctions of subject and object; bliss is its enjoyment and satisfaction. The nondual Reality is the *Turīya* or 'the fourth'. This is the changeless, attributeless, non-functional Brahman. The states that change and pass are produced by Māyā; they are illusory. In both *Viśva* and *Taijasa* states, there are both non-apprehension and mis-apprehension of the real. In the *Prājña* states, there is only non-apprehension, but no mis-apprehension. The *Turīya* is not affected by both the activities of Māyā. It is Consciousness *per se*. There is no trace of ignorance in it. Thus it is seen that there is no unavoidability of having two existing entities for superimposition to work. Śaṅkara, in his Adhyāsa-Bhāṣya, gives the example of seeing two moons in spite of the existence of one moon. Superimposition of the not-Self on the Self is executed by Māyā, the power of Self.[132]

No change of the Real is involved in the manifestation of the universe. Nothing is modified into the pluralities of the universe. When a pot is made out of the earth, a form is obtained and so is a name; the earth itself is not changed. In making a ring of gold a form is obtained and so is a name; the gold itself is not changed. And so does Brahman appear as multiple entities of the universe. When the unmanifested (*avyakta*) becomes manifested (*vyakta*), forms (*rūpa*) are acquired and each form gets a name (*nāma*). What we call modification is really a name arising from speech (*vācārambhaṇaṁ vikāro nāmadheyam*).[133]

Advaita Vedānta rejects the doctrine of transformation (*pariṇāmavāda*) and pleads for the doctrine of illusory appearance (*vivartavāda*).[134] Brahman is not transformed into the world. The single Brahman which is real appears as the manifold entities of the universe which is unreal. In *pariṇāmavāda*, the material cause (*upādāna*) and the effect (*kriyā*) have the same nature of existence. In *vivartavāda*, the material cause (Brahman) has got absolute existence (*pāramārthika sattā*) and the products (universe) have got apparent or illusory existence (*prātibhāsika sattā*).

Īśvara (*God*)

Advaita Vedānta recognizes the existence of a creator, preserver, ruler and controller of the phenomenal universe. He is called *Īśvara* or God. The universe is emanated, maintained and reabsorbed. Before it is manifested from the unmanifested condition, *Īśvara* deliberates[135] on it. Māyā, the power of Brahman, is the material cause (*upādāna kāraṇa*) of the universe. But Māyā is insentient (*jaḍa*) as wood or clay. Wood is not converted into a chair without a carpenter. Clay is not converted into a pot without potter. The carpenter or the potter has got knowledge and skill and is the efficient cause (*nimitta kāraṇa*). *Īśvara* is the efficient cause of the universe.[136]

Before a building or a machine is constructed, its plan is made. The architect does it. The plan is well designed. The construction is executed as per the design. We observe beautiful plan of the world. Not only the plan is beautiful, it is intelligently designed for specific purposes. This is true both in the micro- and the macro-world. In the world of subatomic particles, atoms and molecules, beautiful planning and meaningful design are cognized. In the supergalaxies, galaxies, stars and planetary systems, we see the same thing. The gross and the subtle structures of both the living and the nonliving world exhibit planning and designing. The idiotic atom does not understand plan and design. The insentient star-systems and planetary systems are totally ignorant of these. Man, the most intelligent animal on the Earth, takes a life-time to learn a fraction of how he himself has been planned and designed. We don't have any doubt in the existence of a plan-cum-design of the universe. Some people say that it is there and it is naturally made. They themselves do not understand the meaning of 'naturally' although they use it confidently to satisfy their dogma of materialism. By observing the plan and the design of the micro- and macro-world very minutely and deeply, any rational being shall have to infer that there is an invisible planner and designer of the universe.[137]

Advaita Vedānta does not accept the eternality of the world. The world has a beginning, a life-time and an end. This process is repeated. Modern astrophysics corroborate this concept of Advaita Vedānta. The idea of creation out of nothing is rejected in Advaita Vedānta. In the original manifestation, the universe emanates from Māyā and after the great world period (*mahā-kalpa*), it goes back to Māyā.[138]

The world has a beginning; it has been created. Being insentient and unintelligent, it could not be self-created. The world has a creator, an intelligent creator. Having been created, it cannot be sustained even for a moment without an intelligent and powerful sustainer. All the entities of the micro- and the macro-world not only exist, but also function purposefully in strict adherence to some laws and in co-ordination with others. This action of purposeful functioning and co-ordination is explained away by saying that it happens naturally. Man, the most intelligent animal on the Earth, does not know how it is done in his own system. Without his consciousness and effort, his own system functions purposefully and intelligently. This happens not only in man's system, but also in all systems without exception—in plants, animals, amoeba, bacteria and viruses; planetary systems, galaxies and super-galaxies; molecules, atoms, neutrons, protons, electrons, neutrinos and photons. Thus it is inferred that there is some invisible being who is sustaining the whole universe. This well-planned, well-designed and purposefully functioning well-coordinated cosmos will not live perpetually. It will have involution (*pratiprasava*), the reverse of evolution. In strict adherence to the laws, the whole universe will be dissolved and absorbed into Māyā to remain there in unmanifested condition. This whole process of dissolution will not be chaotic but will be systematic. Under the supervision and execution of some invisible being, the phenomenal universe will disappear. For the threefold cosmic activities, viz., creation, maintenance and dissolution, we infer the existence of a Creator, Preserver and Destroyer.[139] He is *Īśvara*.

In materialistic philosophy, chance (*ākasmikatā*) and randomness (*yadṛcchā*) play important role in the functioning of the universe. The total functioning of the universe is mediated through the resultant force of all random forces working by chance. It is not correct to say that there are no chance-actions. Random functioning of the micro-world is based on facts of observations. But these observations do not reveal the root of the world-tree. What are apparently chances and random actions follow regular patterns and are resultantly guided by laws. Had the universe been functioning by chances alone, it would have a chaotic fate. But that is not exactly the case. The universe is not a chaos; it is a cosmos. We observe order (*ṛta*) amidst disorder. This order is possible due to an invisible controller. That Controller is God.[140]

In order to be Creator, Sustainer, Destroyer and Controller, all-knowledge, all-power and all-pervasiveness become prerequisite conditions. According to the concept of Advaita Vedānta, God is omniscient,[141] omnipotent[142] and omnipresent.[143] He is unborn;[144] He does not die.[145] He is not caused.[146] He is eternal.[147] Anybody with temporal existence cannot discharge the duties of creation, maintenance, control and dissolution, cycles of phenomena that are eternal. Anybody who is unborn and eternal is bound to be uncaused.

Īśvara is not a product. He is not the subsequent state of any antecedent state. Being beginningless, He has no origin and is uncaused. He is not only uncaused, but also is not the material cause of anything.[148] He has no product. He is not the antecedent state of any product. God is not an object that can be converted into products.

The cosmic egg that is produced at the beginning of each *mahākalpa* (world period) is produced from Māyā.[149] It is not produced from *Īśvara*. *Brahmā* is the creative divinity who supervises the creation of all entities of the universe and is produced by *Īśvara*.[150] But *Brahmā*, being *Īśvara* himself, is not a product. This is the *causa sui* concept in Advaita Vedānta. Being self-caused, Brahmā is known as *Svayambhū*.[151]

God is one and not more than one. Advaita Vedānta gives three names to three aspects of the same one God. The creative divinity is *Brahmā*; the sustaining divinity is *Viṣṇu*; and the destructive divinity is *Rudra*.[152] Māyā is the limiting adjunct (*upādhi*) of God. Being associated with this *upādhi, Īśvara* acquires the constituents (*guṇa*) of His *upādhi*. *Īśvara*, acquiring the constituent of activity (*rajas*), is known as *Brahmā*; He is the Creator. *Īśvara*, acquiring the constituent of serenity (*sattva*), is known as *Viṣṇu*. He is the Supporter and Sustainer. *Īśvara*, acquiring the constituent of inertia (*tamas*), is known as *Rudra*. He is the Destroyer.

Thus *Īśvara* is not attributeless. He has attributes,[153] although acquired from His *upādhi*. Had not *Īśvara* acquired attributes, He could not function and the concept of non-functioning *Īśvara* is self-conflicting and unsound. That is why the Chāndogya Upaniṣad describes *Īśvara* not negatively, but in positive language such as "with all works, all desires, all odours, and all tastes".

It has already been said that Brahman is attributeless and is the only Reality. It is again said here that *Īśvara* is with attributes and is the Creator, Preserver, Controller and Destroyer of this universe. Is *Īśvara* different from Brahman and a second Reality?

Some say that Brahman and *Īśvara* are one and the same and are like the two sides of a coin. They are two aspects—without attribute (*nirguṇa*) and with attributes (*saguṇa*)—of the same Reality. This concept does not convince logically. One single nondualistic Reality cannot be both with and without attributes. It is better to accept dualism instead of two aspects of a non-dualistic Reality that is homogeneous, undifferentiated and partless. Some others say that *nirguṇa* Brahman is higher and that *saguṇa* Brahman is lower. This also does not satisfy the conditions of non-dualistic philosophy without positive involvement of dualism. The concept of *Īśvara* in Advaita Vedānta is very much technical and needs comprehension for a thorough understanding of the philosophy. There are two theories pertaining to the concept of *Īśvara* in Advaita Vedānta. According to one of them, Consciousness (Brahman) associated with the limiting adjunct (*upādhi*), *Avidyā* or Māyā, is *Īśvara*.[154] The second one is called *pratibimba-vāda* (the doctrine of reflection). Consciousness is reflected on Māyā and the image (*pratibimba*) created on Māyā is *Īśvara*.[155]

The word '*upādhi*' is translated into English as 'limiting adjunct'. The '*upādhi*' concept is highly technical in Advaita Vedānta. Etymologically this word means "to project one's own image elsewhere while staying nearby (*samīpe sthitvā svīyam rūpamanyatra ādadhāti*)."[156]

Māyā is the power[157] of *Īśvara* and through this power He creates the whole universe as a magician[158] creates pluralities through his magical power. Māyā is under the full control[159] of *Īśvara* who is not controlled by Māyā at all. As a magician is not deluded by his magic, so is *Īśvara* who remains uninfluenced by His magic.[160] The one *Īśvara* assumes many forms according to whatever form He enters into. This is clearly illustrated by the Ṛgveda[161] and the *Kaṭhopaniṣad*.[162]

Īśvara creates, supports and dissolves the universe by His divine power, Māyā.[163] All the cosmic phenomena are the illusory and imaginary products of this Nescience that acts as both material and instrumental[164] cause. God enters[165] into everything that is created, both living and nonliving. Remaining within every created entity, He controls all the activities of all the entities from within. That is why He is called the inner Controller (*antaryāmī*).[166]

God is Controller, inner and outer. It is also said that God does not do anything and Nature (*Prakṛti*) does everything.[167] Is there no contradiction between these two concepts? This contradiction is apparent and not real. Nature is the agency of whatever action is done in the phenomenal world. The photon, the electron, the proton and the neutron are always active and each micro-entity is the subject of its own action. The virus, the bacteria, the protozoa, the snake, the bird, the tiger, the cow and the man have freedom to work and are the doers of their own deeds. Everybody has freedom of action and everybody's freedom of action is restrained by the totality of the cosmic laws. God pervades all entities of Nature and is the Presiding Deity (*adhyakṣa*)[168] of everything. Without this function of the presiding of the Consciousness, insentient Nature does not have the ability to work.

A pertinent question is often asked, "What is the need of God for the creation of the universe?" Advaita Vedānta categorically says that there is no need.[169] This magic is played by the Magician-God as sports (*līlā*)[170] only. In theology, a question like "Why did God create evil?" puzzles scholars. The nondualist philosopher does not entertain such a question. He asserts that in reality there is no creation of good or evil, that the apparent cosmos is a magic show, that it is the sports of God, and that, in the sports, fruits of sweet or bitter taste are eaten by each in accordance with the actions performed by each. "Who created this universe? What for did He create? How did He create?" These and many more questions pertaining to the creation are asked by deluded beings. And how is one to answer these questions without knowledge?[171]

Jīva (individual self)

According to Advaita Vedānta, only Brahman is Pure Consciousness (*Cit*) and everything else is insentient (*jaḍa*). Brahman is Self (*Ātman*) and every thing else is not-self (*anātman*). Not-self, including Māyā and the products of Māyā, is insentient. The inner instrument or organ (*antaḥkaraṇa*) consisting of intellect (*buddhi*) and mind (*manas*) are also insentient.

The body gets some limited consciousness through the mind. But Advaita Vedānta says that mind is a product of Māyā, is material and is insentient. If that is correct, how is it possible for the body to get some knowledge through the insentient mind? This happens due to reflection of Consciousness (*Cidābhāsa*).[172] *Cidābhāsa* may be defined as appearance of something as *Cit* (Consciousness) which is really insentient. This appearance of an insentient thing as conscious is due to the reflection of *Cit* on the insentient thing. The example of the flower and crystal (*kusuma-vacca maṇiḥ*)[173] well illustrates the phenomenon. When a scarlet hibiscus flower is placed in contiguity to a crystal, the latter appears red, although it is still transparent in reality. When the flower is removed, the crystal is no longer red.

The word *antaḥkaraṇa* is used in a technical sense in Advaita Vedānta. Its modifications (*vṛtti*) are intellect (*buddhi*) and mind (*manas*). Further, intellect includes mind-stuff (*citta*) and mind includes egoism (*ahaṅkāra*). Intellect determines the real nature of an object. It has the function of ascertaining (*niścaya*). The mind considers whether a particular object is this or that and whether one will perform a particular action or not. It has got the function of doubting (*saṁsaya*). *Citta* is the memory; one remembers by it. Egoism establishes the relationship of 'I' or 'mine' with the object. These four are the different aspects of the *antaḥkaraṇa*,[174] which is a product of Māyā and is insentient.

The Self does not work and the not-Self works. Every entity of the universe—whether micro or macro, living or nonliving—works and works in co-ordination and harmony. In spite of the prevalence of chaos, the universe is primarily a cosmos. There are natural laws and the functioning of the universe is in strict adherence to these laws. Every individual entity—an electron, a proton, an atom, a molecule, a virus, an amoeba, a plant, an animal, a human being—functions knowingly or unknowingly for its own interest, existence and protection. How can we explain this intelligent functioning of every insentient being? There is a *bhūtātmā* or a *jīvātmā* inside every entity. The former is applicable for the nonliving entities and the latter for the living entities. This embodied *ātman* (self) is consciousness.[175] It is like the hibiscus flower and the *antaḥkaraṇa* is like the crystal. The *jīva* (*jīvātman*) which is consciousness is reflected on the *antaḥkaraṇa* that acquires consciousness although it is itself insentient.

Whenever any entity is created, the Self enters into it and presides over it.[176] In case of a living being, the embodied self is known as *jīva*. This *jīva* is not produced at any time and does not perish at any time. It is unborn,[177] immortal[178] and eternal.[179] It does not change[180] and does not decay.[181]

According to Śaṅkara, anything that is delimited (*vibhakta*) has origin, modification and end.[182] The embodied self or *jīva* is delimited by a body. Hence the *jīva* should have birth, changes and death. But Śaṅkara does not accept such an idea. He says that the limitation of the *jīva* within the body is not real. The internal organ (*antaḥkaraṇa*) is the limiting adjunct (*upādhi*) of the *jīva*. The embodiment of the *jīva* is apparent only. The scriptures declare that *jīva* and Brahman are identical.[183] Brahman being one only and *jīva* being identical with Brahman, there cannot be multiple *jīvas*. All *jīvas* are one and the same[184] and not different from Brahman. Since Brahman is eternal, *jīva*, being Brahman, is also eternal.

As Māyā is the *upādhi* of *Īśvara*, so the internal organ (*antaḥkaraṇa*) is the *upādhi* of the individual self or *jīva*.[185] The concept of the subtle body (*liṅga śarīra*) and that of the five sheaths of the *jīva* have technical meaning in Advaita Vedānta and need elaboration here. The gross body comprises the material sheath (*annamaya kośa*).[186] The five vital forces (*prāṇa, apāna, vyāna, udāna, samāna*) with the five subtle organs of action (*karmendriya*) constitute the vital sheath (*prāṇamaya kośa*).[187] Mind (*manas*) with the five subtle organs of perception (*jñānendriya*) makes the mental sheath (*manomaya kośa*).[188] The intelligent sheath (*vijñānamaya kośā*)[189] is formed by the intellect (*buddhi*) and the five subtle organs of perception. The subtle body (*sūkṣma* or *liṅga śarīra*)[190] is formed by a combination of three sheaths, viz., the vital sheath, the mental sheath and the intellectual sheath. The blissful sheath (*ānandamaya kośa*)[191] is a fifth one which is called the causal body (*kāraṇa-śarīra*).[192] This sheath is a modification of nescience (*Māyā* or *Avidyā*). In the state of profound sleep (*suṣupti*), the mind[193] does not function and in all states the Ātman is functionless; in spite of this, the *jīva* experiences bliss. Ignorance is present even in deep sleep and functions in a very subtle form.[194] This is what is called the blissful sheath. Brahman, that is Bliss Absolute, is reflected in this sheath and the *jīva* (Prājña) experiences bliss.[195] The *jīva* is associated with all these five sheaths[196] whereas the attributeless, absolute Brahman is in the fourth state (*Turīya*) and has no association[197] with any of these.

There are two theories in Advaita Vedānta on the identity of *jīva* and Brahman. These are the theory of reflection and that of apparent limitation.

According to the reflection theory[198] (*ābhāsa-vāda* or *pratibimba vāda*), *jīva* is the image of Brahman as a result of the reflection of Brahman in the internal organ (*antaḥkaraṇa*) like the image of the Sun in the water of a reservoir. There is only one Sun that is reflected in the water of many reservoirs, resulting in multiple images of the one Sun. If one image in the water of one reservoir trembles due to disturbance in that reservoir, the other images in other reservoirs are not affected at all. Similar is the case with the reflection of one Brahman in the multiple *antaḥkaraṇas* of innumberable beings. Each image of Brahman in each *antaḥkaraṇa* is a *jīva* who is affected by the fruits of actions of its own body and not by those of others.

The theory of apparent limitation[199] may be better explained by taking the example of the unlimited space (*mahākāśa*) and the space limited in the pot (*ghaṭākāśa*). Ākāśa (space) is one only. But when the same *ākāśa* is limited in multiple pots, *ākāśa* seems to be more than one. When the limiting pots are broken, we again get one *ākāśa* only. The different entities of the universe, produced by *Māyā* (Nescience), are the limiting adjuncts for Brahman. They are not real adjuncts, since they do not have real existence and are produced by the magical power of *Māyā*. Each *antaḥkaraṇa* is an apparent limiting adjunct (*upādhi*) and the embodied Consciousness in each *antaḥkaraṇa* is a *jīva.*

Scriptures declare that all the *jīvas* do not have different identities, that they are one only and that all of them are identical with Brahman. There are four *Mahāvākyas* (great Vedic dicta). They are: Thou art That (*tattvamasi*),[200] This Self is Brahman (*ayamātmā brahma*),[201] Consciousness is Brahman (*prajñānaṁbrahma*),[202] and I am Brahman (*ahaṁ brahmāsmi*).[203] From the point of view of language analysis, it may need some discussion to show that "Thou art That" is an identity statement. In logic, "A is A" or "Devadatta is Devadatta" is an identity statement (*akhaṇḍārthaka vākya*).[204] In the statement, "Thou art That", the subject (Thou) and the predicate (That) do not seem to be identical. If we take the implied meanings of 'Thou' and 'That', identity is established. A word in a sentence may have direct (*vācya*) or implied (*lakṣya*) meaning.[205] In the sentence "The cowherd village is in the Gaṅgā" (*gaṅgāyāṁ ghoṣaḥ*),[206] the literal meaning of '*gaṅgāyāṁ*' is 'in the Gaṅgā' and its implied meaning is 'on the bank of the Gaṅgā'. Here the literal or direct meaning cannot be accepted since there cannot be a village on the water-stream of the Gaṅgā. We have to take the implied meaning of the statement, "This is that Devadatta", in order to establish the identity of *this* Devadatta and *that* Devadatta. In the Vedic dictum "Thou art That", the direct meaning of 'Thou' is Consciousness associated with individual ignorance, i.e., *jīva*, and the direct meaning of 'That' is Consciousness associated with collective ignorance, i.e., *Īśvara*. The implied meaning of both the term 'Thou' and 'That' is Brahman or Pure Consciousness unassociated with ignorance. Thus the Vedic scriptures authoritatively declare the identity of Brahman and the *jīva.*

It has already been discussed that Brahman and *Īśvara* are not two different entities. Brahman is attributeless (*nirguṇa*) whereas *Īśvara* is with attributes (*saguṇa*). Māyā is the limiting adjunct (*upādhi*) of *Īśvara* whereas Brahman has no limiting adjuncts. We may discuss now the commonness and differences between *Īśvara* and *jīva*.

Brahman apparently associated with Māyā as its limiting adjunct is *Īśvara.*[207] The same Brahman apparently associated with the internal instrument (*antaḥkaraṇa*) as its limiting adjunct is *jīva.*[208] The image (*pratibimba*) of Brahman reflected in Māyā is *Īśvara* whereas that of Brahman reflected in the *antaḥkaraṇa* is *jīva*.[209] *Īśvara* is associated with the material cause; *jīva* is associated with the products of the same material cause. Brahman which is attributeless becomes *Īśvara* with attributes by acquiring (falsely, of course) the constituents (*guṇa*) of the aggregate (*samaṣṭi*) ignorance. The *jīva* acquires the constituents of the individual (*vyaṣṭi*) ignorance. Māyā is under the full control of *Īśvara* who, as the Magician (*aindrajālika*),[210] conjures the universe with His magical power, Māyā. *Īśvara* is never deluded by Māyā.[211] However, this is not the case with the *jīva* who is under the control of Māyā and is deluded by Māyā.[212] *Īśvara* has omniscience, omnipotence and omnipresence. He is the Creator and Controller of the universe.[213] The *jīva* is caged inside the *antaḥkaraṇa*; it has limited power and limited knowledge; it does not have the power of creation.[214] This difference between *Īśvara* and *jīva* is due to the unlimitedness and limitedness of their *upādhis*, Māyā and *antaḥkaraṇa*, respectively.

In Advaita Vedānta, some terms are used for *Īśvara* and *jīva* in comparative states. In waking state, when the *upādhi* is the aggregate universe, the name of Consciousness is *Vaiśvānara*. In the same state, when the *upādhi* is the individual gross body, the name of Consciousness is *Viśva*. In the dream state, when the *upādhi* is the aggregate subtle universe, Consciousness is named as *Hiraṇyagarbha*. When the individual subtle body (*liṅgaśarīra*) is the *upādhi* in the dream state, Consciousness is called *Taijasa*. After dissolution (*pralaya*), when the *upādhi* is aggregate Māyā, Consciousness is *Īśvara*. Consciousness is *Prājña* in the state of deep sleep when individual ignorance is the *upādhi*. Thus, in the three states of experience, Brahman is known as *Vaiśvānara*, *Hiraṇyagarbha* and *Īśvara*, with the three types of aggregate *upādhis* and the same Brahman is known as *Viśva, Taijasa* and *Prājña* with the three types of individual *upādhis*. Between *Īśvara* and *Prājña*, the difference is only the limiting adjunct; in the former case, the *upādhi* is aggregate ignorance (*samaṣṭi avidyā*) whereas in the latter, the *upādhi* is individual ignorance (*vyaṣṭi avidyā*).[215] Otherwise, as Consciousness they are identical.[216] In the state of deep sleep, *jīva* remains, temporarily, united with *Īśvara*.[217] Even at this stage it is covered with ignorance. This ignorance of *Prājña* is the blissful sheath (*ānandamaya kośa*) or the causal body (*kāraṇa śarīra*). The gross things of the waking state are dissolved into the subtle things of the dream state, and finally the subtle things are dissolved into the Ultimate Cause in the state of deep sleep.[218] In the fourth state (*Turīya*) which is transcendental, the *jīva* becomes free from ignorance and realises his identity with Brahman, the Absolute.[219] In all the three states of experience of *Iśvara* and *jīva*, Brahman Absolute is the Consciousness Witness (*sakṣī cetā*).[220]

Īśvara pervades everything (*sarvavyāpī*) and hence is present in every entity of the universe. In each individual body, both *Īśvara* and *jīva* are present. Thus, the scriptures declare: "Two birds, who are companions and always united, sit on the same tree. Of these two, one eats the sweet fruit and the other looks on without eating."[221] The *jīvātman*, while in the body, experiences the pleasant and painful fruits of its past deeds. The *jīvātman*, being non-functional, is not the agent of any action. Nature (*prakṛti*) does everything and the embodied self is not the doer of actions.[222] In spite of this fact, the *jīvātman*, being deluded by Māyā, feels that he is doer and experiencer.[223]

The embodied self or *jīva* is in bondage (*bandhana*). When freed (*mukta*), it is the same as Pure Consciousness or Brahman Absolute. As long as the *jīva* is in bondage, it has to be born and reborn. Taking a body becomes a necessity for the embodied self. The bodies and successive lives are means for the end of attainment of release (*mokṣa*).

It is not the free choice of the *jīva* to enter into any womb and occupy a body. This function is executed by *Īśvara* whose decision is commensurate with the cumulative total of the actions of the *jīva* in the past lives.[224]

How the free and functionless *jīva* is bound due to the actions of the body needs explanation here. It has already been said that the limiting adjunct of the *jīva* is the internal instrument or *antaḥkaraṇa* of the body. In death, the gross body (*sthūla śarīra*) perishes, but the subtle body (*sūkṣma* or *liṅga śarīra*) does not perish. *Jīva*, encaged in *antaḥkaraṇa* leaves the gross body and undergoes transmigration.[225] As the *ākāśa* (space) inside a pot remains bound up, so is the *jīva* who is encaged inside the subtle body. This subtle body is like a tape recorder. Impressions of the individual are recorded on the *antaḥkaraṇa*. This imprint on the *antaḥkaraṇa* is technically known as *karmāśaya*[226] or *Saṁskāra*.[227] These printed impressions must be erased for attaining release (*mokṣa*). There cannot be existence of the *antaḥkaraṇa* with the erasing of all the *saṁskāras*. When that happens, the *antaḥkaraṇa* disappears, and with the disappearance of the limiting adjunct, the *jīva* is freed. That is the *mokṣa* or release of the *jīva*.[228] As long as the *antaḥkaraṇa* is not annihilated, the bondage of the *jīva* cannot be prevented. In such a situation, the *jīva* gets birth repeatedly and, in each life, it erroneously identifies itself with the body and falsely feels that it is the doer of good and bad actions and the enjoyer of their fruits. This pseudo-feeling of the *jīva* is brought about by the deluding power of Māyā.[229]

A *jīva* gets a good or bad life according to good or bad actions done in all of its past lives. The ledger on which the account of these good and bad actions is recorded is the *antaḥkaraṇa* which encages the *jīva*. This account may be termed as *karma*. According to the *karma*-theory, *prārabdha*[230] is that part of our past actions, which through their cumulative force, has given birth to this present body. With *prārabdha*, one's *karma*-reservoir is not exhausted unless this is the last life of the *jīva* before attaining release. The total reservoir of *karma* minus the *prārabdha* is the *sañcita karma*[231] which is the residual reservoir of past actions, still reserved to give birth to future lives. The actions that are being done during this life are stored for future lives and this store is known as *kriyamāṇa karma*.[232]

When the universe was created, all *jīvas*, one may imagine, might have started their careers with a clean ledger—there was no trace of *karmāśaya* or *saṁskāra*. If that were the case, how could *jīvas* become unequal? Why is one rewarded and another punished? How could the *karmāśaya* or reservoir of *karma* be built differently for different *jīvas*? Is not *Īśvara* guilty of partiality? Advaita Vedānta answers this question negatively. *Īśvara* is not responsible for giving good or bad *karma* to anybody. *Karma* is made by the individual and is not given by God. A good or bad *karmāśaya* is built by the good and bad actions, respectively, of the individual.[233] *Īśvara* does not reward or punish any individual. He is completely impartial.[234] The union of actions and fruits thereof is mediated by natural processes.[235] The universe has not been created once only. The creations have been beginningless in the past and will be endless in the future.[236] Hence there is no question of zero reservoir of *karma* for any *jīva*. When it is zero, the *jīva* is Śiva or Brahman Absolute and in that situation it is no longer *jīva* encaged within a subtle or gross body. After the total dissolution (*mahāpralaya*) at the end of each *mahākalpa* (world-period), the unreleased *jīvas* do not disappear. They remain in subtle state, being dissolved in *mūlaprakṛti* (primeval Nature or Māyā) and each *jīva* retains its characteristic *karmic* reservoir.[237] When the next world-cycle begins, each *jīva* is assigned by *Īśvara* womb and a gross body befitting its *karmic* reservoir.

Notes

1. BSŚB, II.3.9; Chā, VI.8.7; Tai, II.1.1; BGŚB, II.17; VPDA Intr., 1; VC, 20; APR, 21.
2. BSŚB, I.1.4; II.1.27; Bṛ ŚB, IV.5.14; BG, II.24; BGŚB, II.18, 25; VC, 134; APR, 25.
3. BSŚB, II.1.14; VPDA, Ch. IV.
4. BS, II.3.9; BSŚB, II.3.9; Kaṭ, I.3.15; Śve, V.13; BG, X.3, XIII.31.
5. Bṛ, II.4.12; Kaṭ, I.3.15; Śve, V.13; Tai, II.1.1.
6. ṚV, X.129.4; BS, I.4.24; II.3.12, 13; BSŚB, II.3.13; Bṛ, III.7.3, 23; Chā, VI.2.3, 4; Tai, II.6.1.
7. BS, II.2.1; BSŚB, I.1.11; II.2.1; Śve, VI.9.
8. BS, I.3.10, 11; BSŚB, I.3.11; II.2.2, 4; Ait, III.3; Bṛ, I.4.7; III.7.4; III.8.7; Chā, VI.3.2; Mā, 6; BG, X.3.
9. BS, III.2.16; BSŚB, I.1.4; II.1.24; III.2.18; Ait, III.3; Bṛ, II.4.12; III.9.28; IV.5.13; Śve, VI.11; Tai, II.1.1, 2; VPDA Intr., 1.
10. BSŚB, I.1.2; MāKā, IV.72; BGŚB, XIII.12.4.
11. Tai, II.1.1.
12. Bṛ, II.5.19; MāKā, I.26.
13. Bṛ, II.5.19; MāKā, I.26.
14. Kaṭ, I.2.18; MāKā, III.26; Mu, II.1.2; BG, II.20, 21; IV.6; VII.25; X.3, 12; VC, 134.
15. Kaṭ, I.2.18, 19; BG, II.19-21; VIII.20; XI.18; VC, 134.
16. BSŚB, I.1.4; Kaṭ, I.2.18; Mu, I.1.6; BG, II.20-21, 24; BGŚB, II.18; VC, 134; APR, 5.
17. Tai ŚB, Intr.
18. BSŚB, I.1.4; Mā, 1.
19. Bṛ, III.8.8.
20. BS, III.2.14; Īśa, 8; MāKā, III.36; Mu, II.1.2; APR, 25.
21. BSŚB, III.2.18; BṛŚB, III.7.23; III.9.26; Kaṭ, I.3.15; II.3.8; Mā, 7; Śve, VI.11; BG, XIII.31; BGŚB, XIII.12.4; APR, 27.
22. BSŚB, I.1.4; BṛŚB, III.9.26; Śve, VI.19; BGŚB, XIII.12.4; APR, 27.
23. Mu, I.1.6; BG, II.21, 25; IV.6; VII.25; XI.18; XIII.31; BGŚB, II.17; XIII.31.1; VC, 134.
24. Bṛ, III.8.8-9; Mā, 1; BG, VIII.3, 11, 13, 21; XI.18.
25. VC, 134.
26. BSŚB, II.3.9; Bṛ, II.5.19; MāKā, I.11, 26; Śve, VI.9.
27. BSŚB, I.1.2; II.1.27; Bṛ, III.8.11; IV.5.15; Kaṭ, I.3.15; Mā, 7; Mu, I.1.6; BGŚB, XIII.12; VP, I.2.23.
28. BGŚB, II.25.

29. BSŚB, II.1.27; III.2.18; Mā, 7; MāKā, III.37; BG, II.25.
30. Bṛ, III.8.11; Ken, I.2-9; DDV, I.
31. BṛŚB, IV.4.18.
32. Bṛ, II.4.13; III.4.2; IV.5.15; Ken, I.2-9.
33. BGŚB, II.18.
34. Kaṭ, II.1.11.
35. BSŚB, II.1.24; Bṛ, IV.4.19; IV.5.15; Chā, VI.2.2; VII.24.1; Kaṭ, II.1.11; Mā, 7; Śve, VI.11; BG, VII.7; BGŚB, XIII.12.4; VC, 478.
36. Bṛ, IV.3.15-16; MāKā, IV.72; BGŚB, XIII.12.4.
37. Bṛ, IV.5.15.
38. BSŚB, I.1.4; II.1.27; Mu, II.2.10; Śve, VI.19; BGŚB, XIII.12.4; APR, 17.
39. VC, 478, 494, 516.
40. Bṛ, I.4.7.
41. Bṛ, II.4.12; IV.5.13.
42. BSŚB, I.1.4; Īśa, 8; Mu, I.1.6; Śve, VI.11; BG, II.17, 24; VIII.22; IX.4; X.12; XI.38; VC, 128.
43. BG, IX.4; VC, 128.
44. Bṛ, III.8.7, 11.
45. BSŚB, I.1.4; VPDA, Ch. II.
46. Ait, III.3; Chā ŚB, VI.2.2; Kaṭ ŚB, II.3.12; Tai ŚB, II.6.1; BGŚB, X.39; VPDA, Ch. VII.
47. BSŚB, I.1.4; MāKā, III.36-37.
48. Chā, III.2.6; Kaṭ, II.2.15; Mu, II.2. 10-11; Śve, VI.14; BG, X.42; XV.12; VC, 128.
49. BS, I.1.12; BSŚB, I.1.4; Bṛ, III.9.28; Tai, II.7-9; III.6; VPDA Intr. 1.
50. Mā, 7; MāKā, III.37; Śve, VI.19.
51. BSŚB, I.1.4.
52. MāKā, III.37; BG, II.24; VC, 513.
53. BSŚB, I.1.4; Śve, VI.19.
54. BSŚB, I.1.5; Bṛ, III.7.23; Śve, VI.11; BGŚB, IX.10.
55. VC, 494.
56. BSŚB, III.2.18; Mā, 7; MāKā, III.37; Tai, II.9.1; BGŚB, XIII.12.4.
57. Īśa, 4-5; Kaṭ, I.2.20-22; Kaṭ ŚB, I.2.21; Mu, III.1.7; Śve, III.20.
58. Bṛ, II.5.19; III.8.8; Mā, 7.
59. Mā, 7; BGŚB, XIII.15.
60. Bṛ, II.3.6; III.9.26; IV.2.4; IV.4.22; IV.5.15.
61. BGŚB, XIII.15; MS, I.5.
62. BS, I.1.1.
63. BSŚB. I.1.1: II.3.7.
64. BSŚB, Intr.; I.1.4; Bṛ, III.4.1.
65. BSŚB, I.1.1; BGŚB, XIII.12.
66. BSŚB, I.1.2; I.1.4.
67. Chā, VI.8.7; VI.9.4; VI.10.3.
68. Bṛ, I.4.10.
69. Bṛ, II.5.19; IV.4.5; Mā, 2.
70. Bṛ, II.4.6; Chā, VII.25.2.
71. Bṛ, II.5.1; Chā, III.14.1; Mai, IV.6; Mā, 2; Mu, II.2.11.
72. BSŚB, Intr.; MāKā, IV.72.

73. Śve, I.3; Śve ŚB, I.3; BGŚB, IV.6; VII.14; IX.10; XIII.19.2; XIII.29.1; XV.1.1; XV.16; Bhā, III.5.25; VC, 108.
74. Śve, IV.10; BGŚB, IV.6; IX.10; XIII.19.1, 2; XIII.29.1; XIV.3.1.
75. BSŚB, I.4.2; I.4.3; Kaṭ ŚB, I.3.11; BG, VIII.20; BGŚB, Intr.; BGŚB, XIII.5; VC, 108.
76. BSŚB, I.4.3; II.1.14; Kaṭ ŚB, I.3.11; BGŚB, IX.10; VC, 108.
77. BSŚB, I.4.3; Śve ŚB, I.3; I.9.
78. VC, 109.
79. BSŚB, I.4.3; Śve ŚB, I.9; Bhā, III.5.25; VC, 109.
80. Śve, IV.5; MāKā, I.16; BGŚB, XIII.19.1; VC, 108.
81. BSŚB, I.2.22; I.4.3; Mu, II.1.2; BGŚB, XV.16.
82. BGŚB, XV.4.
83. BGŚB, Intr.
84. BSŚB, I.2.22; Bṛ, I.4.7; BGŚB, XIII.5.
85. Śve, IV.5; BGŚB, Intr.; BGŚB, IV.6; VII.14; IX.7, 10; XIII.19.2; XIII.29.1; XIV.3.1; VC, 108.
86. VC, 109.
87. BSŚB, I.4.3; II.1.14; Śve ŚB, I.9; VC, 109.
88. BGŚB, VII.25; VC, 113; VS, 51-53.
89. VC, 111, 113, 115; VS, 51, 54.
90. BGŚB, IV.6.
91. BSŚB, I.2.22; I.4.3.
92. BSŚB, I.2.22; I.4.2; I.4.3; II.1.14.
93. MĀ, 5th *prapāṭhakaḥ*.
94. Śaṅkara in *Tattvabodha*.
95. BGŚB, VII.6; IX.7.
96. BSŚB, I.4.3; II.1.14; BGŚB, IV.6; VII.6; IX.7, 8, 10; XIII.19.1-2; XIII.20.1; XIV.3.1; XIV.4; XV.16.1; VPDA, Ch. VII; Bhā, III.5.25; VC, 108; VS, 55.
97. BSŚB, I.4.3.
98. BSŚB, II.1.24-25; BGŚB, XIII.19.1-2; Śve, VI.8.
99. BSŚB, II.1.30.
100. BSŚB, I.4.3; Śve ŚB, I.3; IV.10; BGŚB, Intr.; BGŚB, IV.6; VII.25; IX.7-8; XIII.19.1; XIV.3.1.
101. VC, 123.
102. BSŚB, II.1.9; BGŚB, XV.4.
103. BSŚB, II.1.9; BGŚB, VII.25; IX.8.
104. BGŚB, IV.6; IX.8.
105. BSŚB, I.2.22; II.1.14.
106. VC, 108.
107. Kaṭ, II.1.11.
108. VC, 20.
109. MāKā, II.32; III.48; IV.4, 22, 23, 38.
110. MāKā, IV.73.
111. MāKā, I.17; II.31; III.27; IV.44, 58, 59.
112. MāKā, II.12, 13; III.10, 19, 24.
113. Bṛ, II.5.19.
114. MāKā, III.28.
115. Mā, 2.

116. Mā, 3.
117. Mā, 4.
118. Mā, 5.
119. Mā, 6.
120. Mā, 7.
121. MāKā, I.13.
122. MāKā, I.11.
123. MāKā, I.17.
124. MāKā, II.17-18.
125. BSŚB, II.2.28, 30; Bṛ, II.3.1; Mai, VI.3.
126. Chā ŚB, VI.12.2; Īśa ŚB, 4; Kaṭ ŚB, II.3.1; Mu ŚB, II.1.10; BGŚB, XV.1-2.
127. BGŚB, XIII.26.1; VPDA, Ch. II.
128. MāKā, IV.45.
129. ṚV, I.164.14; YV, 40.1; Īśa, 1.
130. BGŚB, XV.3.1.
131. BSŚB, Intr.
132. BS, II.1.28; BSŚB, II.1.28, 30; Bṛ, IV.3.10; Śve, IV.1.
133. Chā, VI.1.4-6; VC, 228-31.
134. VPDA, Ch. I.
135. ṚV, X.129.4; BS, I.4.24; II.3.13; BSŚB, I.1.5; II.2.2; Bṛ, III.7.3, 23; Chā, VI.2-4; Tai, II.6.1.
136. BSŚB, I.1.10, 11; BGŚB, VII.6; IX.7-8; XIII.19; XIV.3-4; Śve, VI.7, 9-10, 12.
137. BS, II.2.1; Śve, VI.2.
138. BSŚB, II.1.14; BGŚB, IX.7; XV.16; DBhā, I.2.5.
139. BSŚB, I.1.10, 11; BGŚB, VII.6; BG, XIII.16; BGŚB, XIII.19.
140. BS, I.3.43; BSŚB, I.3.10, 11; BG, IV.6.; VIII.9, 19; X.3; XIII.22; Bṛ, III.8.9; IV.4.22; Bṛ ŚB, III.7.23; Kaṭ, II.2.12; Mu, I.1.9; Śve, III.4; IV.12, 15; V.3; VI.7-9, 12.
141. BSSB, I.1.11; II.1.14; BGŚB, VII.6.
142. BSŚB, I.1.11.
143. Īśa, 1; Śve, IV.10; VI.11; BG, II.17, 24; VIII.22; IX.4; X.12.
144. Śve, IV.5; BG, X.3.
145. Śve, IV.18; V.13.
146. Śve, VI.9.
147. Śve, I.12; Mu, I.1.6.
148. Śve, VI.8.
149. BGŚB, Intr.
150. Mu, III.1.3.
151. Bṛ, II.6.3; IV.6.3; VI.5.4; Īśa, 8; Kaṭ, II.1.1; Śve, VI.16; ŚBrā, I.9.3.10; TBrā, III.12.3.1.
152. ABS, Parimal Publications, Delhi, Ist Ed., 1981, Ch. IV, pp. 200-1.
153. BS, II.1.30; BSŚB, I.1.11; Chā, III.14.2, 4; VIII.7.1.
154. VS, 38.
155. VPDA, Ch. VII.
156. ABS, Ch. IV, p. 198.
157. BSŚB, I.2.22; II.1.14; Śve, I.3; IV.10; BG, VII.13-14; BGŚB, IV.6; VII.6, 25; IX.7, 8; XIII.29; XIV.3; XV.16.

158. ṚV, VI.47.18; BSŚB, I.1.17; II.1.22; Bṛ, II.5.19; Śve, III.1.
159. Śve ŚB, I.3; BGŚB, IV.6; IX.8.
160. BSŚB, II.1.9; BGŚB, VII.25; XV.4.
161. ṚV, VI.47.18.
162. Kaṭ, II.2.9, 10.
163. BSŚB, II.1.14; Śve, I.3; VI.10; BGŚB, VII.16; XIII.19; DBhā, I.2.5.
164. BSŚB, II.1.24, 25; Śve, VI.8; BGŚB, XIII.19.
165. Śve, II.17; IV. 11;V.2; VI.11; Tai, II.6.1.
166. BS, I.2.18; BSŚB, II.2.3; Bṛ, III.7.3-23.
167. Śve ŚB, VI.12; BGŚB, XIII.29.
168. ṚV, X.129.7; Śve, VI.11; Tai ŚB, II.8.9; BGŚB, IX.10.
169. BS, II.1.32.
170. BS, II.1.33.
171. ṚV, X.129.6; TBrā, II.8.9.
172. Woodroffe, S.J., *Śakti and Śākta*, Ganesh & Co., Madras, 8th Ed., 1975, p. 198.
173. SPS, II.35.
174. VPDA, Ch. I; VS, 65-9.
175. BS, II.3.18; Kaṭ, I.2.18.
176. BSŚB, II.3.17; Bṛ, I.4.7; Chā, VI.3.2; Tai, II.6.1.
177. Bṛ, IV.4.25; Kaṭ, I.2.18.
178. Bṛ, IV.4.25; Chā, VI.11.3; Kaṭ, I.2.18.
179. Kaṭ, I.2.18.
180. Kaṭ, I.2.18.
181. Bṛ, IV.4.25.
182. BSŚB, II.3.17.
183. Bṛ, I.4.10; II.5.19; VI.8.7; VI.11.3.
184. Śve, VI.11.
185. BSŚB, I.2.20; VPDA, Ch. I and VII; VS, 38.
186. VC, 154.
187. VS, 88; ABS, p. 295.
188. VS, 74; ABS, p. 295.
189. VS, 72, ABS, p. 295.
190. VS, 61, 89; ABS, p. 295.
191. ABS, p. 295.
192. ABS, p. 295.
193. KU, 13.
194. VS, 46.
195. KU, 13; Mā, 5; VS, 46.
196. PD, III.37, 41; VS, 243.
197. VS, 125, 211.
198. BSŚB, II.3.50; III.2.18; BGŚB, XV.7; VPDA, Ch. VII; ABS, p. 198, 202-3.
199. BSŚB, I.1.17; I.2.20; MāKā, III.3-4; 6-7; BGŚB, XV.7.
200. Chā, VI.8.7; VI. 9.4; VI.10.3; VI.12.3; VI.13.3; VI.14.3.
201. Bṛ, II.5.19.
202. Ait, V.3.
203. Bṛ, I.4.10.
204. VS, 148; PD, VII.75.

205. VS, 50.
206. VS, 50.
207. BSŚB, I.2.20; MaiU, 61; VPDA, Ch. I; VC, 243.
208. BSŚB, I.2.20; MaiU, 61; VPDA, Ch. I.
209. BSŚB, II.1.21; VPDA, Ch. VII.
210. ṚV, VI.47.18; BSŚB, II.1.21; Bṛ, II.5.19; Śve, III.1; VS, 40.
211. BGŚB, VII.25.
212. BG, V.15; BGŚB, IX.8.
213. VS, 38.
214. VS, 43.
215. VS, 47-8.
216. Mā, 6.
217. Chā, VI.8.1.
218. KU, 13; VS, II.45.
219. KU, 18; VS, 49-50; Mā, 7.
220. KU, 18; VC, 125.
221. ṚV, I.164.20; YV, IV.3.3; AV, I.24.1; Kaṭ, I.3.1; Mu, III.1.1; Śve, IV.6.
222. BG, XIII.29.
223. BG, III.27.
224. BG, XVI.19.
225. BGŚB, XV. 8-9; VC, 169, 174.
226. PYD, II.12.
227. PYD, I.50.
228. PYD, II.13; VC, 169.
229. BG, III.27.
230. BSŚB, IV.1.15; Chā ŚB, VI.14.2; BGŚB, IV.37; VC, 451.
231. VC, 447.
232. VC, 449.
233. Bṛ, III.2.13; KU, III.8; Kaṭ, II.2.7.
234. BSŚB, II.1.34-36; BG, V.15.
235. BG,V.14.
236. ṚV, X.190.3; BSŚB, II.1.35-36; BG; XV.3.
237. BSŚB, I.3.31; Bhā, I.10.22.

CHAPTER IX

SPIDER

> Certain it is that a conviction, akin to religious feeling of the rationality or the intelligibility of the world lies behind all scientific work of a higher order. This firm belief, a belief bound up with deep feeling, in a superior mind that reveals itself in the world of experience, represents my conception of God.
>
> *Albert Einstein*

> If God has made the world a perfect mechanism, He has at least conceded so much to our imperfect intellect that in order to predict little parts of it, we need not solve innumerable differential equations, but can use dice with fair success.
>
> *Max Born*

ADVAITA VEDĀNTA considers that the universe is not a reality, but is an illusory appearance. It was never born, it has no existence at present and it will never exist in the future.[1] In spite of this extreme view of Gauḍapāda, the empirical existence (*vyāvahārika sattā*) of the universe is recognized by Śaṅkara and other nondualists. Even though all things that appear in a magical show are not real, they have sequence in appearance and are meaningful to the spectators. In our relative and dependent existence, anything that has no absolute existence and that has relative existence cannot be ignored. In this sense, the universe and our lives are meaningful to every philosopher of Advaita Vedānta.

Pantheistic Concept

Unless properly understood, the cosmology and cosmogony of Advaita Vedānta seem to be puzzling and perplexing. In many passages of scriptural texts, there is a clear tone of pantheism. Anything and everything of the visible universe is Brahman or God. Anything and everything of the invisible universe is Brahman or God. There is nothing which is not Brahman or God. All this universe is Brahman or God.[2] Of course, Brahman is more than the universe. As the Vedas declare, only a quarter of Brahman is the universe and three quarters are beyond the universe.[3] The world-image of God, as depicted in the Bhagavadgītā,[4] is apparently pantheistic. Some passages in the Upaniṣads[5] also convey similar idea.

Transformation

A part of Brahman is converted into the universe. Such an idea is clearly given by the following Upaniṣadic text: "That is full (infinite); this is full (infinite); full came out of the full; still full remained after full had come out".[6]

Some scriptural passages describe the doctrine of transformation in a different way. According to this concept, transformation of Brahman into the universe did not take place at any particular instant or definite period; it is a process that has been continually occurring like sparks coming out of fire or fibres of net coming out of the spider's body.[7] One will commit conceptual error if one stretches the simile too much. Fuel burns, fire is produced, energy is produced, energy is consumed and sparking occurs. But a fuel cannot burn eternally and its fire cannot stay eternally. Any particular source of energy is not inexhaustible. This is, however, not the case with Brahman which does not function, does not produce anything and remains without change and decay. The example of fire and spark describes in a figurative way that Brahman is the source of the world-product. It does not convey the idea of transformation.

The concept of partial or complete transformation of Brahman into the universe is not compatible with the philosophy of Advaita Vedānta.[8] Brahman is undifferentiated, homogeneous and partless. It is self-contradictory to say that Brahman is partless and at the same time is divided into parts. In any process of transformation or modification, energy is expended. Brahman being functionless, eternal, timeless, unchangeable and non-modifiable, transformation of whole or part of Brahman is untenable. Hence the doctrine of transformation of Brahman into the universe violates the fundamental concept of Brahman in Advaita Vedānta.

Brahman is Not the Cause

It has been mentioned in a number of scriptural texts that Brahman is the material cause of the universe.[9] Accordingly, everything of the universe has been produced from Brahman in the analogy of a chair or a table produced from wood, or ring, bangle and necklace produced from gold. If y is produced from x, y is the product and x is the material cause of the product. Is Brahman likewise the material cause of the universe? Advaita Vedānta says that it isn't. Brahman is changeless and does not undergo modification. B remains as B; it is not produced from anything; it is not converted into anything. Hence it is not a fact that Brahman is the material cause of the universe.[10] We must find out a different meaning of the Vedāntic texts that declare that Brahman is the source of the universe.

Some scriptures[11] declare that Brahman is the efficient cause of the universe in the analogy of a carpenter who is the efficient cause of a chair or a goldsmith who is the efficient cause of a necklace. Such a declaration is made in a figurative sense and should not be taken literally. Brahman is non-functional. It never does any work. Anything or anybody that is non-functional cannot be the agent of any action. A concept such as "A non-functional entity is the agent of an action" is self-contradictory and hence must be discarded. Thus Brahman is not the efficient cause of the universe.[12]

Source of Universe

Has the world come out of nothing? Is the creation *ex nihilo*? Was there no preceding state of the universe? Is the world-product produced from absolute void, nothingness? The Upaniṣads say that the universe was nothing in the beginning, that it was non-existence (*asat*) and that existence came out of non-existence.[13] But how could it happen? Is it logically consistent for something to have been produced out of nothing? Vedānta does not accept the idea of *ex nihilo* creation.[14] "Nothing cannot be something and something cannot be nothing."[15] The Bhagavadgītā unambiguously declares this. "Nothing=something" and "something=nothing" are self-contradictory concepts and hence cannot be valid. Further, for Vedānta, there is nothing like 'nothing', 'vacuum' or 'void' (*śūnya*). Vedānta recognizes plenum or full (*pūrṇa*) and discards the concept of void.

The non-existence (*asat*) of Advaita Vedānta is in reality existence (*sat*). This has been clearly mentioned in the Upaniṣad.[16] The world of name and form is sense-perceptible. We recognize something as existent (*sat*) when it is perceived by our senses directly or indirectly. What is sense-imperceptible is non-existent (*asat*) for us, although it may really exist absolutely in a subtle form.[17] Thus speaking in this sense, existence and non-existence are two relative terms based on our ability or inability to perceive by our senses. In this context, these two terms are not used in the absolute sense. When we say, "The universe was non-existent before its creation", we mean thereby that the previous state of the universe was sense-imperceptible. When it could be sense-perceptible, it became existent for us. The Upaniṣad says, "The universe was non-existent in the beginning (before its creation)." From this statement, somebody may deduce that the universe was produced out of nothing. In order to eliminate the chance of such a deduction, the seer of the Upaniṣad simultaneously declares that what was non-existent was really existent. The universe is existent in a gross form so that it is sense-perceptible. The precedent state of the universe was present in a subtle form so that it was sense-imperceptible.

'Unmanifested' (*avyakta*) and 'manifested' (*vyakta*) are two other terms that are used in Advaita Vedānta to express the subtle and the gross states, respectively. The precedent state of the universe was unmanifested. The manifestation of the unmanifested state is otherwise known as creation. The word 'creation' is very often understood as *de novo* production or *ex nihilo* generation. Advaita Vedānta does not accept such an idea of creation. The Sanskrit word for a similar concept is '*sṛṣṭi*'[18] (*sṛj+ktin*). It literally means emanation from some already existing source. Thus manifestation conveys better sense than creation in the philosophy of Advaita Vedānta. What is manifested is *sat* (existent) for us. What is unmanifested is *asat* (non-existent) for us, although the *asat* may be eternally existent and the *sat* may be transiently existent.

This *sat-asat* concept was first given in *nāsadīya sūkta*[19] of the Ṛgveda. Before the universe came into being, it was neither *sat* nor *asat*. It was not *sat*, because it was not gross to be sense-perceptible. It was not *asat*, because it was not really nothing and it existed in a subtle state. This concept of the Ṛgveda was later echoed in the Upaniṣads.

Before the universe came into being, there was Brahman alone and nothing else.[20] The universe could not be produced out of nothing. Hence the only deduction that can be made is that the source of the universe was nothing else other than Brahman. A number of scriptures of Advaita Vedānta declare that the universe was produced from Brahman. It made itself[21] and produced the world.

But it has already been said that Brahman cannot be the material or the efficient cause of the universe. Brahman is changeless and functionless. It is partless. It cannot be modified into any product. It cannot be the agent of any action. Hence the cause of the universe must be found out somewhere else.

Advaita Vedānta says that Māyā,[22] the power of Brahman, is the material cause of the universe and that *Īśvara*,[23] the image of Brahman reflected on Māyā, is the efficient cause of the universe. Since Māyā is dependent upon Brahman and is the power of Brahman, the material cause of the universe, in an implied sense, is Brahman. Since *Īśvara* is Brahman with attributes, Brahman is also the efficient cause of the universe in its implied sense. Otherwise, strictly speaking, Brahman is itself causeless and is not the cause of anything.

Formation of Cosmic Egg

Śaṅkara says that a cosmic egg was produced from Māyā and that everything of the universe was produced from the cosmic egg.[24] He is categorical about the fact that the cosmic egg did not originate from God. References to the cosmic egg have been given in a number of scriptures.[25] In the cosmogony of Advaita Vedānta, the appearance of the cosmic egg is an important event. The precursor of the cosmic egg is insentient Māyā. How could the insentient Māyā produce the cosmic egg? It could be the material from which the cosmic egg was produced in the analogy of the wood being the precursor material of the chair. But a carpenter is necessary to be the efficient cause of the chair. Advaita Vedānta says that God is the efficient cause of the cosmic egg.[26] God did not want to be alone.[27] The One wanted to be many.[28] He desired to have a universe.[29] And so He produced the cosmic egg.

First of all God produced *āpaḥ*, *nāra*, *arka* or *ka* (the primeval fluid) and put his seed into it.[30] This developed into the cosmic egg. The word '*āpaḥ*' is translated by some scholars as 'waters'. If they understand '*āpaḥ*' as 'water' whose molecule has been made of two atoms of hydrogen and one atom of oxygen, they are not right. In the evolutionary process, water appeared on the Earth at a much later time. *Āpaḥ* is the first fluid whose exact nature is unknown to us.

The creative principle of *Īśvara* or God is known as Brahmā[31] who took birth inside the cosmic egg. He was self-produced and hence is known as *Svayaṁbhu.*[32] He resided inside the cosmic egg for one divine year.[33] Brahmā is *Hiraṇyagarbha*[34] during the one year (divine) of dormancy inside the cosmic egg and *Prajāpati*[35] after the explosion of the cosmic egg. Individuation takes place during the *Prajāpati* state. He was the first-born.[36] He created the universe.[37] He became the efficient cause in the production of everything in the universe out of the primordial substance of the cosmic egg.

In the Vedic and *Purāṇic* literature, the floating of the cosmic egg has been described symbolically. One of the names of Brahmā is *Āpava,*[38] meaning 'He who sports on the waters.' Lord Viṣṇu sleeps on the hood of the divine serpent who is in the primeval waters.[39] A lotus was projected out of the navel of Lord Viṣṇu and from this lotus the cosmic egg developed.[40] Thus the cosmic egg was not isolated but was attached to Lord Viṣṇu. Brahmā was self-produced inside the cosmic egg and thus has been described as born from the navel-lotus of Lord Viṣṇu.[41] Viṣṇu advised Brahmā to procreate.[42] Brahmā practised austerity.[43] He meditated[44] and by his meditation he disturbed the equilibrium that existed among the three constituents (*guṇas*), viz., *sattva*, *rajas* and *tamas*. Brahmā is *rajas*-dominated. Due to the preponderance of the *rajas* constituent, the dormancy of the cosmic egg was disturbed and cosmogonic processes started. Whenever the three constituents are in equilibrium, there is no activity.[45] This equilibrium must be disturbed for any activity to ensue. *Rajas*-dominance is responsible for creation. *Sattva*-dominance favours maintenance of the creation. *Tamas*-dominance leads to destructive processes. The disturbance of the equilibrium among the three constituents was brought about by the *rajas*[46] of Brahmā. As a consequence, the cosmic egg exploded.[47]

Cosmogony in Superheated Condition

With the explosion of the cosmic egg, *prāṇa*[48] was produced. The violent explosion caused prāṇa to vibrate[49] violently. As a result, excessive quantity of heat[50] was produced. In that superheated condition, *ākāśa,*[51] *kha, aditi* or space was produced from *prāṇa.*

Brahmā who is known as *Prajāpati* at this stage produced energy-particles and matter-particles in opposite-pairs[52] from *ākāśa*.

What is this *prāṇa*? It is not life; it is not vital force of the living beings only.[53] At that time there were no living beings. It is as important for living beings as for non-living entities. It is a subtle energizing substance which is all-pervasive.[54] It had no presence before the cosmic explosion; Brahman does not have it.[55] It is the precursor substance of everything in the universe, whether matter or energy.[56] The only precursor substance of *prāṇa* is *āpaḥ*. Nothing in the universe can function without the help of *prāṇa*. This *prāṇa* is subtler than *ākāśa* or space, but not subtler than *āpaḥ*, *nāra* or *ka*. Subtantially *āpaḥ* (*ka*), *prāṇa* and *ākāśa* (*kha*) are not different.[57] All these three are one and the same entity except their degree of subtlety. Manifestation takes place from the more subtle to the less subtle state and from the subtle state to the gross state. *Prāṇa* is subtler than *ākāśa*, but *āpaḥ* is subtler than *prāṇa*. All these three are interconvertible.

In the extreme superheated state prevailing immediately after the explosion of the cosmic egg, *ākāśa* was producing particle-pairs and the particle-pairs were being reconverted into *ākāśa*. Light-particles (photons) were dominant at this time.[58] Other particle-pairs were also formed. These particle-pairs were symbolically designated as *dakṣa*. There was dynamic state of flux between the particle-pairs (*dakṣa*) and *ākāśa* or *aditi*. The particle-pairs were formed out of *ākāśa* and were again re-united to be merged into *ākāśa*. The Ṛgveda describes this phenomenon as *dakṣa* born of *aditi* and again *aditi* born of *dakṣa*.[59] *Aditi* has also been described in the same Veda as both the parents and the offspring.[60] The particles (*reṇu*) were vigorously dancing in that superheated condition in an extremely chaotic manner and thus there were constant collision, annihilation and transmutation.[61] No atoms could be formed due to the extreme random movements of the particles. It was an energy-dominated state and the minor amount of matter was in the form of particles and antiparticles.

The plasma state as described by the modern physicists has been beautifully narrated in the Ṛgveda.[62] What we call 'field' in quantum physics is described by three words in the Vedic literature, viz., *apāṁ-napāt* or *āpaḥ*, *prāṇa* and *ākāśa*. All these three words represent three sub-states of a single state known as 'field'. The undifferentiated subtlest state of substantial existence is *āpaḥ* or primal waters.[63] The next state of materialization is *prāṇa*. Although *prāṇa* is still subtle, it is less subtle than *āpaḥ*. *Ākāśa* or space is less subtle than *prāṇa*, but subtler than energy and matter particles. All these three states have not yet been differentiated in science and have been combinedly designated as 'field'. *Prāṇa* is produced from *āpaḥ* and *ākāśa* from *prāṇa*. In the reverse process, *ākāśa* may be converted into *prāṇa* and *prāṇa* into *āpaḥ*. In consideration of the importance of these three entities, *aditi*[64] is revered as a goddess, *prāṇa*[65] as a god and *apāṁ-napāt*[66] as another god.

Products of Ākāśa

The *Purānic* literature is full of myth and symbolism. The incest myth involving Brahmā is relevant in the present context. The body of Brahmā became two-fold. One part turned out to be a man and the other a woman.[67] The man was Brahmā himself and the woman was named Śatarūpā.[68] Brahmā was attracted by the beautiful girl. He could not control his lustful desire. He embraced his daughter, copulated with her and produced offspring. The same event has been described as an incestuous affair between Brahmā and Sarasvatī or Sāvitrī or Gāyatrī or Brahmāṇī,[69] who are not different from Śatarūpā. On the surface, this action of Brahmā is immoral. But there is nothing immoral if one finds the symbolic meaning. There was no occasion for two persons—one male and another female—to indulge in sexual union in the early universe in which even atoms could not be formed due to hyperkinesis of the particles affected by too high a temperature. There were no galaxies, no stars and no planets. There were no living beings, no human bodies and no animal bodies. In such a situation, who were there to copulate? The Matsya Purāṇa warns against the misinterpretation of those who say that the Brahmā-Śatarūpā episode is a form of incestuous licence.

After lapse of some time following the explosion of the cosmic egg, appreciable quantity of neutron was converted into proton and electron by the splitting of neutron. The bigger one was proton and the smaller one was electron. As the Upaniṣads[70] say, these two particles interplayed and through them everything in the universe was produced. When an electron is trapped by a proton, and the former revolves around the latter, an atom of hydrogen is formed. This hydrogen atom is the primary element that works as a building block in the nucleogenesis of heavier and more complex elements. The scientific events that are described here have been symbolically narrated as splitting of Brahmā (*neutron*) into a male (proton) and a female (electron), embracing the female (electron) by the male (proton) and production of offsprings (other elements) through copulation.

The cosmogonic sequence given in the different Upaniṣads is not the same. However, if a synthesis is made, it would be clear that *prāṇa* was the first product that appeared subsequent to the explosion of the cosmic egg and that *ākāśa* or space was produced from *prāṇa*.[71] There is an opinion that *ākāśa* is a non-entity, that it is void (*śūnya*), and that it is eternally present. Advaita Vedānta rejects the idea of *ākāśa* being void, and considers *ākāśa* as a subtle form of matter. It has no existence after the dissolution and before the creation and hence is not ever present.[72] It has been created[73] in the process of cosmogony and it will be dissolved in the process of dissolution. It is not inactive either. It is full of activity. Particles and antiparticles are produced from it and again they are merged into it. It expands with the expansion of the universe. As a matter of fact, without the expansion of *ākāśa*, the universe of gross matter cannot expand.

According to the Upaniṣads, gaseous matter (*vāyu*) was produced from *ākāśa*.[74] Many scholars equate *vāyu* with air of the Earth's atmosphere. This is, however, not correct. There was no Earth and not even our Sun in the early universe. In this context, the meaning of *vāyu* is gaseous matter. Hydrogen is a gas and is the simplest gas in consideration of its chemical structure. After the evolution of *ākāśa*, the next important evolute was hydrogen whose source was *ākāśa*. The appearance of proton and electron has already been described. When the temperature of the early universe was just right for the formation of atom, an electron was captured by a proton and thus hydrogen atom was produced.

When the stars were formed out of hydrogen-condensation,[75] too much heat was produced due to the compression of gas and the stars glowed.[76] In the course of evolutionary processes, planets were formed out of some stars. These planets like our Earth underwent gravitational contraction. Due to compression of hydrogen gas, heat was produced and this heat liquefied the gas. These two processes have been described by the Upaniṣads as '*agni*'[77] (fire) produced from '*vāyu*' and '*āpaḥ*'[78] (liquid matter) produced as a result of heated gaseous matter.

In course of time, the surface and exterior parts of the planetary sphere gave up heat to the environment. As a result, the planet became solidified at the periphery. The word used by the scriptures for the solidified condition is *pṛthvī*[79] or *anna*.[80] The literal meaning of *pṛthivī* is Earth and that of *anna* is food. These literal meanings do not convey any meaningfulness in the context of the cosmogonical processes described here. Hence the contextual meanings may be taken for appropriate interpretation. For this purpose, the meanings assigned by Charaka[81] to the five *bhūtas* (primary principles modified out of *mūlaprakṛti* or primordial Nature) may be referred to. In the opinion of Charaka, *kṣiti* or *pṛthivī* is solid matter, *āpaḥ* is liquid matter, *tejaḥ* (meaning literally heat or light) is energy, *marut* or *vāyu* is gaseous matter and *vyoma* is ākāśa or space.

Evolutionary Cosmogony

The cosmogony of Advaita Vedānta is evolutionary. Śaṅkara says that the universe has been evolved gradually and that everything in it has not appeared all of a sudden in the form of finished products.[82] The concept of evolution in Advaita Vedānta is, however, different from that of science. Darwinian evolution is confined to species evolution and is antispiritual. The evolution of modern science has three phases, viz., inorganic, organic and species. Science starts from the cosmic egg, makes a long to-and-fro-sojourn through evolution and involution, and ends in the cosmic egg. The cosmic egg itself starts from the 'singularity' and ends in the 'singularity'. The 'singularity' is nothing else other than zero or nihil. In science, the whole process of evolution is not guided by any intelligent Being. Consciousness, which science understands as consciousness of biological organism, is a manifested symptom of living beings at a certain stage of evolutionary development. Advaita Vedānta does not agree with science in many respects. The fundamental and primary Being is Consciousness (*Cit*) according to Advaita Vedānta. The Power (*śakti*) of that Consciousness evolves under the guidance and supervision of the reflection (*pratibimba*) of Consciousness in that Power. So Nature evolves under the chairmanship (*adhyakṣatā*) of the Spirit.[83] Consciousness is eternal and timeless; its Power is eternal and timeless but unconscious; the Presiding Spirit, which is omniscient, is eternal and timeless. Nothing starts from nihil; nothing ends in nihil. What remains in *Mūlaprakṛti* (Primeval Nature) in a dormant and unmanifested condition becomes manifested in the form of universe and undergoes some sequential development. *Prakṛti* or Nature is insentient. It is devoid of consciousness and intelligence to evolve purposefully and meaningfully. The evolution of Advaita Vedānta takes place under the chairmanship of the Spirit Who is All-Conscious.

The evolutionary sequence given in the Taittirīya Upaniṣad includes, in a nutshell, inorganic, organic and species evolution.[84] The same Upaniṣad describes ascendance of psyche from matter to life, life to mind, mind to intellect and intellect to bliss.[85]

Time as Non-Entity

It is worth mentioning here that time finds no place in the cosmogonic sequence of Advaita Vedānta, although space (*ākāśa*) gets prominence in it. Space is a positive entity; it is a product. On the contrary, time is a non-entity; it is not a product. In reality, there is nothing like time. Advaita Vedānta says that time is a mental construct.[86] In the absence of any activity or events, there cannot be any mental concept of time. With the occurrence of more than one event, the mind constructs time-concept. After the dissolution of the cosmos and before the next creation, Brahman alone remains without the universe and no events occur in that non-functional state. This is a timeless condition.

In the Sāṅkhya system,[87] time is also considered as a non-entity and a mental construct. "Infinite Time is a non-entity objectively considered, being only a construction of the understanding based on the relation of antecedence and sequence, in which the members of the phenomenal series are intuited to stand to one another. These phenomenal changes as intuited by us in the empirical consciousness fall into a series which the understanding conceives as order in Time."[88]

When the cosmic egg is created it is zero time (t_o). When the cosmic egg is dissolved, it is maximum time (t_m). The duration of time between t_o and t_m is termed 'para'[89] in Vedāntic literature. This is the time when the universe exists. Time exists as a concept only due to occurrences of more than one event during the interval after creation and before dissolution.[90] When the universe does not exist, time does not exist. Even when time exists, it does not exist as an entity, but it exists in our mind as a psychological concept.

Formation of Stars and Planets

How stars and planets have been formed and what their precursor material is have been mentioned in the Vedic literature. That stars have been formed out of gas-clouds[91] and dust[92] has been clearly mentioned in the scriptures. The dust of space and that of the Earth have been distinguished without any ambiguity.[93] The stars are products of gas-clouds and cosmic dust that are, in turn, products of the cosmic egg.[94] The technical word used in the Vedic literature for the primary content of the star is *aśmāpṛśniḥ*.[95]

With reference to our solar system, the scriptures clearly say that our Earth and all the other planets of our system have originated from the Sun.[96] The rotundity of the Earth has been mentioned. As a matter of fact, it has been said that all the stars, all the planets, all the satellites and the space as a whole are round in shape.[97] The concept of the motionless Earth was not accepted in the Vedic literature. Again, the Sun moving round the Earth was also not recognized. The Vedic seers definitely knew that the Earth and other planets of our solar system revolve round the Sun.[98] The crust-formation of the Earth at the surface and its molten interior have been narrated in the scriptures.[99]

Galaxies and supergalaxies (clusters of galaxies) have been observed by the modern astrophysicists. It is difficult to say whether the Vedic seers used equivalent words in the Vedic literature. One word '*brahmāṇḍa*' and another word '*loka*' have been used by them. They have said that multiple billions of *brahmāṇḍas* exist in the universe.[100] Perhaps the word '*brahmāṇḍa*' is used for a galaxy or a supergalaxy. The whole universe has been divided by them into fourteen *lokas*.[101] How many galaxies are contained in one *loka* has not been ascertained. The *loka* in which our galaxy is situated is known as *bhūḥ*. The other *lokas* that are located above us are in order of sequence: *bhuvaḥ*, *svaḥ*, *mahaḥ*, *jana*, *tapas* and *satyam*.[102] The seven lokas that are below us are in order of sequence: *atala, vitala, sutala, rasātala, talātala, mahātala* and *pātāla*.[103]

Repeated Cycles

In the Vedic literature, the concept of the eternality of the universe has been rejected. The universe has a beginning. It is born at zero time (t_o). It stays for a long period. After its span of life is over, it no longer stays as the universe; it dies at a time which is maximum (t_m). After t_m and before t_o, there is nothing like time. The time interval between t_o and t_m is known as *para*. The universe does not appear from nothing at t_o. It is manifested from an unmanifested condition. The universe does not disappear as nothing at t_m. It goes back from the manifested state to the unmanifested one at t_m. What happens at t_m is known as dissolution (*pralaya*); what happens at t_o is known as creation or emanation (*sṛṣṭi*). Māyā is the eternal reservoir into which the universe is dissolved and is also the eternal reservoir from which it emanates. During the unmanifested condition or the state of dormancy, everything of the universe stays in Māyā in a seed state. Although there is no time during this state of dormancy, for the convenience of our understanding, we call it the night of Lord *Viṣṇu* (God). *Para* is the day of Lord *Viṣṇu* whose day and night are equal in length. After the end of the night, the seed sprouts; the world-tree germinates, grows, blossoms, withers away and dies. This world-cycle is repeated *ad infinitum*.[104]

Although the universe originates from Māyā and goes back to Māyā, the world-tree is rooted in Brahman.[105] Firstly, Māyā has no independent existence; it depends upon Brahman for its existence and is the power of Brahman. Secondly, *Īśvara* (Brahman with attributes) controls Māyā and its activities. Thirdly, *Īśvara* is the creating agent, the supporter and the destroying agent of the universe as *Brahmā*, *Viṣṇu* and *Rudra*,[106] respectively. Hence it has been given in the scripture that the source of the universe is Brahman, that the universe is supported by Brahman and that the universe is dissolved into Brahman.[107] Advaita Vedānta rejects the idea that the universe has been made by any insentient, primordial matter or eternal atoms; it does not accept the hypothesis of *ex nihilo* creation; and considers the notion of spontaneous generation as absurd.[108]

Three types of creation are recognized by Vedānta, viz., *prākṛta, dainandina* and *nitya*.[109] The creation of the whole universe out of Māyā or *Prakṛti* is the evolutionary cosmogony which is known as *prākṛta* creation. This has already been described in this chapter. There is only one *prākṛta* creation in one *para* (Great World Period). It repeats in every *para*. The word '*dainandina*' literally means 'daily' and the diurnal creation is known as '*dainandina*' creation. In this context, day does not refer to the human or Earth day, but it refers to the day of Brahmā. One day of Brahmā (excluding his night) is known as '*kalpa*'. At the end of a *kalpa*, the three *lokas*, viz., *bhūḥ*, *bhuvaḥ* and *svaḥ*, are destroyed. It is followed by a night of Brahmā. The day and the night of Brahmā are of equal duration. At the termination of Brahmā's night, the next *kalpa* begins and the three *lokas* that had been destroyed are again created. In this type of creation and dissolution, the other *lokas* of the universe are not materially affected. *Nitya* or continuous creation does not refer to the creation of whole universe or that of any *loka* or group of *lokas*. In the macro-world, galaxies, stars, planets and satellites are continually created. In the micro-world, molecules, atoms and micro-particles are constantly created. The creation that takes place continuously or continually both in the macro- and the micro-world is known as *nitya*.

The time of Brahmā may be defined here. One Earth-year or human year is one day-and-night in *Devaloka* (one divine day).[110] One divine year contains 360 divine days; 12,000 divine years make one *caturyuga* (four eras); and 1,000 *caturyugas* make one day of Brahmā or a *kalpa*.[111] In one *kalpa*, there are 4.32 billion human years. One night[112] of *Brahmā* also contains 4.32 billion human years. Thus, 8.64 billion human years make one day and one night of Brahmā. This period multiplied with 360 gives the duration of Brahmā's year, which is 3110.4 billion human years. Brahmā lives for a period of 100 years or 311040 billion (311.04 trillion) human years; this period is known as one *para* and one-half of it is known as *parārdha*.[113]

According to another calculation,[114] the duration of one *para* is 369956.16 billion (369.95616 trillion) human years. There are 14 *Manvantaras*[115] (period of one *Manu*) in one day of Brahmā. One *Manvantara* is made of 0.36702 billion human years. Thus, one day of Brahmā or one *kalpa* is made by 5.13828 billion human years. There is thus a difference in the duration of one *kalpa*, as calculated by the previous method and this method. However, this difference is not much significant in consideration of the long duration of a *para*.

Diurnal dissolution of three *lokas* (*bhūḥ*, *bhuvaḥ* and *svaḥ*) takes place at the end of a *kalpa*, whereas total dissolution of the whole universe occurs at the end of a *para*. *Brahmā* still lives after a *kalpā;* he lives for a period that is twice the length of 100 *kalpas*; but he dies after a *para*. *Parārdha* which is one-half of a *para* has been used in Vedic cosmology. In the first *parārdha* of a *para,* the universe expands, and in the second *parārdha,* the universe contracts.

Four types of dissolution[116] (*pralaya*) have been described in the Vedic literature. These are: *nitya* (continual), *naimittika* (occasional), *prākṛta* (total) and *ātyantika* (absolute). At every moment, things are annihilated both in the macro- and the micro-world. Galaxies, stars, planets and satellites are disappearing continually. In every moment, particles and micro-particles are being annihilated. This sort of annihilation is known as *nitya pralaya.*[117] At the end of a *kalpa* or Brahmā's day, the three *lokas,* viz., *bhūḥ*, *bhuvaḥ* and *svaḥ*, are annihilated. This is known as *naimittika* or occasional dissolution.[118] At the end of a *para* or the life-span of Brahmā, the total universe is dissolved into *Prakṛti* or Māyā. This is *prākṛta pralaya.*[119] The individual self, on attaining release from bondage, is merged into Brahman. This is *ātyantika pralaya* or absolute dissolution.[120]

Total Dissolution

In Vedic literature, there are references to the cosmic egg, explosion of the cosmic egg and consequent expansion[121] of the universe. During the first *parārdha* or first half of the Great World Period which is about 185 trillion (1 trillion$=1\times10^{12}$) years, the universe continues to expand. This is followed by the phase of contraction during the second *parārdha.* This process of the expansion and the subsequent contraction of the universe has been compared in the Upaniṣads[122] with the spider's projection and subsequent absorption of its net. This is the concept of the oscillating universe[123] in modern science. Bonner's oscillating universe in science does not ever disappear. It contracts to the point of singularity and again expands. Thus the universe goes through an unending series of explosions and implosions. This is not the case with the spider's universe of Advaita Vedānta. The universe contracts and finally it is completely absorbed by the spider. Who is this spider? This is a symbolic expression for Brahman. Whatever is movable and immovable, living and nonliving, macro and micro is eaten[124] by Brahman. After everything is eaten, Brahman alone remains.[125] It creates again; it absorbs again. Cycle of emanation and dissolution is repeated *ad infinitum*. From the source of Brahman the world comes out; to the same source of Brahman the world goes back.[126]

In a figurative sense, Brahman is the spider; in creation the universe originates from it; in dissolution the universe is merged into it. This is, however, not correct in entirety. *Prakṛti* or Māyā which is the power of Brahman is the eternal and timeless reservoir from which the universe emanates and into which the universe enters. The process of creation is actuated by *Brahmā* and that of dissolution by *Rudra,* both being two aspects of the same *Īśvara. Rajas* constituent is dominant in *Brahmā* who creates; *sattva* constituent is dominant in *Viṣṇu* who sustains; *tamas* constituent is dominant in *Rudra* who destroys. This difference is functional due to the dominance of one of the three constituents. Otherwise, *Brahmā, Viṣṇu* and *Rudra* are not different from *Īśvara,* who, being One only, plays three different roles. So whatever happens in Māyā and the universe, which is the product of Māyā, is guided and supervised by *Īśvara.*

The sequence of dissolution is the reverse[127] of that of creation. This reverse process is gradual. Gross matter becomes subtle and subtler. Finally, the whole universe is absorbed into *Māyā* or *Prakṛti* in which the universe stays in dormancy in unmanifested condition. In this condition, all the three constituents, viz., *sattva, rajas* and *tamas,* are equipoised. This condition continues until the equilibrium of the three constituents is disturbed and creation starts again.

The *nāsadīya sūkta*[128] of the Ṛgveda is the first and the most important description of Vedic cosmogony. This chapter is better concluded by quoting its English version here (poetic rendering by Prof. Macdonell).[129]

(1)

Non-being, then existed not, nor being,
There was no air, nor sky that is beyond it,
What was concealed? Wherein? In whose protection?
And was there deep unfathomable water?

(2)

Death then existed not, nor life immortal,
Of neither night nor day was any token,

By its inherent force, the one breathed windless,
No other thing than that beyond existed.

(3)

Darkness there was at first by darkness hidden,
Without distinctive marks, this all was water,
That which becoming, by the void, was covered,
That One by force of heat came into being.

(4)

Desire entered the One in the beginning,
It was the earliest seed of thought, the product,
The sages searching in their hearts with wisdom,
Found out the bond of being in non-being.

(5)

Their ray extended light across the darkness,
But was the One above or was it under?
Creative force was there and fertile power,
Below was energy, above was impulse.

(6)

Who knows for certain? Who shall here declare it?
Whence was it born, and whence came this creation?
The gods were born after the world's creation,
Then who can know from whence it has arisen?

(7)

None knoweth whence creation has arisen,
And whether he has or has not produced it,
He who surveys it in the highest heaven,
He only knows or haply, he may know not.

The important thing about cosmogony is: "He (God) may know not". The Vedic seer expresses it to express his total despair in getting definite knowledge on cosmogony.

Notes

1. MāKā, II.32; III.48; IV.4, 22, 23, 38, 58, 59.
2. ṚV, X.90.2; Bṛ, II.4.6; II.5.1; Chā, III.14.1; VII.25.1; Mai, IV.6; Mu, II.1.4; II.1.10; II.2.12; BGŚB, II.16.

3. ṚV, X.90.3; TA, XXX.12; BG, X.42.
4. BG, XI.
5. Mu, II.1.4; Tai, III.2.1.
6. Bṛ, V.1.1; Īśa, Invocation.
7. Bṛ, II.1.20; Mu, II.1.1.
8. BS, II.1.26.
9. ṚV, X.82.3; BS, I.1.2; I.4.23, 26, 27; Bṛ, I.4.10; Chā ŚB, VI.4.4; Mu, I.1.3; III.1.3; Tai, III.1.1.
10. BSŚB, II.1.23, 25, 27; MāKā, I.26.
11. BS, I.1.2; II.1.30-31; BSŚB, II.1.30; Chā, III.14.2 and 4; VIII.7.1; Mu, I.1.9.
12. Bṛ ŚB, III.9.26.
13. ṚV, X.72.2-3; X.129.1; Bṛ, I.2.1; Chā, III.19.1; VI.2.1-2; Tai, II.7; MS, I.5; PD, I.19.
14. BS, II.2.26.
15. BG, II.16.
16. Chā, III.19.1; VI.2.1-2.
17. VP, I.2.23.
18. MBh, XII.229.7; KP, I.7.51-60.
19. ṚV, X.129.1.
20. Bṛ, I.4.1, 9-11, 17; Ait, II.1.1; Mai, VI.17; VP, I.2.23.
21. BS, I.4.26; Tai, II.6.1.
22. BSŚB, Intr.; BGŚB, XIV.3; Śve, VI.10.
23. BSŚB, Intr.; BGŚB, XIV.3.
24. BGŚB, Intr.
25. Chā, III.19.1; ŚBrā, VI.1.2.3; MBh, XII.299.3; MS, I.9; BP, I.1.39; GP, I.4.6-11; HV, I.1.36-38; KP, I.4.40-41; PP, III.3.31; VP, I.2.54-60; BDP, I.1.3.24-27; Vā P, IV.76 b-79; Bhā, II.6.21; III.6.6.
26. BGŚB, XIV.3.
27. Bṛ, I.4.3.
28. Chā, VI.2.3-4; Tai, II.6.1.
29. ṚV, X.129.4; BS, I.4.24; II.3.12-13; Bṛ, I.2.1; III.7.3, 23; Ait, I.1.1; Chā, VI.2.3-4; Tai, II.6.1; ŚBrā, VI.1.2.3.
30. ṚV, X.82.5-6; Bṛ, I.2.1-2; V.5.1; Kaṭ, II.1.6; TĀ, X.22; MS, I.8; MBh, XII.160.11; BP, I.1.38; HV, I.1.35-36; VP, I.4.6.
31. Mu, I.1.9.
32. Bṛ, II.6.3; IV.6.3; VI.5.4; Īśa, 8; Kaṭ, II.1.1; ŚBrā, I.9.3.10; TBrā, III.12.3.1.
33. Chā, III.19.1; MS, I.12; MBh, XII.299.4; HV, I.1.38.
34. ṚV, X.121; BSŚB; I.3.30; BGŚB, XIV.3; VJS, XIII.4; KP, I.7.13; MkP, 47.31; MBh, XII.291.17; VP, I.5.19.
35. Bṛ, I.3.1; V.5.1; Pr, I.4; KP, I.7.13; MkP, 47.31; VP, I.5.19.
36. ṚV, IX.96.9; YV, XIII.4; AV, XIX.22.21; Mu, I.1; Śve, VI.18; MBh, XII.160.12; XII.291.15; BDP, I.1.3.24-25; KP, I.4.38; MkP, IV.5.64; ŚP, V.1.8.22; VII.1.10.22; Bhā, II.5.1.
37. Mu, I.1; BGŚB, XIV.3; Bhā, I.3.2; BDP, I.1.3.24-5; KP, I.4.38; MkP, IV.5.64; ŚP, V.1.8.22; VII.1.10-22.
38. BP, II.1.
39. VP, I.2.64; VI.4.4.

40. PP, III.3.31.
41. ṚV, X.82.6; YV, XVII.30; Bhā, I.3.2; II.6.22; III.20.16; GBrā (*Pūrva-Bhāgaḥ*), I.16; MBh, XII.47.40; XII.175.15; KP, I.9.10, 25, 27, 28; MP, 37.19; PP, III.3.31-32; Vā P, I.24.
42. Śve, VI.18.
43. ŚBrā, X.5.3.1-3.
44. MS, I.12.
45. VP, I.2.33.
46. Bhā, III.20.12; GP, IV.6-9; MĀ, 5th *prapāṭhakaḥ*; VP, I.2.29; BDP, I.1.4.3-12.
47. MS, I.12; Chā, III.19.1; ŚBrā, I.4.1.22; JBrā, I.145; III.72; TdBrā, VII.10.1; KS, XIII.12; TS, III.4.3; BP, I.1.38; HV, I.1.38.
48. BS, I.1.23; II.4.1, 7-8, 17; Bṛ, I.2.6; II.1.20; III.9.9; Chā, V.1.1; Mu, II.1.3; Pr, VI.4.
49. BS, I.3.39; Kaṭ, II.3.2.
50. ṚV, X.129.3; Bṛ, I.2.6; Tai, II.6.1; III.1.1-5; MBh, XII.175.16; XII.248.13; XII.250.17; XII.327.26; XIII.138.18; HV, I.29.
51. Kaṭ, II.1.7; Mu, II.1.3; Pr, VI.4; Tai, II.1.1.
52. Bṛ, I.3.1; I.4.4; Pr, I.4. and 5.
53. BS, II.4.9; Chā, III.18.4.
54. BS, II.4.7 and 13; BSŚB, II.4.13; Bṛ, I.3.22.
55. Mu, II.1.2.
56. BS, II.4.8, 17-19; Chā, I.11.4-5; V.1.1.
57. Chā, IV.10.4-5.
58. ṚV, X.129.5; BS, I.1.24; I.3.40; MBh, III.83.47; III.155.2; KP, I.25.69-70.
59. ṚV, I.164.33; X.72.4.
60. ṚV, I.89.10.
61. ṚV, X.72.6.
62. ṚV, II.35; X.72.6-7; X.121.7.
63. ṚV, X.129.3.
64. ṚV, I.89.10; X.72.4; Kaṭ, II.1.7.
65. Bṛ, III.9.9; Chā, I.11.45.
66. ṚV, II.35.
67. Bṛ, I.4.3; Bhā, III.12.52-3.
68. ṚV, I.164.33; ABrā, III.33-35; TS, VII.1.5.155; Bhā, III.12.52-54; HV, I.1.37; MP, III.30-9; VP, I.7.17; KP, I.8.6-10.
69. MP, III.30-9; ŚBrā, V.2.5.17; 4.2.1; VI.1.2.1-11; VII.3.1.20; VIII.4.3.20; KS, 12.5; 27.1; HV, I.1.37.
70. Bṛ, I.3.1.
71. Pr, VI.4.
72. VP, I.2.23; MBh, XII.160.11; XII.175.13.
73. ṚV, I.164.39; BS, I.1.22; II.2.24; II.3.1-2; Chā, I.9.1; III.14.3; Tai, II.1.1.
74. BS, II.3.8; Pr, VI.4; Tai, II.1.1.
75. ṚV, X.121.5; TBrā, I.5.2.5.
76. Pr, VI.4.
77. Tai, II.1.1.
78. BS, II.3.11; Chā, VI.2.3; Pr, VI.4; Tai, II.1.1.

79. BS, II.3.12; Bṛ, I.2.2; Chā, VI.2.4; Pr, VI.4; Tai, II.1.1.
80. BSŚB, II.3.12; Chā, VI.2.4.
81. Charaka, *Śarīrasthāna*, Ch. XXVI, Quoted by Seal, B. in "*The Positive Sciences of the Ancient Hindus*", Motilal Banarsidass, Delhi, 1985, pp. 57-8.
82. MuSB, I.1.8.
83. Śve, VI.11; BG, IX.10.
84. Tai, II.1.1.
85. Tai, III.2.1; III.3.1; III.4;1; III.5.1; III.6.1.
86. MāKā, II.14.
87. VB, I.44.
88. Seal, B., *The Positive Sciences of the Ancient Hindus*, Motilal Banarsidass, Delhi, 1985, pp. 18-9.
89. VP, VI.4.47.
90. VP, I.2.24.
91. YV, XIII.30; ABrā, IV.20; JBrā, II.62; II.145; ŚBrā, VII. 5.1.8; X.6.5.2; TBrā, I.5.2.5.
92. ṚV, X.121.5.
93. ṚV, I.154.1; YV, XXXIV.32.
94. ŚBrā, VI.1.2.3.
95. ṚV, V.47.3; ŚBrā, VI.1.2.3.
96. JBrā, I.87; TS, VII.3.10; VāP, 50.99.53.
97. JBrā, I.257; II.62; ŚBrā, VII.1.1.37.
98. YV, III.6; ABrā, III.4.6.
99. YV, XI.57; ŚBrā, XIV.9.4.21; TS, V.5.2.
100. VP, II.7.27; BP, ŚP and NP, Quoted in *Advaita-Brahma-Siddhi* of Sadananda, Parimal Publications, Delhi, Ist Ed., 1981, Ch. IV, pp. 201-2.
101. VS, 104; VPDA, Ch. VII.
102. VP, II.5.2.
103. VP, II.7.3-20.
104. ṚV, X.190.3; Śve, VI.1.
105. Kaṭ, II.3.1; BG, XV.1-2.
106. ABS, Parimal Publications, Delhi, Ist Ed., 1981, Ch. IV, pp. 200-1; VP, I.2.66.
107. BS, I.1.2; Tai, III.1.
108. BSŚB, I.1.2.
109. VP, I.7.44-5.
110. VP, VI.3.10.
111. BG, VIII.17; BDP, XXXII.86; VP, III.2.50; VI.3.11-2.
112. BG, VIII.17; Bhā, XII.4.3; VP, VI.4.9.
113. VP, I.3.5.
114. VP, I.3.20-2.
115. VP, I.3.16.
116. VPDA, Ch. VII.
117. Bhā, XII.4.34.
118. Bhā, XII.4.3-4.
119. Bhā, XII.4.22; VP, VI.4.46.
120. Bhā, XII.4.34.
121. Mu, I.1.8.
122. Mu, I.1.7; Śve, V.3.

123. Bonner, W., *The Mystery of the Expanding Universe*, Eyre and Spottiswoode, London, 1964.

124. AV, XI.7.1; BS, I.2.9; Kaṭ, I.2.25; Bhā, IV.7.42.

125. BGŚB, VIII.20; MnU, VI.17.

126. BG, VIII.16-19; IX.7.

127. BS, II.3.14; VPDA, Ch. VII; MBh, XII.339.29; VP, VI.4.

128. ṚV, X.129.

129. Mehta, D.D., *Positive Sciences in the Vedas*, Arnold Heinemann Publishers, Delhi, 1974, pp. 214-5 (Quoted).

PART III

CONFLUENCE

CHAPTER X

SUBSTRATUM

Religion without science is blind.
Science without religion is lame.

Albert Einstein

The wise man regulates his conduct by the theories both of religion and science.

J.B.S. Haldane

Everything that is not forbidden is compulsory.

Murray Gell-Mann

THE WORLD IS IMPORTANT for us. We live in it. We like to live in it. Our life is important for us. We love our life. We enjoy our life. We long for an eternal life. Does the world exist? Is it real? Is it not illusory? Who am I? Whence have I come? Where do I go? What is the meaning of my life? What is the meaning of death? Am I this body or is the body mine? Am I annihilated to nothing in death? Am I the subject? Is the world the object? Man has been trying to get answers to these and such other questions. If the world is not real, what is real?

Real Versus *Illusory World*

The common man does not question the reality of the world. He perceives the world by his five senses, viz., eyes, ears, nose, tongue and skin. Whatever he himself perceives is real to him. His definition of reality is based on sense-perceptibility. Whatever is sense-perceptible, directly or indirectly, is real. Whatever is sense-perceptible is existent. On the other hand, whatever is sense-imperceptible is not real and does not exist. Such a concept of reality is naive. Deeper probe into the subject through scientific and philosophical analysis unravels the futility of the so-called real world.

Acquaintance with epistemology, physiology and psychology

is necessary for a comprehension of how each individual constructs his own world. He sees a red rose. There is a pigment with definite chemical constitution in rose. This pigment absorbs light of wavelengths other than a certain narrow range, which may be called X. This light of wavelength X is reflected by the rose and falls on the retina of his eye. Photochemical changes take place on the retina. An electric impulse is generated in the retina and it is conducted by the optic nerve to the diencephalon of the brain and from there to the occipital lobe of the cerebrum where the visual centre is situated. Some area of the visual centre receives the nerve impulse and then something happens there. That 'something' is not clear to us. The mind makes an idea. That idea is the red colour of the rose.

An individual is in ecstasy on hearing the sweet melody of a song. He gets a pleasant experience. His experience is real to him. But what does he receive from the outside world in listening to the melody? Sound wave in certain frequency comes from the source of music and enters his ears. The external ears receive the wave. The middle and internal ears process it. Electrical impulse that is generated is conducted through the auditory (cochlear) nerve to the cochlear nucleus situated in the medulla oblongata and from there to the mid-brain. The nerve-impulse is transmitted from the mid-brain to the temporal lobe of the cerebrum. There something happens and we do not know what that 'something' is. The mind makes an idea. That idea is the sweet melody.

An individual enjoys a pleasant perfume. Another individual nauseates on getting a foul smell. Why is one odour pleasant and another unpleasant? What is there in odour? Odoriferous substances are volatile chemicals of different constitutions. When such a substance reaches the olfactory cells of the olfactory mucosa, there an electrical impulse is generated. This impulse is conducted through the olfactory nerve to reach the olfactory bulb located at the anterior end of the cerebrum (rhinencephalon). From there it goes to the pyriform lobe of the cerebrum to be interpreted by the amygdaloid nucleus. In this nucleus, something happens and that 'something' is not clear to us. Thereby the mind makes an idea. That idea is our pleasant or obnoxious smell.

One eats a sweet dish and enjoys it. Another eats a quinine pill which gives an unpleasant bitter taste. What is that something 'sweet' in sugar? What is that something 'bitter' in quinine? There is nothing like 'sweet', 'bitter', 'sour', 'burning' and 'astringent' in the substance we eat. There are compounds with specific chemical constitutions. Each type of such compounds influences one specific type of gustatory sense-receptors (taste buds). As a result, electrical impulse is generated and conducted through the gustatory fibres present in three different nerves. The facial nerve transmits gustatory sensation from the taste buds located on the anterior part of the tongue. The glosso-pharyngeal nerve transmits gustatory sensation from the taste buds located on the posterior part of the tongue. Similar message is transmitted from the taste buds on the root of the soft palate through the vagus nerve. The sensation passing through any of these three nerve-pathways reaches the solitary nucleus located in the medulla oblongata and from there it goes to the cerebrum through the solitary tract. In the concerned area of the cerebrum, something happens and that 'something' is unclear to us. Thereby the mind makes an idea. That idea is the sweet, bitter, sour, burning or astringent taste.

We get a pleasant sensation through kissing. We get a painful sensation through a pinprick. A warm-water-bath is pleasant in the winter. A cool-water-bath is pleasant in the summer. It is painful when the skin is scalded with hot water. The tingling sensation of the ear-lobes or the finger-tips is unpleasant when the body is exposed to snow-fall. What is this pleasant or unpleasant touch? What is this soothing or painful touch? What is that which we call cold or hot? For cutaneous sensation, the skin has different types of receptors such as tactile, hot, cold, pressure and pain receptors. All the cutaneous receptors are open terminal nerve endings. They receive the stimulus and transmit the sensation in the form of electrical impulse. From all parts of the body except the face, the nerve impulse reaches the spinal cord and ascends to the brain. It reaches the parietal lobe of the cerebrum through the thalamus. From the facial skin, the cutaneous sensation is transmitted through the trigeminal nerve and reaches the brain directly. Each type of cutaneous sensation is conducted via one type of fibre tract and interpreted in the brain by specific areas. There something happens and that 'something' is unknown to us. The mind makes an idea. That idea is soothing, exciting or painful.

What has been described here in the foregoing few paragraphs may not be misconstrued as philosophical idealism, which regards the mental or ideational as the key to the nature of reality. In the subjective idealism of Fichte, the world is a posit of the judging subject. This is what is called solipsism. Only 'I' exist, and nothing else exists. All this world except the 'I' in me is apparent and is an idea of this 'I'. This is the quintessence of subjective idealism. In contrast to the subjective idealism, the panpsychism of Berkeley and others is called 'objective idealism' which identifies reality with idea, reason or spirit and regards Nature as simply 'visible intelligence'. Hegel accepted subjective idealism as thesis, objective idealism as antithesis and his own 'absolute idealism' as synthesis. Some of the other prominent absolute idealists are F.H. Bradley, T.H. Green, Bernard Bosanquet and Josiah Royce. In Kant's 'transcendental idealism', the contents of direct experience are not 'things in themselves' and space and time are forms of our own intuition. The idealism of philosophers like Descartes and Locke is called 'epistemological idealism'. They do not believe that one makes contact with things. They contend that one makes contact only with ideas or psychic entities. The *vijñāna-vāda* of Buddhist philosophy is a very old form of idealism. It considers the world of external things to be unreal. Any one form of idealism, mentioned here, does not conform to the philosophy of Advaita Vedānta. According to it, the non-existence of external objects cannot be maintained on account of perception.[1] We perceive the external world. It is a fact that our mind makes an idea of the external object on receiving the stimulus. But the stimulus does not originate in the mind; it comes from the external object. Of course, the stimulus is not the external object and there is no way to be sure of the identity of our mental conceptualization and the external thing itself. Again, Advaita Vedānta accepts the mind as insentient matter. Brahman, the fundamental Consciousness, is reflected in the mind that conceptualizes only with the help of the reflected Consciousness. What we perceive is not nothing. But what is the real nature of that something is not known to us. Our idea about that something is not that something. We may perceive J as not-J, as A, B, C, D, X, Y and Z, but not as J (*atasmiṁstadbuddiḥ*).[2] That J is not nothing. Advaita Vedānta does not say that J is reality. Only Brahman or Pure Consciousness is Reality for Advaita Vedānta and *Jagat* or the world is not real. But, *Jagat* which is the product of Māyā, the power of Brahman, is not nihil.

It has been said here that the common man is sure of the reality of the world. One may not be surprised to know that this is not applicable to the common man only. Many philosophers and scientists have also been advocating realism. Among the Indian philosophers, the thinkers of Mīmāṁsā, Nyāya-Vaiśeṣika and Jainism were realists. The Cārvākas of India were also realists. The realists hold that objects of knowledge exist independently of our awareness. The electron, positron, photon, quark, X-ray or gamma-ray exist before we come to know them. All the galaxies had existed before we knew about them. Some of the micro-particles and galaxies, still unknown to us, do exist irrespective of the fact of our awareness. The doctrine of 'representative realism' has been clearly developed by John Locke, who says that our awareness consists of sense-data of various types which more or less represent the world. Thomas Reid developed the 'common sense realism'. He held that the principles of common sense are unquestionably true. Everybody perceives the world. Everybody experiences it. "How can we contradict our own experience?" This is the question that was posed by Reid. A movement of 'new realism' was launched in the early twentieth century. Some of the philosophers who participated directly or indirectly in the movement of 'new realism' were G.E. Moore, William James, Bertrand Russell, E.B. Holt, W.P. Montague, R.B. Perry, W.B. Pitkin, E.G. Spaulding and W.T. Marvin. Moore in fact revived Reid's 'common sense realism'. 'Critical realism', which developed in response to new realism, recognizes a triad. The object, the sense-datum and the act of perception constitute the triad. Lenin was pleading for an 'epistemological realism'. It holds that our mental content must replicate reality outside the mind. Whatever may be the form of realism, whatever detailed philosophical complexities it may contain, it does cherish the doctrine of 'naive realism' which holds that all of the characteristics we sense in objects are truly characteristics of them. Advaita Vedānta does not agree to this view and puts forward arguments to refute the doctrine of realism.

For the scientists of the Newtonian age, the world was real to them. Newton's space was absolute, time was absolute. For him everything of the world was really existent. Einstein proved that both space and time were relative. This was the clash of doctrine between absolutism and relativism. Nevertheless, Einstein was a special type of realist. He did not say that whatever we perceive in the world is real. But he did assert the reality of the world in some form or other. According to his ultimate vision, a piece of matter is a curvature of the space-time continuum; whatever exists in the world, matter or energy, is space-time curvature in motion. Once he accepted 'field' as reality and later his ultimate reality was space.

According to the Copenhagen interpretation of Quantum Physics (1927), reality cannot be comprehended in its entirety. Einstein did not like this approach.

He said: "The most incomprehensible thing about the world is that it is comprehensible".[3]

The Marxist philosophers are realists. Lenin defines matter as follows:

> Matter is a philosophical category, denoting the objective reality which is given to man by his sensations, and which is copied, photographed, and reflected by our sensations, while existing independently of them.[4]

The Marxist concept of matter had precedent in Hegel's philosophy. This becomes vivid by perusal of the following two paragraphs:

> The conception of matter as original and pre-existent, and as naturally formless, is a very ancient one; it meets us even among the Greeks, at first in the mythical shape of chaos, which is supposed to represent the unformed substratum of the existing world.[5]
>
> Space and time are filled with matter ... Just as there is no motion without matter, so there is no matter without motion.[6]

In this context, motion does not mean change of place. It means change in Marxist philosophy. In order to dispel ambiguity and give clarity, Engels gives the contextual meaning of motion in the following paragraph:

> Among natural scientists motion is always as a matter of course taken to mean mechanical motion, change of place ......

Motion, as applied to matter, is *change in general*.[7] He further says:

> Both matter and its mode of existence, motion, are uncreatable and are, therefore, their own final cause.[8]
> *Motion is the mode of existence of matter.* Never anywhere has there been matter, without motion, nor can there be.[9]

Afanasyev, who is a Marxist philosopher, gives his views on matter in the following language:

> If matter is primary and eternal, it is uncreatable and indestructible, it is the inner final cause of everything existing. In a world where matter is the primary cause, the primary foundation of everything, there is room neither for God nor any other supernatural forces ......
> In the material world there is not a single thing, however minute, which can arise out of nothing or disappear without trace. The destruction of one thing gives rise to another and this to a third, and so on *ad infinitum*. Concrete things change, they are transformed one into another, but matter neither disappears nor is created anew in the process.[10]

Afanasyev elaborates the concept of matter and its different states of existence in the following manner:

> Substance is a form of matter. Everything that has a rest mass is a substance.......
> Substance exists in a variety of states. In our everyday life we usually deal with solid, liquid or gaseous substances. And yet the most widespread state of substance in the world is *plasma*, a gaseous condition created by electrically charged particles—electrons and ions ... Plasma is also regarded as yet another, fourth form of matter.
> The field is another basic form of matter. The gravitational field and the electromagnetic field were known already in the nineteenth century.
> The boundaries between substance and field are dinstinct only in the macroscopic visible world. In the sphere of microprocesses, however, these boundaries are relative ... Substance and field are inextricably connected; they interact and under certain circumstances are capable of being transformed one into another.

> The world by its nature is material: all that exists represents various forms and kinds of matter. But matter is not something inert and stagnant. It constantly moves in time and space. Motion, space and time are the basic forms of being of matter.[11]

Materialists, dialectical and otherwise, consider matter as real and enternal and the fundamental basis of the world. In 1905, Einstein declared his mass-energy equation ($E=mc^2$). Consequently, matter is considered as a packet of energy. This knowledge brought about a revision in the doctrine of materialism. At the turn of the twentieth century, many scientists and materialistic philosophers accepted energy as the fundamental basis of the world. The Marxists brought about little reorientation in their doctrine, but did not revise it. In their opinion, there is identity between matter and energy except their forms and hence energy can be called matter and thus matter may be still regarded as the fundamental basis of the world.

At the early part of twentieth century, energetism was the trend in philosophy and natural science. The advocates of energetism think that motion exists by itself.

Marxist philosophers react to the doctrine of energetism. They ask the question: "Does motion exist by itself, without any material carrier?" They blame those who reduce matter to motion and energy. They think that it is nothing more than a refusal to recognize matter. They brand energetism as idealism pure and simple. On this topic, Afanasyev expresses his views as follows:

> Present-day champions of energetism are particularly vociferous in their idealist views. They speak of the 'annihilation' of matter, its conversion into 'pure' energy. To this end, for example, they idealistically interpret the conversion of a pair of elementary particles of substance (electron and positron) into photons, particles of the electromagnetic field (light) ... The photon, however, is a particle of the field, a special form of matter.
>
> There is neither matter without motion nor 'pure' motion divorced from matter, nor could there be any. Matter and motion are inseparable.[12]

The doctrine that matter is primary and real cannot be accepted as fact. The doctrine that energy is primary and real cannot also be accepted as fact. After all, matter and energy are identical and exist in two different states only, and hence a distinction between matter and energy cannot be maintained. The so-called reality of matter or energy is based on empirical verification or verifiability. "Whatever is perceived by one or more of our five senses is existent and real." This is the principal doctrine of the empiricists with reference to the reality of the world. The Indian Carvākas were very much emphatic on this point. The Greek materialists such as Democritus and Epicurus trace all knowledge to an influx of images from things perceived. For them, the world of atoms was real, since they could perceive the world. British empiricism put much stress on sense-perceptibility as the criterion of reality. Roger Bacon advocated for direct inspection and experimentation. In his opinion, speculative argument is never sufficient to establish a conclusion; direct inspection is necessary. "Experimental science", he said, "is superior to speculative science". Francis Bacon, another British empiricist, supported empirical method or induction and argued against excessive generalization. Thomas Hobbes, a British philosopher of the 16th and 17th century, held that all reality is corporeal, and is controlled by rigid causal laws. David Hume established a distinction between 'relations of ideas' and 'matters of fact'. This idea was strengthened by the logical positivists of the Vienna Circle in the twentieth century. Two of the members of this circle, viz., A.J. Ayer and Herbert Feigl, call their view logical empiricism. They divide statements into two types, analytic and synthetic. Identical statements such as "A is A", "Water is water", "Water is aqua", "A triangle has three angles" are analytical statements, where the subject and the predicate are the same or mean the same. No factual verification is necessary to establish the formal truth of analytical statements. On the other hand, synthetic statements such as "The material of this chair is wood" is to be verified by sense-perception in order to establish its truth. The logical empiricists say that a synthetic statement is never true unless and until it is verified or is, at least, verifiable. Of course, it is to be admitted that direct inspection, experimentation and verification are valuable tools in the discovery of Nature. But this truth is acceptable at a certain level, and beyond that level it is no longer valid. The nature and problems of epistemology are to be appreciated. The limits of our senses are to be recognized. It would then be vivid that the sense of certitude we place in our sense-perceptions vanishes.

The epistemological problems have already been discussed in this chapter. Some sense-data come from the external world. Our sensory organs process them, modulate them and transmit some messages in the form of electrical impulses to some specific centres in our brain. In the brain-centre something happens and a concept is created. That feeling of ours is our seeing, hearing, smelling, tasting and touching. Advaita Vedānta says that the insentient sense-organs and mind cannot conceptualize unless these are reflected by the Consciousness which is Brahman. Here the thing observed (*dṛśya*), the observer (*draṣṭā*) and the action of observation (*dṛṣṭi*) are involved. The question is: "Is the action of observation identical with the thing observed?" We see a red rose. Our feeling of the redness is not the same as the rose. "What is the exact nature of the rose?" There is no way for us to answer this question. We can express what we observe, what we experience. We are not aware of anything beyond that. What we observe may have real existence. What is the true nature of that real existence is not known to us. What we observe may be unreal, may be magical. How can we rule out the possibility of illusion and hallucination? We can't. Secondly, the red rose is observed as 'red' by X and also observed as 'red' by Y. Is there any sure method of ascertaining the identity or non-identity of the 'red concepts' of X and Y? There is not. Further, a person, colour-blind to 'red', cannot observe the redness of the flower. Thus our sense-perceptions cannot ensure us of the reality of the world.

Our sense-perceptions have limits too. Our sense-organs have been evolved to perceive within certain specified range. The human eye is sensitive to light of wavelength in the range between 400 and 760 nanometers. The infra-red (more than 800 nanometers) and the ultra-violet (less than 400 nanometers) waves cannot be detected by the human eye. The human eyes are not sensitive to X-rays whereas these rays can be detected by the eyes of the honey-bee. Radiation in the neighbourhood of 580 nanometers produces the sensation of yellow. The same yellow colour can be produced by a mixture of wavelengths. If waves of 700 nanometers, which by themselves produce the sensation of red, are mixed in a definite proportion with waves of 535 nanometers, which by themselves produce the sensation of green, this mixture produces sensation of yellow. The human ear perceives sound waves with frequencies between 20 and 20,000 vibrations or cycles per second. The upper pitch limit of dogs is generally about twice that of man. Bats emit sounds usually with components up to 150 kilocycles per second or higher, having wavelengths short enough to reflect strong echoes off even small targets. These are ultrasonic sounds for man (above our range of hearing). The commonest family of bats uses loud-frequency-modulated (FM) pulses and cries that sweep downward through approximately an octave in the range of 100 to 20 kilocycles per second. These cries are emitted at a rate of 10 to 20 per second, increasing to 100 to 200 per second after detection of an obstacle to be avoided or a target to be caught, while the cruising duration of 2 to 5 milliseconds falls to 0.5 to 1.0 milliseconds during the buzz. The bat sends sound waves, these waves hit the bodies of small insects and then echoed back to the bat's ears. In order to catch prey, the bat's system has developed a sort of radar device. The external ear structures and the brain auditory nuclei of the bat have been evolved for a sensitivity to frequencies as high as 100 to 150 kilocycles per second. Another development is the extremely fast recovery and even short-term (2 to 20 milliseconds) facilitation of the auditory nervous system of the bat to sound. These are a few examples for illustrating the limits of our sense-perceptions. Considering these limits, we cannot afford to say that what we do not perceive does not exist and only what we perceive exists. Secondly, in consideration of the epistemological problems, we cannot claim, with any degree of certainty, that what we perceive really exists. Thirdly, there is no way of becoming sure of the identity of our perception and the thing we perceive.

In our day-to-day living, we experience a number of things that do not exist ontologically. The blue sky we experience is a non-entity. The darkness we experience is a non-entity. Being non-entities, the blue sky and the darkness are empirically existent for us. Advaita Vedānta says that the world has empirical existence, although it is an illusion. In any illusion, X is perceived as Y. This may be better expressed in mathematical symbolism as "B being perceived as non-B". This non-B may be A, C, D, E, F, ..., X, Y, Z, but not B. This concept of illusion is not nihilism. There is something which is perceived as something else. That something which exists is Brahman which is the substratum of all the world-phenomena.

The macro-universe of space, stars, planets, satellites, oceans, seas, mountains, rivers, water, air, earth, light, heat, plants, animals and man is made of atoms that, in turn, are made of sub-atomic particles such as proton, electron and neutron. The sub-atomic particles are made of quarks. The quarks may be the fundamental particles, or, they may be composite particles made of still subtler particles. Are these particles real? If they are not real, the universe made of the unreal particles cannot be real. Let us be conversant with what some prominent scientists say on the unreality of the micro-constituents of the universe.

Like the Upaniṣadic seer answering about Brahman with the word *'neti'* (not this), Oppenheimer answers negatively in the following paragraph:

> If we ask, for instance, whether the position of the electron remains the same, we must say 'no'; if we ask whether the electron's position changes with time, we must say 'no', if we ask whether the electron is at rest, we must say 'no', if we ask whether it is in motion, we must say 'no'.[13]

Śaṅkara, a Hindu monk of the eighth century, declared that the world is an illusion. Sir Arthur Eddington, a renowned physicist of the twentieth century, expresses his opinion in similar language:

> In the world of physics we watch a shadowgraph performance of familiar life. The shadow of my elbow rests on the shadow table as the shadow ink flows over the shadow paper ... The frank realization that physical science is concerned with a world of shadows is one of the most significant of recent advances.[14]

It is surprising that the image of mirage, given by Śaṅkara in explaining his doctrine of illusion, finds a place in Eddington's description of the world as an illusion.

> The world we see and experience in everyday life is simply a convenient mirage attuned to our very limited senses, an illusion conjured by our perceptions and our mind. All that is around us (including our own bodies) which appears so substantial is ultimately nothing but ephemeral networks of particle-waves

> whirling around at lightning speed, colliding, rebounding, disintegrating in almost total emptiness—so-called matter is mostly emptiness, proportionately as void as integalactic space, void of anything except occasional dots and spots and scattered electric charges.[15]

Heisenberg's Uncertainty Principle (Principle of Indeterminancy) may be discussed with reference to the unreality of the world. He advanced reasons to prove that it is not possible to determine both the position and a momentum of a particle simultaneously and with unlimited accuracy. If one determines the position of a particle accurately, one automatically alters its velocity. With change in its velocity, its momentum is changed. Thus, the momentum of a particle becomes uncertain at the time of the exact determination of its position. Again, if one determines the momentum of a particle accurately, one automatically alters its position. Thus, the position of the particle becomes uncertain at the time of the accurate determination of its momentum. The more certain we are of the position of a particle, the less certain we have to be about its momentum, and *vice versa*. In addition to position and momentum, there also is a reciprocal uncertainty of time and energy. In a subatomic event, the less uncertain is the time involved, the more uncertain is the energy involved, and *vice versa*.

The building blocks of the universe are atoms, subatomic particles and subatomic micro-particles. Without position, a particle does not exist. Without momentum, a particle cannot exist. Both position and momentum of a particle are basic necessities for its existence. The particle cannot exist with one only. But, with the accurate determination of one, the other one becomes uncertain. It is deduced from this that the existence of the particle is uncertain. In such a case, does the world exist with certainty? In this respect, Heisenberg himself remarks:

> In the experiments about atomic events we have to do with things and facts, with phenomena that are just as real as any phenomena in daily life. But the atoms or elementary particles themselves are not as real; they form a world of potentialities or possibilities rather than one of things or facts.[16]

According to quantum mechanics, subatomic particles have no objective existence. They are not particles like particles of dust.

They are 'tendencies to exist' and 'correlations between macroscopic observables'. Heisenberg has said: "In the light of the quantum theory ... elementary particles are no longer real in the same sense as objects of daily life, trees or stones."[17] Thus, in spite of all our attempts in the search for the ultimate stuff of the universe, we finally come to the conclusion that there is not any.

It has already been mentioned that Advaita Vedānta holds that the world is an illusion and that it still declares that the world has got empirical existence (*vyāvahārika sattā*). In the opinion of Jeans, modern physics has become epistemological, not ontological. His views may be reproduced here in his own language:

> The Theory of Realitivity shows that we can observe only *relations*, while the Quantum Theory has determined that we can observe only probabilities. Both together result in the following: all the mathematical equations that handle particles or wave packets in their different states or conditions do not actually represent them at all; they merely indicate the different kinds and amounts of knowledge we may have about them. Thus, modern physics has become essentially epistemological and has given up all claims (if it ever entertained any) to be ontological; it deals with the grounds of possible knowledge, not with the essence of a fundamental reality that is beyond its scope.[18]

What the world is without the observation of an observer cannot be said. But the fuzzy and nebulous world sharpens into concrete reality when an observation is made. In this respect, Niels Bohr gives his opinion as follows:

> The fuzzy and nebulous world of the atom only sharpens into concrete reality when an observation is made. In the absence of an observation, the atom is a ghost. It only materializes when you look for it. Look for its location and you get an atom at a place. Look for its motion and you get an atom with a speed. But you can't have both. The reality that the observation sharpens into focus cannot be separated from the observer and his choice of measurement strategy.[19]

Quantum physics prefers the word 'participator' to the word 'observer'. We do not observe a thing without influencing it. As a matter of fact, not only do we influence our reality, but, in some degree, we actually *create* it. We measure property, p_1, when we choose to do it. We measure property, p_2, when we choose to do it. Quantum physicists believe that we create properties when we choose them. A particle with momentum perhaps had not existed before the experimenter conducted an experiment to measure its momentum. A particle with position perhaps had not existed before an experimenter conducted an experiment to measure its position. A particle perhaps had not existed before an experimenter thought about it and measured it. The quantum physicist is reluctant to dispel the idea from his mind that he creates the particles that he experiments with. He does not accept the statement, "Particles exist". He thinks that particles are 'tendencies to exist' or 'tendencies to happen'. The concept of illusion is hidden in the concept of participation of the quantum physicist. In this connection, John Wheeler, a well-known physicist at Princeton, has written like this:

> May the universe in some strange sense be 'brought into being' by the participation of those who participate? ... The vital act is the act of participation. 'Participator' is the incontrovertible new concept given by quantum mechanics. It strikes down the term 'observer' of classical theory, the man who stands safely behind the thick glass wall and watches what goes on without taking part. It can't be done, quantum mechanics says.[20]

Advaita Vedānta and the Copenhagen Interpretation of Quantum Mechanics have complete agreement on the illusory nature of the world. According to the latter, the world which we perceive as physical reality is actually our cognitive construction of it. Although this cognitive construction appears to be substantive, the physical world itself is not. In this connection, the opinion of Henry Stapp may be presented here:

> If the attitude of quantum mechanics is correct, in the strong sense that a description of the substructure underlying experience more complete than the one it provides is not possible, then there is no substantive physical world, in the usual sense of the term. The conclusion here is not the weak conclusion that

there *may* not be a substantive physical world but rather that there definitely is not a substantive physical world.[21]

A chapter on quantum mechanics has been presented in Part I of this book. Here the opinions of some prominent quantum physicists on the unreality of the world have been given. The Marxist and other materialistic philosophers have no sound arguments to contradict the concept that the world is not real, but illusory. The old idea of matter as fundamental, uncreatable, undestructible and eternal is repeated by them. That idea has been obsolete. Those who think that energy is fundamental are also wrong. If matter could not be real and fundamental, so also is energy.

Advaita Vedānta[22] does contain the concept of the matter in motion. The Sanskrit word for the universe is *jagat* (*gam+kvip*), which etymologically means "that which is in motion" or "that which ever changes". But Advaita Vedānta does not accept the eternality of the world. As long as the world exists, it is ever mutable. But it does not exist always as such. It is created at zero time (t_o); it stays in motion up to its maximum time (t_m); it has got a definite span of life ($t_o - t_m$); it is dissolved at t_m. This process of creation, maintenance and dissolution is repeated in cycles. It has already been shown and will again be shown that eternality of the world is scientifically impossible.

Modern astrophysics gives a narration of the singularity, formation of the cosmic egg, big bang explosion, the expanding universe, the big crunch and back to the singularity. This theory has been accepted in science. Hence where is the question of the eternal matter or eternal energy? Is there matter or energy in any form in the so-called singularity? Science gives an evasive answer to this question.

Science tries to find reality in terms of matter, energy, field or space. None of these things can be the reality. Once Einstein has thought 'field' to be the reality. Shortly before his death, he declared that space is the only reality. Any such attempt to find reality in matter, energy, particles, field and space is bound to be a failure. According to Advaita Vedānta, all these are products of Māyā and cannot be real. Brahman is the only reality and nothing else.

Pluralism and Monism

The world which we experience apparently consists of diverse things. We see too many stars, many planets of our solar system and too many things in our planet. Are all these things which are apparently different are really different? Is the world made of a single basic material? Are the basic materials two in number, or, are they too many? Man has been pondering over these questions since very early times of human history.

Any metaphysical view holding that the world is composed of only one basic entity is called monism. Dualism admits two kinds of basic entities. In pluralism it is held that the world is made of more than two kinds of basic entities.

We come across a number of pluralists among Greek philosophers. Anaxagoras was of the opinion that the number of qualitatively different substances in the world were indefinitely great. According to Empedocles, four basic substances, viz., earth, air, fire and water, are the raw materials of which the world is composed. The German philosopher, J.F. Herbart (1776-1841) described his ontology as 'pluralistic realism'. There is nothing like a single entity which may be called reality. There are too many 'reals' which are simple qualitative units. All these form syntheses to give rise to reality. This synthesized one, in Herbart's opinion, is the world we experience. The American philosopher, William James (1842-1910) is one among the modern pluralists. He did not believe the world to be absolutely unified. There is looseness in it. Ours is not a block universe. Its relations are not all internal. James explained the pluralism of the world in terms of external relatedness.

The Greek philosopher, Plato, was a dualist. He attributed true existence to ideas, to the universal forms. Nonetheless, he recognized the individual concrete thing as an inferior but opposing principle. The French philosopher, René Descartes (1596-1650) was a thoroughgoing dualist. He distinguished between the *res cogitans* and the *res extensa*. Thus Cartesian dualism recognized the body and the mind as two opposing fundamental principles. The Western world was beseiged with the dualism of mind and matter for many centuries.

Monism has different shades. The monism advocated by Parmenides and Spinoza represents substantival monism. The Greek philosopher, Parmenides (515-450 B.C.) was a monist.

He considered consciousness (thought) to be identical with being which is changeless and the only reality. The world of sense experience, on the other hand, is full of contradiction and hence is mere illusion. For Parmenides, empty space is not-being and non-existent, and without existent space motion is impossible.

B. Spinoza (1632-97) was a Jewish philosopher who was a monist. He emphasized on a single substance that can exist by itself and that is the whole of reality. This whole of reality is God and only one God. The absolutely infinite Being exists necessarily and is eternal, not temporal. The essence of the Being implies its existence. It is its own cause, *causa immanens* and *causa sui*. This Being has an infinite number of attributes.

Attributive monism encompasses the relevant ideas of Democritus, Leibniz and the contemporary atomic theory. It is a view that holds that many substances existing in the world are all of a single kind.

The Greek philosopher, Democritus (460-370 B.C.) has said that the ultimate constituents of reality are atoms. The atoms of Democritus were internally solid, simple, homogeneous and without void. His idea of 'void' is the idea of empty space in which nothing exists and through which existent things can move. Atoms differ among themselves in size, shape and velocity; their differences are quantitative only. This atomic theory of Democritus has become obsolete now. However, this was his monism.

G.W. Leibniz (1646-1716) was a German philosopher. His ontological unit is primarily a centre of force. He rejected the concept of an 'atom' as the smallest particle of matter. He gave birth to the concept of 'monad' which is an extensionless unit with force. The monads are the simple substances out of which all things of the universe are made. Since monads are devoid of extension, they are not in space. Being partless, they cannot degenerate into something simpler. This monistic idea of Leibniz who considered the monad as the single primary unit of the universe is speculative only.

Bertrand Russell (1872-1970), being apparently a pluralist, was still a neutral monist, at least for some time. On a suggestion of William James, he built a concept of neutral monism. His neutral monism held that reality is neither mental nor physical but some neutral stuff capable of either type of organization.

In the year 1900, Max Planck gave the idea of 'quantum'.

According to this concept, energy is not homogeneous and continuous; it exists in discrete packets or quanta. This is the beginning of quantum physics. The quantum concept of Planck was in favour of pluralism. In 1905, Albert Einstein established his mass-energy equation ($E = mc^2$). Up to this time, matter and energy were considered to be different. Einstein's equation proved that matter is packet of energy. After this discovery, the difference between matter and energy vanished. Matter is energy and *vice versa* except the mode of existence.

Thus the various forms of matter and energy are ultimately converted into energy. There can be transformation. One form of matter can be converted into another form. One form of energy can be converted into another form. Matter and energy are inter-convertible. From these premises, can we deduce that energy is the fundamental and single unit of the universe? Does this give a proof of monism?

Max Planck's discovery of quanta rejected the concept of monism. Energy is both continuous and discrete. It is continuous for certain purposes and discontinuous for some other purposes. Light is electromagnetic wave. As wave it is continuous. Light is particulate; it is made of particles known as photons; as particulate it is discrete. Monism cannot be upheld if energy is accepted as particulate. But the atomicity of energy is no more debatable in science. Thus monism became unacceptable in science in the early part of the twentieth century.

It is ironical that quantum physics has become monistic in the same twentieth century. The first quantum physicist, Max Planck, gave the concept of quanta that favoured pluralism. Later quantum physicists have rejected the concept of pluralism and established the idea of the 'unbroken whole'.

The word 'particle' may be used here in the sense of both matter and energy particles. Both matter and energy manifest in duality. They exist as particles; they also exist as waves. The existence of an entity in the state of particles proves its discontinuous nature. The existence of an entity in the state of wave proves its continuous nature. Thus the world of matter and energy is both continuous and discontinuous.

How are the particles held together? Why are they not flying away? How are the macro-objects—the galaxies, stars, planets and satellites—held together? Why are they not running away and lost to one another? In the search for answers to these questions, scientists could discover four fundamental quntum interactions, viz., the gravitational interaction, the weak interaction responsible for radioactivity, the electromagnetic interaction and the strong quark-binding interaction. Each of these four interactions has an associated gluon.

In 1967, Steven Weinberg and Abdus Salam could mathematically prove that the electromagnetic and the weak interactions are not distinct. They could combine these two in an integrated mathematical description. In 1980, they received the Nobel Prize for this work. Thus, the four fundamental quantum interactions became three. In reality, these are not three, but basically one only. One and only one quantum interaction manifests in four varieties.

Notwithstanding the fact that all the four quantum interactions have been unified, monism is not established in science as long as quanta exist.

Science and many schools of philosophy considered space as non-entity, a void. This idea of space as void has been discarded by quantum physicists. Particles appear from space and disappear into space. Many scientists are of the opinion that space is filled with 'field' from which particles originate and into which particles are dissolved. For them, the ultimate material reality is the 'field'. The quantum field is both continuous and discontinuous. The discontinuities are temporary condensations of space-time where the field is unusually intense, giving rise to corpuscular matter. The field is invisible. But we can determine its effects. Scientists now believe that particles and field are complementary manifestations of the same reality. But, now they discard the idea that particles are the ultimate reality. The ultimate reality which they accept now is the field.

Of course, it is safer for them to avoid the use of the word 'ultimate'. On the empirical plane, they have been recognizing the ultimate reality differently at different times. There was a time when matter was the ultimate reality for them. Atoms became the ultimate reality later. Next, energy became the ultimate reality. Next came field; and then space. The opinion of great scientist like Einstein may be quoted here:

> We may therefore regard matter as being constituted by the regions of space in which the field is extremely intense......There is no place in this new kind of physics both for the field and matter for the field is the only reality.[23]

Shortly before his death, Einstein formulated the quintessence of his world-view in these words:

> Space has devoured ether and time; it seems to be on the point of swallowing up also the field and the corpuscles, so that it alone remains as the vehicle of reality.[24]

Still there is confusion among some scientists as to the nature of space and field. They think that space is the container and field is the content. In their view, space is permeated with field. This view holds in a covert way that space is void. This is, however, not correct. As a matter of fact, space is itself field.

Whatever may be the controversy regarding 'field in space' or 'field as space', science has discarded the concept of pluralism and has accepted field or space as one and a single continuous entity as the basis of the appearance of the multifarious world. This basic entity is one and continuous; it is the source of the heterogenous manifestation of the universe. The one gives rise to many; the invisible gives rise to multifarious invisible-cum-visible ones; the formless gives rise to pluralities of forms. Thus monism is established in science.

At the field or space level, the world is monistic. At the level of the corpuscles, the world is pluralistic. In spite of this apparent pluralism, the micro-particles communicate among themselves although they may be far apart at billions of light-years away and this communication too occurs without any time-interval. Scientists have been very much puzzled to explain this phenomenon. A brief discussion on this topic may be useful here.

During the early 1930s, Einstein made an imaginary test of the quantum rules. He worked in Princeton with Boris Podolsky and Nathan Rosen and published a paper[25] which presents what has been known as the EPR paradox. Two particles, p_1 and p_2, may be imagined to interact with one another and then to fly apart. It may be further imagined that these two particles remain as such without interacting with anything else until the experimenter investigates one of them. When the two particles are close together, we can measure precisely their total momentum and the distance between them. When they are far apart, we can measure the momentum of one of them (say, p_1) and thereby get the momentum of the other one (p_2) since the total momentum is to remain unchanged. After this, we can measure the precise position of particle p_1. This disturbs the momentum of particle p_1 without presumably disturbing that of particle p_2 which is far apart. We now know the position of particle p_1; we can deduce the present position of particle p_2 by use of its momentum and the original separation of the particles. Thus, we have deduced precisely both position and momentum of particle p_2 in violation of the uncertainty principle. In case we presume that the uncertainty principle is not violated, we have to inescapably presume that our measurements on particle p_1 affect its partner p_2 in violation of causality. "How can 'action at a distance' be explained?" "Can there be *instantaneous* 'communication' travelling across space between p_1 and p_2?" If the Copenhagen interpretation is accepted, the EPR paper concluded, it has to be accepted that the reality of a second system p_2, which is not disturbed by system p_1 in any way, depends upon the process of measurement carried out on system p_1. In the opinion of Einstein, Podolsky and Rosen, no reasonable definition of reality could be expected to permit this.

The EPR experiment was a thought experiment. Einstein himself did not do any actual experimentation on this problem. During his life-time, he could not get a chance to know the results of anyone's actual experiments on it. After his death, it could be proved with experimental evidence that the Copenhagen interpretation was correct.

In 1952, David Bohm introduced the idea that spin measurement might be done to experimentally verify the EPR thought experiment. This idea was translated into action by John Bell[26] who published his paper on this in 1964.

The Bell test was based on the premise of the 'local realistic' view of the world. This view was defined by Bernard d'Espagnat, a theorist of the University of Paris-South. The local realistic view of the world is based on three fundamental assumptions. First, there are real things that exist regardless of whether anybody observes them; second, general conclusions can be drawn from consistent observational or experimental data; third, there can be no propagation faster than the speed of light.

Bell derived a mathematical formula, an inequality, which could be checked experimentally. After repeated experimentation, Bell concluded that Bell's inequality was violated.

What are the implications of the violation of Bell's inequality? Objectivity and local causality are crucial in obtaining Bell's inequality. By the experimental violation of Bell's inequality by Bell himself, objectivity and local causality could be rejected. Thus the local realistic view of the world was unacceptable to quantum physics. Bell noticed a strange 'connectedness' among quantum phenomena. At a deep and fundamental level, the 'separate parts' of the universe are connected in an intimate and immediate way.[27]

The scientists at the University of California used photons for conducting tests of Bell's inequality. Their reports were published in 1972.[28] By 1975 six such tests were carried out. The results of four of them violated Bell's inequality. A team of physicists at the Saclay Nuclear Research Centre in France used low-energy protons for the test of Bell's inequality. The results of this experiment clearly demonstrate that Bell's inequality is violated and that the local realistic views of the world are false. In the mid-1970s, experiments were conducted with photons that are gamma rays produced as a result of annihilation of an electron and a positron. The polarizations of the two photons were measured and the results violated Bell's inequality.

After the mid-1970s, further experiments confirmed the earlier finding that Bell's inequality is violated. Ultimately, an experiment was designed by Alain Aspect's team at the University of Paris-South. This was ingeniously designed in 1982 so as to close the last major loophole for the local realistic theories. The results of the experiments of Aspect's team were announced just before Christmas of 1982.[29] These results violate Bell's inequality to a greater extent than those of any of the previous experiments.

Einstein believed in an objective reality. He did recognize an appearance of uncertainty and unpredictability at the quantum level. He realized the statistical variations, the random fluctuations and the occurrences of chance events. But, in his opinion, there is something below these superficial uncertainties, and that deeper 'something' keeps the universe running. He visualizes an objective reality that exists and functions irrespective of the fact whether somebody is observing or not. The particles, having momentum and position, are precisely defined in the opinion of Einstein, even when nobody is not looking at them. Unfortunately Einstein died long before 1982. He would have revised his opinion after getting the evidence from Aspect's experiments. Einstein was an honest man, with open mind to accept sound experimental evidence. In this connection d'Espagnat has said:

> Experiments have recently been carried out that would have forced Einstein to change his conception of nature on a point he always considered essential.........we may safely say that non-separability is now one of the most certain general concepts in physics.[30]

The Aspect experiment and its predecessors provide us sufficient clues to build up a holistic picture of the universe. They tell us that particles that were once together in an interaction continue to remain parts of a single system, even though they are separated by long distance at a later time. Every thing of the world is made of particles. All particles were in close proximity in the 'singularity', cosmic egg and even immediately after the big bang explosion. In the beginning, all particles were interacting in a single system. Hence theorists such as David Bohm and d'Espagnat believe that everything is connected to everything else, and that only a holistic approach to the universe can explain to phenomena of the universe.

The Bohr-Einstein debate has come to a stop by a series of experiements some of which have been mentioned here. The question that is still puzzling scientists is: "How does particle p_2 react instantaneously, when something happens to its partner particle p_1?" Particle p_1 and p_2 may be spinning clockwise and anticlockwise, respectively. By some device we may change the spin behaviour of particle p_1 which may now spin anticlockwise. Simultaneously particle p_2 will change its spinning from anticlockwise to clockwise. We have not done anything to affect p_2 which may be billions of light-years away from p_1. What causes p_2 to react? How does p_2 know that its partner p_1 has changed its spin? How is the message propagated from p_1 to p_2? Does the message travel at superluminal speed? These are the questions that have agitated the minds of physicists.

According to quantum theory, changing the measuring device in area A changes the wave function which describes the particle in area B. Einstein believed in the local causes. He did not accept 'action at a distance'. The principle of local causes says that what happens in area A does not depend upon variables subject to the control of an experimenter in a distant area B, space-like separated from A. Einstein's reaction may be reported here in his own words.

> ....On one supposition we should, in my opinion, absolutely hold fast: the real factual situation of system S_2 (the particle in area B) is independent of what is done with the system S_1 (the particle in area A), which is spatially separated from the former.
> One can escape from this conclusion (that quantum theory is incomplete) only by either assuming that the measurement of S_1 (telepathically) changes the real situation of S_2 or by denying independent real situations as such to things which are spatially separated from each other. Both alternatives appear to me entirely unacceptable.[31]

On the topic of communication between particles at a distance, Erwin Schrödinger remarks:

> It is rather discomforting that the (quantum) theory should allow a system to be steered or piloted into one or the other type of state at the experimenter's mercy in spite of his having no access to it.[32]

Communication requires a signal to go from one place to another. According to the relativity theory of Einstein, signals cannot go from one place to another at a speed faster than that of light. Then how can particle p_2, distantly separated from p_1, know what happens to its partner particle p_1? How does signal propagate from p_1 to p_2 so that p_2 responds simultaneously? Is superluminal communication possible? Some scientists believe that particles in area A and B are of course connected, but not by signals.

In 1975, Jack Sarfatti enunciated his theory—"superluminal transfer of negentropy without signals."[33] According to this theory, each quantum jump is a space-like superluminal transfer of negentropy without transport of energy. There is no propagation of signal from area A to area B. Nothing travels. The coherent structure or quality of the energy in areas A and B changes instantaneously.

There may or may not be signals. We may accept the fact that particle p_2 at area B responds in a correct way to what happens to particle p_1 at area A. Our acceptance of this fact would impel us to conclude that particles are conscious. Śaṅkara,[34] the non-dualist philosopher of India, has recognized the consciousness of particles long back in the eighth century. Some physicists, like Evan H. Walker, speculate that photons may be conscious. He remarks:

> Consciousness may be associated with all quantum mechanical processes.........Since everything that occurs is ultimately the result of one or more quantum mechanical events, the universe is 'inhabited' by an almost unlimited number of rather discrete conscious, usually non-thinking entities that are responsible for the detailed working of the universe.[35]

John Wheeler has come up with a delayed-choice thought experiment, which is a variation of the double-slit experiment of Thomas Young. The photons in the double-slit experiment somehow 'know' whether or not both slits are open and they act accordingly.

All these discussions in this section of this chapter pinpoint one thing. Pluralism has been rejected and monism has been accepted in science; but monism is inadequate to explain the phenomenal world. We have to go beyond monism to get the answer.

Non-Dualism

Advaita Vedānta is not monism, but is non-dualism. Brahman is trans-empirical; it is Reality and the only Reality. The world has got empirical existence, but is illusory. It is the product of Māyā, which is the power of Brahman. Māyā itself is indeterminable, being existent, non-existent and both existent and non-existent. The world is a product of Māyā and cannot be real. It is futile to search for reality in matter, energy, particles, field or space. All these are illusory products of Māyā and cannot be real. Advaita Vedānta does accept the pluralistic nature of the world.

All the diverse things of the world are made of five *mahābhūtas* (elementary products), viz., solid (*kṣiti*), liquid (*āpaḥ*), gaseous (*mārut*), energy (*tejaḥ*) and space (*vyoma*). But these *mahābhūtas* are not primary and fundamental. They are also illusory products of Māyā. None of these is real.

According to Advaita Vedānta, particles originate from space and are again dissolved into space, which is not void, not a non-entity. It is not inactive too. It is a bee-hive of activity in the micro-world. *Prāṇa* is subtler than space or *ākāśa* and *āpaḥ* or the primeval water is subtler than *prāṇa*. All these three entities are interconvertible in the sequence of *āpaḥ→prāṇa→ākāśa* in the process of evolution and *ākāśa→prāṇa→āpaḥ* in the process of involution. *Āpaḥ* is the first evolute and the last involute in the process of creation and dissolution, respectively. *Āpaḥ* manifested from the unmanifested Māyā before the cosmic egg was formed. The whole manifested universe is reconverted into *āpaḥ* which is finally dissolved into Māyā and remains in a dormant way in unmanifested state. Māyā, the source of the universe and the final recipient of the universe, is not real. In such a situation, monism cannot give the answer and science cannot find reality in energy, particles, field or space. The cosmic egg is a product. It appears in creation. It disappears in dissolution. It does not appear *ex nihilo*. It does not disappear as nothing. It is manifested from the unmanifested *mūlaprakṛti* (primeval Nature or Māyā). It becomes unmanifested and merged into *mūlaprakṛti*. There is nothing like 'singularity'. There is Reality (Brahman), but we cannot trace it in matter or energy, particles, field or space.

Brahman which is Reality is Pure Consciousness and Unbroken Whole (*akhaṇḍa*). This Conciousness is reflected in Māyā and the products of Māyā. As a result, all insentient things of the universe gain consciousness. There is nothing, whether macro or micro, stars or photons, that are completely unconscious. When considered in this context, the proton, electron, neutron, neutrino and photon are all conscious within their respective limits.

The substratum is Brahman which is Pure Consciousness. The multiple manifestations of the phenomenal world are waves, ripples and bubbles that are appearances on the surface only. The underlying principle, the support below the apparent phenomenal surface, the substratum is the deep sea—the Unbroken, Pure Consciousness. There is no question of propagation of signal, transfer of information from particle p_1 in area A to particle p_2 in area B. There is no area which is beyond Brahman. All the areas in the empirical universe are connected at the deeper level since everything of the universe has got only one support, only one substratum which is unbroken whole.

We may here correlate the concept of Advaita Vedānta with the ideas of some modern physicists. David Bohm writes:

> Parts are seen to be in immediate connection, in which their dynamical relationships depend, in an irreducible way, on the state of the whole system (and, indeed, on that of broader systems in which they are contained, extending ultimately and in principle to the entire universe). Thus one is led to a new notion of *unbroken wholeness* which denies the classical idea of analyzability of the world into separately and independently existing parts.[36]
>
> We must turn physics around. Instead of starting with parts and showing how they work together (the Cartesian order) we start with the whole.[37]

Bohm talks about the 'explicate order' and the 'implicate order'. Particles are discontiguous in space. This is what Bohm terms 'explicate order'. The unbroken whole is that-which-is. This that-which-is is the implicate order. Particles are contiguous in the implicate order. This that-which-is is the *tat sat* of Advaita Vedānta.

The Aspect experiment and its predecessors have already been discussed. One deduction may be made from the results of these experiments that every entity and every event influence every other. This is the Mach Principle:

> Contemporary physics would concur that every 'event' in the universe involves, more or less, every other. Physicist Ernst Mach rediscovered this fact when he put forth the 'Mach Principle' according to which the inertial of any celestial body or system is dependent upon its interaction with all the rest of the universe (which prompted Einstein to postulate that the presence of matter and energy actually 'curved' space-time).[38]

Erwin Schrödinger has been very much influenced by Vedānta.

In his opinion, contemporary physics finds a more congenial *meta*physical extension in the mystical vision of the Vedānta than in the blurred vision of Occidental metaphysics.[39] He brings about identity of all minds with each other and with the supreme mind. He writes:

> Still, one thing can be claimed in favour of the mystical teaching of the 'identity' of all minds with each other and with the supreme mind—as against the fearful monadology of Leibniz. The doctrine of identity can claim that it is clinched by the empirical fact that consciousness is never experienced in the plural, only in the singular. Not only has none of us ever experienced more than one consciousness, but there is also no trace of circumstantial evidence of this ever happening anywhere in the world. If I say that there cannot be more than one consciousness in the same mind, this seems a blunt tautology—we are quite unable to imagine the contrary.[40]

We may conclude this section by quoting Carl Zung who writes on the subject of cognizance:

> All science (Wissenschaft) however is a function of the soul, in which all knowledge is rooted. The soul is the greatest of all cosmic miracles, it is the *conditio sine qua non* of the world as an object. It is exceedingly astonishing that the Western world (apart from very rare exceptions) seems to have so little appreciation of this being so. The flood of external objects of cognizance has made the subject of all cognizance withdraw to the background, often to apparent non-existence.[41]

Language, Logic and Mysticism

A question is very often asked: "Can trans-empirical Brahman be logically derived?" We cannot perceive Brahman by our senses. Hence there cannot be empirical verification of Brahman. An alternative procedure is to find out logical proof. But logical analysis can be done only with the help of language. There cannot be logic without language. Advaita Vedānta says that no language can be used for Brahman. Hence Brahman cannot be subjected to logical scrutiny.

Language can be used for anything that has attributes and

functions. We use language for the world. We also use language for God and Māyā, although both are not sense-perceptible. For use of language, it is not necessary for something to be sense-perceptible. The particles and micro-particles are not sense-perceptible. Still we do use language for them. Whenever some entity has got attributes and functions or we assign some attributes and functions to it, we use language for it.

In the classical logic of the Aristotelian type, three laws have been considered to be fundamental. These are: (1) the law of identity, (2) the law of contradiction, (3) the law of excluded middle. Everything is what it is or A is A. This is the law of identity. Triangle is triangle. Triangle is a geometrical figure with three angles. Both these propositions are identical. A cannot be both B and not-B. The same predicate cannot be affirmed and denied of precisely the same subject. This is the law of contradiction. This law may be better termed as the law of non-contradiction. A is either B or not-B. A given predicate must either be affirmed or denied of a given subject. This is the law of excluded middle.

The law of non-contradiction and the law of excluded middle refer to contradictory, and not to contrary terms. The terms 'existent' (*sat*) and 'non-existent' (*asat*) are contradictory. The terms 'red' and 'non-red' are contradictory. But 'white', 'black', 'yellow', 'green', 'blue' and 'red' are contrary terms. "This rose is both red and black." Such a statement cannot be true. "This rose (which is red) is not white and not black." Such a statement is true.

The Aristotelian logic that has been described here is not applicable to Advaita Vedānta and quantum physics. In 1803, Thomas Young, by his double-slit experiment, proved that light is wave-like. Only waves can create interference patterns and hence Young concluded this. In 1905, Albert Einstein described the corpuscular nature of light. It won him Nobel Prize in 1921. Einstein showed that light is composed of tiny particles (later called photons). In 1900, Max Planck discovered that energy is absorbed and emitted in integral quanta or packets. Einstein theorized that energy itself is quantized. In 1924, Louis de Broglie, a young French prince, could prove the existence of matter waves. He used the simple equations of Planck and Einstein and formulated a new equation of his own ($\lambda=h/mv$). By the use of this equation, the wavelength of matter waves can be determined. The greater the momentum of particle, the shorter is the length of its associated wave. Thus, not only are waves particles, but particles are also waves.

Is the electron a wave? Yes, it is a wave. Is the electron a particle? Yes, it is a particle. The electron is both a particle and a wave. The terms 'particle' and 'wave' seem to be contrary ones. On deeper analysis, it is realized that they are contradictory terms. Anything that is wave-like is continuous and anything that is particulate or corpuscular is discontinuous. We say that an electron is both continuous and discontinuous. Thus, in quantum logic, A can be both B and not-B.

The wave-particle duality marked the end of the 'Either-Or' way of looking at the world. In 1924, Bohr and two of his colleagues, H.A. Kramers and John Slater, gave suggestion of the existence of probability waves. The photon, in the double-slit experiment, going through hole A represents one possible world (world A). When it passes through hole B, it represents a second possible world (world B). Both these worlds, according to Bohr, are somehow present together; they are superimposed. Bohr asserts that the world of our experience does not represent either A or B and that it is a genuine hybrid of the two.

In this connection, Werner Heisenberg writes:

> It meant a tendency for something. It was a quantitative version of the old concept of 'potentia' in Aristotelian philosophy. It introduced something standing in the middle between the idea of an event and the actual event, a strange kind of physical reality just in the middle between possibility and reality.[42]

The 'Either-Or' or 'True-False' type of classical logic cannot be applied to the quantum world. The law of excluded middle says that A is either B or not-B. The quantum phenomena do not obey this law. Here A can be B; A can be not-B; and A can be any variable between B and not-B. This sort of bizarre possibilities seem to be illogical, but it is factual. How is it possible? It seems we the observers are involved in the nature of reality in a fundamental way.

Einstein is firm in his opinion that there is one-to-one correspondence between physical reality and physical theory. He says:

> Whatever the meaning assigned to the term *complete*, the following requirement for a complete theory seems to be a necessary one: *every element of the physical reality must have a counterpart in the physical theory.*[43]

Quantum physics denies this one-to-one correspondence between theory and reality.

Advaita Vedānta accepts the fact that every created entity of the universe is bipolar, that it is a composite of pairs of opposites (*dvandvas*). It is futile to look for a single pole for the comprehensive understanding of a thing. Both the opposite poles are to be known for understanding anything.

In 1920s, Niels Bohr came up with his principle of complementarity. This principle holds that the wave and particle natures of light are not mutually exclusive to one another but complementary. Both concepts are necessary to provide a complete description of light. Our understanding of light would be incomplete if we know only one of the contradictory properties.

Bohr's principle of complementarity is not restricted to light only. Everything in Nature exhibits multiple pairs of opposite characters. Opposite characters belonging to each pair are complementary to each other. It is impossible for any observer to discern both the contradictory characters at the same time. Only one can be observed at a time.

Whether it is photon in the double-slit experiment or electron in the experiment for the measurement of its position or momentum, Bohr does not recognize an independent reality. He writes:

> ....an independent reality in the ordinary physical sense can be ascribed neither to the phenomena nor to the agencies of observation.[44]

There is an important philosophical implication of Bohr's notion. According to this, the world consists not of things, but of interactions; properties belong to interactions, not to independently existing things. The particle-like and the wave-like behaviours of light do not belong to light itself, but to our interaction with light. Independent of us, light does not possess properties. Devoid of properties, light does not exist. Without light, or in general without the observed object, we the observers cannot interact.

By implication, without any observed object with which we interact, we do not exist. And so Heisenberg remarks: "Strange kind of physical reality just in the middle between possibility and reality."[45]

Quantum physics holds that the observer disturbs the system which he observes. In the opinion of Bohr, it is meaningless to ask what the atoms are doing when we are not looking at them. We should keep in mind that we have to interfere with atomic processes in order to observe them at all. The observer interferes with the system to such an extent that it cannot be said that the system has an independent existence. Whenever the experimenter chooses to measure the position of a particle precisely, he forces the particle to develop more uncertainty in its momentum, and vice versa. If the experimenter chooses to measure the wave properties of light, he eliminates its particle feature, and vice versa. Both the particle and wave aspects cannot be revealed by any single experiment at the same time.

There is built-in provision of opposite characters in everything of the universe. This is universal both in the macro- and the micro-world. This process becomes more apparent in the micro-world.

What happens to an object when it is observed and not observed is a topic of extreme controversy in modern physics. Max Born developed matrix mechanics, whereas Erwin Schrödinger established the concept of wave mechanics. His wave function is denoted by the Greek letter ψ (psi). The probability of an event is given by the square of this wave function. For illustration, an electron may be taken here as a representative of the particle world. In the double-slit experiment, an electron leaves the gun of the apparatus and vanishes when it is out of sight. It is replaced by an array of 'ghost' electrons. These ghosts interfere with one another. They remain as ghosts as long as we are not looking at them. When we look, all the ghosts except one vanish. The one which does not vanish solidifies as a 'real' electron. In terms of Schrödinger's wave equation, each ghost corresponds to a wave, or rather a packet of waves. Max Born interpreted this Schrödinger wave as a measure of probability. Observation crystallizes only one packet of potential wave into a 'real' wave when all of the array of probability waves disappear. The one wave that does not disappear is our 'real' electron. The phenomenon of the disappearance of the waves except one only when observed, is called collapse of the wave function. Whatever has been described here for the electron holds good for all particles. As the wave function collapses during an observation, myriad ghost particles disappear and only one coalesces into a single 'real' particle. Copenhagen interpretation of quantum mechanics requires wave functions to collapse magically when observed. As soon as we stop observing a particle, it immediately splits up into a new array of ghost particles, each pursuing its own path of probabilities through the quantum world. Nothing in the world is real unless and until it is observed. What is real as long as we are observing ceases to be real as soon as we stop observing.

Hugh Everett was working on the many-worlds interpretation of quantum mechanics in the 1950s. He published his first paper on this topic in 1957.[46] In the same journal, John Wheeler[47] published a paper to draw attention to the importance of Everett's work. According to Everett's interpretation, the overlapping wave functions of the whole universe—the alternative realities that interact to produce measurable interference at the quantum level—do not collapse. All of them are equally real. They exist in their respective areas of 'superspace'. When we make a measurement at the quantum level, we are forced by the process of observation to select one of these alternatives. We see what we select as the 'real' world. When unobserved, the alternative realities were bound together. The act of observation severs the tie so that the alternative realities are allowed to go their own separate ways through superspace. Each one may be observed by somebody else. Nobody knows whether all the observations of the alternative realities are identical in nature.

Everett's new interpretation of quantum mechanics was almost ignored for more than ten years until Bryce DeWitt[48] worked on it and popularized it. The book written by DeWitt and Graham[49] is a comprehensive one on the many-worlds interpretation of quantum mechanics. Max Jammer, one of the ablest of quantum philosophers, has said: "The multi-universe theory is undoubtedly one of the most daring and most ambitious theories ever constructed in the history of science."[50]

Here two interpretations have been given. Whatever may be the interpretation, there is nothing like objective world in quantum physics. An entity is real when we look at it; it is not real when we don't look at it. The world branches and rebranches *ad infinitum* to become an infinite number of worlds. An observer observes only one out of the many. Another observer observes a second one. A third observer observes a third one; and so on. Are all the observations identical? Nobody can answer that. Are two observations of the same observer identical? There is no way to know it. Amid such uncertainties, it is natural to expect that no language can be used for *the* whole world, multiple worlds or the constituents of the world(s) to convey any definite and precise meaning.

In 1936, Birkhoff and Neumann published a paper that laid the foundations of quantum logic.[51] In classical logic there is a law of distributivity. It says that "A, and B or C" is the same as "A and B, or A and C". This law which is a foundation of classical logic does not apply to quantum logic. In quantum logic, nothing is either this or that; there is always at least one more alternative, and often an unlimited number of alternatives. Classical logic is based on the use of language or symbols. Quantum logic is concerned with the realm of *experience*, where everything is not either this or that and where more alternatives are available.

Physicists prefer mathematical language to common language to describe quantum phenomena. In this respect, Max Born writes:

> The ultimate origin of the difficulty lies in the fact (or philosophical principle) that we are compelled to use words of common language when we wish to describe a phenomenon, not by logical or mathematical analysis, but by a picture appealing to the imagination. Common language has grown by everyday experience and can never surpass these limits. Classical physics has restricted itself to the use of concepts of this kind; by analyzing visible motions it has developed two ways of representing them by elementary process: moving particles and waves. There is no other way of giving a pictorial description of motions—we have to apply it even in the region of atomic process, where classical physics breaks down.[52]

In the opinion of David Finkelstein,[53] both common language and mathematical language are inadequate to express quantum phenomena. Mathematics, like English, is also a language. The best you can get with symbols is a maximal but incomplete description. A mathematical analysis of subatomic phenomena is no better qualitatively than any other symbolic analysis, because symbols do not follow the same rules as experience.

Suzuki is of the opinion that our inner experience transcends language and symbols. He writes:

> The contradiction so puzzling to the ordinary way of thinking comes from the fact that we have to use language to communicate our inner experience which in its very nature transcends linguistics.[54]

In this respect, the opinion of Werner Heisenberg may be quoted here:

> The problems of language here are really serious. We wish to speak in some way about the structure of the atoms...But we cannot speak about atoms in ordinary language.[55]

There is difference in the use of terminology in physics and Advaita Vedānta. When the physicist speaks about reality, he means atoms, electrons, neutrinos and photons, etc. On scrutiny, he realizes that there is no reality in what is called reality. Advaita Vedānta also says that the world of matter and energy, waves and particles does not *really* exist. But 'something' really exists and that something is reality. That reality is Brahman.

We do use language—common or mathematical—for the illusory world. Our use of language, says Advaita Vedānta, cannot be precise since there is nothing precise in the illusory world. Every A is made of B and not-B and many such pairs of opposites. It is the nature of the world. Nothing of the world is purely B or purely not-B. Only Brahman is beyond the pairs of opposites. Brahman is attributeless and hence the question of having pairs of opposites does not arise. Thus, all worldly entities, being uncertain and imprecise, are bound to be expressed in language in contradictory and uncertain way.

The magical world of Advaita Vedānta cannot be objective. It is a conjured one. It does not exist without the observer. The world we conjure is an interaction of the observer and the observed. Māyā has both concealing and projecting power. It conceals A and the observer does not perceive A as A. It projects A as B, C, D, etc., but not as A. But the fact remains that A is perceived as not-A and this not-A changes in an infinite range. Advaita Vedānta does not isolate the observer from the observed for the purpose of the observation of the world.

Advaita Vedānta stops using language for Brahman, that is attributeless, actionless, formless, changeless, non-dual and non-relational. It is impossible to use language for such an entity. It is *the* Reality in Advaita Vedānta. Language can be used for the phenomena, but not for the noumena of Kant. The Vedāntic seer indicates Brahman without speaking about it (*lakṣyate, na tu ucyate*).

Sometimes the investigator of Brahman makes *vain* attempt to describe Brahman. He tries to do it by use of contradictory language. Brahman is existent (*sat*) and non-existent (*asat*), near and far, inside and outside, larger than the largest and smaller than the smallest. Negative language is also used to describe Brahman; nothing positive about it is said. Brahman is neither gross nor subtle, neither small nor big, it is attributeless, actionless, formless, spaceless, *prāṇa*-less (*viton*less), colourless, etc. In a third way, questions about Brahman are answered negatively by saying 'not this (*neti*)'. Is Brahman this Earth? Not this. Is Brahman the Sun? Not this. Is Brahman the moon? Not this. Is Brahman the space? Not this, and so on.

When John Lennon (1940-80) said, "Nothing is real", he restricted himself to the quantum world of particles. He could not conceive of a Being which is the substratum of the phenomenal world and is the Reality. It is meaningless to search for quantum reality. There isn't anything like that.

When languages fails for the Hindu, he makes use of symbols. He has devised icons for Brahmā, Viṣṇu, Rudra and many such deities. He has geometrical figures or *yantras* that act as symbols for him. He utters the sound 'OM' which symbolizes Brahman. All these symbols are not realities. There is no one-to-one correspondence between the symbol and the reality. Symbols are media for yoking the psychology of an individual who makes effort for ascendance from the level of matter to that of spirit.

But next comes a stage when the symbol is not sufficient, and no media are adequate. Brahman is to be realized without the mediation of anything. The mind is annihilated. In such a state psychic processes stop working. The individual experiences Brahman without any mediation. This is the *aparokṣānubhūti* of

Śaṅkara. Literally, it means 'realization without mediation'. This is the silence of ecstasy. In this condition, one experiences Brahman and thereby oneself becomes Brahman.[56] Perhaps Wittgenstein spoke of this silence when he said: "Whereof one cannot speak, thereof one must be silent".[57]

At the stage of immediate realization, mystic experiences become very much relevant. Bertrand Russell speaks about mysticism in the following words:

> Metaphysics, or the attempt to conceive the world as a whole by means of thought, has been developed, from the first, by the union and conflict of two very different human impulses, the one urging men towards mysticism, the other urging them towards science. Some men have achieved greatness through one of these impulses alone, others through the other alone: in Hume, for example, the scientific impulse reigns quite unchecked, while in Blake a strong hostility to science co-exists with profound mystic insight. But the greatest men who have been philosophers have felt the need both of science and of mysticism: the attempt to harmonize the two was what made their life, and what always must, for all its arduous uncertainty, make philosophy, to some minds, a greater thing than either science or religion.[58]

On the topic of mysticism, Albert Einstein has stated the following:

> The most beautiful and most profound emotion we can experience is the sensation of the mystical. It is the sower of all true art and science. He to whom this emotion is a stranger, who can no longer wonder and stand rapt in awe, is as good as dead. To know that what is impenetrable to us really exists, manifesting itself as the highest wisdom and the most radiant beauty which our dull faculties can comprehend only in their most primitive forms—this knowledge, this feeling is at the centre of true religiousness.[59]

You and I

There was objective thinking in Greek pre-Socratic thought; the subject was completely lost. Democritus has said: "Colour is by convention, sweet by convention, bitter by convention, in truth there are but atoms and the void." The Greek man looked out of himself, rather than within; he looked at the external world, the vast Nature, the universe at large and tried to understand its objective nature. Heraclitus has said:

> It is therefore necessary to follow the common. But while reason is common, the majority live as though they have a private insight of their own ... Those who speak with a sound mind must hold fast to what is common to all... The waking have *one* common world, but the sleeping turn aside each into a world of his own.[60]

Parmenides equated being with pure reason and logical thought. For Plato ideas alone are objectively real. They had already existed before man discovered them. These ideas are the ultimate objects (although mental). The visible and tangible objects of the universe are only imperfect replicas of the ideas. Thus Plato's objective idealism identified reality with the pure ideas and considered the physical world of phenomena as a pale shadow only. In this aspect Riencourt writes:

> In spite of the Delphic Oracle's command *gnothi seautón*, 'know thyself', actual knowledge of the Self had become impossible because of the elimination of the subjective as being ultimately unreal: only the objective was knowable and there was no longer a Self to be known. It never occurred to Greek idealism's naïveté that the human mind's limitations could restrict it to mere appearances—it assumed uncritically that the rational mind could cognize the whole of reality and this reality was the external world of physical phenomena, along with the discursive thinking that comprehends it.[61]

René Descartes cleaved his objective world into two sharply separate entities, viz., mind and matter. He said, "I think, therefore I am (*cogito, ergo sum*)". The intellect of the thinking 'I' was *res cogitans*; the objective material world extended in space and time was *res extensa*. This was the Cartesian partition between mind and matter. This drastic division was in confirmation of the medieval Christian dualism.

In Descartes' philosophy, supported by his mathematics, the

universe and everything in it are automata. The universe is a great automatic machine. He extended his mechanistic view of matter to living organisms. All plants and animals are simply machines. Although he could speculate the seat of the human soul in the pineal gland inside the brain, he did not distinguish the human body from the animal machine. He did not recognize any difference between the mechines made by craftmen and the human and animal bodies that Nature alone composes.

Newton was a believer in God. But the mechanics of Newton's universe did not need any God. The subject of Descartes' Cartesian philosophy was discarded in Newtonian mechanics; only his object remained; and hence the Newtonian universe was purely mechanical without any place or function of God or human souls. The Newtonian physics gave an impression of 'absolute objectivity'. It held that the external world exists apart from us. Such a concept of scientific objectivity was based upon the assumptions that an external world exists, that this world is outside me as the object as opposed to the 'I' which is inside me as the subject, and that the object exists and functions irrespective of the existence or non-existence of any subject.

Quantum physics rejected the concept of the Cartesian division between mind and matter, soul and body, creator and the world, and the subject and the object. Further, there is no such thing as objectivity in quantum mechanics. The Copenhagen interpretation says that it is not possible to observe reality without changing it. The subject cannot eliminate himself from the object.

Even Einstein suffered from the influence of the dualism of subject and object. He could not believe that "God plays dice with the world."[62] He was under the impression that the physical world really exists independently of the human observer. Werner Heisenberg sharply differs from Einstein on this issue. He says: "Quantum theory does not allow a completely objective description of nature."[63] He adds further: "The ontology of materialism rested upon the illusion that the kind of existence, the direct 'actuality' of the world around us, can be extrapolated into the atomic range. The extrapolation is impossible, however."[64]

The Cartesian division between mind and matter or subject and object has made it extremely difficult for the founders of quantum theory to interpret their observations of atomic phenomena. As Heisenberg has said: "This partition has penetrated deeply into the human mind during the three centuries following Descartes and it will take a long time for it to be replaced by a really different attitude toward the problem of reality."[65]

Paul Davies[66] has quoted John Wheeler who has pleaded for a holistic element by rejecting all distinctions between subject and object, cause and effect. It may be interesting to know what Wheeler thinks:

> In 1979, John Wheeler, speaking at a symposium in Princeton celebrating Einstein's centenary, claimed that the precise nature of reality has to await the participation of a conscious observer. In this way, mind can be made responsible for the retroactive creation of reality—even a reality that existed before there were people.
>
> Wheeler's astonishing modification of the Young's two-slit experiment reveals that an observer today can be partially responsible for generating the reality of the remote past.
>
> Quantum theory demolishes the distinction between subject and object, cause and effect, and thereby introduces a strong holistic element into our world view.

Erwin Schrödinger has repeatedly emphasized that subject and object are only one. He writes:

> All this was said from the point of view that we accept the time-hallowed discrimination between subject and object. Though we have to accept it in everyday life 'for practical reference', we ought, so I believe, to abandon it in philosophical thought. Its rigid logical consequence has been revealed by Kant: the sublime, but empty, idea of the 'thing-in-itself' about which we for ever know nothing.
>
> It is the same elements that go to compose my mind and the world. This situation is the same for every mind and its world, in spite of the unfathomable abundance of 'cross-references' between them. The world is given to me only once, not one existing and one perceived. Subject and object are only one. The barrier between them cannot be said to have broken down as a result of recent experience in the physical sciences, for this barrier does not exist.[67]
>
> The reason why our sentient, percipient and thinking ego is

> met nowhere within our scientific world picture can easily be indicated in seven words: because it is itself that world picture. It is identical with the whole and therefore cannot be contained in it as a part of it.[68]
>
> There are two ways out of the number of paradox, both appearing rather lunatic from the point of view of present scientific thought (based on ancient Greek thought and thus thoroughly 'Western'). One way out is the multiplication of the world in Leibniz's fearful doctrine of monads: every monad to be a world by itself, no communication between them; the monad 'has no windows', it is 'incommunicado'. That nonetheless they all agree with each other is called 'pre-established harmony'. I think there are few to whom this suggestion appeals, nay we would consider it as a mitigation at all of the numerical antinomy.
>
> There is obviously only one alternative, namely the unification of minds or consciousness. Their multiplicity is only apparent, in truth there is only one mind. This is the doctrine of the Upaniṣads.[69]

Quantum physics says that the subject changes the object in the process of observation. There is nothing like an 'objective' object which is independent of the subject and remains unaltered irrespective of observation or no observation of any subject. Erwin Schrödinger gives his views on this aspect in the following paragraphs:

> As an appendix to these considerations, those strongly interested in the physical sciences might wish to hear me pronounce on a line of ideas, concerning subject and object, that has been given great prominence by the prevailing school of thought in quantum physics, the protagonists being Niels Bohr, Werner Heisenberg, Max Born and others: Let me first give you a brief description of their ideas. It runs as follows:
>
> We cannot make any factual statement about a given natural object (or physical system) without 'getting in touch' with it. This touch is a real physical interaction. Even if it consists only in our 'looking at the object' the latter must be hit by light rays and reflect them into the eye or into some instrument of observation. This means that the object is affected by our observation.

> You cannot obtain any knowledge about an object while leaving it strictly isolated. The theory goes on to assert that this disturbance is neither irrelevant nor completely surveyable. Thus after any number of painstaking observations the object is left in a state of which some features (the last observed) are known, but others (those interfered with the last observation) are not known, or not accurately known. This state of affairs is offered as an explanation why no complete; gapless description of any physical object is ever possible.[70]

It is thus clear that the ontological dualism which has been deep-rooted in the Western mind in the spheres of philosophy, religion and science has been rejected in the twentieth century due to the advancement in quantum physics. In the non-dualistic philosophy of Vedānta, only one ontological Being is recognized and that is Brahman. There is subject (Brahman) only whose nature is pure Consciousness. There is no object. The world which is the apparent object is illusory; it is the product of Māyā. The illusory object is superimposed on the subject due to the concealing power of Māyā. Owing to this effect of ignorance, Reality is not self-revealed. Due to the projecting power of Māyā, one and only one Reality B is perceived in plural forms as not-B. Śaṅkara compares the subject with light and the object with darkness.[71] Ontologically, darkness does not exist; it is a non-entity. But empirically it exists. The absence of light is perceived psychologically as darkness. Some scholars have erroneously stated that Vedānta admits identity of subject and object. It is however, not fact. Advaita Vedānta accepts the subject only. That subject is Brahman. "That thou art (*tattvamasi*)".[72] That subject is he, you and I. There is nobody who is not that subject.

The quantum physicist vainly tries to find that subject in the object. The object does not really exist. It appears to exist. The proton, neutron, quarks, electron, positron, neutrino and photon cannot be real; it is a blunder to equate any of them with Reality. They cannot be subject. Neither can they be object. They are magical appearances only. They appear and disappear on the vast screen of the quantum world. They are objects for the deluded subject. When the cover of ignorance is removed, the whole magical screen with the dancers and dances vanishes.

Rock Bottom

Both quantum physicists and the non-dualistic philosophers of Advaita Vedānta agree on the point that the world is an illusion. The world which I experience in my daily life is not real. My body is not real. The food I eat, the water I drink, the air I breathe, the Earth I live on, the stars I see are not real. The world I perceive through my five senses is not real. Then what is real?

Advaita Vedānta is not nihilistic. It does not say that nothing is real. It does not recognize void (*śūnya*). It does accept the full (*pūrṇa*). It says that Brahman is Reality and *the* only Reality. This Reality cannot be perceived by our senses. It cannot be seen, cannot be heard, cannot be smelt, cannot be tasted, and cannot be touched. It has got no form, no quality and no function. A pertinent question is asked: "What is the justification of denying the experienced world and accepting the so-called 'nothingness' as reality?"

The justifiability of the unreality and the illusoriness of the world has already been furnished in the discussion on Advaita Vedānta and quantum physics. It is accepted that the empirical world is unreal. If we too accept that nothing else is real, we end in nihilism. This is the opinion of Śaṅkara.[73] He refuses to accept nihilism which does not posit anything and which declares that nothing including this 'I' exists. If nihilism is to be rejected, something positive is to be accepted. That positive something must be unchangeable and eternal. That must be birthless and deathless. That must not undergo modification. That must be formless, attributeless and actionless. That must be sense-imperceptible. Why all these 'musts' are unavoidable for that Being has already been explained in Part II of this book. A name has been given to that Being in Vedānta. That name is Brahman.

Advaita Vedānta says that Brahman is Consciousness and that this Consciousness is not a property of any being, but is the Being itself.

The Marxist philosopher considers matter as primary and consciousness as an evolute of matter in the process of biological evolution. The Marxist idea on consciousness is given below:

> ......*consciousness is a function of the human brain, the essence of which lies in the reflection of reality.* At the same time the problem of consciousness has turned out to be extremely

> difficult for materialist philosophers and psychologists as well. Some materialists, baffled by the problem of the origin of consciousness, came to regard it as an attribute of matter, as its eternal property, inherent in all its forms, higher and lower. They declared all matter animate. This belief has been called hylozoism (from the Greek hyle—matter, and zoe—life).
>
> Dialectical materialism proceeds from the fact that consciousness is a property not of any matter but of *highly organized matter*. Consciousness is connected with the activity of the human brain. As the founders of Marxism emphasized, consciousness can never be anything but consciously apprehended existence, and people's existence is the real process of their life. The dialectical-materialist concept of consciousness is based on the principle of reflection, that is, the mental reproduction of the object in the brain of the individual in the form of sensations, perceptions, representations and concepts. The content of consciousness is ultimately determined by surrounding reality, and its material substratum, or vehicle, is the human brain. It is quite obvious then that without the brain, without the mechanisms providing the paths that connect it with the world there can be no spiritual life.[74]

The Marxist philosopher rejects any concept of consciousness without reference to brain. In this respect, V.G. Afanasyev writes:

> Attempts to divorce thought from the brain are also absolutely untenable. Lenin aptly called a philosophy which endeavours to do so and asserts that thought exists without the brain a 'brainless' philosophy. Natural science, Lenin wrote, firmly upholds that consciousness does not exist independently of the body, that it is secondary, a function of the brain, a reflection of the outside world.[75]

Recent advances in science and technology have complicated the Marxist thinking about consciousness. If there cannot be consciousness without the brain, as the Marxists say, how shall we explain the functioning of computors and robots? To answer this question, Afanasyev writes:

> The world is witnessing the rapid development of a new

science, *cybernetics* which studies various control systems and control process, and has created some remarkable machines. Some of them guide trains, aircraft or intricate production processes, others translate texts from one language to another, still others perform logical operations, extremely complex mathematical calculations, etc. These machines can be fed information, 'memorise' and process it and perform useful functions. In some respects these machines surpass man: for example, they perform calculations hundreds of thousands of times faster than man, study a vast amount of data, analyse a mass of variants, and so forth. Machines are being designed which will be able to perfect the programme of their work and even improve its own structure on the basis of preceding activity. A machine can operate where man cannot work either due to danger (for instance in places where atomic and other harmful processes take place), or inaccessibility (remote outer space).

The process of cybernetics has given grounds to ascribe to automatic machines the ability to experience sensations and even to think. Moreover, there is a talk that it is possible to develop an automatic machine whose intellectual capacity will enable it to surpass, and, in the final count, to replace man. It is claimed that the era of robots will replace the era of mankind. In reality, even the most perfect machine cannot experience sensations, let alone think. A machine does not think, it merely *imitates* or *models* certain logical functions inherent in man, and only those of them which can be formalised or mathematically processed.[76]

The Marxist philosophers have confined the use of 'consciousness' to the functioning of the human brain. This is not a correct use, however. There is no scientific reasoning to say that the animals are unconscious. There is difference in the level of consciousness, of course. In the evolutionary process, the human brain is more developed than the animal brain. Man can think more rationally, can discriminate between good and bad, can have creative thoughts, and can function more intelligently. Animals, due to their less developed cerebrum including the frontal lobe, cannot be compared to man in psychic functioning. But they do have consciousness. They can perceive by their five senses. They are conscious of their environments. They respond positively and negatively to the environment in a way which is self-protecting and self-defensive. Birds have still less developed brain than animals. Their consciousness is at still lower level. Lower animals with brain and spinal cord are further lower in their level of consciousness. Brain is an instrument through which consciousness is revealed or manifested, and depending upon its stage of development, the level of consciousness varies. But, whatever may be the level, consciousness is exhibited both by man and animals. It is not restricted to the human brain only.

It is also not correct to say that consciousness is restricted to the nervous system. There are many lower micro-organisms that do not possess nerve at all. The amoeba is an example. It is a unicellular organism—a shapeless bit of jellylike protoplasm. From its main protoplasmic mass, it sends out, usually in the direction of locomotion, a number of pointed projections, the pseudo-podia. It does not possess any nerve cell or nerve fibre. If a food particle is present in front, it engulfs and digests it. If a sand particle comes on its way, it bridges over it and passes forward, leaving the non-nutrient particle behind. If a drop of sulphuric acid is placed in front of it, it avoids the harmful substance through a bypass route.

How do we explain the behaviour of the amoeba, as has been stated here? Can we say that the amoeba is unconscious? We will be certainly irrational if we reserve the word 'conscious' for a specific use which is convenient to our dogma. Regarding the possession of consciousness with reference to the possession of nervous system, H.S. Jennings writes:

> We find that in organisms consisting of but a single cell, and having no nervous system, the behaviour is regulated by all the different classes of conditions which regulate the behaviour of higher animals. In other words, unicellular organisms react to all classes of stimuli to which higher animals react. All classes of stimuli which may affect the nervous system or sense organs may likewise affect protoplasm without these organs. Even the naked protoplasm of amoeba responds to all classes of stimuli to which any animal responds. The nervous system and sense organs are therefore not necessary for the reception of any particular classes of stimulations.[77]

These facts show the necessity of guarding against overrating the importance of the nervous system. It is doubtful if the nervous system is to be considered the *exclusive* seat of anything; its properties are accentuations of the general properties of protoplasm. Dogmatic statements as to the part necessarily played by the nervous system in given cases must be looked upon with suspicion unless supported by positive experimental results.[78]

All that we have said thus far in the present chapter is independent of the question whether there exist in the lower organisms such subjective accompaniments of behaviour as we find in ourselves, and which we call consciousness. We have asked merely whether there exist in the lower organisms objective phenomena of a character similar to what we find in the behaviour of man. To this question we have been compelled to give an affirmative answer. So far as objectve evidence goes, there is no difference in kind, but a complete continuity between the behaviour of lower and of higher organisms.[79]

But such impressions and suggestions of course do not demonstrate the existence of consciousness in lower organisms. Any belief on this matter can be held without conflict with the objective facts. All that experiment and observation can do is to show us whether the behaviour of lower organisms is objectively similar to the behaviour in man that is accompanied by consciousness. If this question is answered in the affirmative, as the facts seem to require, and if we further hold, as is commonly held, that man and the lower organisms are sub-divisions of the same substance, then it may perhaps be said that objective investigation is as favourable to the view of the general distribution of consciousness throughout animals as it could well be. But the problem as to the actual existence of consciousness outside of the self is an indeterminate one; no increase of objective knowledge can ever solve it. Opinions on this subject must then be largely dominated by general philosophical considerations, drawn from other fields.[80]

The Western scientists and philosophers, even if some of them are atheists and materialists, have not yet been able to free themselves from the influence of a Christian doctrine that man alone has soul and the rest are soulless, that mind and thinking are associated with soul only, and that man only is conscious. This is the genesis of defining 'consciousness' with reference to human behaviour. Through scrutiny of scientific evidences, one realizes, however, that such a reserved meaning of consciousness is untenable.

Not only have animals got consciousness, but plants too. We try to explain the behaviour of plants by use of words such as 'tropism' or 'taxis'. As a matter of fact, instead of explaining, we explain away. A plant in the desert pierces its roots deep into the soil in search of water. We call it 'hydrotropism'. A germinated seed, with root upwards, bends its root towards the Earth. We call it 'geotropism'. A plant in shade bends itself towards light. We call it phototaxis. A creeper plant develops tendrils for binding itself around some support. A banyan tree, some of whose branches grow almost horizontally, is to be supported by prop-roots and so from the branches prop-roots develop. Some varieties of plants try to conserve water by reducing leaf-surface through the infolding of leaves in drought conditions. Some carnivorous plants behave cunningly to catch the prey-animal for eating and digesting. These examples are not exhaustive, but are sufficient enough to indicate that plants are conscious.

The inanimate objects are also conscious. Such a statement is apparently ridiculous when one observes a piece of stone which is immovable and does not cry as a response to any amount of hammering. The quantum physicist does not consider the stone at the macro-level. He observes consciousness in the micro-particles of the stone—in the electron, positrons, photons and quarks. We will quote here the opinions of a few prominent scientists on the topic of consciousness.

Sir Arthur Eddington says that consciousness is fundamental. He is opposed to those who consider matter as fundamental and consciousness as a property of highly organized matter. He asserts:

> Recognizing that the physical world is entirely abstract and without 'actuality' apart from its linkage to consciousness, we restore consciousness to the fundamental position instead of representing it as an inessential complication occasionally found in the midst of inorganic nature at a late stage of evolutionary history.[81]

Advaita Vedānta says that Brahman which is Consciousness and fundamental is Reality, that it is the substratum of the phenomenal world, and that this Reality is trans-empirical. Sir Arthur Eddington says the same thing as given in Advaita Vedānta. In his opinion, Consciousness which is the substratum of the phenomenal world is beyond scientific investigation. He writes:

> We are thrown back, by physical science itself, onto the problem of the nature of consciousness—or rather, our task now is to deal with that part of consciousness that does not emerge in space and time and is therefore not amenable, and never will be, to scientific analysis.[82]

Sir Arthur Eddington makes a distinction between our knowledge on the world and reality. Sullivan has stated the opinion of Eddington as follows:

> Arthur Eddington explains that while the readings truly reflect the fluctuations of the world qualities, our real knowledge is that of the readings rather than of the qualities—and the readings resemble to qualities as much and as little as a telephone number resembles a subscriber.[83]

Advaita Vedānta repeatedly stresses on the point that Brahman is the substratum (*ādhāra, adhiṣṭhāna*) of the phenomenal universe. Werner Heisenberg says the same thing:

> Physics can go only so far and no further in its objective study of nature because it collides with an ultimate barrier set up by nature itself—taking into account the limitations imposed by our sensorial apparatus. Beyond, there remains a whole realm of 'reality' that can *never* be investigated by scientific observation. Physics has to presuppose the existence of a *background* or substratum that shall for ever remain outside the scope of its probings because, as Heisenberg himself pointed out, "...... we cannot make observations without disturbing the phenomena —the quantum effects we introduce with our observation automatically introduce a degree of uncertainty into the phenomenon to be observed.[84]

While commenting on consciousness, Eugene Wigner, a noted physicist, has given the following opinion:

> The formal inclusion of consciousness in physics could well become as essential feature of any further advance in our scientific understanding.[85]

Erwin Schrödinger is a strong advocate of Vedānta. He believes that the multiple appearances of the phenomenal world are produced by the deceptive Māyā. For him, consciousness is only one and the reality. He writes:

> The only possible alternative is simply to keep to the immediate experience that consciousness is a singular of which the plural is unknown; that there is only one thing and that what seems to be a plurality is merely a series of different aspects of this one thing, produced by a deception (the Indian MAYA); the same illusion is produced in a gallery of mirrors, and in the same way Gaurisankar and Mt Everest turned out to be the same peak seen from different valleys.[86]

Thus it is obvious that Advaita Vedānta and quantum physics speak in one tone about reality. Consciousness is fundamental and *the* reality. It is non-dual, one alone without a second. It is named as Brahman in Advaita Vedānta. This consciousness is not a property or manifested symptom of any being. It is Being itself. It cannot be perceived by our senses. It cannot be investigated by science. It is the substratum of the phenomenal world that is deceptive and unreal. The unreal world exists for us empirically, because Brahman, the substratum, exists. Without the substratum or the noumena, phenomena cannot exist. Of course, the reverse is not true. Brahman does not depend upon anything else for its existence. Brahman exists when the empirical world exists; it also exists when the empirical world does not exist; it exists timelessly. The world is not eternal. It is created at zero time (t_o); it is dissolved at maximum time (t_m); it is sustained during the time-interval of $t_m - t_o$. When the world does not stay after dissolution and before the next creation, Brahman exists without the existence of anybody else or anything else.

Advaita Vedānta uses the word *cit* for Brahman. The word

'cit' means 'consciousness'. But it is not the consciousness as understood in common science and common psychology. There is no equivalent expression in English for the word *cit*. When 'consciousness' is used for Brahman in the sense of *cit*, it starts with the capital letter C in this chapter. According to Advaita Vedānta, the consciousness acquired by any living or non-living entity—macro or micro, man, animal or micro-organism, star or photon—is a reflected one. Brahman is the original Consciousness. When it is reflected in any insentient matter including the human brain and mind (mind is material in Advaita Vedānta), the latter becomes conscious as the moon becomes lighted by the Sun. But the original Consciousness and the reflected consciousness are not the same. The former is omniscience; the latter is limited consciousness. All worldly entities—living and non-living—are primarily insentient. They become partly sentient due to the reflection of consciousness. Brahman is all pervasive. Everything is in Brahman, although the reverse is not true. Due to this all-pervasiveness of Brahman, no insentient thing is completely devoid of consciousness.

For the manifestation of consciousness through the insentient entities of the world, a structure or an apparatus is necessary. This structure may be a photon, an amoeba, a banyan tree or a human being. Depending upon the evolution of this structure, its milieu and functioning, the quality and intensity of consciousness vary in the manifestation process.

Very often, there is no external manifestation of consciousness, although there is internal functioning guided by consciousness. The physical scientist, biological scientist, psychologist or the philosopher may refuse to use the word 'consciousness' for such purpose; he may prefer the term 'unconscious' to the term 'conscious'. A short discussion on this controversy may be useful here.

For the purpose of easy communication, consciousness may be qualified as 'subjective' and 'objective'. When man becomes aware of pain in some part of his body, his consciousness may be termed subjective. He feels the urge for eating or drinking and this is subjective consciousness. He comes to know that some social customs are evil and need immediate reform. He decides to act in certain way to bring about the reform. This sort of consciousness is subjective. The individual or the subject is aware of something and this awareness is called subjective consciousness.

Many things happen in the world every moment. We are not aware of those things. The mystery is this that many things happen in our own bodies every moment and we are not aware of them. A person, X, is frightened. His system immediately secretes catecholamines, viz., adrenaline and noradrenaline, that help the individual to cope up with the emergency situation. In spite of this purposeful action, the individual is unconscious of what is happening in his own system. Hepatitis virus enters into the body of an individual, who is ignorant of it. The defensive mechanism of the body starts manufacturing specific 'interferon' that inactivates the virus. Here the body is defended without the conscious effort of the individual. Even if he is conscious of the injection of an infective agent into his body, he consciously does not initiate any defensive action, although his system takes up all immediate measures to fight the infection. A tuberculosis patient knows about his disease long after his system has started fighting against the causative organism. The lesion brought about in the tissue of the patient is cordoned by a defensive wall and thereby some causative organisms are imprisoned. If one kidney of an individual is damaged and surgically removed, the other healthy kidney undergoes compensatory hypertrophy. It enlarges itself by multiplication of cells and functions more efficiently to do its own function and compensate the function of the lost one. This purposeful function is done without the knowledge of the individual. Milk is very poor in iron which is required for the formation of haemoglobin in blood. The baby lives on milk diet only for the first few months after birth. To meet the iron requirement of the baby, the foetus inside the mother's womb collects extra iron from the mother's blood and stores in the foetal spleen and liver for meeting the future deficiency condition. This is done without the consciousness of the mother and the foetus. The new-born baby is prone to varieties of infections immediately after the parturition. The milk that is secreted by the mother's mammary glands during the first few days after delivery is called colostrum which is rich in gammaglobulin that is an antibody to fight against infections. The mother's mammary gland secretes this special kind of milk at this period for a definite purpose without her being conscious about it. These are but few examples cited here to focus the point. Innumerable things like this happen in the body every moment without the consciousness of the subject. As a matter of fact, the subject is not conscious of most of the things happening inside him and all those things are for the survival, protection and well-being of the individual. Without consciousness, the subject can live for many days, as is the case with the coma patient. But without the vital functions that take place while the subject is not aware of, life is not possible even for a single moment. Without the consciousness of the individual, all the vital organs—the brain, heart, lungs, kidneys and liver—function in harmony all the moments. This type of consciousness may be called 'objective consciousness'.

Some physiologists, psychologists and philosophers may be reluctant to associate consciousness with the so-called 'automatic', 'natural' functions of the body. But Advaita Vedānta differs sharply from any such doctrine of naturalism. According to it, no action is initiated, executed and coordinated without consciousness. Again, the action which is purposeful for the survival of the individual cannot be executed naturally or due to chance. The whole body of an individual is called 'subject' here for this purpose. This is, however, a misnomer. Advaita Vedānta calls it 'object' (*viṣaya*) and the individual self (*ātman* or *jīva*) as the subject (*viṣayī*). Again, Advaita Vedānta equates the *jīva* or *ātman* with the *Paramātman* (Cosmic Self). Everything happens in the body and everywhere in the world due to the actions of the insentient Nature. But Nature functions and the body functions only under the chairmanship of the *ātman*. Advaita Vedānta accepts the subject only, which is real and Consciousness. It rejects the empirical object which is unreal. Thus there is no dichotomy of Consciousness; there is nothing like subjective and objective consciousness. The 'unconscious' that guides the vital functions of the body is conscious. When the cerebral centres are not active in creating awareness of the individual, and still purposeful and vital functions are executed inside the body, we say that the subject is not conscious of the actions. It is, however, not correct to limit the use of the word 'consciousness' to the function of the cerebral cortex of human being only. In Advaita Vedānta, Māyā is Nescience, and derivatively all products of Māyā are insentient. In such a situation, the cerebral cortex of man only cannot be called conscious organ and its functioning cannot be called consciousness.

Anything in the world—body, brain, mind, matter, proton, electron, neutrino, photon—becomes conscious in a restricted and limited way only when the universal Consciousness which is Brahman is reflected in it. This is the only version of Advaita Vedānta in regard to consciousness of matter. The individual human cerebrum is not the subject; it is an object out of many objects in the world. The 'subject' which is ignored in materialistic science and philosophy is Brahman who is the only subject and the nondual subject, without any object, of course.

Somehow in the historical perspective, the real subject is lost in both the religious and the scientific culture of the West. The subject and the only subject is the Universal Self or Brahman. Erwin Schrödinger expresses his views on this subject as follows:

> The earliest records to my knowledge date back some 2,500 years or more. From the early great Upaniṣads the recognition ATMAN = BRAHMAN (the personal self equals the omnipresent, all-comprehending eternal self) was in Indian thought considered, far from being blasphemous, to represent the quintessence of deepest insight into the happenings of the world. The strivings of all the scholars of Vedānta was, after having learnt to pronounce with their lips, really to assimilate in their minds this greatest of all the thoughts.
>
> Again, the mystics of many centuries, independently, yet in perfect harmony with each other (somewhat like the particles in an ideal gas) have described, each of them, the unique experience of his or her life in terms that can be condensed in the phrase: DEUS FACTUS SUM (I have become God).[87]

It is generally believed that science has got no dogma. This belief is not untrue in principle. However, in practice, the greatest dogma prevalent in science is its confidence in the notion that atheism has been proved and finally proved. Renowned scientist like Erwin Schrödinger is against a personal God (monotheism) and still exposes this dogma in the following paragraph:

> Let me briefly mention the notorious atheism of science which comes, of course, under the same heading. Science has to suffer

this reproach again and again, but unjustly so. No personal god can form part of a world model that has only become accessible at the cost of removing everything personal from it. We know, when God is experienced, this is an event as real as an immediate sense perception or as one's own personality. Like them he must be missing in the space-time picture. I do not find God anywhere in space and time—that is what the honest naturalist tells you. For this he incurs blame from him in whose catechism is written: God is spirit.[88]

Finally, one point may be discussed here regarding the primacy of Consciousness. It has already been said that, according to the argument of Advaita Vedānta, no action is possible without precedent and concurrent consciousness. If matter is primary and consciousness is a property of highly organized matter (evolution of human brain, as the Marxist philosopher says), how was the material universe functioning during the long period from the big bang explosion to the appearance of the human species (Homo sapiens)? Science now accepts the concept of the oscillating universe. Before the formation of the cosmic egg, there was no matter and no energy. The scientist himself does not know what that 'singularity' was. Could the whole universe evolve out of nothing? Could it be evolved without the guiding factor of consciousness? Rational thinking, without preconceived ideas, without dogmas, cannot afford to deny Consciousness as primary and fundamental Being, as Reality devoid of becoming, and as the substratum of the illusory and phenomenal universe.

NOTES

1. BS, II.2.28.
2. BSŚB, Introduction.
3. Einstein, A., 'On Physical Reality', Franklin Institute Journal 221, 1936, 349 ff.
4. Lenin, V.I., *Materialism and Empirio-Criticism*, Collected Works, Vol. 14, p. 130.
5. Hegel, G.W.F., *Encyclopedia of the Philosophical Sciences*, I, p. 258.
6. Hegel, G.W.F., *Philosophy of Nature*, p. 67.
7. Engels, F., *Dialectics of Nature*, p. 247.
8. *Ibid.*, p. 254.
9. Engels, F., *Anti-Dühring*, Moscow, 1977, p. 77.

10. Afanasyev, V.G., *Marxist Philosophy*, Progress Publishers, Moscow, 1980, pp. 40-1.
11. *Ibid.*, pp. 42-6.
12. *Ibid.*, pp. 51-2.
13. Oppenheimer, J.R., *Science and the Common Understanding*, Oxford University Press, London, 1954, pp. 42-3.
14. Eddington, S.A., *The Nature of the Physical World*, Cambridge University Press, Cambridge, 1928, Introduction.
15. *Ibid.*, p. 290.
16. Heisenberg, W., *Physics and Philosophy*, Allen & Unwin, London, 1959, p. 160.
17. Heisenberg, W. *et al.*, On *Modern Physics*, Clarkson Potter, New York, 1961, p. 13.
18. Jeans, J., *Physics and Philosophy*, Cambridge University Press, Cambridge, 1948, p. 169.
19. Bohr, N., Quoted by Davies, P. in '*God and the New Physics*', J.M. Dent & Sons, London, 1983, p. 103.
20. Wheeler, J.A., Thorne, K.S. and Misner, C., *Gravitation*, W.H. Freeman & Co., Salt Lake City, Utah, USA, 1973, p. 1273.
21. Stapp, H., *Mind, Matter and Quantum Mechanics*, Quoted by Zukav, G. in '*The Dancing Wu Li Masters*', Fontana/Collins, London, 1980, p. 105.
22. YV, 40.1; Īśa, 1.
23. Einstein, A., Quoted by Capek, M. in '*The Philosophical Impact of Contemporary Physics*', D. Van Nostrand, Princeton, New Jersey, 1961, p. 319.
24. Einstein, A., Quoted by Thiel, R., *And There Was Light*, 1958, p. 345.
25. Einstein, A., Podolsky, B. and Rosen, N., 'Can quantum mechanical description of physical reality be considered complete?', Physical Review, Vol. 47, pp. 777-80, 1935.
26. Bell, J.S., Physics, Vol. 1, p. 195, 1964.
27. Clauser, J.F. and Shimony, A., Bell's Theorem: Experimental tests and implications, Rep. Prog. Phys., 41, pp. 1881-1927, 1978.
28. Freedman, S. and Clauser, J., Experimental test of local hidden variable theories, Physical Review Letters, 28, p. 938 ff, 1972.
29. Aspect, A., Dalibard, J. and Roger, G., Experimental test of Bell's inequalities using time-varying analyzer, Physical Review Letters, 49, p. 1804, 1982.
30. D'Espagnat, B., *The Physicist's Conception of Nature*, ed. J. Mehra, D. Reidel, Dordrecht, Holland, 1973, p. 734.
31. Einstein, A., 'Autobiographical Notes' in Paul A. Schilpp (ed.), *Albert Einstein: Philosopher-Scientist*, The Library of Living Philosophers, Inc., Evanston, Illinois, 1949, p. 85.
32. Schrödinger, E., 'Discussions of Probability Relations between Separated Systems', Proceedings of the Cambridge Philosophical Society, 31, pp. 555-62, 1935.
33. Sarfatti, J., 'The Case for Superluminal Information Transfer', MIT Technology Review, Vol. 79, no. 5, p. 3 ff, 1977.
34. Chā ŚB, VI.11.2.

35. Walker, E.H., 'The Nature of Consciousness', Mathematical Biosciences, 7, pp. 175-6, 1970.
36. Bohm, D., Quoted by Zukav, G. in "*The Dancing Wu Li Masters*", Fontana/Collins, London, 1980, p. 315.
37. *Ibid.*, p. 323.
38. Mach, E., Quoted by Reincourt, A.D. in "*The Eye of Shiva*", Souvenir Press, London, 1980, p. 167.
39. Schrödinger, E., *My View of the World*, Cambridge University Press, Cambridge, 1964, p. 19.
40. Schrödinger, E., *What is Life and Mind and Matter*, Cambridge University Press, Cambridge, 1967, p. 140.
41. Jung. C.G., *Eranos Jahrbuch*, 1946, p. 398, Quoted by Schrödinger, E. in "*What is Life and Mind and Matter*", Cambridge University Press, Cambridge, 1980, p. 129.
42. Heisenberg, W., *Physics and Philosophy*, Harper & Row, New York, 1958, p. 41.
43. Einstein, A., Podolsky, B. and Rosen, N., 'Can Quantum Mechanical Description of Physical Reality Be Considered Complete?', Physical Review, 47, pp. 777-80, 1935.
44. Bohr, N., *Atomic Theory and the Description of Nature*, Cambridge University Press, Cambridge, 1934, p. 53.
45. Heisenberg, W., *Physics and Philosophy*, Harper & Row, New York, 1958, p. 41.
46. Everett, H., 'Relative State Formulation of Quantum Mechanics', Reviews of Modern Physics, Vol. 29, pp. 454-62, 1957.
47. Wheeler, J., Reviews of Modern Physics, Vol. 29, p. 463, 1957.
48. DeWitt, B., Physics Today, Vol. 23 (no. 9), p. 30, 1970.
49. DeWitt, B. and Graham, N., ed, *The Many-Worlds Interpretation of Quantum Mechanics*, Princeton University Press, 1973.
50. Jammer, M., *The Philosophy of Quantum Mechanics*, Wiley, John & Sons, New York, 1974, p. 157.
51. Birkhoff, G. and Newmann, J.V., 'The Logic of Quantum Mechanics', Annals of Mathematics, Vol. 37, no. 4, Oct. 1936.
52. Born, M., *Atomic Physics*, Blackie & Son, Glasgow, 1969, p. 97.
53. Finkelstein, D., Quoted by Zukav, G. in '*The Dancing Wu Li Masters*', Fontana/Collins, London, 1980, pp. 276-7.
54. Suzuki, D.T., *On Indian Mahāyāna Buddhism*, ed. Edward Conze, Harper & Row, New York, 1968, p. 239.
55. Heisenberg, W., *Physics and Philosophy*, Allen & Unwin, London, 1963, pp. 178-9.
56. Mu, III.2.9.
57. Wittgenstein, L., *Tractatus Logico-Philosophicus*, Routledge & Kegan Paul, London, 7.
58. Russell, B., *Mysticism and Logic*, Allen & Unwin, London, 1970, p. 9.
59. Einstein, A., Quoted by Frank, P. in '*Einstein*': *His Life and Times*, Alfred A. Knopf, New York, 1947, pp. 340-1.
60. Heraclitus, Quoted by Schrödinger, E. in 'What is Life?', New York, 1956, pp. 206-8.

61. Riencourt, A.D., *The Eye of Shiva*, Souvenir Press, London, 1980, p. 60.
62. Einstein, A., Quoted by Frank, P. in '*Einstein: His Life and Times*', Alfred A. Knopf, New York, 1947, p. 342.
63. Heisenberg, W., *Physics and Philosophy*, Allen & Unwin, London, 1959, p. 96.
64. *Ibid.*, p. 128.
65. Heisenberg, W., *Physics and Philosophy*, Harper & Row, New York, 1962, p. 81.
66. Wheeler, J., Quoted by Davies, P., *God and the New Physics*, J.M. Dent & Sons, London, 1983, pp. 110-1.
67. Schrödinger, E., *What is Life and Mind and Matter*, Cambridge University Press, Cambridge, 1967, p. 137.
68. *Ibid.*, p. 138.
69. *Ibid.*, pp. 138-9.
70. Schrödinger, E., *What is Life and Mind and Matter*, Cambridge University Press, Cambridge, 1980, pp. 134-5.
71. BSŚB, Introduction.
72. Chā, VI.8.7; VI.9.4; VI.10.3; VI.12.3; VI.13.3; VI.14.3.
73. BSŚB, III.2.22.
74. *The Fundamentals of Marxist-Leninist Philosophy*, Progress Publishers, Moscow, 1974, pp. 102-3.
75. Afanasyev, V.G., *Marxist Philosophy*, Progress Publishers, Moscow, 1980, p. 60.
76. *Ibid.*, p. 61.
77. Jennings, H.S., *Behaviour of the Lower Organisms*, Oxford & IBH Publishing Co., New Delhi, 1965, p. 261 (originally published by Indiana University Press).
78. *Ibid.*, p. 264.
79. *Ibid.*, p. 335.
80. *Ibid.*, p. 337.
81. Eddington, S.A., *The Nature of the Physical World*, Cambridge University Press, Cambridge, 1931, p. 332.
82. *Ibid.*, p. 323.
83. Sullivan, J.W.N., *The Limitations of Science*, Penguin Books, Harmondsworth, 1938, p. 141.
84. Heisenberg, W., *Physics and Beyond*, Allen & Unwin, London, 1971, p. 104.
85. Wigner, E.P. in Wigner, E.P., ed, *Symmetries and Reflections*, M.I.T. Press, Cambridge, Mass, 1970, p. 172.
86. Schrödinger, E., *What is Life and Mind and Matter*, Cambridge University Press, Cambridge, 1980, p. 95.
87. *Ibid.*, p. 93.
88. *Ibid.*, pp. 149-50.

CHAPTER XI

SEED AND SPROUT

> But because I have been enjoined, by this Holy Office, altogether to abandon the false opinion which maintains that the Sun is the centre and immovable, and forbidden to hold, defend, or teach the said false doctrine in any manner ...... I abjure, curse, and detest the said errors and heresies, and generally every other error and sect contrary to the said Holy Church ...
>
> *Galileo Galilei*

> No point is more central than this, that empty space is not empty. It is the seat of the most violent physics.
>
> *John A. Wheeler*

> The effort to understand the universe is one of the very few things that lifts human life a little above the level of farce, and gives it some of the grace of tragedy.
>
> *Steven Weinberg*

COSMOLOGY AND COSMOGONY have been discussed in Parts I and II of this book. The concepts of modern sicence on this subject have been dealt with under astrophysics in Chapter VI. Chapter IX gives a brief account of cosmology and cosmogony of Advaita Vedānta. The co-currents and counter-currents of these two streams will be presented here.

Creator

Theologians are firm in their opinion that the world has a Creator. They argue: "Every effect has got a cause. Every product has got a maker. The pen has a maker. The watch has a maker. There is no product which has no maker. The world is a product. How could it be made without a maker? How could it be produced without a producer?" He who has made this world, says the theologian, is God.

The atheist uses the argument of the theologian to establish the fallacy of the latter. "Everything has a maker, a father." Such a statement is not *a priori* truth in logic. Nonetheless, it may be presumed that it is axiomatically true. The world has a maker and that maker is God. Using the same argument, it is said that God must have a maker, a father. But, how can God's father be fatherless? So God must have a grand-father. We can't stop there. God's grand-father must have a father. By the same analogy we continue to trace backward and in this process, we can never stop at any point. In the domain of the past we make an unending sojourn in a series of *infinitum regressum*. In our vain attempt, we march in the backward direction and never reach a destination. What do we gain by this? We gain nothing. The theologian says: "We must stop at the God level. He is unborn, immortal and eternal. He is uncreated. He was in the infinite past. He is at the present. He will continue to be in the infinite future." The atheist argues: "If we can stop at the God level, why can't we stop at the world level? The world is uncreatable and indestructible. Barring transformations, the world-stuff is eternal. It was in the past. It is at the present. It will continue to be in the future. God is imaginary whereas the world, we experience, is concrete. If we can stop at the level of the imaginary God, why can't we stop at the level of the concrete world?"

An ever-existing dynamic state of flux is accepted in Marxist philosophy. Matter and motion are eternal; but matter is ever changing; form F_1 changes to form F_2, F_2 to F_3, F_3 to F_4, F_4 to F_2, F_2 to F_1, and so on. This is the dynamic state of flux. No matter remains in a fixed form. "All that comes into being deserves to perish."[1] Thus, any specific entity of matter is not eternal. But the sum total of matter in motion is eternal. It has got no birth. It was never created by any creator. It will never come to an end. It is uncreatable, and imperishable. Engels says: "Modern natural science has had to take over from philosophy the principle of the indestructibility of motion; it cannot any longer exist without this principle."[2] The following paragraph present a clear concept about the eternally moving matter:

> It is an eternal cycle in which matter moves, a cycle that certainly only completes its orbit in periods of time for which our terrestrial year is no adequate measure, a cycle in which

the time of highest development, the time of organic life and still more that of the life of beings conscious of nature and of themselves, is just as narrowly restricted as the space in which life and self-consciousness come into operation; a cycle in which every finite mode of existence of matter, whether it be sun or nebular vapour, single animal or genus of animals, chemical combination or dissociation, is equally transient, and wherein nothing is eternal but eternally changing, eternally moving matter and the laws according to which it moves and changes. But however often, and however relentlessly, this cycle is completed in time and space; however many millions of suns and earths may arise and pass away; however long it may last before, in one solar system and only on one planet, the conditions for organic life develop; however innumerable the organic beings, too, that have to arise and to pass away before animals with a brain capable of thought are developed from their midst, and for a short span of time find conditions suitable for life, only to be exterminated later without mercy—we have the certainty that matter remains eternally the same in all its transformations, that none of its attributes can ever be lost, and therefore, also, that with the same iron necessity that it will exterminate on the earth its highest creation, the thinking mind, it must somewhere else and at another time again produce it.[3]

Buddhism has doctrine of flux that is similar tothat of Marxism. It is called the doctrine of dependent origination (*pratītyasamutpāda*)[4]. Advaita Vedānta accepts a permanent substratum. There is no such thing in Buddhism (unless *Nirvāṇa* is equated with Brahman). The Buddhistic *anātmavāda*[5] rejects the existence of any self (soul or *jīvātman*). Everything is impermanent (*anitya*) and momentary (*kṣaṇika*) according to Buddhist philosophy.[6] Phenomenal things undergo changes constantly. All cosmic events are in a dynamic state of flux. No event happens in isolation. The changes of substances may be shown on next page.

This is an unending chain which revolves the world into a procession. It is not possible to say which link of the chain is the beginning and which one the end.

The physical phenomenon of flux is based on inductive metho-

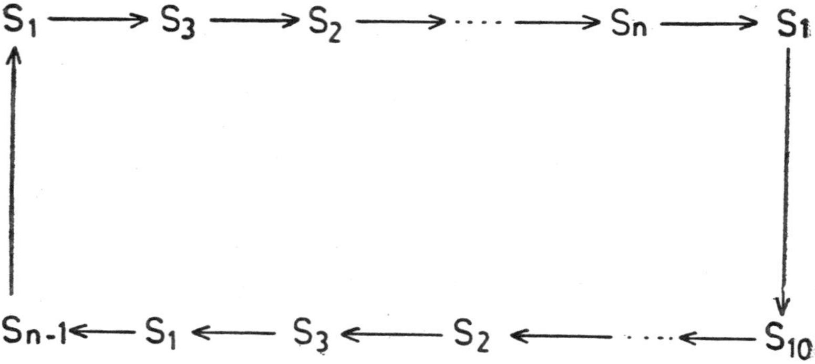

dology. It is recognized in empirical science. From this flux phenomenon, both Buddhism and Marxism draw a conclusion. It is inferred that the universe is beginningless and endless and that it has got no creator and controller God.

The eternality of the world has been accepted in *Mīmāṁsā* that pleads for a steady-state universe. By taking the universe as a unit, *Mīmāṁsā* does not find any net change in it. Neither creation nor dissolution of the universe as a whole is accepted by this old school of Indian philosophy. It declares: "Never was the world otherwise than what it is at present (*na kadācit anīdṛśaṁ jagat*)". "Mīmāṁsā does not admit even the existence of God as the creator and destroyer of the universe. God could not have had the tools to fashion the world with. He could have no motive to create it, either as a cruel or a merciful act. In fact when there were no beings in the beginning, how could he have any good or bad feelings towards them? Moreover if we believe he is the creator, he would require another creator, and so on. So there is no God, no creator, no destroyer and no dissolution. The world is, and has ever been."[7]

In 1948, Herman Bondi and Thomas Gold proposed the steady-state model of the universe. Fred Hoyle tried to substantiate this model by imagining a C-field (a reservoir of negative energy) and continuous creation of matter from this C-field. This model of Bondi, Gold and Hoyle has been discussed in Chapter VI.

Now it may be critically analyzed if the universe can be accepted as an eternally existing, beginningless and endless one. The big bang and the big crunch, conceived by the astrophysicists of the twentieth century, provide evidence for the birth and the death of the universe. In 1965, Arno A. Penzias and Robert W. Wilson detected a homogeneous, isotropic background micro-wave radiation that is the relic of the big bang explosion of the cosmic egg. This was the empirical evidence of the beginning of the universe. From this finding, the present age of the universe has also been calculated. The universe did not exist in the infinite past; time in the past had a beginning and the universe had a beginning too. The universe will not exist in the infinite future; time in the future will have an end and the universe will have an end too.

Śaṅkara says: "Whatever has got a beginning shall be impermanent (*yadārabdhaṁ tadanityam*[8])". Here 'beginning' implies 'becoming an effect or a product'. In the process of becoming an effect or a product, work in involved. There cannot be work without expenditure of energy. What is the exact meaning of expenditure of energy? It is not exactly like expenditure of money. Energy is utilized in work; it decays. Here 'decay' does not mean complete destruction or annihilation, something becoming nothing. It means degradation of energy, workable form of energy being converted to unworkable form, what the physicist terms 'entropy'.

A product, once formed, continues to change unless and until it goes back to its original, potential state. Every product has got a form. To maintain the form, work is necessary. To change to any other form and to maintain the changed form work is necessary. Work implies expenditure of energy, which, in turn, implies decay of energy. Hence a product is bound to be impermanent.

The total amount of energy that was manifested from the unmanifested *Prakṛti* or Māyā (E_{um}) at the beginning of creation was E_m. This E_m is vast, but not unlimited, inexhaustible and infinite. Any product, small or big, including the whole universe, cannot be infinite. It may be termed 'infinite' in the sense that its finitude cannot be determined by man. Thus, E_m, even being too huge in quantity, is still exhaustible. All of this E_m was workable or functional energy (E_f) in the beginning. Every moment some of it has been, is being and will be degraded to non-functional energy (entropy). In course of time, E_f will be gradually depleted and finally there will be a moment when E_f will be zero. With the depletion of E_f, there is corresponding generation of degraded energy (E_d). When all of E_f becomes zero, E_d will be maximum. Maximum E_d will be equivalent to the original E_f in quantity.

The E_d is the E_m, although in degraded, non-workable and non-functional form. It shall have to be reconverted to E_{um} in order that the next cycle of world process would function. The reconversion of the E_d into the unmanifested state (E_{um}) is otherwise known as dissolution. Māyā is the inexhaustible reservoir of unmanifested energy. Manifestation takes place from the source of Māyā. In the reverse process which is called dissolution, the whole universe is merged into Māyā and remains therein unmanifested state.

According to the doctrine of Advaita Vedānta, anything that is functional cannot be eternal and anything that is non-functional is eternal. Brahman is non-functional. It is formless, attributeless and changeless. It is B that continues to be B (B→B→B→B→... →B). If A changes to B and B changes to C, B has got birth and death, beginning and end. In such a situation, the material cause of B is A and the product or effect of B is C. For the changeless B, their is neither beginning nor end. The world has a precedent state. The world has got a consequent state. Of course, in the case of the world, the precedent state and the consequent state are identical, both states being Māyā only. It is meaningless to ask the question, "Who is the father or maker of Brahman?" We go on asking this question for everything of the world. But we must stop at the Brahman level.

Entropy has already been alluded to. This concept is contained in the second law of thermodynamics. According to this law, there will be maximum disorder at a future time, when entropy will be maximum and utilizable energy will be zero. That will be the end of the universe. Thus the future is not infinite. Again, according to this law, the past cannot be infinite. Had it been so, the end of the universe would have come in the past. So far, science has accepted the second law of thermodynamics. That being true, the eternality of the universe is rejected and a universe with a beginning and an end is accepted.

This discussion has enabled us to reject the uncreatability and indestructibility of the universe. The universe has been created. Then who is the creator? Brahman is decidedly not the creator. Brahman is functionless and hence cannot be the efficient cause. Brahman is changeless, partless and homogeneous and hence cannot be the material cause. Again, Advaita Vedānta asserts that Brahman is nondual, is the only Being without a second. It thus becomes puzzling and perplexing to identify the maker of this universe which is magical and illusory.

Māyā has been accepted by Advaita Vedānta as the power of Brahman. It is indescribable, since it exists, does not exist and exists and does not exist. It is the eternal power of Brahman. The existence of Māyā depends upon that of Brahman. Advaita Vedānta holds that Māyā is the material cause of the universe. In creation, it is the source of the universe. In dissolution, it is the final receiver of the universe. Thus, the universe is a manifestation of the power of Brahman. This power is itself illusory. It conceals and projects. This illusory power gives rise to the illusory universe.

It is accepted that Māyā is the material cause of the universe. But it is insentient. Being devoid of consciousness, it cannot assume the authorship of the universe. The wood is not automatically made into a chair. The earth is not automatically made into a pot. The gold is not automatically made into a necklace. The doer is a carpenter, a potter, a goldsmith. The world has been well-designed. It is a wonderful piece of architecture. The world functions according to laws. The cosmic design is well executed. The cosmic laws are well operative. The world functions is harmony. Who is the architect? Who is the engineer? Who is the executor? Who is the controller? The insentient Māyā cannot be the designer, the engineer, the executor and the controller. The universe of insentient matter and energy cannot itself play these roles. Non-functional Brahman is not concerned with any activity. Then who is the efficient cause of the universe?

Various schools of theology assert that God is the Creator and the Controller. Let this concept be accepted first. Any doer of action cannot be eternal for reasons given in the case of the world. If God is a Being and an acting Being, He cannot be birthless and deathless. If God can be accepted as a functionary Being Who is beginningless and endless, the logic of the atheist cannot be wrong when he says that the universe is ever present and functioning in a dynamic state of flux, without birth and death.

Advaita Vedānta has a God-concept. But it is different from that of the theological schools. Brahman which is pure Consciousness is reflected in Māyā which becomes the limiting adjunct (*upādhi*). This reflected Consciousness in Māyā is God. Similarly, the reflected Consciousness in any individual being is the individual self. As one Sun appears like many Suns in many pools of water, so also one Brahman appears as many individual selves in many individual beings. The cosmic reflection of Consciousness on Māyā, otherwise called God, controls Māyā and all individual entities of the universe. There is no question of birth of God and death of God. When Brahman and Māyā have no birth, the reflection of Brahman on Māyā has no birth. When Brahman and Māyā have no death, the reflection of Brahman on Māyā has no death. Brahman is Consciousness. God, who is the reflection of Brahman on Māyā, is omniscient. He is the efficient cause of the universe.

Some religions give over-emphasis on the efficient cause only. They say God is the efficient cause and there is no material cause. They favour *creatio ex nihilo* (creation out of nothing). The whole universe has been created by God out of nothing.

According to the genesis given in the Bible, God created the stuff of the universe *ex nihilo*. He created light on the first day; sky on the second day; dry land with plants and waters in seas on the third day; sun, moon and stars on the fourth day; and sea-creatures and birds on the fifth day. On the sixth day, He made all the beasts and finally man. He made man in His own image. He took rest on the seventh day which was Sunday. Thus He created the whole universe out of nothing in six days only. Having created, He sustains the ordered universe. If His sustaining power were withdrawn, the universe would collapse back into nothingness again.

The Quran does not subscribe to the concept of *creatio ex nihilio*. It says: Allah sustains by His will a cosmos formed by Him from the pre-existing and eternal chaos of matter.

Conceptual analysis does not support *ex nihilo* creation. Some thing becomes nothing (something=nothing, X=not-X). Nothing becomes something (nothing=something, not-X=X). These identity expressions have been given in the analogy of chemical reactions. Carbon combines with oxygen to become carbon dioxide and heat energy. This is otherwise expressed as $C+O_2=CO_2+E$. The identity expressions such as "something=nothing", "X=not-X", "nothing=something", "not-X=X" are self-contradictory and hence cannot be true. Thus *ex nihilo* creation is refuted. On logical ground, Advaita Vedānta rejects the idea of something becoming nothing and nothing becoming something.[9] Empirical evidences are too many to support evolutionary cosmogony. It has taken eons for the universe to come to this stage. Nothing has been made at a particular time in a finished form. Man was not made by God instantaneously. Man appeared on Earth very late in comparison with other forms of life. There is no life on many other celestial bodies. There may be life somewhere else in some other star's planets of our galaxy or other galaxies. But there too evolution might have taken place through ascendance from stage to stage—inorganic, organic and biological. Evolution in other star-systems might have traversed different paths and the evolved beings in all celestial systems might not be identical. In spite of these possible diversities, evolution has been observed empirically on the Earth and elsewhere in other celestial systems. Becoming is a universal phenomenon. Only Brahman which is the Real Being is free from becoming. On the other hand, every entity of the universe, whether small or big, ever becomes; not only does matter exist, but also it exists in motion. Everything ever changes. There is ascendance through the changes; some say it is linear, others say it is spiral; but whatever the course may be, it is upward. The cosmogony described in the Upaniṣads is evolutionary. In this regard Śaṅkara says: "Gradually, not suddenly at a specific time (*krameṇa, na yugapat*)[10]. Of course, the evolution, as described in Advaita Vedānta, is material-cum-spiritual, not materialistic. It is not like the evolution of Darwin who gave a materialistic picture of species evolution only. Before species evolved, organic compounds culminating in formation of RNA and DNA had already evolved. Inorganic evolution must have taken place before organic evolution. Before the formation of elements, particle-evolution must have been the dominant becoming consequent to the big bang explosion. The preceding event was the formation of the cosmic egg. Science stops at this point and refuses to march further backward. The materialistic evolution, just mentioned in a nutshell, fails to present an integral picture. It depends entirely on chance. Everything happens randomly. The universe has taken this shape by pure chance alone. Intelligence is an evolved property of matter at a stage of higher organization. Evolution, the materialistic evolutionist says, has not been guided by any intelligence. Advaita Vedānta does not agree to such a mechanical interpretation. Evolution is mechanical, of course. But this mechanical evolution is guided by Spirit. *Īśvara* is the Chairman (*adhyakṣa*)[11] under whose guidance Nature evolves. The universe is not a product of chance. It is destined to undergo evolution in a certain ways; it is destined to undergo involution in the reverse way. It appears from Māyā; it stays and evolves; it is absorbed into Māyā. It stays in Māyā in dormancy, in unmanifested condition; again it manifests, it evolves. Cycles of creation and dissolution are repeated *ad infinitum.*

Cosmic Egg

Both modern science and Advaita Vedānta agree on the point that formation of the cosmic egg was the first step in the creation of the universe. The cosmic egg exploded. Matter was formed. Stars and galaxies were formed. The universe expanded and is still now expanding. It will not expand for ever. It will not expand to infinitum. There will come a time when the universe will contract. It will contract to smaller and smaller volume. Too much heat will be produced. This condition is called the 'big crunch' by the astro-physicist. The big crunch will proceed; the universe will contract finally to a point. Will it further contract and vanish or will it stop there? Some scientists conjecture that the universe will vanish and vanish for ever. They lament the final death of their dear universe. Some other scientists develop optimism. Although they are not able to devise any mathematical model for the retreating of the universe from the point before the final disappearance, they expect something to happen, natural or miraculous, so that the universe will bounce back from the final singular point. They call this point 'singularity'. The universe will contract to the singularity and will again expand. Expansion from the singularity and contraction to the singularity will go on alternately and this process will continue *ad infinitum*. This is the concept of the oscillating or pulsating universe.

Before the concept of the pulsating universe was born, scientists were very much puzzled over the appearance of the cosmic egg. Wherefrom did the cosmic egg appear? How did it stay as such for a long time? Why did it burst? What made it burst? Scientists were not answering these questions. They were evading replies. They were afraid lest God would creep in. There are really no ghosts. But the biggest ghost of which scientists are afraid is God. They think it sacrilegious to contaminate science with God. The most sacred thing for them is to keep science secular, with complete banishment of the God concept. There is justifiable reason for this sort of psychosis of the scientist. Modern science developed in the Western world. Religion made serious attempt to strangulate science. For centuries, antagonism developed between science and religion. Finally, science triumphed and religion receded. After this struggle was over, there could not be reconciliation at a later date. Still now, there is no scope for compromise, because there is very little thing in religion that could accommodate scientific thought and mutually enrich both the schools of thought. This was the background of the animosity between science and religion.

Advaita Vedānta upholds the notion of the pulsating universe. The cosmic egg is formed. The egg explodes. The universe expands. The universe contracts. All these phenomena of the pulsating universe are recognized by Advaita Vedānta. It, however, does not accept the notion of 'singularity'. In the pulsating model of science, singularity is the starting and the ending point. The scientist is satisfied with this notion. He is confident of having got a solution. He feels that his theory is salvaged. He believes that his theory is saved. He is happy for getting the plea that he could keep away the ghost 'God' from his 'fundamentalism' by using a single word 'singularity'. But words are used to explain and also explain away. Perhaps the scientist here is explaining away. Use of the word 'singularity' gives a positive impression. The world finally contracts to a 'singularity' which is something, not nothing. Is it really something? Is it not nothing? The whole universe contracts to a point—like geometry whose volume tends to zero. Is there any known scientific device that can stop the contracting process to a zero volume? There is nothing like that. Advaita Vedānta says that finally the volume of the universe becomes zero. The universe disappears altogether. It, however, does not become nothing. The manifested universe becomes unmanifested and absorbed into Māyā.

The concept of dissolution (*pralaya*) has not yet been adopted by modern science. In the model of the pulsating universe of modern science, there is a continuation of the physical universe which ever stays in any form, singularity or otherwise. The scientists have not yet been able to explain the perpetual running of the world-machine, which is impossible on the basis of the first and the second law of thermodynamics. What happens to the maximum entropy and how is it reconverted to utilizable energy?

The modern cosmologists of science have not answered this question.

Marxist philosophers are very much upset by the entropy concept of the second law of thermodynamics. This law says that there will be a time when the entropy of the universe will be maximum and the utilizable energy will be zero. After that point in time, the universe cannot be functional. It cannot stay either. Matter cannot stay without position and momentum and for this purpose energy has to be spent. In Marxist philosophy, motion is eternal, matter in motion is permanent and the world process is ever operative. The second law of thermodynamics clashes with this Marxist doctrine. Marxist philosophers plead that there is transformation of energy, that the heat produced as a result of the world activities will be reconverted into energy of other forms and that matter in motion will be eternal. They cite the examples of negentropy. In the conversion of steam into water, water into ice, solar energy into plant products, coal and fossil fuel, nutrients into animal tissues and many other natural processes, matter from a state of disorder changes to matter of a relative state of order. The refrigerating system is one common example. In all such examples, entropy is converted to negentropy. The same thing should happen to the whole universe. In this regard, Frederick Engels says:

> What becomes of all this enormous quantity of heat? Is it for ever dissipated in the attempt to heat universal space, has it ceased to exist practically, and does it only continue to exist theoretically, in the fact that universal space has become warmer by a decimal fraction of a degree beginning with ten or more noughts? Such an assumption denies the indestructibility of motion; it concedes the possibility that by the successive falling into one another of the heavenly bodies all existing mechanical motion will be converted into heat and the latter radiated into space, so that in spite of all 'indestructibility of force" all motion in general would have ceased. (Incidentally, it is seen here how inaccurate is the term "indestructibility of force" instead of "indestructibility of motion".) Hence we arrive at the conclusion that in some way, which it will later be the task of scientific research to demonstrate, it must be possible for the heat radiated into space to be transformed into another form of

motion, in which it can once more be stored up and become active.[12]

Engels speaks of negentropy here. It must be remembered that, in case of two or more open systems, one system may have increase in entropy while a second system may have corresponding increase of negentropy (or decrease in entropy); that in one closed system there may be increase in entropy in one individual entity with corresponding decrease in entropy in another entity; and that the closed system as a whole will always show increase in entropy until the maximum is reached. The universe is finite and an isolated, closed system. When the whole universe is concerned, it cannot give its entropy to some other system which does not exist. Hence Marxist philosophers cannot substantiate their claim that motion is indestructible.

The concept of total dissolution, prevalent in Advaita Vedānta, provides a solution to the problem. So far no second solution has been suggested. The contraction of the universe does not stop at the singularity stage. The volume of the universe becomes less and less until it becomes zero. The sequence of dissolution is just the reverse of that of creation. The last product in the sequence (solid matter→liquid matter→excess of heat→gaseous matter, viz., hydrogen→plasma state→energy→space→*prāṇa*→*āpaḥ* or primeval waters) is *āpaḥ* that is finally merged into Māyā. In this system, heat or entropy will not continue to stay as such. It will lose its identity in the process of dissolution. The next world-cycle will start afresh.

In the pulsating model of the universe, materialistic science does not involve a Conscious Being although it necessitates one. This is the greatest dogma of science. Order is visualized in the pulsating model. The same processes of singularity formation of cosmic egg, big bang explosion, nucleogenesis, expansion of the universe, inorganic, organic and species evolution, contraction of the universe, big crunch and singularity will be repeated again and again. The same laws of Nature will operate. The same cosmic designing and execution will be necessary. How do all of these happen? Is it possible without a Conscious, Intelligent and Omniscient Designer, Executor and Controller? Science dogmatically answers: "Such a Conscious Being is not necessary. Everything happens naturally." There is nowhere in science an explanation why singularity does not disappear, how it initiates another world-cycle and why a subsequent cycle is not anything else other than the precedent cycle. How is the rhythm of the pulse maintained? Why is the regularity? Why is the order? Science avoids these questions. Advaita Vedānta does not evade the issue. It clearly says that *Īśvara* is the designer, executor and controller of the world-cycles. He deliberates to have the universe and then only *āpaḥ* is manifested from Māyā and the cosmic egg is formed. He disturbs the equilibrium of the three constituents (*sattva, rajas, tamas*) and then only the creation process is initiated. As *Hiraṇyagarbha*, He enters into the cosmic egg. When the egg explodes, energy and matter particles are formed and cosmogonic sequences become operative. Īśvara as *Prajāpati* executes and regulates all these phenomena. As *Viṣṇu*, He sustains and nourishes all entities of the universe. As *Rudra*, He annihilates all entities of the universe. Creation and annihilation are perpetual phenomena in the functioning of the universe. All these functions are carried out by Nature under the Chairmanship of *Īśvara*. Thus, the spider (*ūrṇanābhiḥ*)[13] model of the universe, as enunciated by Advaita Vedānta, although resembles the pulsating model of modern science, differs in few significant details and is material-cum-spiritual in nature.

Space and Time

Among different schools of ancient Indian philosophy, variations are observed in their concepts on space and time. It may be useful to present a summary of those concepts here.

In Mīmāṁsā. In the earlier Mīmāṁsā, Jaimini did not discuss space seriously. He vaguely referred to it as one of the substances.[14] In contrast, he has considered time as a mental construction.[15] The idea of time is associated with action.[16] Nature changes and this idea of change gives a notion of time.[17] The notion of time arises with the succession of events.[18] It is linked with desire.[19] Although the flow of time is continuous and uninterrupted, it originates from desire, one desire succeeding the other in an endless chain. It is always associated with two successive desires.[20] Thus time is an ideal construct and not a reality. It exists for other things, but not for itself.[21] It is a continuous whole, although it is divided for empirical use.[22] Jaimini categorically asserts that the world is not created out of time. It is not the cause or the result of action.[23] It is considered as the greatest destructive force.[24] It does not really mean that time, as a specific entity, destroys the things in the world. Since change is associated with time, and destruction is associated with change, time is treated as a destructive force.

In later Mīmāṁsā, the concepts of space and time had sharp deviations from those of Jaimini. Two such schools of Mīmāṁsā were developed—one by Prabhākara and the other by Kumārila.

Both Prabhākara and Kumārila make a difference between *ākāśa* and *dik* (space). Their *ākāśa* is the substratum of sound.[25] Prabhākara maintains that *dik* or space is an eternal substance.[26] Kumārila also treats *ākāśa* and *dik* as eternal.[27] For him, *ākāśa* is eternal, indivisible and all-pervasive.[28] Anything that is eternal is uncreated. Hence it may be concluded that Prabhākara and Kumārila considered space to be an uncreated substance. For Prabhākara, time is an eternal substance.[29] Kumārila also says that time is one, eternal and all-pervasive.[30]

In Nyāya-Vaiśeṣika. The Nyāya-Vaiśeṣika system treats both space and time as realities. This school upholds the objective existence of metaphysical time. It also accepts the reality of space.

Nyāya-Vaiśeṣika school makes a distinction between *dik* (space) and *ākāśa*. According to this school, *ākāśa* is the material cause of sound and *dik* is the general cause of all effects.[31] *Ākāśa* is a substance (*bhūta dravya*) while dik is not.

Ākāśa and *dik* are like wall and cord for hanging pictures. The picture is hung on the wall by means of the cord. The wall provides place; the cord holds the picture in its relative position. Likewise *ākāśa* provides place for the things and *dik* holds the things in their relative positions.[32] *Dik* is eternal.[33] It is the cause of the notions of farness, nearness, etc.[34] Like the Newtonian concept of space, the Nyāya-Vaiśeṣika school considers *dik* as the receptacle (*ādhāra*) of everything in the world.[35] Time (*kāla*) and space (*dik*) constitute the background of the entire cosmic order.

Dik is unitary in Nyāya-Vaiśeṣika philosophy. It is spoken of as east, west, above, below, etc. Such a use is in vogue due to its different limiting adjuncts.[36]

Both space (*dik*) and time (*kāla*) are taken as the efficient cause of the entire universe in the Nyāya-Vaiśeṣika system.[37] They are necessary common conditions in the production of effects.[38]

Time (*kāla*) is eternal[39] and ubiquitous[40] in this system. It is the substratum of motion.[41] It is the cause of changes and modifications.[42] It is the eternal background of the creative processes. It is the cause of things that are produced.[43] It is regarded as the efficient cause of everything in the world.[44] The origination, maintenance and destruction of all objects of the world are done by it.[45] The distinction in time such as moments (*kṣaṇa*), hour (*ghatikā*), etc. is made due to its various limiting adjuncts.[46]

In Sāṅkhya-Yoga. In the Sāṅkhya system of evolution, space (*ākāśa*) is an evolute. It is a modification (*vikṛti*) of *Prakṛti* (Nature). Being a product, it cannot be eternal. In the involution process, all the evolutes of *Prakṛti* are reabsorbed into *Prakṛti* which becomes a single, homogeneous entity. Unlike *ākāśa*, time does not find any place in the evolutionary process of the Sāṅkhya. The concepts of space and time in Sāṅkhya are shared by the Yoga system.

In the Sāṅkhya-Yoga system, time is not real; it is a product of mind; the idea of time arises in mind as a result of perceptions or of words (*sa khalvayaṁ kālo vastuśunyo'pi buddhinirmāṇaḥ śabda-jñānānupātī*).[47]

Every evolutionary product is characterized by activity, change or motion (*vyaktaṁ sakriyaṁ parispandavat.*)[48] Moment (*kṣaṇa*) is the minimum limit of time taken by an atom in motion to leave one point and reach the next point. The moment rests on sequence of events (*kṣaṇastu vastu-patitaḥ kramāvalambī*). Every moment the whole universe undergoes changes (*tenaikena kṣaṇena kṛtsno lokaḥ pariṇāmānubhavati*).[49] Succession involving a series of changes or a series of events is associated with moments.[50] The continuous flow of time is the result of the sequence of moments. Moment M_2 follows moment M_1; moment M_3 follows moment M_2; and thus the sequence continues. Without events, mind cannot construct the idea of time.

In Jain Philosophy. In Jain philosophy, both space[51] and time[52] are real. Space is that in which things exist. It is devoid of qualities. It is eternal, formless, all-pervasive, inactive and unconscious.[53] The existence of substances (*pudgala*) depends upon accommodation in space.[54]

Although space is a single substance, it consists of infinite units called *pradeśas*. There are two kinds of space, viz., *lokākāśa* and *alokākāśa*. Things exist and move in *lokākāśa*. *Alokākāśa* is pure, transcendental space in which there is no movement. Unlike in the Vaiśeṣika system, no distinction is made between *ākāśa* and *dik* in Jaina philosophy.

Time (*kāla*) which is real in Jaina philosophy is an independent entity which functions chiefly in assisting other substances in undergoing changes. It is the auxiliary cause of change.

Time (*kāla*) consists of time-atoms (*kālāṇus*), that are the smallest units of time. Each time-atom is indivisible and eternal. Time-atoms are independent units; they don't mix with one another. The whole universe is filled with time-atoms.

There are two kinds of time, viz., empirical time (*vyavahāra kāla*) and transcendental time (*niścaya kāla*).[55] Empirical time has a beginning and an end whereas transcendental time is eternal and infinite.

In Buddhist Philosophy. Buddhism has a number of sects. All the sects do not have identical concepts of space and time.

Hīnayāna and *Mahāyāna* are two principal branches of Buddhism. The former has two sub-branches, viz., *Vaibhāṣika* and *Sautrāntika*. *Sarvāstivāda* and *Vibhajyavāda* are included in the *Vaibhāṣika* school. The Mahāyāna branch has also two sub-branches, viz., *Yogācāra* and *Mādhyamika* (*Śūnyavāda*).

Sarvāstivāda divides *dharmas* into two classes, viz., *saṁskṛta* and *asaṁskṛta*. *Saṁskṛta dharma* is made up of parts whereas *asaṁskṛta dharma* is non-composite. Space (*ākāśa*) is an *asaṁskṛta* dharma. It is unborn, uncaused, immutable, indestructible and eternal. It is an all-pervasive, positive entity according to the *Vaibhāṣika* school.

Space is that which does not impede.[56] Its chief nature is freedom from obstruction (*anāvṛtiḥ*)[57]. The *Vibhāṣa* distinguishes infinite space from local space. Infinite space is immaterial, invisible, non-resistant and unconditioned. Local space is a hole or cavity in which there are no material objects.[58] It is a part of the material universe.

The *Sautrāntikas* do not posit any uncaused category. Hence they reject the idea of the eternality of space. They regard space as pure nothing.[59] It is the mere absence of a touchable or resistant body. It is a conceptual form bereft of any objectivity.

Yogācāra is an idealistic school. For it, consciousness alone is real and the whole world of appearance is unreal.[60] Hence the question of space being real and eternal does not arise. This school regards space as a form.[61]

The *Mādhyamikas* regard space as a mental notion devoid of objective existence. In their opinion, those that are uncaused are non-entities, and those that are not dependent do not exist anywhere. They do not accept anything like permanent entity that exists in reality anywhere.[62] They criticise the *Vaibhāṣikas* who conceive space and time as uncaused, immutable and eternal. For the *Mādhyamikas*, space and time have no objective existence even from the empirical standpoint.[63]

The *Vaibhāṣikas* consider time as uncaused, immutable and eternal. *Sarvāstivāda* recognizes the existence of past, present and future.[64] The *Sautrāntikas* maintain that only the present exists.[65]

Vibhajyavāda[66] could make a reconciliation of these two opposing ideas. It accepts the reality of the present and only that part of the past that has not yet lost its force. It denies the reality of the future. It also says that the part of the past that has lost its force no longer exists.

Yogācāra, being an idealistic school, does not accept the reality of time.

Nāgārjuna, who is the exponent of the *Mādhyamika* school, refutes the realities of the past, present and future.[67] According to him, time does not exist apart and aloof from the changing objects. The changing objects are unreal; and consequently time is unreal.[68]

There are other Buddhist schools that describe non-void nature of space and *nirvāṇa*. *Milinda-pañha*[69] describes space as unborn, undecaying, permanent, static, absolute, independent, non-obstructive and infinite. The same scripture considers time as existent and non-existent.[70] It is interrelated with *saṁskāras* (accumulated impressions on the mind). Time exists for those *saṁskāras* that are still producing effects, or have the potentiality to produce effects in future. It does not exist for those *saṁskāras* that have ceased to exist. It exists for those who suffer from the cycles of rebirth. It does not exist for those who have attained *nirvāṇa*. This *nirvāṇa* is a timeless state.

The *sthavira* texts[71] of the *Mahāyāna* school reject the idea that space and *nirvāṇa* are void or *śūnya*. Instead of being *śūnya*, they are *pūrṇa* (full). It is a state of perfect calmness. It is a timeless, changeless and actionless state. It is devoid of attributes. Nothing can be predicated of it.

The *ākāśa* or 'cosmic space' of the mystical seer of the *Mahāyāna* school of Buddhism is not the same as the 'mathematical space' of Einstein. We shall be totally confused if we do not make a distinction between these two concepts.

Concept of Space in Advaita Vedānta. According to Advaita Vedānta, *ākāśa* or space is a substance (*dravya*). It is a product[72] that is not eternal and has a beginning. The nihilist Buddhists maintain that space is a negative entity that is simply absence of obstruction. Śaṅkara[73] refutes this idea. It is too subtle; subtler than matter and energy particles.[74] By virtue of its subtlety, it functions as a receptacle (*ādhāra*). As water is receptacle of aquatic animals like amoeba, fish and whale, so is *ākāśa*. Water is subtler than the solid fish and thus functions as a receptacle. It is not necessary to become a void to serve as a receptacle and to be non-obstructive to movement. Void or *śūnya* is a meaningless term in Advaita Vedānta. It recognizes plenum or fullness (*pūrṇa*). Space is a substance, subtle enough to hold macro-objects like the Earth and the Sun and micro-particles like the electron and photon.

Five primordial substances (*mahābhūta*) have been enlisted by the ancient Indian philosophers. These are: earth, water, energy, air and space. Three terms, viz., earth water and air, have been used symbolically. They stand for solid, liquid and gaseous substances, respectively. All forms of matter and energy of the universe are made of these primordial substances. It may be pointed out here that no difference was maintained between matter and energy in Vedānta and space was considered as a form of matter.

Space was created with the creation of the universe. The Taittirīya[75] Upaniṣad gives the cosmogonical sequence. Space or *ākāśa* was the first product from which hydrogen gas originated through generation of a series of particles. The 'field' of modern science is this *ākāśa*. Some scientists are of the opinion that space contains field. In such a notion, the void nature of space is still maintained. Advaita Vedānta says that space *is* field. Three subtle entities are recognized in Advaita Vedānta. These are the primeval waters (*āpaḥ*, *ka* or *ambhas*), *prāṇa* and space (*ākāśa*, *kha* or *aditi*). There is no equivalent word for *prāṇa* in English language. A new word 'viton' may be coined for it. It is the vital entity that vitalizes all entities of the world. *Āpaḥ*, *prāṇa* and *ākāśa* are in decreasing order of subtlety. Otherwise they are not different.[76] *Āpaḥ* is the first product to appear.[77] It precedes the appearance of the cosmic egg. It originates from Māyā. *Prāṇa* is produced from *āpaḥ* and *ākāśa* is produced from *prāṇa.*[78] *Āpaḥ* and *prāṇa* are interconvertible. Likewise, *prāṇa* and *ākāśa* are interconvertible. All these three entities constitute the 'field' of modern science.

Āpaḥ[79], *prāṇa*[80] and *ākāśa*[81] are not inert; they are vigorously active. Things are produced from them and again are merged into them. *Aditi* or *ākāśa* is an active participator in the cosmic drama. It dances and perpetually dances. From it particles are produced; into it particles are merged. Particles appear and disappear. This sort of particle-dance gives a false notion of something appearing from nothing and nothing appearing as something. In reality, *ākāśa* is manifested as particles and particles are dissolved into *ākāśa.* The Vedas[82] describe this phenomenon as mother *Aditi* producing offspring and the offsprings producing mother *Aditi.*

In dissolution, all of matter and energy of the universe is converted into *ākāśa* in the reverse order of creation.[83] *Ākāśa* is converted into *prāṇa* which, in turn, is converted into *āpaḥ*. Finally, the *āpaḥ* or primeval waters merge into Māyā and remain there in unmanifested condition till the next creation. Thus, *ākāśa* is present when the world manifests. It is one constituent entity of the world. But it does not exist in the absence of the world. Thus Brahman is spaceless *(anākāśam).*[84]

The spatio-temporal concept of Einstein was present in a seminal state in Advaita Vedānta. Events are invariably associated with time-concept. In the phenomenal world which is in motion and full of events, *āpaḥ*[85] and *ākāśa*[86] are woven like warp and woof.

Concept of Time in Advaita Vedānta. Advaita Vedānta does not recognize the objective existence of time. It is a mental construction, generated by the occurrence of more than one event.[87] Had there been no change, there could not have been time-concept.

Brahman is the creator of time (*kalākāra*). The origin of conceptual time is simultaneous with the beginning of creation.[88] There was no time before the cosmic egg appeared. There will also be no time after the phenomenal world is dissolved. In dissolution, the entire universe is converted, through reverse steps, into *ākāśa* (space) that changes to *prāṇa* (viton) and finally to *āpaḥ* (primeval waters). Lastly *āpaḥ* are merged into Māyā. No events occur after dissolution and before the subsequent creation. Hence there is no time in the absence of the world. Brahman is the devourer of time. The world is with time and Brahman is timeless.[89]

Time is neither the material nor the efficient cause of the universe.[90] It is the divine power (*devātmaśakti*) or Māyā from which the universe originates.

Apparently a contrary view regarding time has been given in a number of scriptures. It has been regarded as the originator and the destroyer of everything in the world.[91] It would be wrong if we understand such statement in its literal sense. Its allegorical sense must be taken for a proper interpretation of the function of time. Since events or changes are interrelated with time-concept, everything in the changeable world ever undergoes changes, and everything has an origin, life-span and death in the ocean of time like bubbles and waves. Thus it is allegorically said that time is the cause of the origination, maintenance and death of everything. In reality, time that has got no objective existence and that is a mental construct only cannot be the originator and destroyer of anything. Rightly the Maitrī Upaniṣad[92] says: "Time cooks all things indeed in the great self. He who knows in what time is cooked is the knower of the Veda."

Without space-time, the phenomenal world cannot be conceived of. Advaita Vedānta recognizes this. But it is further recognized that Brahman is above spatio-temporal sequence.[93]

Western Concept of Space. In ancient Greece, Thales, Anaxamenes, Heraclitus and Empedocles considered water, air, fire and earth, either singly or collectively, as the primordial substances out of which everything of the universe has been made. Space was a non-entity for them. Greek philosophy contrasted the plenum and the void. For Democritus, space was void; it was that in which atoms moved. Parmenides considered space as plenum. Zeno of Elea, the disciple of Parmenides argued that empty space was contradictory. Plato held that space is 'receptacle'. Forms are individualized in it; they are instantiated in it, i.e., they become instances of the universal. Aristotle conceived of space as place. He defined place as the inner boundary of the containing body. Epicurus and Lucretius continued to interpret space as void.

Descartes reverted to the notion of the plenum. He defined matter as extension. Although matter fills all space, motion in space is possible due to the subtlety of space. Descartes recognized the full space instead of the empty space. But, when he said, "Matter fills all space", he had a covert notion of space as void.

For Newton, space is absolute. Like Plato, Newton considered space as a receptacle to hold everything of the universe. His space was eternal, unchanging, inert, absolute, infinite and void. He thought of space to be the divine sensorium in which God works His will, and senses the results.

Kant regarded space as the *a priori* form of external phenomena. Space is the form of the external sense. We never experience space although we don't experience anything except in space. Hence space does not come from sensation but from ourselves.

Western Concept of Time. Plato defined time as the moving image of eternity. Aristotle thought of time as the numbering of motion with reference to before and after. Since every 'now' implies a 'before', he argued, time must be beginningless. Parmenides and his disciple Zeno did not accept the reality of time on the grounds of unreal change and motion. For Newton, time was absolute, flowing equably from the infinite past to the infinite future without relation to anything external. Kant considered time as an *a priori* form of the inner sense. He held that space is the form of the external sense and time the form of the internal sense. We do not experience time and space. In Kant's opinion, time is an empirically real but transcendentally ideal form of intuition. In Hegel's notion, space and time are creations of the Absolute Idea, occurring at certain stages of its development, in such a way that space appears first and then follows time.

Marxist Concept of Space and Time. In Marxist philosophy, both space and time are real and objective. "Space is an objectively real form of the existence of matter in motion. The concept of space expresses the co-existence and separateness of things, their extent and the order of their disposition in relation to one another."[94] "Time is an objectively real form of the existence of matter in motion. It characterizes the sequence of the occurrence of material processes, the separateness of the various stages of these processes, their duration and their development."[95]

Space and time are universal forms of the existence of matter. In this connection, Lenin wrote: "There is nothing in the world but matter in motion, and matter in motion cannot move otherwise than in space and time."[96]

The idealist philosophers deny the objectivity of space and time and assert that the concept exists in the human consciousness. Dialectical materialism refutes the idealist notions of space and time, theorized by philosophers such as Kant, Mach and Hegel. Lenin wrote: "The existence of nature *in time*, measured in millions of years, *prior* to the appearance of man and human experience, shows how absurd this idealist theory is."[97]

In Marxist idea, space and time are objective, eternal, boundless and infinite. They are inseparably linked with matter in motion. Just as there can be no matter outside space and time, so there is not and cannot be any space or time outside matter. Space and time exist only in and through material things. Engels has pointed out: "The two forms of existence of matter are naturally nothing without matter, empty concepts, abstractions which exist only in our minds."[98]

Space, time and matter are inseparably connected in dialectical materialism. In metaphysical materialism, however, space and time, being objective realities, are independent of matter. Space is empty receptacle in metaphysical materialism. In the classical mechanics of Newton, space and time were objective, independent of moving matter and unconnected with each other. For Newton, space and time were immutable and absolute. The notion on space and time of the Marxist philosophers differs from that of metaphysical materialism and Newton.

Einstein's Space-Time. Newtonian absolute space and absolute time were not accepted by Einstein, who established the relativity of space and time. Space is not independent of time and *vice versa*. Einstein conceived of space-time continuum. Space has got three dimensions. The time-dimension was added to the space-time continuum. Thus all events and objects are four-dimensional. Simultaneity can be established only within a given inertial system; it has no validity for observers in systems moving in relation to the given inertial system.

Hermann Minkowski (1864-1909) taught mathematics to Albert Einstein. It was Minkowski who joined the three dimensions of space to a fourth dimension, time. By considering the four dimensions as co-ordinates and getting their specification, he could precisely locate anything whatsoever. For such location, a set of world-points are required. These points become world-lines by virtue of the time-dimension. Thus every event or object has got a position on some set of world-lines. The time-dimension includes both past and future. Hence, all events, Minkowski said, are determinately present in the space-time continuum.

Einstein was very much motivated by the concept of the determined universe of Minkowski. He attempted to construct a unified field theory. In the four-dimensional space-time continuum, every event is determinately fixed. The space-time continuum is stretched out into world-lines with future occurrences as fixed as those in the past. According to this concept, the future is already determined and predictable. This effort of Einstein ran counter to the probabilistic features of quantum theory. Einstein could not accept the idea of the quantum physicists who pleaded for chance, randomness and probability in the functioning of the world. It was the firm belief of Einstein that God would not play dice with the universe.

Every entity, micro and macro, that exists in the universe, has position and momentum. The position refers to the three dimensions of length, breadth and height of space; the momentum refers to time that constitutes the fourth dimension. Thus, motion (change) has in-built implication of time. In the space-time concept of Einstein, time relates to change or motion or occurrence of events.

Space and Relative Space. Very often distinction is not maintained between space and Einstein's relative space. When Einstein says, "Space is relative", he means thereby the dimensions of length, breadth and height to be relative. Space, as an entity, as a subtle form of matter, is not relative, however. An example may be taken here. The water of a river is flowing. In connection with this flowing, four dimensions, viz., the length, breadth and height of water and time, are concerned. Water is flowing in space; water is flowing in time; actually water is flowing in space-time. But the water that flows is matter, different from its length, breadth and height. The three dimensions of matter are not themselves matter. A brick has got length, breadth and height. The brick, however, is not identical with its three dimensions. The length of a train in motion may be more or less to different observers. But the length of the train is not the train itself. Similarly, space which is a subtle form of matter has length, breadth and height that are relative. But space itself is not relative.

Quantum physics has accepted space as plenum. It generates particles; it reabsorbs particles. It is something positive. It is not void. Einstein has accepted space as a positive entity. Advaita Vedānta had a clearer understanding of space, much clearer than modern quantum physics.

Notes

1. Quoted in '*Dialectics of Nature*' by Frederick Engels, Progress Publishers, Moscow, 1974, p. 35.
2. Engels, F., *Dialectics of Nature*, Progress Publishers, Moscow, 1974, p. 36.
3. *Ibid.*, p. 39.
4. Pande, G.C., *Studies in the Origin of Buddhism*, 3rd ed., Motilal Banarsidass, Delhi, 1983, p. 424.
5. (a) Digha Nikāya, P.T.S. Edition IX. 53.
   (b) Katz, N., (Ed.), *Buddhist and Western Philosophy*, Sterling Publishers, New Delhi, 1981, pp. 267-86.
6. (a) As in [5b], p. 355.
   (b) Kirthisinghe, B.P., ed., *Buddhism and Science*, Motilal Banarsidass, Delhi, 1984.
7. Bahadur, K.P., *The Wisdom of Mīmāṃsā*, Sterling Publishers, New Delhi, 1983, p. XV. (Intr.).
8. Tai ŚB, Introduction.
9. BS, II.2.26; BG, II.16.
10. Mu ŚB, I.1.8.
11. BG, IX.10.
12. Engels, F., *Dialectics of Nature*, Progress Publishers, Moscow, 1974, p. 38.
13. Mu, I.1.7.
14. JS, X.3.68-70.
15. *Ibid.*, VI.4.35-42.
16. *Ibid.*, II.4.27.
17. *Ibid.*, V.4.22-4.
18. *Ibid.*, VI.4.43-7.
19. *Ibid.*, XI.2.20-2.
20. *Ibid.*, X.8.69-70.
21. *Ibid.*, X.6.64.
22. *Ibid.*, IX.2.58-60; X.6.3.
23. *Ibid.*, II.3.28-41.
24. *Ibid.*, IX.2.52-60.
25. Prabhākara, *Prakaraṇa*, p. 145.
26. *Ibid.*, p. 84.
27. *Tantravārttika*, p. 236.
28. *Mānameyodaya*, p. 186.
29. Prabhākara, *Prakaraṇa*.
30. Kumārila, *Śabara-Bhāṣya*.
31. *Bhāṣya of Praśastapāda*, p. 22.
32. *Tarkasaṅgraha*, p. 133.
33. *Vaiśeṣika Upaskāra*, II.2.11.
34. *Bhāṣā Pariccheda*, p. 46.
35. *Nyāyakandalī*, p. 22.
36. *Bhāṣā Pariccheda*, p. 94.
37. *Bhāṣya of Praśastapāda*, p. 25.

38. *Nyāyakandalī*, p. 25.
39. *Bhāṣya of Praśastapāda*, p. 64.
40. *Kiraṇāvalībhāskara*, p. 137.
41. *Vaiśeṣika-Sūtra*, V.2.26.
42. *Nyāyakandalī*, p. 65.
43. *Nyāyakandalī*, p. 22; *Bhāṣā Pariccheda*, p. 45.
44. *Nyāyasūtra*, II.1.23.
45. *Bhāṣā Pariccheda*, p. 45.
46. *Ibid.*, p. 46.
47. *Yoga-Bhāṣya*, III.52.
48. *Tattvakaumudī*, 10; *Yoga-Bhāṣya*, III.13.
49. *Yoga-Bhāṣya*, III.52.
50. *Yoga-Sūtra*, IV.33.
51. Mahadevan, T.M.P., *Introduction to Indian Philosophy*, Arnold-Heinemann, New Delhi, 1982, p. 98.
52. *Tattvārtha*, V.30.
53. *Tattvārtha-Sūtra*, IV.7.
54. *Pañcāstikāya*, 90.
55. *Ibid.*, 100.
56. *Abhidharmakośa*, I.5.5.
57. *Ibid.*, I.
58. *Ibid.*, I.4.28.
59. *Sphuṭārtha*, II.55.
60. *Viṁśatikā*, Verse 1.
61. *Laṅkāvatāra Sūtra*, 53-4.
62. *Mādhyamikā Kārikā* of Nāgārjuna, 24.19.
63. *Ibid.*, 9.5.
64. *Abhidharmakośa*, V.25-6.
65. *Mādhyamikā Vṛtti* of Chandrakīrtti, 1894, Calcutta.
66. *Abhidharmakośa*, V.24.
67. *Mādhyamikā Kārikā* of Nāgārjuna, 19.1-3.
68. *Ibid.*, 19.4.
69. *Milinda-Pañha*, IV.8.81.
70. *Ibid.*, II.2.17-20.
71. Conze, E., *Buddhist Thought in India*, George Allen & Unwin, London, 1983, pp. 165-6.
72. BSŚB, II.3.7.
73. BSŚB, II.2.24.
74. Chā ŚB, VIII.14.1.
75. Tai, II.1.1.
76. Chā, IV.10.4-5.
77. Ait, I.2.
78. BP, I.1.38; HV, I.1.35-36; TBrā, I.2.1.3; ṚV, X.129.1 & 3; ṚV, II.35; ṚV, X.82; Mu, II.1.3; MS, I.10; Pr, VI.4; Kaṭ, II.1.7.
79. Ait, I.3; III.2.
80. Chā, I.11.5.
81. Chā, I.9.1; VII.12.1; VIII.14.1.
82. ṚV, X.72.4.

83. BS, II.3.14.
84. Bṛ, III.8.8.
85. Chā, III.8.3.
86. Chā, III.8.4.
87. MāKā, II.14.
88. Śve, VI.2.
89. Mai, VI.15; MāKā, III.2, 19-20, 24, 27, 38; IV.14, 22, 38, 40; Mā ŚB, I.1; Kaṭ ŚB, II.1.5.
90. Śve, I.2.
91. AV, XIX.53-4; BG, X.33; XI.32; Bhā, III.5.26-8; VP, I.2.26; YVā, I.23.4.
92. Mai, VI.15.
93. BSŚB, IV.3.14.
94. *The Fundamentals of Marxist-Leninist Philosophy*, Progress Publishers, Moscow, 1974, p. 85.
95. *Ibid.*, pp. 85-6.
96. Lenin, V.I., *Materialism and Empirio-Criticism*, Collected Works, Vol. 14, p. 175.
97. *Ibid.*, p. 178.
98. Engels, F., *Dialectics of Nature*, Progress Publishers, Moscow, 1974, p. 312.

Chapter XII

CHANCE AND NECESSITY

Everything existing in the universe is the fruit of chance and necessity.

Democritus

Chaos is ubiquitous.

John Barrow

The ancient covenant is in pieces; man at last knows that he is alone in the unfeeling immensity of the universe, out of which he emerged only by chance. Neither his destiny nor his duty has been written down. The kingdom above or the darkness below: it is for him to choose.

Jacques Monod

THERE IS A WIDE RANGE of views on the notion of casuality *versus* acausality. Some thinkers hold that everything is strictly caused while others adhere to chance, randomness and probability to explain the functioning of the phenomenal world. The concept of cause arises in two different contexts, viz., empirical and cosmogonical. We observe empirical events; we try to know the doer of the event, the reason for which he did, his purpose of doing and the antecedent state of the effect. We try to pinpoint the conditions without which the event would not have occurred. This is the empirical context to which it is referred here. A few questions are asked about the universe as a whole. Who created the world? What were the precursor materials of which the world was made? Were some instruments used in making the world? Why was the world created? What was the purpose of the Creator in creating the world? This is the cosmogonical context in which causality is sought for. Since very ancient time, Indian philosophers have remained busy in their search for causality. The Greek philosopher Aristotle[1] was very much seized with this problem.

Causal Principle

Every effect is caused. "Every event has a cause." This is known as the Principle of Universal Causation. This principle was considered in the past to be universally and invariably true. Of course, the reverse of the statement was not always accepted to be necessary.

The Principle of Universal Causation has been rejected in modern philosophy. There may or may not be any cause of an event. Events may occur due to chance. The functioning of Nature may be purely random. This is the modern trend in thinking with reference to causality or acausality. Bertrand Russell writes:

> ....the word 'cause' is so inextricably bound up with misleading associations as to make its complete extrusion from the philosophical vocabulary desirable;.........
>
> The law of causality, I believe, like much that passes muster among philosophers, is a relic of a bygone age, surviving, like the monarchy, only because it is erroneously supposed to do no harm.[2]

Why do many modern philosophers despair of making any sense of the word 'cause'? Why do they associate so much muddle and complexity with the notion of 'cause'? We get the answer after being acquainted with some Western notions of 'cause'.

Temporal Precedence. Temporal precedence is a notion that is connected with cause. It is said that cause precedes effect. Whenever C causes E, C precedes E. This concept has been questioned. Can we rule out the possibility of simultaneous C and E? Can't E precede C? This second question will be discussed when the 'final cause' is taken up. But the first question cannot be ignored and evidence of simultaneity in certain cases has been obtained in quantum physics. Thus it may not be correct to say that cause *always* precedes effect. After Einstein's theory of relativity has been known, the words 'before', 'after' and 'simultaneous' have relational meanings and hence it is not safe to base the causal law on temporal precedence. Moreover, an event C preceding a second event E may not have any bearing on E and may be totally unrelated. Hence temporal precedence does not help the empirical identification of the cause of an effect.

Necessary Connection. When we say, "Cause C brings about

effect E", we have the idea that, there is some 'necessary connection' between C and E. When C occurs, E *must* occur. In our common experience, we do not observe such a 'must'. A cause C does not *always* produce an effect E. We know that by getting infection of Mycobacterium leprae a human being can get the disease, leprosy. But at the same time we also know that leprosy has not been caused even by injecting its causal micro-organism into some persons. All persons exposed to influenza virus and cold do not suffer from influenza; some are affected and some are not. It is not the causal agent only to produce the disease; many other factors such as the dose of infection, the resistant power of the individual's system and others decide the onset of the disease. The effect in this case is the result of the interaction of the infective agent, the effector organ and the environmental factors. Since the scientist does not *always* observe E due to C, he establishes the causal connection by taking help of statistical probability.

Constant Conjunction. David Hume (1711-76), while attacking the necessary connection theory, tried to establish cause as 'constant conjunction'.[3] If we say, C causes E, we mean thereby that C is constantly conjoined with E. In other words, David Hume said that "C is regularly followed by E". He stressed an invariable sequence in his notion on cause.

Thomas Reid[4] (1710-96) pointed out against the invariable sequence of David Hume. He argued: "Day is seen to be invariably followed by night and night by day. Can we say that day is the cause of night and *vice versa*?"

John Stuart Mill[5] (1806-73) defended Hume by trying to meet the criticism of Reid. He introduced the notion of 'unconditionality' in defining the notion of cause. Mill argued as follows: "If there be any meaning which confessedly belongs to the terms, it is *unconditionalness*...........The succession of day and night evidently is not necessary in this sense. It is conditional on the occurrence of other antecedents." According to Mill, day and night are not unconditionally conjoined, and hence, not causally connected. This argument of Mill does not seem sound and, by reintroducing the notion of necessity disguised as unconditionality, he could not defend Hume effectively.

Necessary Condition. The scientist equates the idea of cause with necessary condition. By 'necessary condition', he means a condition in the absence of which no effect occurs. In other words it may be expressed as: If not C, then not E. He designs experiments to test his causal hypothesis. He takes a control group which is not exposed to the suspected causal agent. He takes experimental group which is exposed to the causal agent. If he observes the effect in most individuals of the experimental group and does not observe in the control group, he thereby establishes the cause.

Sufficient Condition. John Stuart Mill made an attempt to remedy the defects in Hume's account of causality. He defined 'cause' as 'sufficient condition'. It is said that C is sufficient for the occurrence of E if, invariably, whenever C occurs, E occurs. Symbolically speaking, if C, then E, or in other words, if not E, then not C.

A seed becomes a seedling. A number of factors, viz., (1) seed, (2) moisture, (3) right temperature and (4) oxygen, are necessary for germination. Each of the conditions *alone* is necessary, but no one of them alone is sufficient. The combination of conditions which combinedly constitute the sufficient condition is the cause of the event according to Mill.

Mill defines cause as follows: "The cause is the sum total of the conditions, positive and negative taken together, the whole of the contingencies of every description, which being realized, the consequent (event) invariably follows."

In mill's 'cause', both cause and contributory factors are taken together. Mill says that there is no basis for such a distinction. He thinks that all are conditions and that all of them are causally relevant to the occurrence of the event.

Mill's notion of cause as 'sufficient conditions' is not identical with the general idea of cause used in day-to-day life. Secondly, even in scientific investigations, it is not so easy to determine and enumerate all the sufficient conditions of an event. The most precise scientific work of modern time has not been able to observe invariably E if there is C. C cannot be definitely ascertained and invariability in getting E if C is an idle dream in practical life.

Reasons and Reasonableness. In asking for the cause of an action, sometimes we want to know the reason of doing it. In daily life, we very often ask the question 'why'. John turned his head. Why did he turn his head? He might have done it to see a cat running. This is the reason or cause of his turning his head. He might have turned his head without knowing what he was doing. He might not have any justifiable reason for his action. We demand rationality, reasonableness or justifiability in order to accept something as a cause. According to this notion, any absurd or meaningless action has no cause. In the micro-world of micro-particles, movement of particles is random and apparently chaotic. Even in human society the so-called 'rational' man acts not infrequently without justifiable reason. There does not seem to be reason of some actions both in the living and non-living world and the macro- and the micro-world. Even if there may be reason, it may not be justifiable. It is not true that action of every entity of the world is based on rationality. Some actions have justifiable reasons; some others have reasons that are not justifiable; there are rather actions that are illogical, irrational, nonsensical and absurd. It is not correct to tag reason and justifiable reason to the causal principle.

Teleology and Final Cause. The concept of final cause has been working in the Western world from the time of Aristotle. It is used in two senses—empirical and ontological. A few examples may be taken here to illustrate the empirical sense.

A sperm fertilizes an egg to form a zygote. Varieties of embryological processes operate with the distant goal of making a complete foetus. All the embryological phenomena operate to serve a purpose and to meet a final goal.

A baby needs milk for its survival. Long before the baby is born, preparations are under way to build the milk plant—the mammary glands of the mother. Anatomical, physiological and biochemical processes become operative without the knowledge and conscious effort of the mother for the full-fledged development and ultimate functioning of the mammary glands. There is a definite purpose for all these actions; there is a definite final goal.

Milk is deficient in iron, which is a constituent of haemoglobin of blood. Without iron, blood cannot be formed and man cannot live. The baby has to depend on milk alone for the first few months of his/her life. In order to tide over the critical period of the first six months after birth, the foetus inside the uterus of the mother draws surplus iron from the mother's blood and makes a buffer stock in his/her spleen to meet the future contingency. The foetus does it without knowing it. The mother is unaware of it. Nevertheless, what is done in this case is purposeful and goal-oriented.

The electron spins around its own axis and revolves around the nucleus of the atom in an elliptical orbit. Had it been stationary, it would be dragged to the proton due to the attractive forces between the negative charge of the electron and the positive charge of the proton. The constant motion of the electron safeguards its survival. In its elliptical orbit it accelerates its speed when it is nearer the nucleus and relatively slows down its speed when it is farther away. The motion of the electron and the precisiveness of its speed depending upon its changing distance from the attracting nucleus are meant to be protective to its survival. Whether we consider the electron to be idiotic or intelligent is a different issue. But we have to admit that there is a purpose behind the motion of the electron.

Examples of teleology are numerous in both the living and non-living world. These few examples, cited here, refer to teleology of the empirical world.

In an integral sense, teleology refers to the total universe and Absolute God. According to the religious belief of the Western world, the final stage of the universe will be the culmination of the world-development. Finally, it will be the Ideally Perfect One, identical with the Absolute. The ideal, perfect and final state is exerting attractive force under the influence of which the past and the present cosmic processes have been and are being in operation. That final state is the final cause of the past, present and future of the world.

Newtonian physics has rejected teleology. Many scientists and philosophers in the post-Newtonian age have rejected teleology. Max Planck, the father of quantum physics, was in favour of teleological explanations of the empirical phenomena of the world. The ontological teleology does not belong to the domain of science and is not acceptable to the oriental religions. However, the teleological phenomena of the empirical world cannot be ignored, in spite of the fact that they may be explained or explained away.

We may restrict our discussion to purpose and final cause in connection with the notion of cause. A future goal cannot be the cause of the present action. The final product, the finished architecture, cannot, through any mechanism, control and influence the present actions. The chair is a finished product. It cannot be the cause of the wood or the carpenter. It cannot exert any influence on the making of the chair. The effect E comes before the cause C in the concept of final cause. Such a concept cannot be logically validated.

The carpenter has a purpose before he starts functioning. He intends to make a chair. He has a volition for it. He makes a design of the chair in his mind (may be on paper subsequently). He takes wood and works on it according to his mental model of the would-be chair. The intention or volition of the carpenter and his mental model of the chair are antecedent to the final product of the chair. Hence there is no question of E coming before C. The mental model of E is not E itself.

Action is very often done with a purpose projected to the future. Of course, it is not logically necessary to act with a purpose. There are many purposeless actions. However, the purpose is not the cause of the action wherever and whenever an action is purposeful.

The Western concepts of cause have been briefly described here. They are diverse and have empirical usefulness only, without any logical necessity. Some respectable modern philosophers like A.J. Ayer[6], R.G. Collingwood[7] and C.J. Ducasse[8] have found usefulness in the causal concept, although it was logically unacceptable to them.

Of course, the empirical use of the cause-concept cannot be undermined. Whether somebody is Bertrand Russell or Emmanuel Kant, he has to bother for the empirical use of cause when he suffers from tetanus, tuberculosis or lukaemia. He does ask the doctor what the cause of the disease is. The world is empirical; life is empirical; pleasure and pain are empirical; and suffering is empirical. Hence anything empirical is not unimportant for us.

David Hume says that there is no such thing as *a priori* knowledge of causes. "There are no objects", wrote Hume, "which by the mere survey, without consulting experience, we can determine to be the causes of any other; and no objects, which we can certainly determine in the same manner not to be the causes."

This is an important point which has confused many philosophers. They have erred by mixing up two issues, viz., the Causal Principle (the Principle of Universal Causation) and the empirical methodology of the identification of a specific cause of a specific action or effect. The empirical identification of the cause of an effect is not the business of philosophy. It is done through experience by controlled observation and intelligent analysis.

It is not correct to think that an effect has necessarily a single cause or a cause has a single effect. There may be single-cause-single-effect, single-cause-multiple-effects and multiple-causes-single-effect relationships. These may be represented as follows:

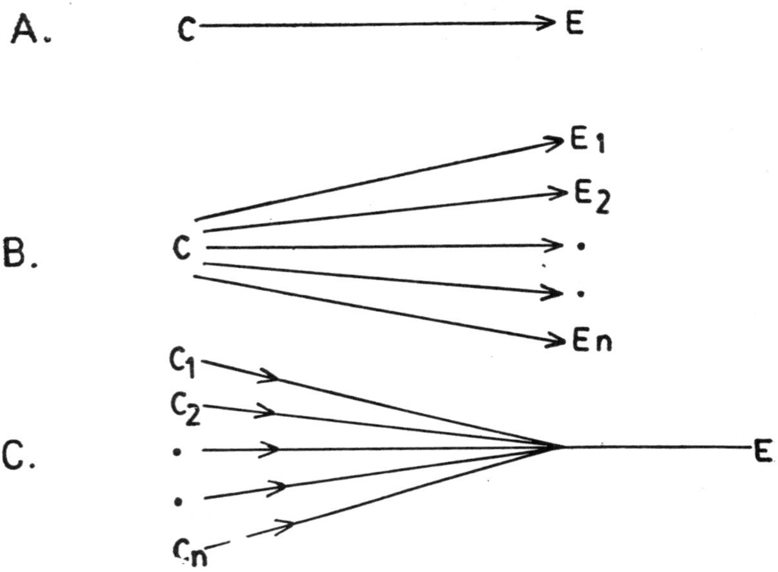

Fig. 12.1

The organism, Mycobacterium leprae causes leprosy in man. No other organism can cause this disease. This is an example of a single-cause-single-effect. Alcoholism causes liver cirrhosis, hypertension and hyperacidity. This is an example of a single-cause-multiple-effects. Virus-infection, excessive smoking, excessive betel-chewing, excessive drinking or over-exposure to radiation may cause cancer. This is an example of multiple-causes-single-effect.

Science makes distinction of the primary cause, the secondary cause(s) and the contributory factors. A person may be primarily infected with the influenza virus. Due to his loss of vitality, his lower respiratory tract may be invaded with the bacteria that are normally present in the tract. Exposure to cold may contribute to the aggravation of the disease. In this example, the influenza virus is the primary cause, the bacteria of the respiratory tract are the secondary causes and chill is the contributory factor.

The scientist does not observe any necessary connection or constant conjunction between cause and effect. A cause which produces an effect in ninety per cent of the cases may fail to evince the effect in ten per cent individuals. A cause may produce effect E_1 in sixty per cent cases and E_2 in the rest forty per cent cases. In scientific experimentation, probability of occurrence of an event is well appreciated and statistical analysis is resorted to especially in biological investigations where individual variations are not uncommon. There is nothing like certainty in the empirical identification of cause and effect. The finding is probable, not certain; and the degree of probability is mathematically estimated and indicated.

Acausality in Quantum Physics

Every event was thought to be caused in classical physics. Newton considered that it would be possible to predict the entire course of the future if we knew the position and momentum of every particle of the universe. The universe of Minkowski, the mathematics teacher of Einstein, was determined. In the four-dimensional space-time co-ordinates, every object and every event are fixed; the past, the present and the future are all determined. Einstein believed in a deterministic universe and was very much reluctant to accept that God plays dice with the world.

In contrast to the classical physics, quantum physics became acausal. This idea started with Heisenberg's principle of indeterminacy. We cannot know the position and momentum of even *one* particle precisely. According to quantum physics, it would be impossible to predict the future. Even for the present, Heisenberg has said in his paper in the Zeitschrift, "We *cannot* know, as a matter of principle, the present in all its details."

The conclusion of acausality derived from Heisenberg's principle of indeterminacy can also be obtained from the other findings of quantum physics—the wave mechanics, the Heisenberg-Born-Jordan matrices and Dirac's q numbers. In 1927, Niels Bohr presented the Copenhagen interpretation of quantum mechanics that altogether rejected the concept of causality. The 'collapse of the wave function', the principle of complementarity, the participatory universe, the many-worlds hypothesis, the vacuum fluctuation, the inflationary universe and many such other notions of quantum physics could not accommodate the principle of causality.

Scientists working on particle physics observed particles appearing from nowhere and disappearing into nowhere; they noticed particles of higher masses originating from those of lower masses and *vice versa*. The micro-world appears to be chaotic. Particles rush about, collide against one another and rush in other directions for further collision against others. Chaos prevails in the total scenario of the micro-world.

Appearance of a particle, disappearance of a particle, collision of particle p_1 against particle p_2, a particle traversing a particular path and, in general, all events of the micro-world occur randomly. In the world of particles, with which quantum physics is principally concerned, all events occur by chance alone. The would-be occurrence of an event has a probability, not a certainty. By means of statistical laws, one can predict the probability of the occurrence of an event. But that the predicted event must occur cannot be foretold. Quantum physicist observes chaos in the micro-world; but, amid chaos, statistical regularities are observed. Hence acausality is accepted in quantum physics.

This concept of acausality exerted profound influence on philosophers, litterateurs and thinkers in the 1930s and afterwards. This was fostered in its extremity and even great thinkers did not hesitate to say that the world came into existence by chance alone, that it functions in a chaotic way and that there is no place of order and rationality in the world, where everything and every action are absurd. The opinion of Jacques Monod may be quoted here:

> The enigma remains, masking the answer to a question of profound interest. Life appeared on earth: what, *before the event*, were the chances that this would occur? The present structure of the biosphere certainly does not exclude the possibility that the decisive event occurred *only once*. Which would mean that its *a priori* probability was virtually zero.
> ...."Among all the events possible in the universe the *a priori* probability of any particular one of them occurring is next to zero. Yet the universe exists; particular events must occur in it, the probability of which (before the event) was infinitesimal. At the present time we have no justification for either asserting or denying that life made only one single appearance on earth, and that, as a consequence, before it appeared its chances of occurring were almost nil.
> This idea is displeasing to biologists, not only because they

are scientists. It offends our very human tendency to believe that everything real in the world is necessary, and rooted in the very beginning of things. We must be constantly on guard against this notion, this powerful feeling of destiny. Immanence is alien to modern science. Destiny is written as and while, not before, it happens.[9]

Cause and Effect in Marxist Philosophy

The Marxist philosophers do not reject the principle of causality. Frederick Engels says: "In order to understand the separate phenomena we have to tear them out of the general inter-connection and consider them in isolation and *then* the changing motions appear, one as cause and the other as effect."[10]

V.G. Afanasyev, a Marxist philosopher, defines cause as follows:

> A phenomenon or group of interacting phenomena which precede and give rise to another phenomenon or group are called *cause*. The phenomenon produced by the action of the cause is called *effect*.[11]

Marxist philosophy holds that cause always precedes effect, but does not consider succession in time as an adequate criterion of cause. A cause not only precedes the effect, but also inevitably *gives rise* to the latter.

Cause is differentiated from *occasion* in Marxist philosophy. Occasion is an event E_1 which immediately precedes another event E_2 and sets E_2 in motion; but E_2 is not necessarily engendered or determined by E_1. Occasion and effect are superficially and inessentially connected.

Cause is also distinguished from the *conditions* in which it operates. The bacterium *Clostridium tetani* causes the disease known as titanus. This organism does this in the absence of oxygen or in anaerobiosis. In this case, anaerobiosis is the condition and not the cause.

According to Marxist philosophy, there is no event which is acausal. The universal character of causality is expressed in the following paragraph:

> The causal connection of phenomena is objective and universal in character. All phenomena in the world, all changes and

> processes must be induced by certain causes. There is no such thing as a causeless phenomenon, nor could there be. Every phenomenon must have its cause. We are able to detect the causal connection of phenomena with varying degrees of accuracy. The causes of some are still unknown to us, but they objectively exist. Thus, medicine has not yet fully discovered the cause of cancer, but this cause exists and will eventually be discovered.[12]

Causality, in Marxist philosophy, is objective. It has not been introduced into reality by man's reason or by some supernatural force. The law of causality leaves no room for God or any kind of miracle, mysticism, or the like. The Marxist understanding of causality is opposed to the religious interpretation of the world, according to which God is the cause of everything existing. Religions hold that God created the world and He refashions and supports it. Teleology is also preached by religions. According to this the development of the world is the realization of the preordained aims of God. Engels ridiculed teleology by saying that cats were created to eat mice and mice to be eaten by cats and that all of Nature was created with some definite purpose of wise God. Marxist philosophy discards supernaturalism, miracles and God; it rejects teleology that upholds preordained aims. According to Marxism, natural causes and objective laws decide the development of everything. But Nature does not and cannot have any purpose. Only human beings may act with some aim, objective and goal. These aims, however, are not pre-ordained by any Almighty, who does not exist. Even the human aims are determined by objective causes, by the entire course of historical development.

The law of causality says that all phenomena are causally conditioned. Philosophers who acknowledge this law are *determinists*. Philosophers who deny this law are indeterminists. Mechanistic determinism prevailed in natural science in the 17th and 18th centuries. It reduces the whole diversity of causes to outward mechanical influences. It is well applicable to the movement of macro-bodies and functioning of machineries. But it is erroneous to explain all biological processes, mental activities and social developments in terms of mechanistic determinism. The phenomena of the micro-world are not mechanistically determined.

Hence quantum mechanics which operates in the micro-world does not obey the laws of mechanistic determinism. Dialectical materialism is opposed to both indeterminism and mechanistic determinism.

Quantum physicists, after realizing the inapplicability of mechanistic determinism to micro-objects, declared the collapse of determinism and the triumph of indeterminism. They discarded the law of causality and explained the quantum phenomena on the basis of chance alone. Marxist philosophy accepts the law of causality and denies the so-called collapse of determinism.

In dialectical materialism, both necessity and chance are recognized. An event is a necessity when it must take place under definite conditions. Necessity is constant and stable for the given phenomenon. It follows from the essence of the phenomenon. In contrast, an event is a chance when it might or might not occur in the given conditions. If it is chance, the event need not necessarily happen. Chance does not follow from the nature of the given object. It is unstable and temporary. The Marxist philosopher says that chance is not causeless; but its cause is not in the object itself.

The Marxist philosophers are very much critical of the acausal concept or the subjectivity of the causal concept of the Western philosophers. The Marxists believe in the objectivity of the law of causality. The English philosopher Hume denied the objectivity of causal connection. He says that we obtain our knowledge of the causal connection of phenomena from our experience. This is regarding the identification of cause and effect and there is nothing wrong about it. But Hume reduced experience to subjective sensations and denied the objectivity of causality. Through our experience we come to know that one event follows another. Hume says that logically we cannot deduce that the former is the cause of the latter. He further says that there is no ground for us to draw conclusions about the future from our experiences of the past and the present. Hume's version of causality boils down to the fact that causality is merely a sequential, habitual connection of sensation and idea, on the basis of which expectation of that connection is predicted. The Marxist philosophers do not agree with Hume on the lack of objectivity of causality. In this connection, Engels wrote:

> ......the regular sequence of certain natural phenomena can by itself give rise to the idea of causality: the heat and light that come with the sun; but this affords no proof, and to that extent Hume's scepticism was correct in saying that a regular *post hoc* can never establish a *propter hoc*. But the activity of human beings *forms the test of* causality. If we bring the sun's rays to a focus by means of a concave mirror and make them act like the rays of an ordinary fire, we thereby prove that heat comes from the sun.[13]

The causal view of Emmanuel Kant was also idealistic like Hume's. But Kant differed from Hume in a significant way. For Hume, causality was merely a habitual connection of sensations. In contrast, Kant considered the existence of causal connection as necessary. Of course, his causality did not exist in the objective world; it existed in the mind. It existed as an *a priori* innate category of intellect. Our various perceptions are linked together into a judgment on the basis of this innate mental character.

The idealistic views of Hume and Kant on causality exerted profound influence on the neo-Kantians and the positivists. The Machists were very much vociferous about the acausality of phenomena. Ernst Mach did not recognize any cause and effect in Nature. He asserted that all forms of causality originate from our subjective desires. Bertrand Russell held that the concept of cause is a pre-scientific generalization which serves only as a guide to action. Russell wrote: "Belief in the external causation of certain kinds of experiences is primitive, and is, in a certain sense, implicit in animal behaviour."[14] According to Hume, causality is based on human habit. On the concept of cause, Russell agrees with Hume except on this point. In the opinion of Russell the concept of cause is not based on human habit; it is based on animal faith which has become deeply embedded in language.

'Cause' has gone out of fashion in contemporary philosophy. Many modern philosophers insist on the expulsion of the word 'cause' from philosophical terminology. They reject the concept of causality and brand it as obsolete and outdated. They replace the law of causality by the law of *functional connection*. They are enamoured by mathematical jargon and take pleasure to emulate the formula Y = f (X), where Y is a function of X. Accordingly, it is prohibited to say that event A causes event B; this much can be said that A and B depend on each other, A is always accompanied by B, A precedes B, or, B follows A.

Marxist philosophy discards this concept of causality, which is really the concept of acausality, propounded by the quantum physicists and many contemporary philosophers. At the same time, it does realize that the causal inter-connections of phenomena are only one type of inter-connections out of many, which are also important. Lenin wrote: "Causality, as usually understood by us, is only a small particle of universal inter-connection, but.........a particle not of the subjective but of the objectively real inter-connection."[15]

Dialectical materialism is opposed to the metaphysical separation of cause and effect. There is no effect without cause; there is no cause without effect. Cause and effect are inseparably connected. Effect, which is engendered by cause, exerts reverse action on the latter. Thus, the relationship between cause and effect is reversible. Due to this two-way action, one phenomenon may be the cause in one connection and the effect in another. "What is characteristic of causality is this endless chain of reciprocal connections, the *universal interaction* of objects and phenomena of the world where each link is simultaneously both a cause and an effect."[16]

Concept of Cause in Advaita Vedānta

'Cause' has been defined in different ways. With reference to the concept of cause in Advaita Vedānta, a definition is furnished here: "A cause is an agent of an action, in which modification or transformation may or may not be involved, or, a precursor material which is modified into a product."

The etymological meaning of the Sanskrit word *kāraṇa* (cause) is "that which acts". Thus the agent of any action or the subject (*kartā*) of any activity is the cause of that action. The term used in Advaita Vedānta for action is *kriyā*. Action like sitting, walking, laughing and sleeping does not bring about any modification or transformation. Action of becoming such as 'clay becoming pot', 'gold becoming necklace' or 'water becoming ice' involves transformation or modification. If C becomes E, the product is E. The product is called effect in the causal theory. The effect is called *kārya* in Advaita Vedānta. Transformation or modification may or may not be involved in a *kriyā* or action. The agent (*kartā*) of an action, with or without involvement of modification or transformation, is the operative or efficient cause (*nimitta kāraṇa*). In actions where modification is involved, the precursor substance which becomes the product is the substantial or material cause (*upādāna kāraṇa*). Functioning without becoming is an action. Becoming is also an action. When we say, "C becomes E", we mean thereby that C is the substantial or material cause of E. In an action of modification or transformation, there is necessarily change. In any change, the precursor substance is the substantial cause and the product is the effect. A carpenter makes a chair out of wood. In this case, the carpenter is the efficient cause, the wood is the material cause and the chair is the product. There are other types of modifications where the precursor substance is itself modified into the product without the agency of any external being or thing. The decay of a radioactive element may be taken as an example. Uranium-238 breaks down by a series of decays to lead-206 by emitting eight alpha particles in the process. In such a process, no external agency is involved. Uranium-238 acts as both efficient and material cause in the decay process.

The concept of cause of Advaita Vedānta, as defined here, is clear and specific. It says: the subject of an action is the efficient cause of that action; if the action involves modification, the precursor substance which is modified is the material cause. What has been said may be expressed in propositional form. Śaṅkara has done this by saying (*yat kāryaṁ tat sa-kartṛkam*): Every verb has got a subject; wherever there is an action, there is a doer of that action. Such a statement is analytical. Being *a priori*, it does not need empirical verification for proving its truth or falsity. Thus, every action has an efficient cause. It is a formal truth. Secondly, in every modification, there is a precedent state C and a consequent state E. Whenever we say, "E is a product", we mean thereby that something C has been modified into E. In every sort of transformation, a preceding form is changed into a consequent form. If we analyze the concept 'transformation' or 'modification' (*vikāra*), we must reach the conclusion that every product (consequent state in the process of transformation) has necessarily a precursor material (precedent state in the process of transformation). This precursor material is the material cause of the action of modification or transformation. That an action involving modification has necessarily a material cause is *a priori* truth.

What has been said here in connection with the concept of cause of Advaita Vedānta is true universally. A carpenter makes a wooden chair. The action of chair-making has got two causes here, viz., the carpenter as the efficient cause and the wood as the material cause. In this example, the efficient cause is external to the material cause and has a separate identity. In the world of micro-particles, particle p_1 changes to particles p_2 and p_3. Here p_1 is both the efficient and material cause of the action of particle transformation. Particle p_1 may jump and dance without undergoing any modification. In such an action there is no product. But the action of jumping and dancing is done by the particle itself. In this case, the particle is the efficient cause of the action. According to the law of causality of Advaita Vedānta, it is not necessary to introduce a human being or supernatural being as the doer of an action. The quantum-physicist observes particle p_1 appearing suddenly from nowhere. He asks himself: "Is this *creatio ex nihilo*?" "Did something appear from nothing?" Particle p_1 changes to particles p_2 and p_3. The product particles p_2 and p_3 have mass higher than that of p_1. The quantum physicist asks himself: "Does it not violate the law of conservation of mass and energy?" It has already been said that the micro-particles are themselves the efficient causes of their own actions. If the quantum physicist did not find a God or a man as the mover of the particle, he could not establish acausality. The particle itself can function as its own mover. Śaṅkara does recognize consciousness of all entities in Nature.[17] By virtue of this consciousness, every entity can function as its own efficient cause. Advaita Vedānta does accept the fact that Nature acts.[18] Hence, in the actions of the entities of Nature, the doer of the action may be either the entity itself or some other agency external to the entity. Advaita Vedānta rejects the idea of *creatio ex nihilo*. Nothing cannot be something; something cannot be nothing; only something can be something else.[19] In this concept, there is no mention of what that something is. That something may be matter, may be energy, may be space or field (*ākāśa*), or may be unmanifested *Prakṛti* or *Māyā*. It is not necessary for that something to be sense-perceptible. We cannot perceive everything by our senses. We cannot claim that whatever cannot be perceived by us does not have existence. Such a misconception is the cause of the erroneous deduction of the quantum physicist about the appearance of particles from nowhere and their disappearance into nowhere. The concept of vacuum, of the creation of particles from vacuum and of the dissolution of particles into vacuum is dangerously misguiding. Vacuum, nothingness or *śūnya* is a non-sensical concept in Advaita Vedānta. Plenum (*pūrṇa*) is recognized by Advaita Vedānta; but *śūnya* is rejected. Space or *ākāśa* is not void in Advaita Vedānta. Particles appear from space and disappear into it. Space is a positive entity. It is converted into particles and particles are reconverted into it. This is a phenomenon of transformation. This is not a phenomenon of nothing becoming something and something becoming nothing. Moreover, the transformation of the energy of motion into mass of particle and *vice versa* may be taken into account in the process of particle transformation. Thus, it has been made clear that, in the micro-world of particles, every action is caused, that an action may have efficient cause only, or may have both efficient and material causes.

The earlier quantum physicists did not realize the importance of field and space in the creation and dissolution of particles. The idea of void was still predominating their thought process. This situation has changed in the latter half of the twentieth century. Now the quantum physicists have appreciated the role of space in the creation and dissolution of particles. In the process of appearance of a particle from space, the particle is the product and space is both the efficient and the material cause. In the reverse process, i.e., in the dissolution of a particle into space, the particle is both the efficient and the material cause and space is the product.

The quantum physicist observes chaos in the micro-world. All micro-particles appear and disappear chaotically. They move randomly. They run a mad race, collide and annihilate one another. They behave erratically. They function irrationally and aimlessly. They don't have any objective; they don't have any goal; they don't have any reason. Their appearance is meaningless; their existence is meaningless; their annihilation is meaningless. All of the micro-world seems to be absurd. There is no law in the micro-world where every entity functions eccentrically as it takes. The quantum physicist asks himself: "What is the reason of particle p_1 or p_2 to act in this way or that way? What is the purpose of such random action? What is the goal of the chaos? Why is this absurdity?" No satisfactory answer to these questions is available. And so the quantum physicist concludes that there is nothing like causality.

This is, however, an erroneous conclusion. The non-dualist philosopher says that the concept of cause of Advaita Vedānta does not connote anything such as purpose, reason, rationality, justifiability, objective and goal. The action may be rational or irrational, wise or absurd, purposeful or non-sensical; if it is action, it has a doer and that doer is the efficient cause. If the action involves modification, a product is the outcome of the action and the precursor of the product is the material cause of the action. The concept of cause does not entail anything else. Advaita Vedānta holds that God has no necessity of creating the world[20] and that it is merely for the sports (*līlā*)[21] of God, who, as the magician, conjures the world-magic. Māyā is in the control of God. Māyā conceals and projects. Advaita Vedānta, which considers the phenomenal world as the sports of God and as illusion, does not expect reason and justifiability of each and every action of each and every entity of the world. Although man is conscious, his consciousness is very much limited. Matter which is insentient has also very limited consciousness due to reflection of the Universal Consciousness. In spite of this fact that Consciousness is reflected, even man is affected more by Nescience (*avidyā*) than by knowledge. For every action to be reasonable and justifiable, the doer of the action must have full knowledge. Where is the question of sound reasoning and justifiability in the magical performances, illusory appearances and deluding functioning of Māyā?

There is, however, a misconception about the lawlessness and causelessness of chaos. It has already been said that every action has cause, either efficient or efficient and material. Random actions are actions and hence have causes. There are also laws for random actions. The whole discipline of statistics has been developed to discover the laws of chance actions. A familiar example may be cited here to explain the order in chaos. The sex-ratio in the human society is ordinarily maintained at about 50:50. No individual regulates it. There is built-in mechanism in Nature, by which it is self-regulated in unison with the laws of probability of statistics. Ejaculated semen carrying millions of sperms enters the female genitalia. The sperms enter into the uterus and participate in a sweeming race. The sperm that first reaches the ovum and enters into the latter is the winner. The sperm that fertilizes the ovum may carry an X or Y chromosome, since each sperm contains either X or Y chromosome. Every ovum invariably carries an X chromosome. The fertilized zygote thus becomes XX or XY. The former combination gives rise to a female child and the latter a male one. Since a sperm has got 50 per cent chance of carrying an X or Y chromosome, the probability of producing a male or a female baby in a *large* population is always 50 per cent (this is marginally altered due to other complicating factors such as presence of lethal genes and others). Whether an individual foetus will be male or female cannot be predicted before fertilization takes place. But the total sex-ratio in the population at large can be predicted with almost one hundred per cent precision. The seemingly mad race of the sperms in the female genital tract is chaotic. But, below the surface of the chaos, order prevails. Whether some phenomenon occurs by following the binomial theorem of statistics or some other phenomenon follows the normal curve of error, it boils down to the fact that there is order (*ṛta*) in disorder (*anṛta*). As Śaṅkara has said, order and disorder are coupled (*satyānṛte mithunīkṛtya*)[22]. All the equations of quantum mechanics depict laws of Nature in mathematical language; the micro-world with which these laws are concerned is chaotic, but these laws present a picture of order. Laws and order are interrelated. There cannot be laws without order and *vice versa*. Disorder is superficial, but order is deep; disorder is superstructure, but order is base. Thus, it is not correct to say that the whole world is absurd.

Heisenberg's principle of indeterminacy has tremendously influenced the quantum physicists to think in terms of acausality. This is the result of sheer misconception. We can determine the position of a micro-particle with accuracy. We can also determine the momentum of the same micro-particle with accuracy. But the higher is our precision in the determination of position, the lower is our precision in the determination of momentum, and *vice versa*. Heisenberg says that it is impossible to accurately determine both the position and the momentum of any particle. The uncertainty principle does not contravene the law of causality of Advaita Vedānta. The causal law of Advaita Vedānta is formal and is universally true. If there is an action (*kriyā*), there must be an operative cause (*kartā* or subject) of the action. If there is some change, modification or transformation in the action, something must be changed to something else. The preceding stage of the transformation is the substantial cause and the consequent stage of the transformation is the effect or product. If man cannot determine something with exact precision, that does not prove that a verb (*kriyā*) has no subject (*kartā*) and that a product or a changed substance has no preceding stage. Identification of cause is an empirical activity and there may or may not be accuracy in such activity. Since sense-perception is necessary in identification of cause and effect, we may have limitations in a number of cases to accurately determine the exact cause of a particular effect. But, our success, partial success or failure in the accurate determination of the cause and effect does not affect the causal law which is *a priori* in Advaita Vedānta. The world which is a product of Māyā and which exists in illusion and delusion cannot be a world of precision. Advaita Vedānta does assert the uncertainty of everything of the world. The ever-changeable world (*jagat*) and the certain world are contradictory concepts; Advaita Vedānta supports the former and rejects the latter. Hence it is not logical to say that the law of causality is violated by the uncertainty which is inherent in the world.

Cosmogonical Causes in Advaita Vedānta

The law of causality of Advaita Vedānta, which has been described in the foregoing paragraphs, refers to the world-phenomena. This does not say anything about the cause of the world-creation—both efficient and material cause. Advaita Vedānta has definite views on this aspect of causation.

Advaita Vedānta holds that the world is not eternal. It had a beginning; it will have an end; the world-cycle will be repeated *ad infinitum*. The world did not originate from nothing; on its termination, it will not disappear as nothing. The material cause of the world is Māyā; the final reservoir into which the world will be dissolved is Māyā.[23] The universe is manifested. Māyā is unmanifested (*avyakta*). Creation is the manifestation of the unmanifest; dissolution is the reverse process.

According to Advaita Vedānta, Māyā is insentient and hence cannot be the efficient cause. God controls Māyā and is the efficient cause[24] of the universe.

The Marxist philosophers do not accept any cause of the world. In their view, there is no God, the world was never created, it ever existed in the past and it will ever exist in the future. It has already been discussed that the world cannot be eternal. Further, the cosmologists have already got empirical evidence for the beginning of the world and they are theorizing on the end of the world. The universe was born with the formation of the cosmic egg and started functioning with the big bang explosion. What was it before the cosmic egg was formed? The scientists do not have an answer. They express their dilemma, as is evidenced from the following paragraph:

> On the far side of the Big Bang is a mystery so profound that physicists lack the words even to think about it. Those willing to go out on a limb guess that whatever might have been before the Big Bang was, like a vacuum, unstable. Just as there is a tiny chance that virtual particles will pop into existence in the midst of subatomic space, so there may have been a tiny chance that the nothingness would suddenly be convulsed by the presence of a something.[25]

Science has not solved this mystery. It will never solve as long as it remains confined to matter only. The scientists become escapists when they confront the problem of cosmogony. The concept of acausality that was erroneously deduced from the findings of quantum physics consoled the twentieth century materialists who were already afraid of the ghost of God. But escapism does not solve the riddle of cosmogony. Hence the mystery continues to be a mystery.

Of all religions and all philosophical systems, Advaita Vedānta is the only system that solves the mystery of cosmology and cosmogony. It takes care of all of science and presents an integral picture which answers all probable queries satisfactorily.

Concept of Acausality in Advaita Vedānta

Brahman is attributeless and functionless. It does not change. Brahman, B, remains as B (B→B→B→B→······→B). Thus there is no previous state of Brahman; it is unborn, beginningless and causeless.[26] Since Brahman is actionless, it cannot be the efficient cause of any activity of the world.[27] Brahman does not undergo any sort of modification. Hence it does not give rise to any product. Thus Brahman is not the material cause of anything of the world.[28] Brahman is endless.[29] It continues to be B without any termination. The concept of cause and effect is not applicable to Brahman which is acausal.

God is also causeless. Timeless Brahman is reflected in its power Māyā and this cosmic, reflected Consciousness is God. Since Brahman and Māyā are timeless and without birth and death, so also is God. Nobody or nothing is the cause of God who is also not the material cause of anything. But God is not actionless and attributeless. He controls Māyā that operates. He creates, sustains and destroys the world. Thus He is the efficient cause of the world.

There are some references[30] in the scriptures, where Brahman has been considered as both the efficient and material cause of the world. Such scriptural statements may be interpreted in a figurative sense. Advaita Vedānta is non-dualistic. It accepts Brahman and nothing second to Brahman as reality. Thus God and Māyā are not second and third entities. There is no Māyā without Brahman and so also there is no God without Brahman. For this reason, the causal role of God and Māyā has been figuratively ascribed to Brahman.

Advaita Vedānta considers that action is not possible without efficient cause, that modification is not possible without material cause, and that causality is not applicable to the functionless, attributeless and changeless Absolute.

Identity of Cause and Effect in Advaita Vedānta

Different views are expressed on the relation between cause and effect. The Nyāya-Vaiśeṣika school does not find any identity between cause and effect. Its causal theory is called *ārambha-vāda* (the theory of new beginnings). According to it, the effect does not pre-exist in the cause but originates freshly. The effect is different from its cause. The Nyāya contends that the whole is something other than the parts from which it is made up.[31] In the later Nyāya, the effect is defined as the 'counter-entity of the antecedent negation' (*prāgabhāvapratiyogī*)[32]. *Asatkāryavāda* is another name of *ārambha-vāda.*

The causal theory of Sāṅkhya is called *satkārya-vāda* or *pariṇāma-vāda*. It opposes the causal theory of Nyāya. In the statement, C becomes E, the Sāṅkhya means thereby that it was a manifestation as E of what was in latent condition in C. The effect exists already in the cause in a potential state. The causal operation makes patent what is latent in the cause. Causation is the actualization of the pre-existing potentialities. It is nothing more than manifestation of transformation (*pariṇāma*).

Advaita Vedānta accepts the *satkārya-vāda* of Sāṅkhya, but rejects the notion of transformation. To distinguish from the theory of transformation, Advaita Vedānta has got the theory of phenomenal appearance (*vivarta-vāda*). Brahman is immutable; B remains as B; it never becomes non-B. Again, Brahman is non-dual, there being nothing second to it. We can talk about transformation when B becomes C, D, E or anything else. There cannot be transformation when the non-dual B remains as B. But, in spite of the fact that Brahman is immutable and there is nothing else other than the non-dual Brahman, we experience the world and its multiplicity. How do we explain this? Advaita Vedānta does it by the *vivarta-vāda*.[33] There is no real transformation of the whole or part (Brahman is partless)[34] of Brahman into the world. The world is but an illusory appearance in Brahman. Multiple forms appear; a name is given to each form by the experiencer. Thus the whole world of name and form (*nāma-rūpa*)[35] is not real in the absolute sense. The *vivarta* world is empirical and relative (*vyāvahārika*); it is not absolute (*pāramārthika*).

There is a rope. It gives an illusory appearance of a snake. Here R is the substratum (*adhiṣṭhāna*)[36] and S is its illusory appearance. According to Śaṅkara's terminology, it is superimposition (*adhyāsa*), one appearing as the attributes of another (*anyasya anyadharmāvibhāsaḥ*)[37]. The universe is superimposed on Brahman. But for this superimposition, there is no *vivarta* and there is no world.

Advaita Vedānta rejects the idea that there is some necessary connection (*samavāya*) between cause and effect.[38] Vaiśeṣika accepts a non-material or non-inherent (*asamavāyī*)[39] cause. The threads that are the causal substrates of the cloth are the material cause of the cloth. But the threads remain as bundle of threads unless they are conjoined. The conjunction (*saṁyoga*) is the non-inherent cause. This *asamavāyī* or non-inherent cause is not admitted by both Sāṅkhya and Vedānta that hold that only the efficient cause may be non-inherent.

The identity of cause and effect has been stressed by Advaita Vedānta.[40] For this purpose, cause means material cause and not efficient cause. Māyā, the power of Brahman, is the material cause of the world. The cause, Māyā, and the effect, the world, are identical. There is no difference among gold, gold-necklace, gold-ring and gold-bangles as far as the gold-substance is concerned. The same substance has assumed different forms and names. Without the form, there is no name, and without name and form, there is the original substance only. Two atoms of hydrogen and one atom of oxygen combine to form a molecule of water (H_2O). Whether it is liquid water, solid ice or gaseous steam, it is H_2O only in substance. The primordial substance (*Māyā* or Mūla *Prakṛti*), S, is formless and potentially existent. It assumes forms and is manifested as S_1, S_2, S_3, ..., S_{n-1}, S_n. The subscripts 1, 2, 3,......, n – 1 and n stand for forms. If considered as devoid of forms, the subscripts disappear, but the substantiality, S, remains unchanged. If S is the material cause of S_1, S_2, S_3,.........,S_{n-1} and S_n, the substantiality of the cause and the effects is identical. This is exactly what Advaita Vedānta says. Māyā (the material cause of the world) and the world (the product of Māyā) are substantially identical.

It, however, may be mentioned here that Advaita Vedānta does not accept the identity of Brahman and the world. Brahman is Self (*Ātman*) and the world is not-Self (*anātman*). It would be a self-contradictory statement if we say "Self and not-Self are identical". Brahman is formless, attributeless and changeless whereas the world is just the opposite. Śaṅkara compares the subject (*viṣayī* or *ātman*) with light and the object (*viṣaya* or world) with darkness.[41] In Advaita Vedānta, God and the world are also not identical. God is the efficient cause of the world. Clay and pot are substantially identical. But pot and potter can never be identical. The efficient cause and the product are different. Of course, in a figurative sense, Brahman and the world are said to be identical in Advaita Vedānta.[42] Śaṅkara says that the world-effects have no existence apart from Brahman (*brahma-vyatirekeṇa kāryajātasyābhava iti gamyate*)[43]. By this, he does not affirm the absolute oneness of Brahman and the world; he only denies their difference.

The whole world, we partly experience and partly don't, is a product of Māyā. Our own bodies are products of Māyā. Substantially, the precursor substance or the material cause which is Māyā and the world-products including our own bodies are identical. Māyā is unmanifest; the world-products are manifested.

Physics deals with manifested Māyā, which is full of illusion and delusion through concealment and projection. The world is unreal. The substratum of this Māyā-world is Reality which is unfathomable but realizable.

NOTES

1. Sorabji, R., *Necessity, Cause and Blame*, Duckworth, London, 1980.
2. Russell, B., *Mysticism and Logic*, Allen & Unwin, London, 1970, p. 132.
3. Hume, D., *A Treatise of Human Nature*, The Clarendon Press, Oxford, 1951, p. 172.
4. Reid, T., *Essays on the Intellectual Powers of Man*, Essay 4, included in Works, ed. Sir William Hamilton, Maclachlan & Stewart, Edinburg, 1846-63.
5. Mill, J.S., A *System of Logic*, 8th ed., Book III, Ch. V., Sec. 6, Harper, New York, 1881.
6. Ayer, A.J., *Foundations of Empirical Knowledge*, Macmillan & Co., London, 1951, Ch. 4.
7. Collingwood, R.G., *An Essay on Metaphysics*, The Clarendon Press, Oxford, 1940, Part 3-C.
8. Ducasse, C.J., *Nature, Mind and Death*, The Open Court Publ. Co., La Salle, Illinois, 1951, Part II.
9. Monod, J., *Chance and Necessity*, Collins/Fontana, London, 1974, pp. 136-7.
10. Engels, F., *Dialectics of Nature*, Progress Publishers, Moscow, 1974, p. 232.
11. Afanasyev, V.G., *Marxist Philosophy*, Progress Publishers, Moscow, 4th ed., 1980, p. 137.
12. *The Fundamentals of Marxist Leninist Philosophy*, Progress Publishers, Moscow, 1974, p. 170.
13. Engels, F., *Dialectics of Nature*, Progress Publishers, Moscow, 1974, p. 230.
14. Russell, B., *Human Knowledge. Its Scope and Limits*, Simon and Schuster, New York, 1962, p. 456.
15. Lenin, V.I., *Collected Works*, Vol. 38, p. 160.
16. Afanasyev, V.G., *Marxist Philosophy*, Progress Publishers, Moscow, 4th ed., 1980, p. 140.
17. Chā ŚB, VI.11.2.
18. BG, XIII.29.
19. BG, II.16.
20. BS, II.1.32.
21. BS, II.1.33.
22. BSŚB, Introduction.
23. BSŚB, I.4.3; II.1.14; BGŚB, IV.6; VII.6; IX.7-8, 10; XIII.19. 1-2; XIII.20.1; XIV.3.1; XIV.4; XV.16.1; VPDA, Ch. VII; Bhā, III.5.25; VC, 108; VS, 55.
24. BSŚB, I.1.10-11; BGŚB, VII.6; IX.7-8; XIII.19; XIV.3-4; Śve, VI.7, 9, 10, 12.

25. Crease, R.P. and Mann, C.C., *The Second Creation*, Affiliated East-West Press, New Delhi, 1987, p. 405 (originally published by Macmillan Publishing Co., New York).
26. BSŚB, II.3.9; Kaṭ, I.2.18; I.3.15; Śve, V.13; BG, X.3; XIII.31; MāKā, I.26; III.36; Mu, II.1.2; Bṛ, II.5.19.
27. BSŚB, II.3.9; Bṛ, II.5.19; MāKā, I.11 & 26; Śve, VI.9.
28. Bṛ, II.5.19; MāKā, I.26.
29. Bṛ, II.4.12; Kaṭ, I.3.15; Śve, V.13; Tai, II.1.1.
30. ṚV, X.82.3; BS, I.1.2; I.4.23, 26-27; II.1.30-31; Bṛ, I.4.10; Chā, III.14.2; Mu, I.1.3; III.1.3; Tai, III.1.1.
31. NS, IV.1.48-54.
32. *Tarka-Saṅgraha*, 39.
33. BSŚB, II.1.26.
34. Śve, VI.19.
35. BSŚB, II.1.14; Chā, VI.1.4.
36. Ait, III.3; Chā ŚB, VI.2.2; Kaṭ ŚB, II.3.12; Tai ŚB, II.6.1; VPDA, Ch. VII; BGŚB, X.39.
37. BSŚB, Introduction.
38. BSŚB, II.1.18.
39. *Praśastapāda*, *Padārtha-dharma Saṅgraha*, ed., Durgadhar Jha, Sanskrit Visvavidyalaya, Varanasi, 1963, pp. 244, 246.
40. BSŚB, II.1.14-19; MāKā, III.15; IV.11-20, 40.
41. BSŚB, Introduction.
42. ṚV, X.90.2; Bṛ, II.4.6; Chā, III.14.1; VII.25.1; Mai, IV.6; Mu, II.1.4; II.1.10; II.2.12; BGŚB, II.16.
43. BSŚB, II.1.14.

CHAPTER XIII

EPILOGUE

> I am God. I do not recognize the hell. I do not recognize the three worlds of heaven, hell and earth. I am the Lord, the Controller. I am the unbroken whole. I am still the witness after everything else is dissolved. Nobody else is God for me; nobody else controls me. I am I-less; I am my-less.
>
> Śaṅkara
> in *Vivekacūḍāmaṇi*, 494

FRANCIS BACON SAID: Knowledge is power. There is knowledge explosion in the twentieth century that is shortly going to welcome the twenty-first. Has man become powerful? The answer is 'yes'.

Is man afraid of his own power? Does man think that humanity, at any moment, may commit suicide?

We may quote a few sentences from the beginning and end of the book "Has Man a Future?" written by Bertrand Russell:

> MAN, or *Homo sapiens*, as he somewhat arrogantly calls himself, is the most interesting, and also the most irritating, of animal species on the planet Earth.
>
> This might be the first sentence of the last chapter of a report on our flora and fauna by a philosophic Martian biologist.[1]
>
> Man has made a beginning creditable for an infant—for, in a biological sense, Man the latest of species, is still an infant. No limit can be set to what he may achieve in the future. I see, in my mind's eye, a world of glory and joy, a world where minds expand, where hope remains undimmed, and what is noble is no longer condemned as treachery to this or that paltry aim. All this can happen if we will let it happen. It rests with our generation to decide between this vision and an end decreed by folly.[2]

The tone of Bertrand Russell is both optimistic and pessimistic. It is a conditional tone. It depends upon the wisdom or the follies of man. Carl Sagan thinks in a similar way:

We see here a conflict between our passions and what is sometimes called our better natures; between the deep, ancient reptilian part of the brain, the R-complex, in charge of murderous rages, and the more recently evolved mammalian and human parts of the brain, the limbic system and the cerebral cortex. When humans lived in small groups, when our weapons were comparatively paltry, even an enraged warrior could kill only a few. As our technology improved, the means of war also improved. In the same brief interval, we also have improved. We have tempered our anger, frustration and despair with reason. We have ameliorated on a planetary scale injustices that only recently were global and endemic. But our weapons can now kill billions. Have we improved fast enough? Are we teaching reason as effectively as we can? Have we courageously studied the causes of war?[3]

A few million years ago there were no humans. Who will be here a few million years hence? In all the 4.6-billion-year history of our planet, nothing much ever left it. But now, tiny unmanned exploratory spacecraft from Earth are moving, glistening and elegant, through the solar system. We have made a preliminary reconnaissance of twenty worlds, among them all the planets visible to the naked eye, all those wandering nocturnal lights that stirred our ancestors toward understanding and ecstasy. If we survive, our time will be famous for two reasons: that at this dangerous moment of technological adolescence we managed to avoid self-destruction; and because this is the epoch in which we began our journey to the stars.

The choice is stark and ironic. The same rocket boosters used to launch probes to the planets are poised to send nuclear warheads to the nations. The radioactive power sources on Viking and Voyager derive from the same technology that makes nuclear weapons. The radio and radar techniques employed to track and guide ballistic missiles and defend against attack are also used to monitor and command the spacecraft on the planets and to listen for signals from civilizations near other stars. If we use these technologies to destroy ourselves, we surely will venture no more to the planets and the stars. But the converse is also true. If we continue to the planets and the stars, our chauvinisms will be shaken further. We will gain a cosmic perspective. We will recognize that our explorations can

> be carried out only on behalf of all the people of the planet Earth. We will invest our energies in an enterprise devoted not to death but to life: the expansion of our understanding of the Earth and its inhabitants and the search for life elsewhere.[4]

Why is this apprehension of self-destruction of mankind? Is this the symptom of the power of man or the weakness of man? Due to some reason, weakness has contaminated the power of man. We are to search for the root of that weakness.

Today's man is more affluent. Although there are still many people who do not get two square meals a day, in general many get enough and some get more than enough to eat. Housing, clothing, facilities for education and health care have improved a great deal. Comforts of life have multiplied. Life-expectancy has increased. Then why is the increase in the rate of suicide, mental sickness and divorce? Why is the physically affluent man mentally unhappy? Today's man is subject to severe stress and strain; he is about to break down due to constant tension. Anxiety, despair, fearfulness and frustration affect him all the time. Overtly he smiles and laughs; covertly he weeps and cries. He does not find a person before whom he can open his heart, with whom he can share his feelings. He suspects everybody; he suspects himself. He finds nobody with whom he can confide. He feels that he is alone. He is bored with his loneliness. He is bored with his life itself. What is the purpose of living? What is the meaning of life? What for is he suffering from? Is this life, full of pain and suffering, worth living? He poses these questions before himself. He fails to find answers. He becomes schizophrenic. His personality splits into two, and often, into many. He does not know which half of his personality truly represents him. He cannot think lucidly. Every thought of his is haunted by duality. Life becomes unbearable for him. Is suicide the answer? He does not know.

The propensity of possession has become very strong in man. He desires more and more. He desires better and better. If he has got one building, he is not satisfied with it; he wants two, three, four and more. If he has got one million dollars, he is not satisfied with it; he needs ten millions, hundred millions, one thousand billions and billion trillions. He or she indulges in sex. But one partner is not enough. More and more partners and more and more beautiful partners are needed. Modern man is ever thirsty.

His thirst is never quenched. Possession of more and more and indulgence in more and more enhance the size, colour and heat of the flame of his fire of lust which is never extinguished. Today's man is ever hungry and thirsty.

In the affluent world of today, everything is in abundance (not applicable to the poor) except peace. Why is peace a rare commodity for affluence? Why is the physically rich man mentally unhappy? The poor man is unhappy; the sick man is unhappy; the hungry man is unhappy. We can account for that. But why is the man of plenty unhappy? Why is the man with wealth, health and power unhappy? We have to probe into it.

Poverty, unemployment, class-conflict, inequality, social injustice and many other politico-socio-economic factors are strong enough to engender unhappiness. They are potent forces to be reckoned and should not be belittled and ignored in any circumstances. But these issues will not be considered here. One fundamental factor that has deteriorated human quality and dehumanized man in the society irrespective of its politico-socio-economic system—capitalistic, communistic and socialistic—will be analyzed here.

Primitive Society

For the primitive man, most of the natural phenomena were supernatural. Multiple gods and goddesses existed for him. Gods and goddesses inhabited the trees, stones, hills, mountains, streams, rivers, sky and everywhere else. They blessed when they were pleased with man. They cursed when they were angry with him. They were talking to him. They were asking for human or animal flesh and blood whenever they were hungry and thirsty. For giving a good harvest of a turmeric crop, they were demanding the bloody sacrifice of a man or woman. All diseases were caused by them. Birth and death were caused by them. Man was afraid of the deities. He was afraid of doing anything wrong, if, in his tribal belief, that action was *immoral.* He was not feeling guilty at all by killing a man for sacrificing at the altar of the deity. He was not very much perturbed at the death of his only son who was eaten by tiger since, in his belief, that tiger was sent for that purpose by some deity. Life was all the time uncertain for him. Every moment anything might happen to him. Life was unsafe and full of risk. In that helpless condition, he had to be a fatalist; he had to be a pawn in the hands of the so-called supernatural spirits. He lived with live Nature. He made company with playful Nature. He conversed with Nature. He was in ecstasy for a moment. He was in agony for the next moment. A simple man with simple belief was playing innocently in the cradle of Nature. Although his life was uncertain and unsafe, he had certainty in his belief. He was never a sceptic. He was ever happy even amid unhappy moments of loss of near and dear ones. If the deity was doing everything, how could he avoid? If whatever happened was unavoidable, why not to accept everything without grudging and grumbling?

The primitive man had little knowledge and was full of ignorance. He was simple and kind. He was simple and cruel. He was both human and inhuman, depending upon his beliefs and customs in vogue. But, on the whole, he was happy.

Medieval Society

In the medieval age, the society had already gained much experience and knowledge. But this knowledge was not scientific. Most of it was through trial and error. Nature was still mystical. Man did not get key to open most of the secrets of Nature. Knowledge was not adequate to solve the riddles of Nature. Hence many natural phenomena could be explained through the natural way and many others had supernatural explanations. Time was not yet ripe to give up all the beliefs of the primitive society.

In different regions of the world, different religions developed. Some were monotheistic, some others were polytheistic, and a few were even agnostic or atheistic. Most religions preached what they called revealed truths. God Himself revealed the truths. God revealed the truth through His son or prophet. Whatever was revealed could not be wrong. God's own words were infallible and incorrigible. They were the last words. The son of God or the prophet of God was the last revealer. Nobody can come after him to reveal anything. Anyone who casts doubt in God's words and the Holy Scripture is a heretic and sinner. It is sacrilegious to question the Holy Scripture. Everybody must obey it. Whosoever does not obey is to be punished. Whosoever believes something else or speaks something else is a heretic who deserves the cruelest punishment. In a nutshell, this was the spirit of the medieval age.

The scriptures of all the religions did contain many things that could purge out the brute in man and made man more humane.

All religions of the world played a definitely positive role in improving the quality of humanity. But the goodness of religions was not free from the contamination with some evil effects. All religions do not speak the same things, although many things are common. But, with reference to some other things, contrary beliefs are upheld in different religions. Again, some things mentioned in some religions have already been proven wrong by empirical science. How could one and the same God reveal different 'truths' in different religions? The existence of one God for one religion is not likely to be acceptable. If it is presumed that only one particular God of one particular religion is real and the others are fake, it is not possible to prove the infallibility of a specific scripture with infallible evidence. When some things of a scripture are good enough to be acceptable and some others are rejectable in the light of the findings of empirical science, experience and logical analysis, God's authorship of the scripture becomes unacceptable. Religions would have done a better job, had they accepted human authorship of their scriptures. To err is human. So a few things of scriptures could have been rejected or modified with more refinement of man's knowledge and this updating activity would have been continual. To accept something as the 'last word' is the greatest blunder of the 'rational man'. This folly has stifled human progress through the ages.

The claim for the revelatory nature of the scriptures and divine authorship was made in the defence and interest of religions. In every age, there are some passionate critics and incisive sceptics who question the validity of beliefs, practices and doctrines and demand evidences. In order to escape from the attacks of these intellectuals, religious leaders had to devise a technique to protect the interest of religions. Revelation and divine authorship were the techniques devised to combat the attack of the intellectuals. The masses were very much influenced by such a doctrine. It was repeatedly injected into the minds of the masses that God Himself uttered the words written in the scriptures. The masses believed it partly out of devotion and partly out of fear. Indoctrination had its desired effect. Nobody dared to question the authority of the scriptures.

A medieval society that did not get much benefit of knowledge had to depend upon religious scriptures and the interpretations thereof by the religious leaders for its guidance. But for that, the brutalizing influence of ignorance could have caustically eroded the base of the society. When considered from this angle, religions played a positive role. Man was made humane. He cherished values in life. He tried to be good with an intention of being blessed by God. He tried to refrain from being bad in order to avoid God's wrath. He developed personal and social ethics for his own guidance and for that of the society. Religion was a shock-absorber for the medieval man. God was his saviour. In perilous situations, amid storms in life, he did not collapse because he sought refuge in God. He faced dangers with courage because he believed that he was not alone and that an omnipotent, omniscient, omnipresent and benevolent God was beside him to come to his rescue. However, he did not always escape from danger. He was a frequent victim to the vagaries of Nature and to inevitable natural losses. He was also harassed by his neighbours, punished by rulers and exploited by society in many ways. He had to tolerate all sufferings since he believed to have been destined to suffer that way. The social order, whether good or bad, had to be accepted without grudge. God's ruling had to be respected even though the individual was to be tortured. This was the world of the medieval man with half knowledge and half ignorance. He was ruled by God, God's scriptures, godmen, king, exploiters, oppressors and natural calamities. He was always the most obedient servant.

The Age of Scientific Revolution

Before 1500 A.D., Western society of the Middle Ages did not experience any impact of science. It was mainly guided by the Church. The ideas of the Greek philosopher-scientist Aristotle had some influence on the thinking of the Church-men. Thomas Aquinas combined Aristotle's comprehensive system of Nature with Christian theology and ethics. The medieval thinker of the Western world was a spokesman of Christian science that contained topics on God, human soul and ethics.

The concept of the spiritual and organic universe, prevalent in the medieval age, was discarded during the period between 1500 and 1700 A.D. The world was considered a machine during the sixteenth and seventeenth centuries. This was the Age of Scientific Revolution. The impact of the thoughts of five geniuses in bringing about scientific revolution will be briefly discussed here. These five thinkers were: Nicolas Copernicus (1473-1543), Francis Bacon

(1561-1626), Galileo Galilei (1564-1642), René Descartes (1596-1650) and Isaac Newton (1642-1727).

The ideas developed in the Age of Scientific Revolution clashed with those of the Church. The Church was not only a religious organization, but also had the controlling power over kings. Galileo was about to die like Socrates for the 'fault' of his empirical findings in favour of the motion of celestial bodies. In order to save his life, he was compelled by the Church to declare that what he found was wrong. The social environment at that time was very much inimical to the development of science and free thinking.

The Scientific Revolution began with the discovery of Copernicus. The Bible preached a geocentric view. Ptolemy supported such an idea. Copernicus presented his heliocentric notion. According to this, all the planets of the solar system revolve round the Sun. This was published in 1543 just before the death of Copernicus, who intentionally delayed the publication, with the apprehension of getting unfavourable response from the Church for the 'offence' of offending the religious consciousness.

The heliocentric view of Copernicus was only a hypothesis. It was further fortified by the discoveries of Johannes Kepler. When Galileo observed the sky with his newly constructed telescope and confirmed the heliocentric view of Copernicus, the scientific community was convinced and scientific opinion could be finally shifted from religion.

Galileo is considered as the father of modern science. He introduced experimentation in science. He also combined scientific experimentation with the use of mathematical language for the formulation of natural laws.

Francis Bacon was contemporary of Galileo. The former was in England while the latter was in Italy. Bacon formulated a clear theory of the inductive procedure—the method of experimentation, drawing general conclusions from the results of experiments and testing the conclusions through further experimentation. He did not believe in ideas that have not come from the conclusions of experimental results. Further, Bacon set the goal of science. It was to obtain knowledge to be used to dominate and control Nature. To co-exist with Nature was the previous ideology. But Bacon said: "Nature has to be hounded in her wanderings, bound into service and enslaved. The scientist is to put her in constraint;

he is to torture Nature's secrets from her." The foundation of the anti-ecological view of science and technology was laid by Bacon.

René Descartes is regarded as the founder of modern philosophy. He held that science was synonymous with mathematics. He wrote: "I admit nothing as true of them that is not deduced, with the clarity of a mathematical demonstration, from common notions whose truth we cannot doubt. Because all the phenomena of nature can be explained in this way, I think that no other principles of physics need be admitted nor are to be desired."[5]

Galileo used mathematics as the language of Nature. Descartes did the same thing. But he developed a philosophy from this use of mathematical language with regard to the certainty of scientific knowledge. "All science is certain, evident knowledge", he wrote, "We reject all knowledge which is merely probable and judge that only those things should be believed which are perfectly known and about which there can be no doubts."[6]

Quantum physics of twentieth century has already proved that Descartes was wrong. There is nothing like certainty of scientific knowledge. There is no absolute truth in science. Scientific concepts and theories are limited and approximate. In spite of this, Cartesian belief in scientific certainty is still exercising strong influence on the thinking of people, both scientists and non-scientists. Scientism has become typical of the Western culture and, for this, the Cartesian philosophy takes major responsibility.

Although Descartes believed in the certainty of scientific knowledge, he was a radical sceptic. He doubted everything. He doubted all traditional knowledge and the knowledge obtained through his own sense-perceptions. He went to the extreme of doubting the existence of his own body. "Have I got this body?" He asked this question to himself. He did not get a certain answer. He could not doubt only one thing, i.e., the existence of himself as a thinker. He said: "*Cogito, ergo sum*" ("I think, therefore I exist"). From this, he deduced that the essence of human nature lies in thought.

According to Descartes, all the things which we can conceive clearly and distinctly are true. Such clear and distinct conception of the pure and attentive mind is intuition for him. He says: "There are no paths to the certain knowledge of truth open to man except evident intuition and necessary deduction."[7]

Descartes' method is analytic. It breaks up complex thoughts into simple fragments and arranges these in their logical order.

This analytical method of reasoning given by Descartes, is a significant contribution to modern science. This is a potent tool in the hands of scientists and technologists for clear understanding of complicated processes and phenomena. But too much emphasis on analytical method has sometimes proven to be bad. It has engendered reductionism in science. It is a belief that any complex phenomenon can be better grasped by reducing it to its constituent parts. This is, however, oversimplification.

The concept of dualism, the sharp distinction between mind and matter, as still prevalent in the Western world, was the product of the thought of Descartes. Mind was more certain for him than matter. For him, mind and matter were exclusive of each other. He said: "There is nothing included in the concept of body that belongs to the mind; and nothing in that of mind that belongs to the body."[8]

The whole of Nature was divided by Descartes into two independent and separate entities, viz., *res cogitans* (thinking thing) and *res extensa* (extended thing). The former was mind and the latter was matter. To the scientific philosophy of Descartes, the existence of God was essential. He believed that God created both mind and matter.

This dichotomy of Nature into mind and matter has created ample confusion in our vision. In this connection, Heisenberg had to struggle a lot to get rid of this confusion.

Descartes conceived of the universe as a machine. This machine works according to mechanical laws. Matter functions as machine without any purpose, life or spirituality. This was the world-machine view of Descartes.

To Descartes, the non-living world was a machine. But, what about plants, animals and human beings? Descartes also extended his mechanistic view to the living world. Plants and animals were simply machines. The human body was a machine, but it was inhabited by a soul. This was the only difference between man and other living organisms. To him living organisms were nothing but automata. He wrote: "We see clocks, artificial fountains, mills and other similar machines which, though merely man-made, have nonetheless the power to move by themselves in several different ways .... I do not recognize any difference between the machines made by craftsmen and the various bodies that nature alone composes."[9]

Descartes' view of the world as a machine and the living beings as machines has exerted profound influence on the philosophy of science. The Vedic seer worshipped the Earth as mother.[10] He worshipped the Sun, the space, the air, the water, the fire, the rivers, the mountains and the trees. He was never pantheistic. He was not henotheistic either. He was staunchly monotheistic. He felt the presence of the all-pervasive Spirit everywhere. He had an organismic view of the world. The anti-ecological effect of science and technology was the result of a faulty vision that sprang from the mechanistic philosophy of Descartes.

This mechanistic philosophy had dangerous implications in the human society. Animals and birds are soulless machines. These machines are to be ruthlessly exploited. Plants are soulless machines. The forests, the mountains and the trees are to be indiscriminately exploited. Let the human soul exist in the pineal gland of the human brain. The machine of the human body is to be enjoyed. The woman's body is also a machine. It may be used for maximum pleasure. All these machines—inanimate and animate—are means for us. This is a dangerous concept which erodes the base of Kant's moral philosophy. According to Kant the practical imperative will be as follows: "So act as to treat humanity, whether in thine own person or in that of any other, in every case as an end withal, never as means only."[11]

Descartes' view of Nature as a perfect machine, governed by exact mathematical laws, functioned as a paradigm in scientific philosophy. But this remained as a vision only in the life time of Descartes. This got a complete shape by the work of Isaac Newton, who developed detailed mathematical formulation of the mechanistic view of Nature. Newton completed the scientific revolution that was initiated by Copernicus and Kepler, Bacon, Galileo and Descartes. Newton invented differential calculus and was ahead of his contemporaries in other branches of mathematics. He laid the foundation of the mathematical precision of the working of the world-machine.

In the seventeenth-century science, two trends opposed each other. Bacon's method was empirical and inductive whereas Descartes' method was rational and deductive. Newton unified these two opposing trends. He was of the view that a theory could not be based simply on experiments without systematic interpretation or on deduction from first principles without experimental evidence. He mixed both Bacon's empirical method and Descartes' method of mathematical analysis to establish a sound scientific methodology.

Descartes was a God-believer. His God created mind and matter. Newton was also a God-believer. His God created the world-machine and set it in motion. After that, the machine functioned automatically. In Newton's system, God later became unnecessary for the functioning of the world-automata. Newton was a strong believer and he did not like the dispensability of God. Hence he felt the necessity of God for correcting the world-machine if some part of it ever got out of order. But, irrespective of the belief of Newton, his concept of world-machine working precisely according to mathematical laws made God superfluous and redundant. Thus the Age of Scientific Revolution culminated in an atheistic, mechanistic view of the world.

Age of Enlightenment

The eighteenth and nineteenth centuries made use of Newtonian mechanics with great success. The scientific concepts that the world is a machine and that there can be rational approach to human problems exerted tremendous effects on the society of the middle class in the eighteenth century which was known as the Age of Enlightenment.

In science, Newtonian mechanics was extended to the continuous motion of fluids and to the vibration of elastic bodies. It was also extended to thermal physics. John Dalton (1776-1844) formulated his atomic hypothesis. Thus Newtonian mechanics was applied to micro-bodies in addition to macro-bodies. The behaviour of solids, liquids and gases, including the phenomena of heat and sound, was studied in terms of the movement of particles.

Being very much influenced by Newtonian mechanics and Cartesian philosophy, the thinkers of the eighteenth century discovered the so-called 'social physics'. In this respect, philosopher John Locke (1632-1704) played a very dominant role. Locke developed an atomistic view of society. As atoms are the building blocks of matter, so are human individuals who constitute the building blocks of the society. The atomic or molecular motion imparts properties to the gases. So, in Locke's view, the individual behaviours of human beings give a composite pattern to the society. This idea of Locke was the basis of his economic and political philosophy. He studied the nature of human individuals in order to formulate the social patterns.

In Locke's opinion, the actions of a person are motivated by his own interest. He says that men possess by nature rights to life, liberty and property, that these are the gifts of God, and that society should not arbitrarily deprive an individual of these rights. He thinks that all men are equal at birth and depend for their development entirely on their environment. In the philosophy of the 'social physics' of Locke, the gas-atom or the individual was given more importance than the congregate of gas-atoms or the society. In historical perspective, this was the seed of individualism.

Thomas Hobbes (1588-1679) declared that all knowledge was based on sensory perception. Locke adopted Hobbe's theory of knowledge. He did not recognize any innate ideas stored in the mind at birth. Man, at birth, is a blank slate, a *tabula rasa*, on which experience writes. Experience gives rise to all ideas, and experience is made up of sensation and reflection. This idea of Locke exerted strong influence on psychologists and political thinkers at a later period. Two schools of psychology, viz., behaviourism and psychoanalysis, were very much influenced by this notion of *tabula rasa*.

Indian psychology differs from Locke's idea of *tabula rasa*. According to the former, a person's mind at birth is not empty and it contains past impressions of former lives in latent form. Without any residual impressions (*karmāśaya*), rebirth is not possible. The psyche that is to be developed in the life of an individual is resultant of three factors, viz., residual impressions at birth, genetic constitution and environmental influences.

Nineteenth Century Thought

The development of thought of the nineteenth century was a continuation of that of the eighteenth century. The major ideas that exerted tremendous impact on the society will be mentioned here.

Electromagnetic field was discovered during this century. Michael Faraday (1791-1867) was a great experimenter who contributed significantly to the concept of the 'field'. James Clerk Maxwell (1831-79) was a brilliant theorist who completed the attempt made by Faraday. The discoveries made by Faraday and Maxwell were departures from the Newtonian and Cartesian concepts and were forerunners of the twentieth-century concept of 'field'.

One important concept that revolutionized human thought was 'evolution'. Geologists were studying fossils and theorizing about the evolution of the Earth. The evolution of the solar system was proposed by Emmanuel Kant (1724-1804) and Pierre Laplace (1749-1827). Jean Baptiste Lamarck (1744-1829), at the beginning of the nineteenth century, propounded his theory of evolution of species in biology. He was the first thinker of biological evolution. According to this theory, all living beings have evolved from earlier, simpler forms under the pressure of environment. A.R. Wallace (1823-1913) anticipated Darwin. As a naturalist, he spent years in studying plant and animal life. In February, 1858, the 'idea of the survival of the fittest' suddenly flashed before his mind. He wrote it down and sent to Darwin. Charles Darwin (1809-82) laid a strong foundation of the theory of evolution by presenting a mass of evidences. He published *The Origin of Species* on November 24, 1859. All living species undergo mutation. They also have a tendency to pass on these variations by inheritance. The changed ones may survive or perish depending upon their ability or disability in adapting to their environments. This is natural selection. "Struggle for existence and survival of the fittest" is the guiding force of Darwinian evolution. The discovery of evolution in biology induced scientists to abandon the Cartesian conception of the world as a machine.

In the nineteenth century, a number of discoveries were made in physical sciences. By the application of Newtonian mechanics to the study of thermal phenomena in fluids (liquids and gases), the science of thermodynamics was developed. This resulted in the discovery of the law of the conservation of energy. Physicists discovered this law in their studies of steam engines and other heat-producing machines. This is known as the first law of thermodynamics.

The second law of thermodynamics was formulated first by Nicolas Léonard Sadi Carnot (1796-1832). According to this law, the amount of useful energy in any particular process diminishes with increase in heat by corresponding quantity, the total amount of energy in the process remaining constant. Any isolated physical system proceeds spontaneously in the direction from order to ever increasing disorder. Rudolf Clausius (1822-88) introduced the term entropy, representing quantitatively the degree of disorder. Ludwig Boltzmann (1844-1906) showed that the second law of thermodynamics is a statistical law. Thus it is not expected that in every process there must be increase in entropy. As a matter of fact, in biological systems and also in some physical systems, there are a number of processes where entropy decreases. However, in any isolated system, there must be net increase of entropy. If this principle is applied to the whole universe which is an isolated system, cosmic 'heat death' is inevitable, unless some other process intervenes. The second law of thermodynamics goes against the concept of the eternality of the universe. It has significantly influenced the cosmology and cosmogony of the twentieth-century science.

A political philosophy, advocated by a number of political thinkers of the eighteenth and nineteenth centuries, exerted profound influence on the politico-socio-economic thoughts of both the nineteenth and twentieth centuries. It preached individualism and *laissez faire*. Among the thinkers of *laissez faire* were David Hume (1711-76), William Paley (1743-1805), Edmund Burke (1729-97), Jean Jacques Rousseau (1712-78), William Godwin (1756-1836), Jeremy Bentham (1748-1832), Samuel Taylor Coleridge (1772-1834) and others. They did not belong to any harmonious group, and rather they happened to come from diversified and warring schools. This is an idea which is individualistic and anti-altruistic. It is against any control of society and the State. It holds that any individual who prospers economically, politically and socially is intrinsically superior to those who are underdeveloped. It further holds that the more capable individuals should flourish and the weaker ones should perish. Herbert Spencer (1820-1903) uses the concept of the 'survival of the fittest' in sociology and economics.

The concept of *laissez faire* which primarily developed in political philosophy infiltrated to economics. The economists who favoured this idea had capitalistic flavour. They were against socialism. What these economists considered of *laissez faire* may be represented in the following quotation from *A Manual of Political Economy* written in 1793 by Bentham who himself was not an economist.

> The general rule is that nothing ought to be done or attempted

> by government; the motto or watchward of government, on these occasions, ought to be—*Be quiet*.........The request which agriculture, manufacturers, and commerce present to governments is as modest and reasonable as that which Diogenes made to Alexander: Stand out of my sunshine.[12]

The idea of individualism and *laissez faire* was counteracted by Marxist philosophy. Karl Marx (1818-83) laid the foundation of his new doctrine of socialism and communism, which was translated into action for the first time in Soviet Russia in 1917. In his system, the individual was subordinated to society which became the sole custodian of the means of production. He did not believe in God. In Marxist philosophy, religion is the opium of the masses and God is something of an airy nonsense. Spirituality was completely banished from the dialectical materialism of Marx.

Twentieth Century Thought

In the domain of science, relativism and quantum physics were the major discoveries in the twentieth century. Cartesian concept was discarded. Newtonian mechanics was limited to the macro-world only for some specific purposes. The Newtonian concept of absolute space and absolute time was discarded. Neither matter nor energy remained reality for the twentieth century scientist. Instead of 'certainty', 'probability' become the catchword. Quantum mechanics was applied to the micro-world.

The discovery of genetics and genetic engineering was a major progress in biology and biochemistry. Electronics and cybernetics had tremendous impact in technology. Space-technology could shatter the concepts of geocentrism and heliocentrism of man.

The science of Western psychology developed in the eighteenth, nineteenth and twentieth centuries. In contrast, Indian psychology took a developed shape in the first and second millennia before Christ. Thus, in comparison with Indian psychology, Western psychology is relatively recent in origin. But the world has not yet been very much acquainted with the psychological concepts of ancient India due to lack of serious discussion.

Scientific discoveries in the subjects of anatomy and physiology were utilized in formulating psychological theories. David Hartley (1705-57), an English philosopher and psychologist, combined neurological reflexes and mental ideas to develop an associational psychology. Hartley's associationalism was a form of empirical psychology. His theories influenced Jeremy Bentham (1748-1832), David Hume (1711-76), James Mill (1773-1836) and John Stuart Mill (1806-73) who contributed in their own ways to the school of associationalism.

Experimental psychology established correlations between mental activity and brain structures. It gained secure footing in the work of Ernst Weber (1795-1878), Gustav Fechner (1801-87) and Hermann Helmholtz (1821-94). Wilhelm Wundt (1832-1900), a German philosopher and psychologist, established the first psychology laboratory in 1879. He maintained that all mental functioning could be analyzed into specific elements. He introduced a sort of elementarism, atomism and reductionism into psychology. The concept of element was applied to the basic units of consciousness, in a manner analogous with its usage in chemistry. The system in experimental psychology, closely associated with the writings and empirical findings of Wilhelm Wundt and Edward B. Titchener, was labelled as structuralism. It presumed that all human mental experience, no matter how complex, could be viewed as combinations of simple processes or elements. Titchener is recognized as the founder of structuralism.

Research on reflexology was initiated by Russian scientists, viz., Ivan Sechenov and Ivan Pavlov (1849-1936). Pavlov's discovery of conditioned reflexes had great impact on development of learning theories.

The reductionist and materialistic theories of psychology evoked strong opposition among some psychologists who favoured the unitary nature of consciousness and perception. Two schools of psychology, viz., Gestalt psychology and functionalism developed as a reaction to the elementist orientation and structuralist position. Both these schools adopted a holistic approach.

Gestalt psychology was founded by Max Wertheimer (1880-1943) who developed his theory in collaboration with Kurt Koffka and Wolfgang Köhler, in the 1910s. Gestalten refers to unified wholes, the nature of which is not revealed by simply analyzing the several parts that make it up. Thus, Gestalt psychology is antithetical to atomistic psychology, behaviourism and structuralism.

William James (1842-1910) was an American psychologist/philosopher. He was pragmatist in philosophy and functionalist in psychology. He was the foremost exponent of functionalism. He emphasized the unity and dynamic nature of the 'stream of consciousness'. His view clearly supported a functional theory of consciousness. In his opinion, the term 'consciousness' does not stand for an entity but that it does for a function.

Functionalism was developed in the 1910s and 1920s at the University of Chicago under J.R. Angell and H. Carr. It disfavoured structuralism in psychology. It gave more emphasis on the analysis of mind and behaviour in terms of their functions rather than their structures.

In the 1910s, behaviourism was founded by John B. Watson (1878-1958). He was an American psychologist. He rejected all introspection. In his opinion, all psychological investigations should be restricted to the observable and measurable behaviours only. Consciousness, purpose and the concept of mind were ruled out by the methods of his radical behaviourism. He limited behaviour to specific peripheral muscular and glandular responses.

Sigmund Freud (1856-1940) introduced Depth Psychology, distinguishing between conscious and unconscious levels of mentality. He used the method of free association to develop psycho-analysis. He had a tripartite model of mind, viz., *Id, Ego* and *Super-Ego*. These three components are, however, not anatomical structures of the brain. They are metapsychological constructs for a descriptive device only. *Id* is the primitive, animalistic, instinctual element. It is the libidinous energy demanding immediate satisfaction. It constitutes the deepest component of the psyche and is the true unconscious. It is isolated from the world about it. It is entirely self-contained. It is bent on achieving its own aims. It always seeks pleasure. The ego is the centre of rational awareness and effective action. The super-ego is the hypothetical entity associated with ethical and moral conduct. It is developed in response to the punishments and rewards of parents and other significant persons. It embodies the interiorisation of the moral code of the community. The *id* is concerned with the pleasurable, the *ego* with the actual and the *super-ego* with the ideal.

The *id* is the source of the flow of libido into the psyche. This energy is essentially sexual in nature. The *ego* is pressurized from both below (*id*) and above (*super-ego*) and tries to adjust by satisfying some demands of the *id* and rejecting some others. When the demands of the *id* are at blatant variance with the *super-ego*, they are repressed combinedly by *ego* and *super-ego* into the unconscious of the psyche. This repressing act is called the censor. What is repressed, however, is not deactivated. The repressed contents continue to have a lively existence at the unconscious level. They make themselves felt through projections in disguised symbolic form in dreams, parapraxes and psychoneuroses. Thus, the unconscious processes play significant role as motivators of human behaviour. They influence our conscious life in hidden ways.

The deep, primitive, libidinous impulses coming out of the unconscious would not be socially acceptable. They are redirected and refined into new, learned 'noninstinctive' behaviour. The learned behaviours are socially acceptable. This process of re-direction of energy from socially unacceptable to the acceptable is called sublimation. The creative, artistic tendencies are manifestations of sublimation. Neurosis occurs when the normal repression-sublimation channel becomes non-functional due to some reason.

Freudianism presumes that early experiences are the causes of later behaviours. The most troublesome repressed contents centre around incestuous relations, especially the *Oedipus* and *Electra complexes*.

The *Oedipus complex* is a group of unconscious wishes, feelings and ideas focusing on the desire to 'possess' the opposite-sexed parent and 'eliminate' the same-sexed parent. According to Freud, this complex emerges during the Oedipal stage, i.e., in the age of three to five years. At first, *Oedipus* referred only to the male complex and *Electra* to the female. Later, both were subsumed under *Oedipus* mainly for convenience.

In Freudian psychology, *Eros* refers to the whole complex of life-preservative instincts, including the sexual instincts, and *Thanatos* refers to the instinct for death as expressed in such behaviours as denial, rejection and the turning away from pleasure.

To find out some effective means of avoiding war, Einstein wrote a letter to Freud. He put the question: What is to be done to rid mankind of the war-menace? A few sentences of that letter are quoted below:

> I have so far been speaking only of wars between nations; what are known as international conflicts. But I am well aware

that the aggressive instinct operates under other forms and in other circumstances. (I am thinking of civil wars, for instance, due in earlier days to religious zeal, but nowadays to social factors; or, again, the persecution of racial minorities.) But my insistence on what is the most typical, most cruel and extravagant form of conflict between man and man was deliberate, for here we have the best occasions of discovering ways and means to render all armed conflicts impossible.[13]

Freud's reply to the letter of Einstein was not optimistic for the avoidance of war. A few sentences of his letter may be quoted here:

We assume that human instincts are of two kinds: those that conserve and unify, which we call 'erotic' (in the meaning Plato gives to Eros in his Symposium), or else 'sexual' (explicitly extending the popular connotation of 'Sex'); and secondly, the instincts to destroy and kill, which we assimilate as the aggressive or destructive instincts. These are, as you perceive, the well-known opposites.[14]

You are interested, I know, in the prevention of war, not in our theories, and I keep this fact in mind. Yet I would like to dwell a little longer on this destructive instinct which is seldom given the attention that its importance warrants. With the least of speculative efforts we are led to conclude that this instinct functions in every living being, striving to work its ruin and reduce life to its primal state of inert matter. Indeed it might well be called the 'death-instinct'; whereas the erotic instincts vouch for the struggle to live on. The death instinct becomes an impulse to destruction when, with the certain organs, it directs its action outward, against external objects. The living being, that is to say, defends its own existence by destroying foreign bodies. But, in one of its activities, the death instinct is operative *within* the living beings and we have sought to trace back a number of normal and pathological phenomena to this *introversion* of the destructive instinct. We have even committed the heresy of explaining the origin of human conscience by some such 'turning inward' of the aggressive impulse. Obviously when this internal tendency operates on too large a scale, it is no trivial matter, rather a positively morbid state of things;

> whereas the diversion of the destructive impulse towards the external world must have beneficial effects. Here is then the biological justification for all those vile, pernicious propensities which we now are combating. We can but own that they are really more akin to nature than this our stand against them, which, in fact, remains to be accounted for.
> The upshot of these observations, as bearing on the subject in hand, is that there is no likelihood of our being able to suppress humanity's aggressive tendencies.[15]

Freud who was a great genius in psychology deserves respect for his opinion. However, some thinkers do not agree with him for his universalization of his concepts. He studied psychologically abnormal patients and built up theories to be applicable to all normal people. His application of *Oedipus complex* universally for everybody does not seem to be right. That most of the mental maladies of man are due to repression of sexual desires during the Oedipal age of three to five years is over-simplification of facts. Freud is right in recognizing the possession and manifestation of the opposing life and death instincts in man. But this is true in the common man. As long as man is not free from ignorance, he is unknowingly guided by life and death instincts. But, Advaita Vedānta says that the evolved man can suppress the death instinct and that the man free from ignorance can annihilate all instincts—relating both life and death. The man, free from bondage, is Brahman himself. According to Advaita Vedānta, it is possible for everybody to become Brahman since he is really Brahman and seems to be non-Self, being alienated due to ignorance. We may not think of the released soul. Even the evolved persons are free from aggressiveness. Not to talk of Gandhi and Einstein, there are many common persons who passionately long for prevention of war. And their number will be multiplied if more awareness is created in the world.

Freud's psychology is purely materialistic. It is definitely anti-religious. He writes:

> The scientific spirit engenders a particular attitude to the problems of this world; before the problems of religion it halts for a while, then wavers, and finally here steps over the threshold. In this process there is no stopping. The more the fruits of

knowledge become accessible to man, the more widespread is the decline of religious belief, at first only of the obsolete and objectionable expression of the same, then of its fundamental assumptions also.[16]

What Freud says in the preceding paragraph is correct. He is correct as far as most religions are concerned. But, if his tone is anti-spiritual, he is wrong. Science and spirituality will fuse together to form a compatible amalgam. After that, it would be very difficult to distinguish spiritual science and scientific spirituality. Reincourt writes:

> Wolfgang Pauli is correct in hinting that it took the scientific revolution in the midst of which he was working and to which he contributed so much, to restate the respective spheres of science and religion—which old Victorian Freud could never begin to understand. But, by and large, the philosophical implications of this revolution have not yet percolated down to the world of Western philosophy, art and literature where meaninglessness and despairing purposelessness still hold full sway.[17]

Carl Gustav Jung (1875-1961) was a Swiss psychologist. Unlike Sigmund Freud, Jung did not place much emphasis on the role of sex and sexual impulses in modelling the psychological behaviour of a person. His psychology was not materialistic. He had a strong faith in Vedānta and believed in the existence of Self. In contrast to Freudian psycho-analysis, Jung insisted upon the term Analytic psychology to characterize his own approach. He focused on the deep, inherited collective unconscious with its universal ideas of images, the archetypes.

What do we conclude from the resume of the development of psychology during a period of three centuries? The advance of knowledge is definitely spectacular. But, for what end is this advance? It is to humanize man or dehumanize man? Are all men sexual demons, always attempting to kill the father and sexually assault the mother? Are all the women always passionately lustful with a mad craving for becoming the sex-partner of the father? Cannot man supress or annihilate his death-instinct? Is mankind *inevitably* waiting for its doomsday, ready for self-destruction with its nuclear weapons to be used in a star-war? This may happen and Freud may be correct. But, is man helpless in avoiding this final disaster? Optimism and pessimism oscillate on a very sensitive pivot. The final decision rests on the wisdom or the folly of mankind. But there is no reason to believe that man hasn't got wisdom.

What do we gain from Watson's behaviourism? It has reduced man from a conscious being to one of insentience. In studying man, the behaviourists observe the movements of the parts of the human machine. Is it rise of man or fall of man?

We may analyze the trends in philosophy in the twentieth century. The main emphasis has been on language analysis. Philosophers have remained busy in determining the meaning of language. Metaphysics is nonsensical in logical analysis of language and concepts. Philosophy has been cleansed off the *impurity* of ethics. Morality has been interpreted in terms of relativism. Many modern philosophers do not cosider any activity as philosophical unless it is restricted to language analysis.

The Logical Empiricists or Positivists tried to establish a scientific philosophy in the 1920s and 1930s. They wanted to eliminate the pseudo-propositions, including those of metaphysics. Any proposition is true for them if and only if its truth can be verified by senses or at least is verifiable. They laid too much emphasis on verification through sense-perception. Alfred J. Ayer (1910-) is a strong advocate of Logical Empiricism. In the tradition of David Hume, Ayer holds that all genuine statements are either empirical (synthetic) or analytic. Analytic statements are devoid of factual content and empirical verification is not necessary for their truth-determination. But one has to determine the truth of synthetic statements through sense-perception only.

Empiricism is the doctrine that the source of all knowledge is to be found in experience. Aristotle was a Greek empiricist and Plato was a rationalist. But a combination of rationalism and empiricism was apparent in the views of Platonists and Aristotelians. Democritus and Epicurus were staunch empiricists among the Greek philosophers. The *Cārvākas* of India were die-hard empiricists.

There was a movement for empiricism in Britain. Roger Bacon (1214-94) put stress on 'direct inspection' and 'experimental science'. Francis Bacon (1561-1626) worked out inductive methods and attacked rationalism. John Locke (1632-1704) was antirationalist and traced all ideas to experience. George Berkeley (1685-1753) identified being with the perceived. David Hume (1711-76) distinguished between matters of fact and relations of ideas. John Stuart Mill (1806-73) stressed inductive logic and empirical methods. This was the tradition of British empiricism.

William James (1842-1910), the American philosopher of pragmatism, meant by empiricism a test of meaning and truth. He used the term 'radical empiricism'.

In the twentieth century, the logical positivists of the Vienna Circle made an effort to purify philosophy of its non-empirical elements. Two of the members of the circle, viz., A.J. Ayer and Herbert Feigl, call their view 'logical empiricism'.

All these thinkers who have pleaded for empiricism are not totally wrong. Empiricism has its own value if properly applied. But it is not the sole truth. It has got applicability for empirical purposes only, for our day-to-day living, for exploring the universe and for all scientific purposes. But it cannot be claimed that what we perceive is the sole truth. What we perceive may be illusion only, useful for our empirical living. We cannot claim that what we don't perceive does not exist. What we perceive is *the* reality and what we don't perceive is unreal; such a statement is not valid.

Existentialism was a philosophical movement challenging essentialism. It had both theistic and atheistic varieties. Sören Kierkegaard (1813-55) developed the concepts of theistic existentialism. He challenged the Hegelian philosophy. He placed emphasis on the individual; he gave much importance on subjectivity; and for him anguish was the central emotion of human life. Friederich Nietzsche (1844-1900) developed the school of atheistic existentialism. He raised the slogan, "God is dead". Regarding morality, he held that each individual must seek his own values. Martin Heidegger (1884-1976) stresses man's freedom. He thinks that man should live authentically; he should discover himself, should be capable of genuine understanding, originative thinking and genuine discourse. This authenticity is possible only for one who has the attitude of 'care'. Attitude of care comes for one who throws his being into question through anguish. Through anguish one discovers oneself which is radical finite nothingness. Then is one able to accept oneself as being destined to die. Heidegger has elaborated his concept of *daş Nichts* or Nothingness. He gives ontological status to Nothing. He asks the question: "Why is there anything at all and not rather Nothing?" He holds that one becomes aware of Nothingness initially through the dread one feels over his prospective non-being. He further holds that logical negation is possible because of the Nothing which was in the beginning.

Jean-Paul Sartre (1905-) brings together all of the themes of atheistic existentialism. He does not place any limitation upon man's freedom. In his opinion, existence precedes essence. He says: "Man is a noughting nought." By this he means that man and the world are merely given, and that man then invents a nature for himself and a nature for the world. Man creates an essence for himself and a structure for the world in order to negate the nothingness of the world. Like Nietzsche, Sartre also thinks that "God is dead". Since there is no God and man is free in the opinion of Sartre, he says that man is free to invent his own values. He also stresses authenticity and anguish (*Angst*) in his philosophy.

It is to be critically analyzed if existentialism is really not non-existentialism. By putting so much stress on Nothingness, anguish, death, atheism, amoralism, etc., one may miss everything positive in life.

Crisis in Perception

There has been a turning point in the course of historical development since the year 1500 A.D. During these five centuries there has been accumulation of knowledge in every branch of human endeavour. There has been knowledge-explosion in physical sciences, biological sciences, social sciences, technology and humanities. In spite of all this advancement, man has become more informed but less wise. This knowledge has not helped man in getting peace and happiness, in protecting mankind, in preserving environment and in developing a cosmic outlook. It has helped man in knowing the external world; it has utterly failed in helping man in knowing himself. The maxim "Know thyself" (*ātmānaṁ viddhi*) has been totally lost. Man has been alienated from himself. He feels lonely. He cannot enjoy his life which is painful to him. He has become cynical and skeptic. He does not believe anybody. He does not believe his kith and kin. He does not believe himself. He fails to find meaning of his life. He does not know for what purpose he lives. Life is unbearable for him. Everything is absurd for him. God is dead for him. He wants to escape from this world. He attempts to forget his existence by taking drugs and intoxicating his body and mind. But drugs don't help him, alcohol does not help him. He tries to get pleasure from excess of food, drink and sex. But those too do not please him. He commits suicide. He does not know if that is the end of his misery. Why is this predicament of the affluent, informed, civilized and modern man?

Newtonian mechanics and Cartesian philosophy taught that the universe is a machine and that man is a machine. In one respect, there is nothing wrong in it. Actually, the macro- and the micro-systems, the living and the non-living worlds are all machines. Man has not made a machine which is as good as the brain, heart, kidneys and lungs. The Bhagavad Gītā declares that the human body is a machine.[18] But the same Gītā urges us to appreciate that the machine is not everything and that there is something else.

Empiricism is right in its own perspective. If we are to claim that certain micro-organism is the pathogen of certain disease, we are to follow the inductive methodology and establish the fact by empirical procedure. We cannot do it by speculation. But we would be wrong if we demand an empirical verification of God or Brahman. We infer the existence of quarks as components of protons and neutrons. We rarely realize that many such things we claim in science have not been empirically verified. "We cannot see God and hence there is no God." This is an unwise and naive argument.

Darwinian evolution, molecular genetics and genetic engineering are important events in the historical development of biology. There is nothing wrong in biological evolution. Before species evolution, there was organic evolution, which was preceded by inorganic evolution. Before the elements were formed, there had been nucleogenesis and particle formation. That was preceded by the big bang explosion of the cosmic egg. How did the cosmic egg appear? We develop allergy to answer that. It is wrong to presume that Darwin finally disproved the existence of God. When did Darwin do that and how could he do that? It is surprising that wise man like Sir Julian Huxley could also think that Darwin had successfully dispelled the idea of God. (His utterance perhaps referred to Genesis in the Bible). In this connection, Hitching writes:

> In 1959, at the time of Darwin's centenary, few wise heads would have shaken in open disagreement when Sir Julian Huxley said on a television programme: 'Darwinism removed the whole idea of God as the creator of organisms from the sphere of rational discussion'.[19]

Laissez faire has been practised and overstretched in political philosophy and economics. Capitalism favours it and socialism disfavours it. "Those who are more capable in the society will prosper and those who are less capable will perish. There is nothing like altruism. One should work for oneself. One should enjoy all the fruits of one's achievements." This is the sociological version of biological Darwinism—"Struggle for existence, survival of the fittest". *Laissez faire* is a self-centred philosophy based on purely individualism.

One type of argument goes like this. All men are born equal. And hence all should share everything equally.

Is this reasoning valid? Are all men really born equal? The constitution of capitalist country like America declares that all men are born equal. Is this really a true statement?

The science of genetics says that the genotype (genetic constitution inherited from father and mother) of each individual is different from that of any other individual unless two individuals are identical twins. Again, identical twins also change in their performances due to variation in environment and training. If training is considered as a component of environment, genotype and environment are the two broad factors that decide the performances of an individual. It is the duty of society and political systems to provide equal (as far as practicable) environments to all individuals. But, even if equal environments are furnished, individuals would differ in their performances due to differences in genotypes.

In a society, very few people are geniuses and very few are dullards. Most people belong to the modal group; they are average in intelligence and performance. Some are above average and some are below average. This trend cannot be ruled out even in communist countries. An individual with less than average genotype may perform better if he is exposed to more congenial environment and if he is more sincere and hard-working. On the other hand, an individual with a very good genotype may not perform well if he is subjected to an unfavourable environment and if he develops an attitude of lethargy. But whatever may be the area in the spectrum of genotype and environment, it is true to state that all men are not born equal.

If individuals are intrinsically and potentially different, *laissez faire* has a strong point. The lion should get a lion's share and the hare should get a hare's share. Why should the small and timid hare get a share equal to that of the lion?

The argument given here in favour of *laissez faire* is an error in perception. Nobody speaks of equality which will ever remain a utopia. The main emphasis is equitable opportunity and equitable sharing for the basic needs of life. All intellectuals and geniuses of the world, from the early civilizations to the contemporary age, have given more to society and taken less from it. They have never preached nor practised *laissez faire*. As the Vedic and Upaniṣadic seers say, "Enjoy by giving up"[20], geniuses have taken pleasure in suffering, self-denial and self-dedicating for the good of the world. An intellectual is not an intellectual if he is self-centred and individualistic. The Vedic seer exhorts us to live an altruistic life through the following hymn:

May your counsel be common,
May you belong to one fraternity,
May your minds move
With one accord.
May your hearts work in harmony
For one goal.
May you be inspired
By common ideal.
May you offer worship
With common oblation.
May you resolve
With one accord.
May your hearts be in unison.
May your thoughts be harmonious,
So that you may live together,
With happiness and hilarity.[21]

"Live and let live" is not the principle of *laissez faire*. Application of Darwinian "Struggle for existence and survival of the fittest" in its naked form to sociology, politics and economics has been a blunder in perception. Due to this wrong application, there is scarcity for some people amid plenty for some others. Man is exploited by man with a false plea that the latter is a lion and the former is a hare. As a reaction to it, communism has declared war against God and anything that is spiritual. This antagonism must go. Mankind should practise the sermon of the Vedic seer, "You may live and let me also live".[22]

Freud's psychoanalysis is correct in its own perspective. It cannot be ruled out that some sons might have covert desire for sex-indulgence with their mothers. There also may be some daughters having covert desire for sex-participation with their fathers. In a society, normal individuals are many and abnormal ones are few. Even all the normal ones are not identical and nobody can ensure the continuance of the normalcy. Freud was a practising psychiatrist. He studied the psychology of his patients and universalized his observations. He held that most of the mental problems of human beings are due to repression of sexual desires. Taking the data of a few particulars and making them universal was wrong on the part of Freud.

Elementarism, atomism, reductionism, structuralism and behaviourism in psychology are not wrong in their own perspectives. But, if these are stretched too far and accepted as universal truth, there is something seriously wrong in our thinking process. How can Gestalt psychology and the holistic approach be refuted especially when we get ample evidences from our observations of Nature. One such instance may be cited here.

> The egg of a frog at the beginning of its development divides into two cells, which, if artificially separated, grow, each of them, into a *whole* individual, instead of half a one—implying that the development of each cell is different from what it would have been, had it been allowed to remain in a two-cell embryo. This would be rather difficult to explain on a pure physico-chemical basis!
>
> Unlike dead, inorganic matter, an organism is an *organized* system in which each part is related in a specific way to the whole, aiming at a certain peak of development while maintaining along the way a state of delicate balance of function that will automatically attempt to re-establish itself if altered. Thus an organism is not so much an aggregate of cells as an *architecture*,

> a dynamic whole that is far more than the sum of its parts—here again, nature displays its 'holistic' tendency. The visible expression of its organizing activity is its *form* which owes nothing to chance but appears to be the goal toward which its organic development strives.[23]

In Newtonian science, there was invariable relation between cause and effect. Scientists believed that there cannot be an event without a cause. In the last decade of the nineteenth century and in the twentieth century, physicists observed the so-called acausal events. Radioactive uranium automatically disintegrates. The particles jump up from space automatically. They disappear automatically. One particle becomes two, four, many and in a billionth of a second all that appear disappear. One electron and an anti-electron, separated by a long distance, still work in unison with correct response to the stimulus to its partner. The quantum physicist does not find any local cause of such an event. And hence causality has been discarded in quantum physics. The philosophers have imitated the quantum physicists and banned the causal law. The litterateur introduced acausality in his writings and produced absurd literature. But all that happened with reference to causality or acausality in the twentieth century thinking was completely misconceived. This has already been discussed in Chapter XII.

The quantum physicist finds illusoriness in the world. Everything is transient and unreal for him. He does not perceive any changeless entity. He is still in search of reality. Matter that was real is no longer real. Energy that was real is no longer real. Particles that were real are no longer real. Space and time were previously real and eternal. Einstein himself declared that space is finite, that space is with beginning and end, that time is with beginning and end and that spacetime has both beginning and end. Then what is real in the universe? Some physicists, including Einstein, believe that 'field' is real. Before the death of Einstein, he held the opinion that field is not real and that space is really real. But how can space be real? What is the meaning of reality? Can anything that is changeable and that has beginning and end be real? Science has not yet accepted the 'Brahman' of Advaita Vedānta and is still in search of reality. This is why there is utter confusion.

Twentieth century philosophy abhors any discussion on cosmology and cosmogony. Astrophysics is quite active in solving the riddles of cosmology. We come to know from science that the universe had a beginning. It started with the cosmic egg and the big bang explosion. We further come to learn that the universe will not remain for ever, that it will contract to the initial condition. We accept the concept of the oscillating or the pulsating universe. Our mathematics points out that the contracting universe will be finally zero in volume. But we try to avoid that zero volume by coining a term 'singularity'. We are determined dogmatically to explain everything in terms of empiricism and objectivity. We fail to explain. We don't confess our failure. The result is self-deceit.

Descartes who was passionately a sceptic surprisingly declared the certainty and precision of scientific knowledge. The concept has been changed and rather discarded especially after Heisenberg's principle of indeterminacy has been known. But persistence of vision is a normal phenomenon in physiology and that is why we see the three different blades of a moving fan as a continuous one. Most of the people in the world—both scientists and non-scientists—are still addicted to scientism. They believe that scientific findings are *absolutely* precise and true, and that science can do anything and everything. Of course, the achievements of science cannot be belittled. The potentialities of science have not been exhausted. We do not know exactly what science can do in future. We are quite hopeful that science can achieve many more things that we cannot imagine now. But science has limitations too. In science, we make attempt to answer questions like what, why, how, how many, etc. We discover Nature by removing the cover of man's ignorance. But we do not create Nature and enact natural laws. We only imitate Nature. We cannot do anything which contravenes the laws of Nature. The modern philosopher says that there are no laws of Nature and that they are uniformities only. Whatever the case may be, we cannot also contravene the uniformities. Thus, it is not correct to say that science does not recognize impossibilities. Scientism is born out of sheer misunderstanding.

It is a fact that humanity faces a crisis. It is paradoxical that knowledge explosion and crisis go together in the twentieth century. Why has it happened so? What is wrong with knowledge? There does not seem to be anything wrong with knowledge *per se*.

Capra has rightly said that there is crisis in perception.[24] With reorientation in our perception, we can do away with this crisis.

Total Vision

During the last five centuries we have undoubtedly enlarged our vision. But, in every sphere of our thinking, our vision has been fragmentary. The six blind men described the elephant. Each one gave a clear and faithful description of the elephant as perceived by him. There was nothing wrong in his perception and description. But the perceptions were fragmentary and the descriptions pertained to the respective fragments. The total vision of the elephant could not be obtained. That is what has exactly happened with our fragmentary and analytical world outlook.

It is time now to bring about a synthesis of science and spirituality. The question is: "How to do it?" The scripture says that the world was created by God in only six days in its finished form. Science says that there has been evolution which is still going on. This is only one example of the innumerable incompatibilities between science and religions. There are many such incompatibilities. How can immiscible entities be homogenized?

Synthesis can be made if Advaita Vedānta and science are coalesced. All modern theories of science can be assimilated by Advaita Vedānta. It may be cosmic egg, big bang explosion, particle formation, element synthesis, star and galaxy formation, biological evolution, big crunch, relativity and quantum mechanics. There is no difficulty for Advaita Vedānta to assimilate all these concepts of science. But the scientific concepts are also fragmentary. They begin from nowhere and end in blind alley. They do not present an integral picture. They cannot answer all questions to make a complete theory.

Now there is need for science to assimilate the concepts of Advaita Vedānta. If we do that, we get a total vision, we make an integral philosophy and we answer all questions pertaining to the cosmos, its functioning and the Reality.

Science does not lose its purity by its amalgamation with Advaita Vedānta. It does not become unscientific. Advaita Vedānta is more scientific than science itself. We have to forsake our dogma, which is purely psychological, in order to bring about a synthesis of science and spirituality. Science condemns religions for their dogmas. Unfortunately, science is not free of its own dogma. There is a conception of the scientist that he always deals with empirically verifiable entities and that Brahman, God and Māyā are metaphysical speculations. Does the particle physicist handle sense-perceptible entities when he deals with quarks, the hitherto supposed primary building blocks of matter? Does the quantum physicist really work on empirical entities that can be seen, heard, smelt, touched and tasted? If he can use logically or mathematically inferable entities to explain empirical phenomena, why is he afraid of Vedāntic metaphysics to explain the cosmic integral totality? After all, the Vedāntic metaphysics is logically inferable rather than speculative. The scientist cannot present an integral cosmology even if he resorts to *scientific* mysticism. His cosmology is fragmentary; it starts from nothing and ends in almost nothing. If he unites science with Advaita Vedānta, he gets an integral cosmology, an integral philosophy, a total vision and a cosmic spirituality (if not a cosmic religion).

Every religion has three main facets, namely, metaphysics including cosmology and cosmogony, ethics and rituals. With reference to the first facet, sharp distinctions exist among religions. Moreover, on some basic issues, scientific observations and theories are at variance with the so-called revelations of some religions. It is almost impossible to bring about a consensus of all religions and of all religions and science. In the field of ethics, there is less divergence among religions, although sharp differences do exist on some moral issues. Science is secular and amoral. It does not deal with moral issues, although a scientist, being a human being, may do. Rituals vary from religion to religion. Any enlightened, liberal, religious person does not give too much emphasis on rituals and take them as mere traditional practices. But, that is not the case with the average religious man. For him, rituals are the be-all and end-all of his religion. He tenaciously sticks to his rituals, and at the same time, he has a distaste and sometimes hatred for the rituals of religions other than his. To think of the fusion of all the religions into a single one seems to be almost impracticable. The feasibility of their confluence is beyond the horizon of vision. There could be mutual tolerance, co-existence of faiths, avoidance of dogmas and non-insistence on the inviolability of scriptures. But, so far, this has remained as a dream to prove the falsity of the statement "Man is a rational animal". Science and religion could interpenetrate. The former could be humanized and the latter rationalized. This should be the goal of humankind, if not yet achieved, to be achieved some day in future.

It is time now for a transition, for all religions to graduate to spirituality. The age of religion is over. It guided humankind in the past, although it sometimes misguided too. Now, in the first decade of the 21st century, we feel that all religions should glide into spirituality and that science and technology too should be humanized and spiritualized.

Science has already proved that monism is true at the material level. The original material source, at the appearance of the cosmic egg and the birth of time, was one only. All the diversity of the manifested universe sprang from a singularity, an almost volumeless monoblock, undifferentiated and homogeneous. With this scientific discovery, material monism is established and pluralism is proved to be apparent and empirical. Logic demands that the cosmic egg did not appear from nothing. That nothing is something or vice versa, being contradictory, is necessarily false in language analysis. With this type of impasse, we have to trace the origin of the cosmic egg to Brahman (its power Māyā being the mother principle and its association with Māyā being Īśvara or the father principle, both being coupled to produce and maintain the universe) that is timelessly Existence and fundamentally pure Consciousness. But for this intelligent Being, the Big Bang could not have been fine-tuned and the subsequent cosmological processes could not be well-controlled and co-ordinated.

The fundamental Being—Existence, Consciousness and Bliss—is nameless and can be algebraically expressed as X. The Advaita Vedānta has given a name 'Brahman' to that X. In a mood of intense realization and deep ecstasy, the Vedāntic seer truly feels and exclaims: "He is I (so' ham)", "I am Brahman (*ahaṁ brahmāsmi*)", "That thou art (*tattvamasi*)", "All this verily is Brahman (*sarvaṁ khalvidaṁ brahma*)". He does admit the cosmic diversity, but ascribes the diversity to empirical phenomena only. For the purpose of reality, however, he says: "There is no diversity whatsoever (*neha nānāsti kiñcana*)".

The nondualism of the Advaita Vedānta forms the basis of scientific spirituality or spiritual science in which all religions should merge. All materialists, communists or non-communists, do not have a basis to substantiate the equality which they plead for. This spiritual science, just described, provides the basis for them. A potent criticism of nondualism is the existence of evil in the world. A veil of ignorance becomes necessary for the sportive play in the cosmos. It is up to the individual to pierce the veil. But, he is often alienated from his source of light and makes his darkness of ignorance denser and densest by his bad actions and thoughts. It is this ignorance that is the cause of evil.

Advaita Vedānta is an ancient Indian philosophical school. It is not Hinduism. It is recommended that Hinduism too should graduate to the cosmic spirituality by its ascendance from the religious level.

The concept of cosmic spirituality seems to be a Utopia. But, there is no reason to think that this Utopia shall never be attainable. From the trend of the evolution of human consciousness, one may safely extrapolate that we are ascending the rungs of the ladder towards cosmic spirituality.

In the first phase, religion antagonized science. In the second phase, science antagonized religion. In the dialectical helix, the third phase is bound to come, whether we like it or not. It would be the synthesis of science and religion. In the process of the synthesis, science will be dematerialized and religion, divested of fundamentalism, will be dedogmatized. The outcome of the synthesis will be the cosmic spirituality, working at a level higher than the present levels of science and religion.

Notes

1. Russel, B., *Has Man a Future?*, Penguin Books, Harmondsworth, 1961, p.7
2. *Ibid.*, p. 127
3. Sagan, C., *Cosmos,* Macdonald Futura Publisher, London, 1981, p. 326.
4. *Ibid.*, pp. 339 and 342.
5. Descartes, R., Quoted in '*The Turning Point*' by Capra, F., Fontana/ Collins, London, 1983, p. 43.
6. *Ibid.*, p. 42.
7. *Ibid.*, p. 44.
8. *ibid.*, p. 45.
9. Rodis-Lewis, G., "Limitations of the Mechanical Model in the Cartesian Conception of the Organism". In Hooker, Michael, ed., *Descartes,* John Hopkins University Press, Baltimore, 1978.

10. AV, XII.1.
11. Kant, I., Quoted by Titus, H.H. and Keeton, M.T. in "*The Range of Ethics*", Affiliated East-West Press, New Delhi, 1972, p. 102.
12. Bentham, J., Quoted by Ebenstein, W. in "*Great Political Thinkers*", Oxford & IBH, New Delhi, 3rd ed., 1977, p. 658 (originally published by Holt, Rinehart Winston, New York).
13. Einstein. A., in [12], pp. 861-2.
14. Freud, S., in [12], p. 865.
15. *Ibid.*, p. 866.
16. Freud, S., Quoted by Coulson in '*Science and Christian Belief*', Oxford University Press, London, 1964, p. 18.
17. Riencourt, A.D., *The Eye of Shiva, Souvenir Press, London, 1980, p. 35.*
18. BG, XVIII.61.
19. Huxley, S.J., Quoted by Francis Hitching in 'The Neck of the Giraffe', Pan Books, London, 1982, p. 113.
20. YV, 40.1; Īśa, 1.
21. ṚV, X. 191.3-4, English rendering by Talreja, K.M. in '*Philosophy of Vedas*' Talreja Publication, Bombay, 1982, p. 241.
22. AV, XIX.69.1.
23. Sinnott, E.W., *Cell and Psyche*, New York, 1961, p. 29.
24. Capra, F., *The Turning Point*, Fontana/Collins, London, 1983, p. 7.

INDEX

ābhāsāvāda, 257
abhidharma Piṭaka, 124
absolute zero temperature, 212, 226
absolutism
  — Newtonian, 55, 297
absurdity, 398, 400
acausality, 83, 96, 103, 389-91, 394-95, 397
  — in *Advaita Vedānta*, 402, 403
  — in quantum physics, 397, 399, 400, 402
action at a distance, 18, 109, 136, 314, 317
adhiṣṭhāna, 160, 214, 246, 319-20, 341-42, 343-44, 404
adhyakṣa, 278
adhyāsa, 248, 249, 404
aditi, 161, 274-75, 370
Afanasyev, V.G., 337, 391
age of enlightenment, 420-21
agni, 199
agnosticism, 99
ahaṅkāra, 255
ajātivāda, 244
ākāśa, 5, 7, 160-61, 242, 257, 274-76, 277-79, 319, 367-68, 371-72, 397-98
  — field, 5
  — void, 5, 7
akhaṇḍa, 319
Alekseev, G.N., 220, 221, 225
alpha particle, 30-31, 39-40
alpha rays, 38-39
altruism, 435, 436
Amontons, G., 207, 211
analytic method, 14
analytic psychology—Jungian, 430
analytic statement, 301
anātman, 123, 405
anātmavāda, 355
Anaxagoras, 309
Anaximenes, 6, 373
Anderson, C.D., 27, 104
Angell, J.R., 426
Angst, 433
anguish, 432-3
angular momentum, 42-43
  — its conservation, 197
anirvacanīyā, 214
anitya, 123
anityavāda, 355
anna, 278
anṛta, 400
antaḥkaraṇa, 236, 255-59, 260-61
antideuteron, 28
antigalaxy, 29
antimatter, 27-28, 105
antineutrino, 40
antineutron, 27-28
antiparticle, 27, 41, 104
antiproton, 27
antiquark, 46
anti-universe, 28
āpaḥ, 273-76, 277-78, 318-19, 371-72
apāṁ-napāt, 161, 275-76
aparokṣānubhūti, 329
Āpava, 273-74
ārambha-vāda, 403
Aristotle, 10, 12, 164, 322, 370, 381, 385, 431
asat, 161, 271
Aspect, A., 108-109, 315-16
Aspect's experiment, 315-16, 320
Associationalism, 425
atheism of science, 348
ātman, 249, 256, 346-47, 405
atom, 6
atomic concept
  — Dalton's, 10
  — Democritean, 6, 7
  — of Kaṇāda, 7
  — Newton's, 17
  — *Vaiśeṣika*, 4
atomic number, 25
atomic pluralism, 4
atomic spectra, 36-37
atomic structure
  — Bohr's model, 80
  — Rutherford's planetary model, 30, 32
  — Thomson's model, 30
atomistic view of society, 420
automata, 332
  — living organisms, 15
available energy, 218, 221, 223
avidyā, 241, 246, 248, 253, 257, 259, 399
avyakta, 160, 241, 272
Ayer, A.J., 301, 387, 431-2

Bacon, F., 12, 21, 301, 409, 415-16, 419, 431
Bacon's method
  — empirical and inductive, 15-16
Bacon, R., 591, 301
Barrow, J., 381
baryon, 42, 45, 47
Becquerel, A., 38, 172
behaviourism, 421, 425-6, 431
Bell, J., 107, 314-15

— unified, 54, 65
field equations, 57, 68, 203
Finkelstein, D., 71, 327
Fitzgerald, G.F., 58
Fitzgerald-Lorentz contraction, 58
Fizeau, A.H.L., 177
flux
— in Buddhism, 356
— in dynamic state, 124, 246
— in Marxism, 354
Freedman, S., 108
Fresnel, A.J., 76
Freud, S., 426, 427-9, 430, 437
Friedmann, A.A., 176
full and void, 17
functionalism, 425
fundamental forces, 53, 122, 136

galactical mass, 169-70
galaxy formation, 189-90
galaxy types, 190
Galileo, G., 11-2, 14, 21, 57-8, 166, 205, 208, 353, 416-17, 419
Gamow, G., 176, 178, 179
Gauḍapāda, 244-46, 269
gauge field theory, 122
Gay-Lussac, J.L., 211
Gay-Lussac Charles' law, 211
Gay-Lussac equation, 211
Gay-Lussac law, 211, 213
Gell-Mann, M., 46, 293
geocentric universe, 11, 164, 416
geometry
— Euclidean, 68
— non-Euclidean, 68
geotropism, 341
Germer, L.H., 87
ghaṭākāśa, 257, 260
Gibbs, J.W., 225
Glashow, S., 46, 52, 122
gluon, 50-3, 122, 136-37, 312
— coloured, 52
— weak, 51
God, 322, 353-54, 359-60, 362-63, 401, 403, 405, 420, 421, 424, 434, 435, 437, 441
— Creator, 353
— efficient cause, 243
Godwin, W., 423
Gold, T., 183, 356
Goldstein, E., 23
Graham, N., 115, 326
gravitational field equations, 203
graviton, 51
Green, T.H., 296
Gribbin, J., 122
guṇa
— equilibrium, 242, 366
— *rajas*, 241, 253, 274, 284, 366
— *rajas*-dominant, 242
— *sattva*, 241, 253, 274, 284, 366
— *sattva*-dominated 242
— *tamas*, 241, 253, 274, 284, 366
— *tamas*-dominated, 242
Guth, A.H., 123

hadron, 45, 47-8
Haldane, J.B.S., 293
Hamilton, W.R., 88
Hamiltonian, 103
Harkins, W.D., 24, 173
Hartley, D., 424-5
Hawkins, 24
heat
— as matter, 208
— caloric theory, 209
— conduction, 210
— convection, 210
— radiation, 210
— transfer, 209
— vibrational theory, 208-09
heat death of universe, 218-19, 221, 223, 225-26, 423
heat theorem, 226
Hegel, 296, 298, 374-75
Heidegger, M., 432
Heisenberg, W., 15, 20, 23, 88-9, 91, 92-5, 98-9, 100, 102, 103, 106, 120, 137, 153-54, 233, 305-06, 323, 325, 328, 332-33, 334, 342-43, 389, 400, 418
Heisenberg's equation, 93
Heisenberg's principle of indeterminancy, *see Heisenberg's uncertainty principle*
Heisenberg's uncertainty principle, 92-6, 102-3, 106, 120, 135, 233, 247, 305, 389, 400
heliocentric universe, 11, 164, 166, 416
Helmholtz, H.L.F., 172, 174, 215, 425
henotheism, 419
Heraclitus, 6, 331, 373
Herbart, J.F., 309
Hertz, H., 76
Hīnayāna, 124
Hipparchus, 164, 165
Hiraṇyagarbha, 259, 274, 366
Hitching, 434
Hobbes, T., 301, 421
holism, 110, 113, 119, 316, 333, 437-8
Holt, E.B., 297
Hoyle, F., 183-84, 356
Hubble, E.P., 176-77, 190
Hubble's law, 177
Huggins, W., 177
Humason, M.L.S., 177
Hume, D., 301, 330, 383-84, 387, 393-95, 425, 432
Huxley, S.J., 435
Huxley, T.H., 163